MW00676832

HANDBOOK OF RESEARCH IN ENTREPRENEURSHIP EDUCATION, VOLUME 2

Handbook of Research in Entrepreneurship Education, Volume 2

Contextual Perspectives

Edited by

Alain Fayolle

EM Lyon and CERAG Laboratory, France and Visiting Professor, Solvay Business School, Belgium

Edward Elgar
Cheltenham, UK • Northampton, MA, USA

© Alain Fayolle, 2007

All rights reserved. No part of this publication may be reproduced, stored in a retrieval system or transmitted in any form or by any means, electronic, mechanical or photocopying, recording, or otherwise without the prior permission of the publisher.

Published by
Edward Elgar Publishing Limited
Glensanda House
Montpellier Parade
Cheltenham
Glos GL50 1UA
UK

Edward Elgar Publishing, Inc.
William Pratt House
9 Dewey Court
Northampton
Massachusetts 01060
USA

A catalogue record for this book
is available from the British Library

Library of Congress Cataloguing in Publication Data

Handbook of research in entrepreneurship education/edited by Alain Foyolle.
    v. cm.
  Includes bibliographical references and index.
  Contents: v. 1. A general perspective.
           v. 2. Contextual perspectives.
  1. Entrepreneurship—Study and teaching. 2. Business education.
3. Entrepreneurship—Research. I. Fayolle, Alain.
HB615.H26595   2007
338'.04071—dc22

                        2006017881

ISBN 978 1 84720 059 4

Printed and bound in Great Britain by MPG Books Ltd, Bodmin, Cornwall

Contents

PART III   NATIONAL CONTEXT

PART IV   POLITICAL CONTEXT

Figures

Tables

Contributors

Bjørn Willy Åmo, Bodø Graduate School of Business, Norway

Robert Anderson, University of Regina, Canada

Jean-Pierre Boissin, CERAG, IAE Grenoble, France

Véronique Bouchard, EM Lyon, France

Maryse Brand, Rijksuniversiteit Groningen, The Netherlands

Gian Casimir, Graduate School of Business, University of Newcastle, Australia

Barthélemy Chollet, IREGE, Université de Savoie, France

Cécile Clergeau, University of Nantes, France

Hans Crijns, Vlerick Leuven Gent Management School and Ghent University, Belgium

Léo-Paul Dana, University of Canterbury, New Zealand

Dirk De Clercq, Brock University, Canada

Fernando Dolabela, Fundação Dom Cabral, Belo Horizonte, Brazil

Valérie Eeckhout, IPM – Institute for university Pedagogy and Multimedia, Université catholique de Louvain, Belgium

Sandrine Emin, GRANEM-LARGO, Université d'Angers, France

Alain Fayolle, EM Lyon and CERAG, France, Solvay Business School, Belgium

Louis Jacques Filion, Rogers–J.A. Bombardier Chair of Entrepreneurship, HEC Montréal, Canada

Benoît Gailly, IAG – Louvain School of Management, Université catholique de Louvain, Belgium

Martine Hlady-Rispal, IRGO, University Montesquieu of Bordeaux, France

Ulla Hytti, Turku School of Economics, Finland

Frank Janssen, Brederode Chair in Entrepreneurship, IAG – Louvain School of Management, Université catholique de Louvain, Belgium

Norbert Kailer, University Johannes Kepler of Linz, Austria

Jill Kickul, University of Miami, USA

Lars Kolvereid, Bodø Graduate School of Business, Norway

Paula Kuopusjärvi, Turku School of Economics, Finland

Scott MacAulay, University College of the North, Canada

Sylvia Maxfield, Simmons School of Management, USA

Michael T. Schaper, School of Business, Bond University, Australia

Nathalie Schieb-Bienfait, University of Nantes, France

Bernard Surlemont, University of Liège, Belgium

Marijke van der Veen, Syntens Nieuwegein, The Netherlands

Thierry Verstraete, IRGO, University Montesquieu of Bordeaux, France

Ingrid Wakkee, Vrije Universiteit Amsterdam, The Netherlands

Warren Weir, University of Saskatchewan, Canada

Harold P. Welsch, De Paul University, USA

Wanda Wuttunee, University of Manitoba, Canada

Foreword

This book contains an eclectic collection of new approaches to entrepreneurship education. With a base of international scholars, this work ranges from building the dream via
the opportunity recognition process to harvesting the fruits of entrepreneurial endeavors.
In the middle of this milieu is a generous and insightful set of recommendations about
structuring successful entrepreneurship education programs. With millions of potential
entrepreneurs coming through the pipeline, it behooves us to make sure that we have
turned every leaf to expose our best thinking to the design and implementation to reach
the most effective programs available.

The approach incorporates not only traditional graduate and undergraduate degree
programs, but also considers new groups such as adult learners, certificate programs,
workshops, seminars, case studies, high school initiatives and women entrepreneurs. The
history of entrepreneurship shows a remarkable resiliency that entrepreneurs have exhibited, continuously adapting to changing conditions, learning new strategies to exploit new
opportunities with a book providing innovative approaches to the training and education
process.

The authors are to be commended not only for their innovativeness in their approach
but also in the depth with which each of their topics is covered. New paradigms, models
and templates are provided which should give entrepreneurship educators and adminis-
trators plenty to think about and contemplate as they design evolving educational
systems. With such guidance and insights we cannot fail to produce more effective entrepreneurs as an outcome!

Harold P. Welsch, PhD
Coleman Foundation Chair in Entrepreneurship
DePaul University, Chicago, USA

1 New and emerging perspectives for future research in entrepreneurship education
Alain Fayolle and Jill Kickul

As stated in the first volume of this *Handbook of Research in Entrepreneurship Education* (Fayolle, 2007), entrepreneurial organizations have witnessed a variety of substantial changes and transformations during the decade in order to compete successfully on a global scale. Sustaining revenue growth and increasing shareholder value as well as adding value to products/services have become the key ingredients in defining organizational success. In order to achieve many of these goals, the entrepreneurs within these firms must find alternative and innovative ways to increase levels of efficiency, lower operational costs, and improve overall processes throughout the organization. In addition, these entrepreneurs must also be able to formulate strategies and tactics that are flexible to allow for continual redesign and restructuring of the organization as it grows and matures (Hitt, 1998; Teece and Pisano, 1994; Teece et al., 1997).

With all of these changes and demands on an entrepreneur's skills and abilities, entrepreneurship educators must find innovative and non-traditional methods of teaching entrepreneurship. Entrepreneurship educators need to be more proactive in how they develop, design, and implement their programs to develop entrepreneurs. More specifically, educators need to be more responsive to the changing conditions of the marketplace in order to develop future aspiring entrepreneurs. Additionally, they also need to teach students concepts and skills that can be directly applied toward starting, managing, and growing an enterprise. Skills that require nonlinear learning and thinking (Hitt et al., 1998; Kerr and Jackofsky, 1989) may become critical to the survival of their business. In addition, a diversity of knowledge in finance/cash management, accounting, strategic thinking, and entrepreneurial leadership are often the most cited requisite areas of development for successful entrepreneurship (Hood and Young, 1993).

Thus, it is evident that such changes in entrepreneurship education and pedagogy call for newness in research aimed at providing entrepreneurship educators with 'learnable' specific knowledge, skills, and abilities. The first volume of this handbook introduces innovative research perspectives around three levels of change, including (1) paradigm, (2) methodology and (3) content. In line with the first volume, this second volume underlines the role and the importance of contextual changes by presenting theoretical and empirical research classified within four types of context:

- cultural,
- institutional,
- national and,
- political.

Although the classification we have adopted in both of the volumes is slightly different from those proposed by Béchard and Grégoire (2004), the research contributions which

1

are introduced within this volume confront a number of obstacles that need to be addressed in order for the entrepreneurship education research to advance. For example, Béchard and Grégoire (2004, pp. 36, 37) underline, among other obstacles, the lack of pedagogical expertise of university professors and the difficulty of pursuing interdisciplinary research. In regards to this first obstacle, the authors of this second volume (and those who contributed in the first volume) have a significant number of years in the field of entrepreneurship, designing courses, teaching students and entrepreneurs, and improving step-by-step their pedagogical material. In regards to the second obstacle, this collective book offers several chapters based on the interdisciplinary approach (see for example, Chapters 8 and 9).

Therefore, in the following chapters of this *Handbook of Research in Entrepreneurship Education*, the authors are drawing a new roadmap of entrepreneurship education and training. This first chapter introduces their work and their overall contribution around four main domains which refer to the different types of context we have presented earlier. For each of the contributing authors and their chapters, we introduce their work and conclude with additional remarks and perspectives aimed at moving the entrepreneurship education field and its domain forward for future research and practical implications for our classrooms.

Cultural context

This first part of the *Handbook* (Volume 2) includes four chapters which approach the notion of culture under different view angles. Chapter 2 ('The making of a revolution in Brazil: the introduction of entrepreneurial pedagogy in the early stages of education') written by Louis Jacques Filion and Fernando Dolabela can be perceived as a cultural revolution in a South American country. As stated by the authors, a Canadian and a Brazilian, the Entrepreneurial Pedagogy Methodology (EPM) is a pedagogical approach designed to support entrepreneurial learning in elementary education. Based on systems and visionary thinking, EPM was developed to support the learning of thinking and acting processes geared toward entrepreneurial expression. The program incorporates tailor-made resource materials. EPM was pilot-tested in 2002. In 2003 and 2004, 6352 teachers and 173 304 students enthusiastically participated in the program in 1566 elementary schools in the state of Paraná, Brazil. A total of 340 000 students throughout Brazil were involved in the project in 123 cities over the two-year period. This chapter presents the content and application results of EPM and discusses the program's importance for the blossoming of entrepreneurial spirit and action. In discussing the Paraná project, Chapter 2 examines entrepreneurship education through the lens of self-identity, democracy, cooperation and learning – all elements considered the building blocks of development.

Chapter 3 ('The entrepreneurship gender gap in global perspective: implications for entrepreneurship education and programming') written by Sylvia Maxfield, an American scholar who emphasizes the gender dimension and cultural differences between men and women. From the author's point of view, contemporary research highlights the role women play as entrepreneurs in the US, Canada, and to some extent the United Kingdom. In less developed countries, it appears that fewer women participate in entrepreneurial activities, although rates of female entrepreneurship vary dramatically across nations. The entrepreneurship gender gap measures the difference between the number of men and the number of women participating in entrepreneurial activity. The latest data show that among the countries with the largest entrepreneurship gender gaps are nations as varied as Poland, Argentina, Norway, and Greece, while countries with among the lowest gaps include South Africa, Peru, Portugal, and Japan. Entrepreneurship policies and educational programs are often imported from one country to another and rarely differentiate by gender. But if the impetus for entrepreneurial activity varies with gender, national culture, or economic circumstance, similar policies will work well in some situations but not in others. To the extent that we can explain variation in the entrepreneurship gender gap, we can better design programs and policies aimed at increasing women's entrepreneurial activity. This chapter identifies and summarizes research on five categories of motivators for female entrepreneurship and briefly discusses how existing programs for women entrepreneurs address these five different categories of motivation.

Chapter 4, 'Teaching entrepreneurship to non-business students: insights from two Dutch universities', is coming from a Dutch team including Maryse Brand, Ingrid Wakkee and Marijke van der Veen. By focusing on entrepreneurship programs at academic institutes, the authors' assume that cultural differences may exist among the variety of academic disciplines. According to the authors, teaching entrepreneurship at the academic level is particularly relevant for several reasons. First, ventures founded by highly educated entrepreneurs tend to be more innovative, experience higher growth levels and survival rates, and are more often involved in international activities. Second, teaching entrepreneurship at an academic level stimulates entrepreneurship research and raises the knowledge level about entrepreneurship both as a research object and as a career domain. This in turn, leads to improved policy-making and better entrepreneurship curricula at all levels of education. Finally and however, the authors limit the discussion to teaching entrepreneurship minors and electives to non-business bachelor and master students at academic institutes, a subject which is still scarcely researched. They examine how entrepreneurship programs can be geared toward stimulating non-business students, in various disciplines, to consider an entrepreneurial career through start-up or corporate entrepreneurial activities. They scrutinize what essential ingredients should be incorporated in a program catered toward non-business students. To that end, they first briefly describe the history and current state of entrepreneurship education, and then present a theoretical model that depicts entrepreneurship as a process aimed at the pursuit of opportunities. This model allows for a systematic analysis of the entrepreneurial process aimed at the identification of elements to be included in entrepreneurship courses for non-business students. Their analysis leads us to a framework that can be used as a tool to construct or evaluate entrepreneurship courses or programs.

In Chapter 5 ('Teaching corporate entrepreneurship the experimental way'), a Canadian/French professor, Véronique Bouchard posits that cultural variables between corporate entrepreneurship and independent entrepreneurship are quite different. The teaching of Corporate Entrepreneurship in business schools is far less widespread than that of Independent Entrepreneurship. Given the scarcity of empirical research on the topic and the ambiguity of the term 'Corporate Entrepreneurship', this is hardly a revelation. And as a result, Corporate Entrepreneurship cannot be taught relying on tested and solid theoretical, empirical or methodological foundations: it is necessarily a pioneering endeavor. As with all pioneers, those who throw themselves into the adventure have to make choices that can first appear arbitrary. They have to take positions on unsettled questions such as 'What is Corporate Entrepreneurship?', 'Where does Corporate Entrepreneurship stand vis-à-vis independent Entrepreneurship?', and 'What is the practical value of Corporate Entrepreneurship?' They also have to decide what, within a mixed and uneven body of literature, is relevant for future managers. And they have to set objectives, determine contents and select a pedagogy in absence of tested models. In these circumstances, it seems prudent to envision the teaching of Corporate Entrepreneurship as an experimental process, that is, one whose outcomes need to be closely monitored and which is susceptible to be redirected at any moment. This chapter recounts the author's own experience and trajectory, from the moment she (with a colleague) took the decision to launch an elective course in Corporate Entrepreneurship to the most recent edition of the course. The first part of the chapter briefly describes and justifies the course's positioning and general orientations. The second part summarizes the organization and content – to a large extent original – of the course. The third part describes the pedagogical approach and highlights the benefits of co-teaching. The fourth part summarizes what the professors have learned in the 'experiment' and how they plan to orient their teaching in the future. The conclusion reviews some of the theoretical, pedagogical and managerial implications of what remains a very idiosyncratic process.

Institutional context
This second part of the book includes four chapters which underline the role of institutions and systems seen in a broad sense. Chapter 6 ('From theoretical production to the design of entrepreneurship study programmes: a French case') written by two French scholars, Thierry Verstraete and Martine Hlady-Rispal, begins with a development on the main stakes related to the multiplication of teaching in entrepreneurship. A key issue for the authors is to point out a difficulty which remains in the teaching of entrepreneurship is the failure of our field to define the notion of entrepreneurship. Their conception, presented in the first section, falls under the paradigm of the creation of a new organization. Any teaching gains by falling under a relatively circumscribed conception (which does not mean partitioned), first, in order to help the students with determining the field for which the program is conceived, then, help them with holding the train of thought on which he/she can attach the whole of the knowledge. Based on this conception, entrepreneurship courses are designed and proposed to the students. The core of these programs is aimed at 'acting', It consists in putting the students in action so that they can assimilate certain dimensions that cannot be given through a course that one would describe as more 'traditional,' except by preparing them by presenting them with the entrepreneurial process. In this chapter, the authors do not state the two opposing debates: the question of nature versus nurture versus the question of technique and art. They believe that certain individuals have predispositions, while others have gaps in which solutions exist that reveal potential. That is, as for the less entrepreneurial students, teaching in entrepreneurship reveals that they need entrepreneurs who make them aware of the realities of the economic world, especially the students of the artistic, literary or scientific fields.

Chapter 7 ('The impact of tertiary education courses on entrepreneurial goals and intentions') from two Australians, Michael T. Schaper and Gian Casimir, poses the following question: what impact do entrepreneurship courses have on students' intentions to start their own businesses? It is commonly assumed that undertaking an appropriate education or training course will enhance students' propensity to launch or purchase their own business ventures. However, such presumptions have not been well-tested. This chapter reports on a recent study on the relative impact of formal tertiary-level courses on subsequent entrepreneurial goals and intentionality. The study set out to determine if studying a semester-long entrepreneurship course increased students' self-reported level of knowledge about business ownership skills. One hundred and thirty-eight undergraduate students who were enrolled in entrepreneurship courses at two Australian universities were surveyed both at the beginning and at the end of their semester-long course. The results indicated that students' self-reported knowledge of how to run their own businesses increased significantly over the semester. However, this did not appear to raise the overall proportion of students who wanted to launch their own enterprise (overall intentions). Although there were significant changes within the student cohort: some became more confirmed in their desire to launch a venture, while other students who had previously been enthusiastic became dissuaded, and vice versa.

Two French women, Cécile Clergeau and Nathalie Schieb-Bienfait, have written the Chapter 8, 'Operating an entrepreneurship center in a large and multidisciplinary university: addressing the right issues'. They discuss the overall interest and the importance of a defined structure, that is, entrepreneurship center, on the development and the diffusion of the entrepreneurial culture. In the quest for more and better ways of nurturing enterprising individuals, and especially ways of developing entrepreneurs, the role of education and training is considered as a prerequisite. This chapter offers further insights into the interests in and the challenge of setting up an entrepreneurship education center within a large and multidisciplinary university. After reviewing major key research issues and debating various entrepreneurship education and training models, this chapter relates this education process experience when introduced into a French university, which is based on the different pedagogical means used for developing entrepreneurship educational programming. The authors introduce the implementation strategy by describing the detailed operations proposed by the center program. Following this, the discussion highlights the integration and the acceptance process.

Chapter 9 ('Interdisciplinary approaches in entrepreneurship education programs') is coming from a Belgian academic group including Frank Janssen, Valérie Eeckhout and Benoît Gailly. From an educational perspective, these authors consider that entrepreneurship education cannot limit itself to firm creation, but has to be broadened to the development of an entrepreneurial spirit which consists of, in business or in any other human activity, identifying opportunities and gathering different resources in order to create richness which meets a solvable demand. Nascent or mature, entrepreneurship as an academic field is by nature interdisciplinary, and therefore requires adapted teaching methods. Several universities have tried to develop such educational approaches, dedicated to the specific objectives and requirements of their entrepreneurship education programs. However, only a few universities appear to have adopted educational approaches that are truly interdisciplinary. Indeed, universities are often locked into their disciplinary structures while entrepreneurship classes are school-specific and only offered to students from one or sometimes two disciplines. In this context, the aim of this chapter is to discuss the link between entrepreneurship and interdisciplinary teaching approaches, through the case analysis of a cross-faculty entrepreneurship education program run since 1997 in the Université catholique de Louvain. Hence this chapter tries to contribute an answer to one of the criticisms toward entrepreneurship education literature recently stressed by Béchard and Grégoire (2004). Because this literature very seldom borrows concepts or theories from disciplines other than management, these authors underline the necessity to develop research and expertise at the intersection between entrepreneurship and education science. Additionally, the authors discuss the potential learning objectives of entrepreneurship education programs and the corresponding teaching strategies involved. They then review, on the basis of Rege Colet's conceptual framework, the link between entrepreneurship and the interdisciplinary approaches it involves. Finally, they discuss this aspect through the analysis of an existing program and in particular its interdisciplinary features. The authors conclude the chapter by a discussion of the entrepreneurial impact of the interdisciplinary entrepreneurship education program.

National context
The third part of the *Handbook* is composed of four chapters, each highlighting a national situation or issue. They are discussed in the order of presentation: Belgium, Canada, New Zealand and Norway. Two out of these countries are European, two are out of Europe in different continents. Chapter 10, 'Entrepreneurship and education in Belgium: findings and implications from the Global Entrepreneurship Monitor', written by Dirk De Clercq and Hans Crijns, is aimed at providing the empirical findings from a research project with regard to the role of entrepreneurship and education in Belgium. More specifically, the authors highlight the findings with respect to the role of education in fostering, or inhibiting, entrepreneurial activity in Belgium as found by the Global Entrepreneurship Monitor. This study fits into an increasing awareness of policy makers and educators across the world that the level and success of entrepreneurial activity within a country is to an important extent related to the quality and focus of its educational programs. Several reasons have been given for why a country's educational system may be important for stimulating entrepreneurship. For example, education may provide individuals with a feeling of autonomy, independence, or self-confidence, which are all characteristics potentially important when starting a new business. Furthermore, education broadens the horizons of individuals, thereby making people better equipped to perceive new business opportunities. However, it has also been suggested that a distinction needs to be made between 'general' education on the one hand, and more 'specific' education focusing on the promotion of entrepreneurship and the stimulation of entrepreneurial skills and knowledge on the other. For instance, the educational system can be used specifically for the encouragement of commercial awareness, and for the development of necessary entrepreneurial skills such as negotiations and opportunity recognition.

Chapter 11 ('Building Aboriginal economic development capacity: the Council for the Advancement of Native Development Officers') from Robert Anderson, Scott MacAulay, Warren Weir and Wanda Wuttunee investigates a less known topic – indigenous entrepreneurship. In their chapter, Aboriginal is used when referring to the Indigenous people in Canada and indigenous is used in a broader sense to describe 'original people.' Aboriginal people in Canada and Indigenous people around the world have suffered greatly as the result of the spread of the western European economic system to the rest of the world and the resulting emergence of the global economy. Once self-reliant and socially cohesive, communities have suffered severe dislocation. What has received less attention, but is very important, is the degree of cohesion that remains and the burning desire among Indigenous people to rebuild their communities on this foundation. Remarkably, they intend to do so by participating in the global economy; but on their own terms. Business development lies at the heart of their approach to this participation. One organization in Canada, the Council for the Advancement of Native Development Officers (CANDO), is playing a key role in the development of the entrepreneurial capacity that is essential to successful Aboriginal business development. This chapter describes the activities of CANDO, in particular its development of a national training and professional certification program for economic development officers working for Aboriginal communities and organizations. It is argued that the very structure of CANDO itself contributes to this capacity-building.

Léo-Paul Dana is the author of Chapter 12, 'New Zealand graduates in entrepreneurship: toward a paradigm of interdependence', which starts with a key question: what do students do after they graduate university? This chapter is the result of research about graduates of the University of Canterbury in Christchurch, New Zealand. Christchurch is the largest city on New Zealand's South Island and opportunities for careers with government or with large firms are limited here. Methodology involved seven focus groups conducted with former students of the University of Canterbury. Those who have opted to get involved in entrepreneurship, rather than seek employment, were invited for open-ended interviews. In contrast to the American stereotype of the entrepreneur, who is individualistic and seeks independence, interviewed graduates tended to seek cooperation in networks. This was manifested in two forms: (1) an attraction to becoming franchisees; and (2) active participation in existing networks. Much literature discusses networks that are created along ethnic lines, as entrepreneurs are comfortable doing business with like-minded people, whom they understand, and with whom they get along. Rather than using ethnicity as the basis for networking, respondents of this study have been networking with others who share the same techno-culture. The first sections of this chapter discuss this techno-culture and review the literature relating to education and entrepreneurship. This is followed by a literature review of the classic independent entrepreneur, revealing that interviewees do not fit this traditional image. A literature review of networking in New Zealand is followed by a discussion of techno-culture networking in the country (for example, franchising is discussed as one form of networking). The chapter concludes with a discussion of implications and suggestions for future research.

To conclude this third part, Chapter 13, 'Entrepreneurship among graduates from business schools: a Norwegian case', from Lars Kolvereid and Bjørn Willy Åmo, offers an opportunity to contrast the previous situation in New Zealand with a European one in Norway. The aim of this chapter is to provide insights from a long-running major program in entrepreneurship. Such an insight could prove useful for those who would like to evaluate a running educational program in entrepreneurship and for educational institutes on the brink of establishing such programs. This chapter addresses to what extent the entrepreneurship major offered at Bodø Graduate School of Business, Norway, has been a success. In doing so, the chapter discusses the aim and the purpose of the educational program and compares this with empirical findings based on statistics from the student database and four different surveys addressing all alumni. The chapter displays how the learning goals of the educational program are related and connected to the overall purpose of the program. It also considers the suitability of different measures of success of an offered major program in entrepreneurship and concludes that the major in entrepreneurship has been a success. Finally, this chapter highlights additional work and research needed to measure success in educational programs in entrepreneurship.

Political context
The fourth and final part of this Volume 2 of the *Handbook* includes four chapters which address key issues in entrepreneurship education such as the promotion of entrepreneurship and the evaluation of entrepreneurship education. Both are closely related to the political dimension. Chapter 14, 'Evaluation of entrepreneurship education: planning problems, concepts and proposals for evaluation design', written by an Austrian scholar, Norbert Kailer, states that Entrepreneurship Education is a growth industry itself. Massive public investments led to an expansion of the support infrastructure and to a growth on the supply side of training, coaching, information and financing for nascent entrepreneurs and start-ups. The boom in entrepreneurship education and the increasing criticism of missing data about the impact of these measures begin this chapter. The author focuses on the question of how a practice-oriented model of evaluation can be developed and established. After discussing definitions of evaluation, the chapter provides an overview about recent empirical studies analysing the usage and deficits of evaluation and the evaluation studies of university entrepreneurship programs. The chapter also discusses problems connected with the introduction of evaluation. Finally, questions and decisions during the evaluation planning process are discussed and evaluation models are presented. The conclusion emphasizes practical proposals for designing and implementing evaluation studies.

In the same line of research, Chapter 15 ('Evaluating entrepreneurship education: play of power between evaluators, programme promoters and policy makers') written by two Finnish women, Ulla Hytti and Paula Kuopusjärvi, considers that evaluation studies have become a common practice in enterprise education and entrepreneurship training programs. However, it should be mentioned that the evaluation studies are used for different purposes, such as tools for program planning and monitoring and for measuring impacts and economic efficiency of the programs. Besides the instrumental use of evaluation (the evaluation results are applied to change the program or policy), the process use (the actual conduct of the evaluation may lead to changes) is also an important element in the evaluation process. The different stakeholders in evaluation studies have differing expectations for the evaluations. Program promoters generally regard running the program as their first priority. They prefer internal and interim evaluations that continually provide information to assist them in the program planning and implementing the decision-making process. Policy makers and financiers are primarily concerned about measuring the impact of programs. Evaluators position themselves to support primarily either the decision-making of the program promoters or policy makers. The differing aims for evaluations lead to evaluation processes and reports that do not serve the needs of all the interest groups involved. It is only recently that research has focused on these forces that shape evaluations and evaluation processes, and the knowledge claims that follow it. This chapter is analysing the tripartite play of power between financiers, program promoters and evaluators with regard to evaluations of enterprise education and entrepreneurship training. The authors argue that it is not possible to create an evaluation scene without this power aspect attached to the process. However, they can become more aware and conscious about these forces that help them to understand different stakeholders and their views, and become more skilled in reading evaluation reports. Discussing the evaluations and their results in a more open environment will help to prevent the misunderstandings and will help the different stakeholders themselves to gain insights of all the agents involved in the programs. As a result the authors recommend that the process use of evaluations is made more open and visible. This could be done by organizing workshops and other events for the different stakeholders to discuss the evaluations. Furthermore, a more open environment for the evaluations should be created by also publishing and distributing the evaluation reports more widely.

In Chapter 16 ('Promoting enterprising: a strategic move to get schools' cooperation in the promotion of entrepreneurship') is written by a Belgian scholar, Bernard Surlemont who first claims that most countries experience a number of difficulties in implementing entrepreneurship programs, particularly at the secondary level, in the classroom. Consequently, in a first step, the chapter explores how such resistance might be associated with the fussiness of what entrepreneurship really means. It supports the argument that it is crucial to make a clear distinction between the technical competencies generally associated with entrepreneurship (that is, business planning, opportunity recognition, fund raising, and so on), and the strategic competencies associated with enterprising (self-realization, perseverance, creativity, teamwork, and so on). Thus, subtle semantic nuance, can make a substantial difference to how well entrepreneurship education is perceived and can be accepted by teachers and educators in secondary schools. In a second step, the core of the chapter develops the arguments to promote enterprising education in secondary school as a way (1) to develop entrepreneurship skills and attitudes to pupils and (2) to ease the introduction of an 'entrepreneurship culture' in secondary schools. The chapter closes with some key implications and suggestions for further research.

A French team, Jean-Pierre Boissin, Barthélemy Chollet and Sandrine Emin, contributes Chapter 17, 'Explaining the intention to start a business among French students: a closer look at professional beliefs'. This chapter studies students' beliefs and attitudes toward entrepreneurship, and how such beliefs and attitudes impact their intention to start a business at the end of their student life. The authors propose a model intended to explain intention, rooted in the theory of planned behavior (TPB). According to the model, intentions result from the combined effect of perceived desirability of starting a business, intensity of social pressure toward starting a business, and individual confidence in one's capacity to achieve entrepreneurial process (self-efficacy). The model is tested on data from 908 French students via multiple regressions. Desirability appears to have a prevailing weight in the explanation of intention. Such a result shows that, beyond just providing the required skills, entrepreneurship courses should also focus on promoting entrepreneurship as an attractive career choice. The theory of planned behavior states that desirability and self-efficacy are themselves explained by personal beliefs. Desirability is influenced by beliefs about the kind of professional life self-employment can bring. Self-efficacy is influenced by beliefs about the typical skills that an entrepreneur needs. Another set of regressions show what kinds of professional beliefs best explain desirability, and what kinds of self-efficacy for critical tasks best explain self-efficacy for starting a business. Results provide significant help for entrepreneurship scholars intending to design courses. Indeed, such design should be oriented toward influencing positively specific beliefs that lead to poor levels of both desirability and self-efficacy.

Concluding comments
As we place the final touches on this introductory chapter of the second volume of the *Handbook of Research in Entrepreneurship Education*, a couple of new perspectives and

insights have emerged. First, there is a great variety of research topics and themes along with a diversity of theoretical and methodological approaches that have been studied in each of the selected research contributions. This indicates once more the richness, but also the complexity, of the field. The second perspective and comment is on the plurality of the contributors. There are 37 from 10 countries and three continents. To make a collective contribution in entrepreneurship education research from a contextual perspective, it seems particularly interesting to have a plethora of different points of view, in terms of culture, geography, institutional, ethical and political systems. Although still much work remains in the entrepreneurship education field, it is our hope that this research will collectively assist entrepreneurship educators to develop new programs and pedagogical approaches that considers the affluence and diversity of these multiple perspectives.

References

Béchard, J.P. and Grégoire, D. (2004), 'Entrepreneurship education research revisited: the case of higher education', *Academy of Management, Learning and Education*, **4** (1), 22–43.
Fayolle, A. (2007), *Handbook of Research in Entrepreneurship Education: A General Perspective*, vol. 1, Cheltenham, UK: Edward Elgar.
Hitt, M.A. (1998), 'Twenty-first century organizations: business firms, business schools, and the academy', *Academy of Management Review*, **23** (2), 218–24.
Hitt, M.A., Keats, B.W. and DeMarie, S.M. (1998), 'Navigating in the new competitive landscape: building strategic flexibility and competitive advantage in the twenty-first century', *Academy of Management Executive*, **12** (4), 22–42.
Hood, J.N. and Young, J.E. (1993), 'Entrepreneurship's requisite areas of development: a survey of top executives in successful entrepreneurial firms', *Journal of Business Venturing*, **8**, 115–35.
Kerr, J. and Jackofsky, E. (1989), 'Aligning managers with strategies: management development versus selection', *Strategic Management Journal*, **10**, 157–70.
Teece, D.J. and Pisano, G.P. (1994), 'The dynamic capabilities of firms: an introduction', *Industrial and Corporate Change*, **3** (3), 537–56.
Teece, D.J., Pisano, G.P. and Shuen, A. (1997), 'Dynamic capabilities and strategic management', *Strategic Management Journal*, **18** (7), 509–33.

PART I

CULTURAL CONTEXT

2 The making of a revolution in Brazil: the introduction of entrepreneurial pedagogy in the early stages of education[1]

Louis Jacques Filion and Fernando Dolabela

Introduction

Entrepreneurship development is often regarded as something that can be achieved mainly through the introduction of policies to stimulate and structure new venture creation. This chapter, however, suggests that one of the most powerful means of developing entrepreneurship in a society is through educational programs that incorporate entrepreneurial thinking at every level of the educational system, starting with elementary school. Entrepreneurship is regarded here as a culture that is expressed through a particular type of thinking and action. We suggest that this type of thinking requires the development of faculties using the resources of the right side of the brain (imaginative and intuitive thinking). This can be achieved by means of exercises in which subjects learn how to dream and then transform their dreams into reality by defining and then implementing entrepreneurial projects.

A pedagogical methodology known as Entrepreneurial Pedagogy Methodology (EPM) was designed and implemented at elementary schools with a view to facilitating entrepreneurial learning at a young age. The methodology is based on a sequential dream initiation structure. The premise behind it is that the education system is focused too heavily on the transfer of knowledge and not focused enough on the learning of independent imaginative thinking methods. The text shows that, based on the Brazilian experience, entrepreneurial learning can start at a very young age, provided people are trained to think in terms of defining dreams or contexts. This particular approach was designed as a radical change to the traditional educational methods used in schools, which tend to concentrate on knowledge transfer rather than learning how to think independently and proactively.

An experiment such as this involves changing the existing culture by creating well-structured interactions between the components of a social system that do not usually interact – for example, teachers, economic development officers and municipal political leaders. The text presented here describes a different way of designing and practising education, along with a new way of organizing its implementation. Within this method, teachers are called upon to play a new role, that of catalyst and facilitator whose job is to help the students to learn a new way of thinking. Instead of simply transferring content, they must now help their students to learn how to think in entrepreneurial terms.

The need for revolutionary learning approaches to change the social order

If society is to change, we must put in place revolutionary – even radical – approaches that allow change to happen. From an entrepreneurship perspective, change should come from the bottom, not the top. But, first, structural changes that will generate the desired entrepreneurial changes must be integrated in the social system. Entrepreneurship offers fresh perspectives for modifying existing learning patterns and processes. It reveals a secret as old as civilization itself: the capacity of human beings to be the protagonists of their own destinies is becoming accessible to all, within both less developed societies and organized, sophisticated social structures. Anyone can act intentionally to alter their relationships with the world and with others, and to continuously re-create themselves.

Mass education, which has existed since the 1800s, has really been made widely free and available only in the last 50 years. Entrepreneurship appears to be something accessible to the masses, who previously had little exposure to how to acquire the tools to become self-sufficient and even prosperous. The learning patterns and processes of entrepreneurship are now attracting the attention of specialists from many fields: economists, psychologists, sociologists, engineers, management scientists, strategists – and educators (Béchard and Grégoire, 2005).

Entrepreneurship is a craft that can be learned (Fayolle, 1999; 2003; 2004; Filion, 2004) and its development in a society can be supported (Kao et al., 2002, 2004; Lundström and Stevenson, 2005; Van der Horst et al., 2005). It has often been seen as an isolated and individualistic activity, but Julien (2005) showed that entrepreneurship is also a social phenomenon and that its blossoming reflects the social values, cultures and dynamics from which entrepreneurs emerge. This view of entrepreneurship has contributed insights about how to instill learning that helps young students acquire skills that can free them from existing cultural patterns and social structures, particularly in developing countries. They will be able to break the chains of new forms of slavery and dependence on the existing social order and become free agents of their own destiny.

This is the revolutionary approach to the pedagogy of development put forward in opposition to the pedagogy of the status quo. The pedagogy of the status quo exists to reinforce the social order. It socializes students to accept the social roles into which they were born and offers little or no hope for the poor, the uneducated and the less educated, who will become part of the machinery that keeps society as it is. Figure 2.1 illustrates the dynamic between learning that implies the logic of entrepreneurship, the selection of appropriate pedagogical approaches, and the impact generated on social change and local development.

Entrepreneurship as a human activity system

Classical economic theory regards the entrepreneur – along with other 'imponderables' such as the climate, government, politics, plagues and wars – as an 'external force' (Shane, 2002a; 2002b). The entrepreneur has come to be seen as playing a major role in economic development.

This is especially true since Joseph Alois Schumpeter (1883–1950), revisiting the ideas of Jean-Baptiste Say (1767–1832), turned the focus to the tripod of 'entrepreneur, innovation and economic growth' (Schumpeter, 1934). Say (1803; 1996), born a century after Richard Cantillon (1680–1734), is considered Schumpeter's precursor and the pioneer of entrepreneurship in economic history (Filion, 1998). While Cantillon (1755) associated the entrepreneur with risk-taking, Say was the first to distinguish between entrepreneurs and capitalists: he linked entrepreneurs with innovation and saw them as agents of change. They were individuals who could get better results using fewer resources. However, it was Schumpeter who in fact launched the field of entrepreneurship. He clearly associated entrepreneurship with innovation and made it known through the publication of his works in English.

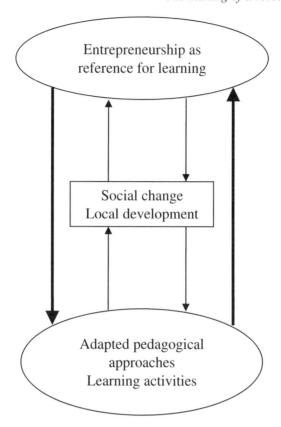

Figure 2.1   Entrepreneurship learning and radical change

A key element of innovation lies in perceiving and seizing opportunities (Filion, 1998; Filion and Dolabela, 2000; Sexton and Smilor, 1997; Shane, 2003; 2005). Timmons defined the entrepreneur as someone able to identify, seize and take advantage of opportunities, searching for and managing resources so as to transform opportunities into successful businesses (Filion, 1991b; Timmons, 2004; Shane, 2005).

Filion (1991a; 1991b) looked at entrepreneurs from a systems thinking perspective (Checkland, 1999). He tried to map how entrepreneurs think in order to do what they do. After studying dozens of entrepreneurs through fieldwork interviewing, he was struck by the fact that in designing their activity systems, they do more projective thinking and anticipatory learning than other organizational actors. There is a close relationship between what entrepreneurs plan to do and how they identify the learning required to do it. They tend to design and structure organizational activities in an organic and adaptive way by following less than other organizational actors the 'known existing rules' about organization management (Filion, 1988). They dream and vision.

Thus, Filion defined an entrepreneur as 'someone who imagines, develops and realizes visions' (Filion, 1991b, p. 26). Theories about conceptualization in entrepreneurship differ, generally according to the perspective and discipline of the theoretical approach. Yet most who study the field do so to learn about those who generate an added value

(Bruyat and Julien, 2001), very often by creating an enterprise or by contributing to the renewal of an existing organization. An entrepreneur can thus be seen as an individual 'who defines contexts'. It was from this reference point that we began to look at designing learning approaches to prepare students to think in ways that would allow them to design new contexts (Filion, 1989).

From that systems perspective, Dolabela (1999; 2003a; 2003b; 2004) wrote books about proactive learning approaches to designing pedagogical methodologies and activities that support the education of entrepreneurs. These approaches to entrepreneurial pedagogy (EP) associate the concept of entrepreneur with a state of being – a lifestyle, a world view, a way of thinking, an orientation towards innovation and a capacity to produce changes in oneself, the environment, and the means and forms of seeking self-realization, including reaction patterns to ambiguities and uncertainties (Dolabela, 2000a).

Dreams as the basis for entrepreneurship activities and learning
We thus essentially saw entrepreneurs as *individuals who are able to dream and able to organize themselves to make their dreams come true.* The approach we are proposing includes three categories of dreams. The first, the *collective dream* (CD), is the dream that the society, or parts of the society, forms implicitly or explicitly about its future. The second, the *structuring dream* (SD), has the capacity to give birth to a life project; the realization of individual SDs will lead to the realization of the CD. The third, the *activity dream* (AD), allows the entrepreneur to conceive of and structure projects that will produce the SD.

This concept of dream applies to all human beings, but especially to children. They are learning to learn, and to think about the world and about themselves. The concept concerns potential entrepreneurs of all kinds, categories and types – those who contribute innovations to enterprises, government, the tertiary sector and non-profit organizations as employees, managers, autonomous professionals and business owners. Dreams imply projective thinking that allows people to become better organized, identify more clearly what they need to learn and increase their level of self-efficiency.

Collective dreams
Collective dreams are the basis from which entrepreneurship is expressed, and they include society's values and expectations. In his research (1961) on the role of heroes in history, David McClelland demonstrated that the CDs that were formed after these heroes appeared in the literature greatly influenced how the generations that followed expressed the need for achievement and power. Structuring dreams were imagined and structured that led to the making of more entrepreneurial, developed and prosperous societies.

Like present-day movie stars, heroes inspire young people's behavior and choice of career. Magazines, newspapers and best-selling books express collective dreams daily through the types of heroes they project and value. But CDs can also be made more explicit by having people in a society specify the types of leaders they want to produce. These types can then be presented as models. For instance, in many societies entrepreneurs have received a multiplicity of awards, and this has helped show that entrepreneurship can be a career valued by society.

We can go a step further. In the late 1990s, Quebec passed a law making it compulsory for every elementary and secondary school to organize a school council of student, teacher and community representatives who decide the type of community they want to become, the subjects that should be studied in the school, and so on. The council chooses the main topic for its school: music, art, entrepreneurship or certain crafts, for example. It has been suggested that, as it is small businesses that create the majority of new jobs, the councils should pay particular attention to the types of small businesses that exist in their communities, so as to better prepare the kind of manpower required by the organizations that are actually going to recruit and hire people (Filion, 2005).

All CDs in today's world should integrate entrepreneurial components. Enterprises throughout the world need more highly developed entrepreneurial behaviors, and all societies need more entrepreneurs (Filion, 2005). Entrepreneurship is a form of leadership; entrepreneurship-related learning implies the learning of leadership life skills that are essential for the organizations of the future (Roberts, 2004). All societies need to generate more entrepreneurial behavior and more people who create and can share the wealth. These people are commonly called *intrapreneurs and entrepreneurs.*

Structuring dreams
Collective dreams will be realized through individual SDs and ADs. A structuring dream is a dream one dreams about one's own future. It leads to self-realization. A structuring dream should answer the questions, 'What is your dream in life?' and 'What would you like to achieve?' It is *the one dream* that makes the eyes sparkle when one talks about it.

Anyone, regardless of circumstances, has the capacity to formulate dreams: this is an attribute of human nature. Within the realm of EP, dreams that are not classified as entrepreneurship related are seen as 'peripheral dreams' (PD). This means that these other dreams, be they single or multiple, do not have potential to be the foundation of a life project or entrepreneurial activities and to lead in a structured way to self-realization.

Dreams that lack emotional content lack sufficient energy to drive the dreamer into action and are not considered SDs or ADs. Dreams bear a structuring character only when they boast the energy necessary to drive the dreamer into an involvement that leads to action about self-realization. Experiencing the emotion of the dream thus transports the individual into a state where the way of seeing and feeling about the world and perceiving one's own abilities is transformed into a drive for action.

BOX 2.1   THREE TYPES OF DREAMS

A few words must be said on the different types of dreams. Depending on the perspective, typologies of structuring dreams and activity dreams have several different configurations. We have kept three: overachievement (OA), coherence (C) and underachievement (UA). These three types apply to all categories of dreams: CDs, SDs and ADs. In the OA dream, children express SDs and ADs with overly ambitious targets that are difficult, and usually impossible to reach. In a C dream, children express SDs and ADs that are achievable and coherent with what they are capable of accomplishing. In the third type, the UA dream, children express SDs and ADs that are below – sometimes far below – their potential.

When first conceived, most SDs may appear embryonic. They may seem abstract; they may contain nothing that can be applied as is or that can be translated immediately into a plan of action. Generally, the dreams first manifest in modes of social interaction: contributing to social justice, the elimination of poverty, the dissemination of knowledge or the improvement of living conditions. Structuring dreams address ways of earning a living, achieving independence, mapping out one's destiny, providing a better future for one's family, making oneself respectable and so on. We have observed that children implicitly develop SDs through which they can express their natural abilities and in areas that are part of their evoked systems (ES). These are areas with which they are somewhat familiar – they have developed a mental image because they have been exposed to the area through personal contact, reading, education or the media.

Activity dreams
Structuring dreams are realized through the design and implementation of ADs. Activity dreams are entrepreneurial projects. The kind of abstraction expressed in an SD depends on the dreamer and the dreamer's stage of life. A 6-year-old child, for instance, tends to formulate more ADs than SDs: children at that age focus on concrete dreams such as a certain toy. If an SD is to materialize for an adult, however, it must first become an AD that can be achieved through a plan of action. Most SDs will be realized through ADs that are entrepreneurial ideas.

The imagery (Block, 1981) that derives from dreams is neither static nor permanent. In fact, the imagery produced by following one's ES and life events becomes stimuli for both new SDs and ADs yet to be designed. Structuring dreams are strongly induced by value systems, including models and social roles. Activity dreams are influenced by the same factors, and especially by expertise expressed around children. They are designed taking into account contingencies, circumstances, abilities, competencies, knowledge and behaviors. Activity dreams will be used to plan activities. When children grow up and become experienced adults, they will be able to formulate visions of the space they can occupy in the marketplace and the organizational systems they need to help them get there (Filion, 1991a; 1991b). The dreaming process they have learned will serve as a useful background to help them vision in a more precise and organized way. Table 2.1 provides examples of each kind of dream.

Table 2.1   Examples of dreams

Collective dreams (CDs)	Structuring dreams (SDs)	Activity dreams (ADs)
To improve health conditions	To become a doctor	To study medicine
	To develop a new kind of hospital	To build a hospital
To preserve animal life	To become a wildlife specialist	To create a non-governmental organization to take care of wild animals
To improve the living conditions of the poor, and especially to improve housing for the millions living in favellas	To become an architect To become a politician	To set up a business that builds houses for the poor To create laws for the financing of low-income housing

The children who become involved in the learning process discussed in this chapter constantly build and rebuild their SDs and ADs as they themselves change and evolve. Their reference group also plays an important role in the evolution of the SDs and ADs. Structuring dreams may be transitory, as they are influenced and determined by the changes in the self and the changes brought to the ES. There is a continuous dynamic between the dreamer and the dream and, among children, especially between the dreamer and the SD. As long as it endures, or until it is replaced or metamorphoses into another dream, the SD provides a meaning, a purpose and a motivation, and influences the formation of identity in youth. Figure 2.2 illustrates this dynamic.

Only the dreamer can distinguish between PDs, SDs and ADs. The dreamer does this by assessing the intensity of the emotion that the dream produces. An SD tends to persist and to endow itself with the load of emotions necessary for its realization. In attempting to realize a dream, the individual continuously makes adjustments between the perception of

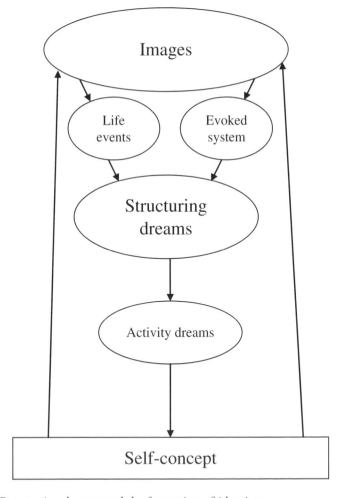

Figure 2.2   Structuring dreams and the formation of identity

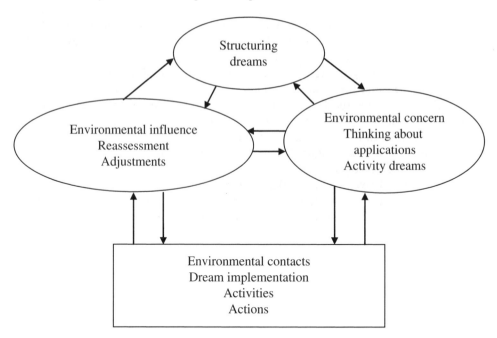

Figure 2.3   Cycles of design and redesign of structuring and activity dreams

the self and the capacity to realize SDs and ADs, and between self-knowledge and the potential for realization of an SD.

The social roles and models that surround the child, and the level of self-esteem that these generate, are key determinants in the self-concept that forms (Filion, 1999). In seeking to realize the SDs and ADs, the individual acts, makes mistakes, reassesses, transforms the self, transforms the SDs and ADs, and acts again. The individual follows a self-creative dynamic motion that implies a continuous creation of the self through a constant interchange of components that characterize living beings – especially young ones – in the making of what they will become. The type of relationship the individual maintains with the environment considerably influences that process. This is where entrepreneurial education can make a difference.

By establishing a relationship of reciprocity with the environment, the individual designs the ideal self he or she wishes to become. In this way, the individual can absorb, in an idiosyncratic manner, the environmental disturbances that necessitate continuous adaptation and readaptation efforts to re-establish the balance. This is constantly repeated in the cycle 'dreaming SDs and ADs and seeking their realization', in which the individual initiates a relationship with the environment. Entrepreneurs continuously cut and polish compatibilities with their ego, the self-realization model represented by the SDs and the environment in which they perform their activities. Figure 2.3 expresses this.

Collective dreams as inspiration for individual dreams
Dreams are expressed within a social context. If the social structure of a society is to be changed, changes have to be brought to the social environment that influences the imagery

from which CDs, SDs and ADs are derived. But how do dreams arise anyway? Leaving aside the psychological aspects of dreams (Fishbein, 1981; Freud, 1955; Winget and Kramer, 1979), we will look instead to sociological dimensions related to SDs and ADs (McClelland, 1961; Piaget, 1962; Richardson, 1969; Segal, Huba and Singer, 1980; Singer, 1973; 1981; Singer and Pope, 1978) and especially to the projective effects on the future of the life structure that follows projective thinking and dreaming (Feather, 1982; Gollwitzer, 1999; Klinger and Cox, 2004; Oetingen et al., 2001; Rabin, 1981; Schmuck and Sheldon, 2001; Semeonoff, 1976; Snyder, 1994; Wong and Fry, 1998).

The nature of the individual dream is strongly determined by the values of the culture to which the dreamer belongs. Why is this so? Human beings are social products. Individual dreams are referenced to the individual's social context. Imbued with cultural values, each individual produces dreams according to a particular representation of the world, the individual's own history, the processes of construction of the self, and the relationships established with others and with the world.

If the dream is determined by culture, and our goal is to appropriate the educational process to establish a foundation for entrepreneurial and ethical values that were absent from the individual's environment and that still may not feature in the society where the individual evolved, relevant new values and culture must be conveyed. This can be done by introducing new types of social models. This is a straightforward application of McClelland's findings (1961) on the influence of heroes in the literature.

This process can also be achieved by other means, including educational programs that present the desired values and social behavior. The desired values could be love and cooperation. The activities shown would always have the common good of the community in mind, thus promoting an improved quality of life and greater freedom for everyone – with all that means in societies that experience violence daily. The educational program could focus on activities that generate more evenly distributed income, wealth, knowledge and power. As society is the source of individual dreams, it can be said that the implicit social models behind the learning and the identification process of children will lead to the reproduction of the status quo. Beings tend to reproduce what they see, what they know and what they are taught to value. Education can present models that will influence change in the social order if those social models are appealing enough to influence the SDs of young students and powerful enough to influence new types of aspirations for their future.

Here are some of the questions we can ask: are the social models presented in a given society by the media desirable for children? Should these models be used in education? If not, what alternatives would support a sane and promising CD and SD for young children? Here, collective dreaming becomes a means of helping educators, parents, children and representatives from society concerned with education to design the desired educational programs that will prepare young children for the society of the future – for the type of entrepreneurial society we wish to see happening in the future (Dolabela, 2003a; Filion, 2005).

If, however, only a small part of society looks at education in this way, other members of society could perceive that small group as a threat. 'A community that dreams and is comprised of individuals whose dream is to realize the community's dream is a threat to those who try to perpetuate the structure of power and prevent changes. It is for this reason that dreaming can be dangerous' (Dolabela, 2003b, p. 43).

Focus on entrepreneurship oriented towards value-added contributions to society
However individual in its conception, an SD implies collective dimensions in its purpose: it should add value to, rather than take value from, the community. And even though it is individual in its conception, the dream is strongly influenced by the values of the community to which the dreamer belongs. Moreover, the SD will bear collective dimensions in its implementation, as it will become the fruit of the cooperation of the various players, resources and support elements that make it happen.

From that perspective, the practice of entrepreneurship that is to be supported by societal support systems, such as education, should include collective values. It should contribute to the quality of life of a society, and generate more than economic activity and individual profit. In relation to this social contribution, we can identify four types of entrepreneurs, which are introduced in Table 2.2.

Educators need to focus on the types of entrepreneurship that carry both individualistic and collectivist values. The emphasis in entrepreneurship is on the capacity to identify and seize opportunities in one's field of work, but these opportunities should generate an added value for society in the form of knowledge, well-being, freedom, health, democracy, material wealth, spiritual enrichment, improved quality of life and so on. These are the values on which the proposed Entrepreneurial Pedagogy Methodology focuses. Entrepreneurial education should make explicit a will to contribute socially. It should focus on the humanitarian type of entrepreneur – in both non-profit and for-profit businesses – more than it has in the past. Many entrepreneurs who made fortunes can be classified as individualistic, but they also contributed an added value to the quality of life in society: Henry Ford, Ichiro Honda and Bill Gates are examples.

Collective dreams may be defined as the desired images members of a society envision for the future of their community, images formed by the convergence of the multiple and diverse images held by the society's individual members. Collective dreams should be associated with specific projects that can be transformed into reality through the dynamic interaction of the human, social and natural potential of the society itself. As the source, nourishment and framework of many individual dreams, CDs offer a reference that inspires individual SDs. These SDs will be shaped taking into account the resources and support available. Individual SDs should overlap and comply with what is socially acceptable, what was defined implicitly or explicitly through social consensus. Contrary to what many think, entrepreneurship is rarely an isolated act. It follows a set of social structures and values, which is why some types of entrepreneurship are expressed in certain societies and ethnic groups more than others.

The defining of collective dreams has implications. Organized societies often define their collective dreams – the type of society they desire – through political parties. But

Table 2.2   Types of entrepreneurs and social contribution

Values	Type of entrepreneur	Social contribution
Egocentric	Destructive	Negative
Egoistic	Static	Neutral
Individualistic	Efficient	Positive
Collectivist	Humanitarian	Positive

CDs can also be defined locally through the education program of each school. Certain conditions and implications of CDs will affect both those now living in the society and those yet to come: how the society is organized, the social structures that result, the types of interpersonal relationships that develop, the types of dialogue that emerge to establish cooperation between the various social actors, and the capacity to resolve conflicts democratically and stimulate the expression of values and emotions that allow higher levels of self-actualization.

Enriched by social diversity in all its forms, by alternatives for social involvement and by an abundance of technological options, CDs should inspire and create the conditions for greater humanity and a richer multiplicity of individual SDs. Collective dreams that are founded on the principles of freedom and acceptance of others and on a process of negotiation towards social consensus about constructing the future will more likely inspire entrepreneurs inclined to design SDs that promote social welfare. Societies that have contributed and developed knowledge about themselves and the world, that have stimulated collective manifestations of emotions and dreams, humor and adventure, beliefs and hopes, and that, by respecting their past, are prepared to reinvent the future and construct the new, will be more appealing for individual SDs that wish to improve the collectivity. The future seems to lie with societies where institutional structures allow negotiation towards social consensus.

Entrepreneurial pedagogy: a key approach to support development
Designed to support social development and social inclusion, entrepreneurial pedagogy begins by constructing a CD. This CD implies a collectivist approach in defining a future for that society.

The school as a representation and a microcosm of the society
By using the existing public and private school systems in its implementation strategy, entrepreneurial pedagogy values the school for its role as a representation of the community. Schools are understood to be the locus for acquiring a capacity to deal with and construct the future. In this sense, the school represents a microcosm of society that can help forecast what the future holds for a given community. One of the characteristics of EP is that the community must actively participate as both a learner and a supporter. The community is the source of education and it sets educational objectives; it determines the uses that can be made of education.

The CD process of constructing a community's future requires projective thinking about scenarios that are often far removed from that society's existing models and structures. This is particularly true in developing societies such as Brazil. For this reason, it is critical that the members of the community develop a reflective relationship about a probable and desirable future for their reality. Entrepreneurial pedagogy offers an environment for CDs related to the collective design of ways of living, being and working that imply new forms of knowledge. The first level of concern is education that will prepare for life, rather than for a specific job or occupation.

Gradual progression in forming new identities
The learning environment that results should nurture and develop the learner's confidence and self-esteem. It should immerse the student in a learning system where there is

a coherent relationship between the learner and the world. A meaningful education should take into account the learner's cognitive, emotional and social background.

The evolution of children in forming new identities must be gradual and coherent with their past, and there should be no drastic rejection of their past. There are nuances here. Forming new identities in a gradual manner is essential to reducing the tensions between the learners and the world around them. The knowledge the children acquire will help them design and implement individual SDs; it will stimulate them to express creative powers as their level of self-confidence increases.

Cultural roots: methodology conditioning factors
Designing a country's development agenda affects not only the role of entrepreneurs, but also the roles of most other players in the society: everyone will be expected to adopt a level of entrepreneurial behavior. Brazil is in great need of entrepreneurial education to allow a higher proportion of its human capital to express their entrepreneurial potential. Otherwise, large segments of society will continue to be denied the opportunity to generate income and experience the fulfillment of self-actualization. While it is interesting and useful to look to the experiences of countries with higher income levels, more equitable distribution, welfare, democracy and freedom of entrepreneurial expression, these experiences and social models cannot be applied in Brazil as such. Brazilian society, like every society, has unique specificities, diversities, regionalisms and complexities that must be recognized and respected. The Brazilian social and cultural fabric is creative due to its diversity, but unevenly developed because of its history. It is open to new approaches to reach better levels of development and offers a fertile ground for EP and for its application in the basic education[2] system.

There are other conditioning factors. We must consider the Brazilian education system. Historically, the education system has often been threatened by ideological and political polarization, a lack of democratic practice and community participation, and a process that undervalues teachers. Teachers, parents and communities have never participated in the system to any degree or been involved in defining learning needs; in that respect EP is breaking new ground. To these factors, we can add a lack of knowledge of and prejudices about entrepreneurship, and little awareness of the importance of entrepreneurship and entrepreneurial education and of what they may contribute to individuals and development. Entrepreneurship is often seen in a negative light, entrepreneurs portrayed as exploitative and unethical.

Ethics must be taken into account. As a pedagogy focused on development, EP associates the results of applying individual dreams primarily with social and human values that will improve the community's standard of living. Our interest lies in entrepreneurship approaches that both produce income and distribute the wealth generated by the entrepreneurial activities. Entrepreneurial pedagogy must lead to more than entrepreneurial expression: it must also support cooperation, democracy and humanity. The implementation of individual dreams should improve the community's quality of life. The implementation of individual dreams must be done in a way that enhances a society's moral and ethical values.

Entrepreneurial Pedagogy Methodology (EPM)

Entrepreneurial Pedagogy Methodology (EPM) was designed for elementary education to develop in youth a more fertile ground for creative and entrepreneurial expression.

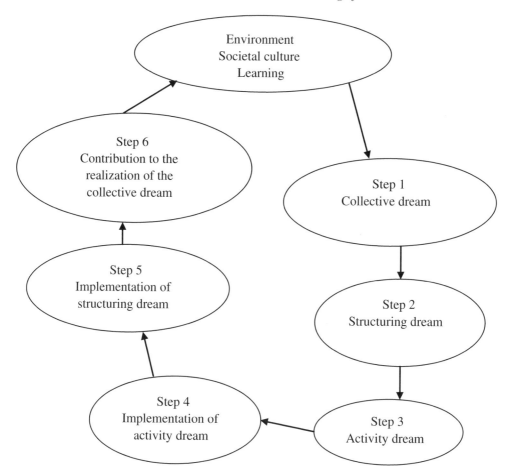

Figure 2.4   The six steps of the dreaming process and the entrepreneurial learning cycle

Entrepreneurial Pedagogy Methodology presents the students with a learning plan that has two objectives that are the basis of the approach: the formulation of dreams and the implementation of these dreams. They are expressed in six steps as illustrated in Figure 2.4. The program, a class of two hours a week for 40 weeks a year, should be part of the students' curriculum from the beginning to the end of elementary school. It can be extended to secondary education using the same principles and, in some schools, might even begin with nursery school or pre-school activities. Thus, it can begin at age 4 and be applied every year up to the last year of secondary education, when the children reach 16 or 17 years of age.

The pedagogical task each school year consists of the 'dreaming dreams and seeking their realization' cycle. The year begins with the question, 'What is your dream and how will you make it happen?' At the end of each school term, the students give individual presentations somewhat as follows: 'Here's what I've done to formulate my dream. Here's how I structured it, and this is what I've done to realize it. Here's what I achieved and what I still need to do to make it happen. Here are the problems I encountered and the lessons I learned that will make it easier next time.'

A classroom application

In August 2002 a pilot test of the Entrepreneurial Pedagogy Methodology was carried out in the municipal school Israel Pinheiro in the slum Loud Vera Cruz. The teacher, Adriana Moura, began the class by asking the students two questions: 'What is your dream?' and 'What will you do to make it happen?' (Two very basic questions almost never asked in Brazil either in the schools or by most parents, apart from the 'social' question, 'What do you want to become when you grow up?' that adults ask when they meet a child.)

'I want to traffic drugs,' responded one 15-year-old, 'because my mother is starving.' The student wanted to be what in Brazil is known as an 'airplane' – the person who provides the 'merchandise' to the customer. This seemed to be the only activity he could envision as a way of making money to help feed his mother and the other children.

One can imagine how a teacher might react in a regular class – she might consider it an act of delinquency, or she might offer to help the mother. And it is likely she would then continue explaining, for example, how to extract a square root . . .

However, the incident took place in the entrepreneurial class – the 'class of dreams' as the students nicknamed it from the beginning – and two things happened.

First, as trafficking drugs was one student's dream, it had to be discussed, commented on and discarded as a possibility by the teacher. Second, the boy's classmates then 'entered' his dream. They opened the discussion and made suggestions: if the problem was a plate of food, he must think of another way to get it. And they found one. They decided to create a company that produced cleaning products. Together, they developed a logo, a folder and six products, for which the science teacher suggested formulas, and 'Tá limpo' ('Very clean') was born. The student had an alternative to entering the drug world, and his mother and younger brothers and sisters had a means of feeding themselves.

The language and process of the proposed Entrepreneurial Pedagogy Methodology (EPM)

Entrepreneurial pedagogy uses a clear and simple language. It explicitly formulates two basic questions: *what is your dream about what you want to become? What is your project to help make this happen? In other words, what do you plan to do to realize your dream?* The methodology uses a variety of support elements, mainly examples of what could be done and what other students have done in previous years.

The idea is to begin with structuring dreams that can be implemented easily. For instance, in poor communities, the SD might be to buy food for the mother, build a small house, buy a filter for potable drinking water at home, provide the means to celebrate birthday parties, go to a swimming pool or buy a new pair of shoes. As the students mature, the program will model the SDs on local entrepreneurs, but in the early years, the objective is to have students acquire positive reinforcement by accomplishing simple, easily achievable tasks.

Entrepreneurial pedagogy is designed to develop increasing levels of freedom and self-confidence in making choices. In formulating an SD and a specific AD and attempting to make these materialize, children learn how to master an activity process: how to design and implement projects and what is required to succeed at this. They learn how to initiate and be responsible for their own accomplishments. The pedagogical exercises invite the children to projective and systemic thinking at incremental levels of complexity related to their level, a process that will influence decisions about future activities. Evaluation of entrepreneurship education programs shows there is an effect on entrepreneurial intention as it influences perceived behavioral control (Fayolle et al., 2005).

Thus, the entrepreneurial learning cycle that results from the dreaming process may be summarized in six steps, as follows. The process begins with a given society's culture and values and implicit or explicit CD. It is then expressed through thinking exercises about an SD that presents an image of the future one wishes to experience, be or become. Individuals then develop an image of something that could be realized – an AD – that will lead to the realization of the SD. This is the project component. Next, the individuals seek to implement the AD and, to do so, identify and learn whatever is necessary to realize this AD. The realization of one, but usually of several, AD will contribute to realizing the SD. The realization of the SD will contribute to the realization of the CD. Learning takes place, a new situation is reached and the cycle begins again. The nature of the relationship between these moments will determine whether an entrepreneurial character is born and how intense that character will be. Figure 2.4 illustrates the process.

This learning exercise produces knowledge in various forms: know how to be, know how to become, know how to design and to implement activities, know how to do, know how to manage, know how to learn, and know how to get along with and make proper use of social capital. This knowledge is entrepreneurship related and is called 'entrepreneurial knowledge' (EK) or 'enterprising knowledge'. It will be acquired in a dream-realization context where the ease of the student will become greater and greater. The tensions between the design, implementation and realization of CDs, SDs and ADs should come to a point where the student finds enjoyment, and even pleasure, in practicing the cycle of entrepreneurial design and the carrying out of entrepreneurial activities.

The path to achieving ADs and SDs and the constant search to realize dreams should become the source that generates and maintains a high level of motivation and the emotional levels that foster in the individual both persistence and a capacity to endure, despite mistakes, difficulties and outside pressures. The ability to learn from one's own mistakes makes the construction of EK a very different experience from the acquisition of other forms of knowledge, as it influences not only the acquisition of knowledge and know-how but also the formation of the self. Thus, individuals are constantly making explicit or implicit decisions about what they want to become and continuously assessing what can be achieved. Acquiring EK therefore implies an ongoing set of decisions about the making of the self.

Entrepreneurial behavior also implies innovation – a contribution that will bring added value through the implementation of what was conceived. This is another factor that influences the acquisition of knowledge about what entrepreneurs-to-be are going through in their learning process. Figure 2.5 expresses this.

Seeking the realization of the dream
The dynamics of EPM include the entrepreneurial learning cycle as shown in Figure 2.4: the dreams and the search for their realization. When involved in the task of realizing a dream, individuals will ponder the adequacy of the dream, the environment and the self. They will seek, in a self-sufficient manner, to deepen their self-knowledge and their understanding of the dream's environment. They will thus gain an increased awareness of the world and of others around them. Two phenomena are always present in this learning process. The first is an increased awareness of the self, others and the world around; the second is a set of decisions about the self and the activities to be undertaken.

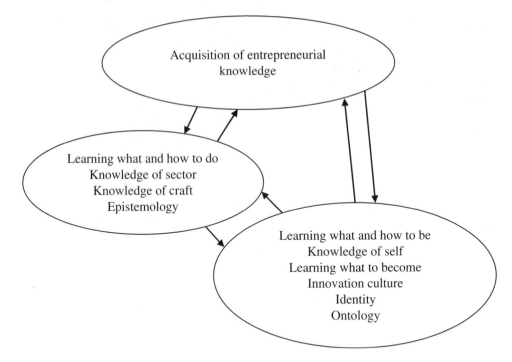

Figure 2.5   Acquisition of entrepreneurial knowledge, epistemology and ontology

This could well explain why the level of anxiety is often high among entrepreneurship students. They must learn to continuously make decisions about things to be done that have consequences for what they will become. At the same time, they are acquiring knowledge and know-how, just as other students are. Like the dream, the self undergoes alterations and continuous change. This is also expressed in Figure 2.5. Entrepreneurial decisions engender both epistemological consequences and ontological effects, particularly at the beginning of the entrepreneurial career.

Thus, the construction of EK is dynamic and often profoundly affects the shaping of the character the entrepreneur will become. This makes it a powerful form of education. Imagining SDs and ADs may be easier for some students than for others, but implementation and the final realization are the most difficult tasks for most students. These must fit the individual's system so that the individual remains in a state of equilibrium. We have called this decision-making process the structuring of the 'ecological system of one's life' (Filion and Dolabela, 2000). Entrepreneurs-to-be who do not learn to do this harmoniously have a difficult time lasting as entrepreneurs as they are in a continuous state of disequilibrium.

The structuring of that 'ecological system' is part of the basic learning that must be done to master the entrepreneurial craft. It requires an adequate knowledge of one's potential and sharp judgment about how to use oneself. Basic self-awareness skills must be acquired. The realization of dreams leads to ever-greater accomplishments. Such dynamic motion tells us that the formulation of a dream and then the search to realize it is a ceaseless process. This is so because the process must absorb and contemplate the changes taking place in the dreamer's life and environment. An ascending spiral motion, in which all parts are interrelated in a cause-and-effect manner, gradually shapes the person's entrepreneurial system.

Because entrepreneurship is a field of action, the connection between dreaming and seeking the realization of the dream is the essence of the process. The value of what is designed lies in its implementation and eventual realization. Entrepreneurs are action oriented, another characteristic of entrepreneurship. Few other areas in the management education system require as much thinking about implementing activities, and few others are as action oriented.

Nothing is more important than this connection. It will almost always lead one to redefine the elements of the dreaming process presented in Figure 2.4. On the one hand, dreams are in a constant state of mutation; on the other hand, the abilities, competencies and resources to realize these dreams are in a constant state of change. Hence, nothing is static. The greater the number of entrepreneurial projects, the more the entrepreneurial environment changes. In the process, one becomes used to dealing with situations characterized by both uncertainty and unpredictability; these become characteristic elements of the entrepreneurial environment.

This is why creativity is needed, and why entrepreneurs have to learn so much about what it means to be creative. Through creativity, entrepreneurs articulate who they are and, especially, what makes them different. This is expressed in the dreaming process. The expression of this differentiation leads to innovation, to do what is unique. The dream's author is always faced with the question, 'What is the next step?' and the dream's author alone is able to find the answer that leads to new activities. In short, the pedagogical process is dedicated primarily to establishing a connection between the dreams, their implementation and their realization. This is because the latter, in its various forms, contains the dynamic elements from which the acts of dreaming and realizing dreams will continuously be constructed in the future.

Educational material[3]
The teachers' material includes *Pedagogia empreendedora* (Entrepreneurial pedagogy) (Dolabela, 2003b), which contains the theoretical and methodological principles of the EPM program as summarized in the preceding section. The 'Cadernos' (Appendix 2.5) provide a bank of exercises designed to help the educator effectively use the EP approach in the classroom. There are also two educational novels to be used by both teachers and students, *A Ponte mágica* (The magic bridge) (Dolabela, 2004) for students aged 10 to 15, and *O Segredo de Luisa*[4] (Luisa's Secret) (Dolabela, 1999) for students 16 and older. These books offer a rich reading experience and explain entrepreneurial activities and new venture creation through fascinating, real-life narratives. Teachers will find them an inspirational source for designing innovative courses and colorful teaching sessions. 'Mapa dos Sonhos' (Dream map) (Dolabela, 2002) is the student guide for all grades. It leads students through a series of graduated exercises to formulate their dreams and their enterprising proposals and describe their proposed paths for implementation – see also Dolabela (2000b).

The application of the Entrepreneurial Pedagogy Methodology (EPM)
This Entrepreneurial Pedagogy Methodology is probably the first methodological approach to have applied entrepreneurial learning on such a large scale. It was designed for elementary and secondary levels but has so far been used only at the elementary level.

Hundreds of people have been involved in thinking about ways to apply the methodology in their schools; thousands of teachers have used it; and hundreds of thousands of elementary-level students have come in contact with it in their classrooms. This methodology is not primarily about creating a pedagogical approach exclusively to prepare students to become entrepreneurs and create ventures. Entrepreneurial Pedagogy Methodology conceives entrepreneurship as a state of being rather than just a way of doing and was designed to develop students' creative potential. Those involved in the program, and especially the teachers, are convinced the course will influence a large proportion of students to become entrepreneurs. Students demonstrate greater entrepreneurial behavior immediately following the course, which indicates that a greater number will act more entrepreneurially in any activity in which they engage and in any area of employment they choose. They will also accept, and be more supportive of, other entrepreneurs and those who want to do something new and creative. The choice to become an entrepreneur is, of course, the student's and only the student's, but when the time comes for the students to choose a craft or professional activity, anything that concerns entrepreneurial activities will be part of their evoked system.

As the program continues to expand to other parts of Brazil, EPM is being disseminated through teacher workshops that introduce teachers to EPM and train them to offer the program to their students. The methodology training is both democratic and interactive. Processes are not imposed, and teachers learn from one another how to use EPM. Teachers design their own way of applying the basic principles: they can use EPM as it is or they can adapt it to suit their individual needs.

It could not be otherwise. Entrepreneurial Pedagogy Methodology has to be applied in a wide variety of contexts. Moreover, what the methodology proposes does not deal with traditional cognitive content. It requires that the teacher be truly motivated and convinced of the methodology's suitability and effectiveness. The social and political aspects of the implementation cannot be underestimated. With a remarkably humanistic approach, EPM prepares the individual to actively participate in social development through the generation and, more importantly, the distribution, of income, keeping in mind the principles of quality of life, democratic practice and the elimination of social exclusion.

Results of the application of Entrepreneurial Pedagogy Methodology (EPM): the experience in the state of Paraná, Brazil
In an unprecedented undertaking, as of September 2003, EPM had been implemented in 123 cities in the state of Paraná as part of a major local development project promoted by Sebrae-Paraná.[5] The cities selected had a maximum HDI-M[6] of 0.800. Each city created a Forum of Local Development, a democratic umbrella organization of local leaders, to coordinate PSDL (*Programa Sebrae de Desenvolvimento Local* [Sebrae Local Development Program]).

Fernando Dolabela coordinated the implementation of EPM, and 16 consultants were trained to manage and coordinate the teacher workshops. Sebrae-Paraná financed the program, which had a global cost of US$400 000. See also Table 2.3.

The program guidelines in Sebrae-Paraná were as follows:

1.   EPM was implemented through the teachers of participating schools. In preparation, the teachers attended two types of training workshops:

Table 2.3   Implementation of EPM through Sebrae in the state of Paraná, Brazil, 2002–04

Number of cities involved	123
Total population of cities involved	2 257 150
Number of schools involved	1566
Number of teachers involved	6352
Number of students involved	173 304
Cost	US$400 000

(a) Methodology Workshop: 50 teachers learned how to apply EPM in the classroom.
(b) Multiplier Workshop: 20 participants from the first workshop were trained to teach the Methodology Workshop to other teachers.

The number and proportion of teachers who attended the first and second workshops varied from state to state. For instance, the city of São José of Campos in the state of São Paulo has 2000 public sector teachers. Two hundred teachers participated in the first Methodology Workshop and 20 teachers from that group were selected to give the Multiplier Workshop. These 20 teachers then offered methodology workshops to the remaining 1800 teachers.

The teachers had never before participated in training of this type on such a scale. The experience changed their view of their work, and their motivation and level of involvement increased.

2. EPM was developed for pre-school through secondary school.
3. Objectives.

General: Over the long term, to generate cultural changes and develop competencies in all levels and classes of the population for the promotion of economic, human and social development.

Specific: To develop the students' entrepreneurial capacity, applicable to any legal activity.

4. To participate, cities had to meet the following conditions:
(a) Have in place programs that promoted local development.
(b) Have a maximum HDI–M of 0.800.
(c) Be represented by an association (a non-governmental organization). The constituted local powers (mayor, municipal administration) were responsible for the decision to accept the program, but the local leadership of the various organizations involved in local development had to commit to, and become involved in, implementation of the program.

5. Responsibilities of Sebrae-Paraná:
(a) Finance the program.
(b) Offer EPM, as developed and taught by Fernando Dolabela, to teachers who become trainers of other teachers.
(c) Publicize the program.
(d) Provide local political coordination.
(e) Monitor the program through evaluation reports from each of the participating cities.

6.   Responsibilities of the cities:
     (a)   Mobilize the leadership and all major organizations involved in local develop-
           ment in each of the cities involved.
     (b)   Organize the necessary infrastructure for the teacher-training workshops and
           the students' courses and classes.
     (c)   Monitor the application of the program content by the students in each munic-
           ipal district.
     (d)   Complete a program evaluation report for Sebrae-Paraná at the end of the
           school year.
7.   Any city that failed to carry out any of its responsibilities would be prohibited from
     working with Sebrae-Paraná for a period of up to two years.
8.   All teachers of the schools in the selected cities were invited to teach the entrepre-
     neurship program.

Phases of teacher training
A city leader in each municipal district gave a presentation to introduce the program. This
phase was followed by two teacher-training workshops delivered by Fernando Dolabela.

1.   Presentation.
     Target group: Local support systems (political, economic, social leadership).
     Objective: Demonstrate commitment to, and build support for, the Entrepreneurial
     Methodology Program.
     Duration: 2 hours.
2.   Methodology Workshop.
     Target group: Directors, supervisors and teachers from the schools involved.
     Objective: Prepare teachers and educators to implement EPM.
     Duration: 16 hours – two days of immersion.
     Maximum number of participants: 50.
3.   Multiplier Workshop.
     Target group: Teachers with the profile of multiplier (a subgroup selected from
     among the participants of the Methodology Workshop).
     Objective: To generate self-sufficiency in the municipal district by training the teachers
     to become 'trainers' of other teachers and to monitor the EPM implementation process.
     Duration: 16 hours – two days of immersion.
     Maximum number of participants: 20.

   Problems that arose during the implementation process were mainly political in nature
and fell into two categories:

1.   Opposition to using the structured political process to support development.
2.   Opposition to the term 'entrepreneurship'. The term was rejected by those who con-
     sider themselves on the 'left' and who associate entrepreneurship with capitalism and
     exploitation.

Evaluation
The program was evaluated at each stage of the process.

First evaluation   The first evaluation took place after the teacher-training workshops. It consisted of a subjective analysis of the strengths and weaknesses of the implementation process that had been suggested during the workshops to allow teachers to make adjustments to the methodology before beginning to use EPM in the classroom.

Sources of information:

- teachers and educators
- EPM consultants
- Sebrae technicians.

Second evaluation   The second evaluation is designed to measure the degree of satisfaction of the program's principal actors and sponsors. Scheduled for 2005, it is financed by Sebrae-Paraná.

Questionnaires will be distributed, through sampling, to those involved: support actors, teachers and students. The evaluation will focus on the relationships between the various actors involved in the program.

The following are examples of what will be assessed:

1. Relationship between the school and the local body representing the Ministry of Education. (This body may differ from one state to another.)
2. Relationship between the local body representing the Ministry of Education and City Hall.
3. Teachers' assessment of EPM.
4. Students' assessment of EPM.
5. Teacher–student relationships.
6. Student–family relationships: what is the family's assessment of the changes in the student?
7. Family–EP relationship: what is the family's assessment of EP?
8. School–community relationship: how has EP changed the relationship between the school and the community?

The experience has shown that teachers easily understand the process. They have worked enthusiastically to implement EP wherever it has been proposed. In many cases, they also began to formulate and implement their own dreams.

The decision of whether or not to implement EPM was left to either the school or the teachers who had taken the training, rather than to the educational hierarchy. This proved to be appropriate to the nature of the project. The teachers based their decisions on whether they perceived a need to incorporate the acquisition of life skills, as proposed by EPM, into the students' curriculum.

The teachers were motivated and enthusiastic, and all decided to use the program. The community's involvement and the general will to develop the entrepreneurial expression of children provided further evidence of EPM's effectiveness. The general perception was that the program allowed the children to acquire additional tools that could be useful for them in life.

Entrepreneurial Pedagogy Methodology has already produced extraordinary results. The reception has been far greater than anticipated, suggesting that perhaps a revolution in basic education is in process in Brazil. In every school that has implemented EPM, student dropout rates have decreased, academic results have improved,[7] and students have demonstrated a greater desire to learn. The results offer encouraging support for continuing to develop and expand EPM.

Conclusion
Education should contribute to developing one of society's principal natural resources: its human capital. This implies the involvement not only of teachers, but also of others concerned with children's development – in particular, the parents and those working in social and economic development.

The idea behind EPM is to identify a minimum of human resources to help build bridges that will allow entrepreneurial education to establish itself and begin to develop. This perspective implies that people perceive a common interest in cooperation that may help them put aside individual differences. In choosing to work with EPM, those involved in primary and secondary education show they are determined to apply the six steps of the dreaming process as presented in Figure 2.4. In secondary education, the program may lead to the creation of real business ventures where students sell their products in school fairs at the end of the school year.

A key EPM innovation is involving the community to develop CDs and discuss the type of world people wish to live in. This clearly contributes to increasing the legitimacy of public sector institutions in a country where there is an increasing awareness of the need to improve quality of life, personal safety and equality of opportunities. Entrepreneurial Pedagogy Methodology helps create social consensus in social microcosms around education projects that can be implemented in the education system. This process could be expanded and applied to a greater extent in other areas of society.

Another contribution concerns the teachers and the effectiveness of the education system. Education often serves to maintain and reinforce the existing social order, but in a country undergoing rapid development, such as Brazil, education can also become a key element in supporting rapid social change. Entrepreneurial Pedagogy Methodology was designed to offer a path to freedom for as many young children as possible – all those who want to start dreaming and to bring these dreams to fruition. The program should improve self-esteem and the level of control people are able to exercise over their destiny.

Entrepreneurial Pedagogy Methodology's primary contribution, of course, is to the students, who will leave school with a range of tools that prepares them in a better way for today's world. It is hoped the program will encourage a greater commitment to social responsibility and contribution. Entrepreneurial Pedagogy Methodology aims to increase not only achievement and entrepreneurial consciousness, but also the ethical and social concerns of students.

Entrepreneurial Pedagogy Methodology will need to be refined and further adapted for both individual cities and curriculum levels. Those who have been involved in the program are already advocating having it made available in the other levels of their schools. And they want the program to work along the same lines every year: dreaming and implementing the dreams. It is obvious that a need has been only partially met. The program has opened a door for developing further educational approaches and material that will allow students to reflect on themselves and their future and develop their imaginations, and that will give them tools to better satisfy their desire for achievement. The experiment described here is probably unique in the world, and could serve as a model for transforming other education systems, both in countries with emerging economies and those wishing to revitalize the development of their greatest natural wealth – the entrepreneurial potential of their human resources.

The experiment is based on a systemic and visionary theory by which entrepreneurship is first and foremost a way of thinking and acting that can be learned. To go further along this road, new research will be required in the fields of entrepreneurship and education. In entrepreneurship, a better understanding of the steps in the development of visionary thinking is needed. In education, the relationship between the different steps in the development of intelligence must be clarified by reference to models such as those of Piaget and the learning methods that are most appropriate for introducing the entrepreneurial and visionary viewpoint.

Notes

1. Many thanks to Judith Richer for her comments, questions and skillful revision of the text.
2. What is known as 'basic education' in Brazil consists of the following: pre-school (three grades, 4 to 6 years of age); primary education (8 or 9 grades, 7 to 14 years of age); secondary education (three grades, 15 to 17 years of age).
3. Appendices 2.1 to 2.4, at the end of this chapter, present a summary of each of the books used in EPM. Appendix 2.5 describes the 'Cadernos', a series of teaching exercises developed to support the application of EPM in the classroom.
4. *O Segredo de Luísa* is the top best-seller ever written by a Brazilian and published in Brazil. By the end of 2004, it had sold over 100 000 copies.
5. Sebrae is a governmental organization that supports small and medium-sized enterprises.
6. HDI–M (Index of Human Development – Municipal) is developed from a data bank of education indicators (literacy and rate of school frequency), longevity and income of the population of a city.
7. Data are being gathered and will be made public.

References

Béchard, J.-P. and Grégoire, D. (2005), 'Entrepreneurship education research revisited: the case of higher education', *Academy of Management Learning and Education*, **4** (1), 22–43.

Block, N. (ed.) (1981), *Imagery*, Cambridge, MA: MIT Press.

Bruyat, C. and Julien, P.-A. (2001), 'Defining the field of research in entrepreneurship', *Journal of Business Venturing*, **16** (2), 17–27.

Cantillon, R. (1755), *Essai sur la nature du commerce en général*, London: Fletcher Gyles. (Also edited by Henry Higgs, London: Frank Cass, 1931).

Checkland, P. (1999), *Systems Thinking, Systems Practice*, 2nd edn, New York: Wiley.

Dolabela, F. (1999), *O Segredo de Luísa*, São Paulo: Cultura Editores.

Dolabela, F. (2000a), *Oficina do Empreendedor*, São Paulo: Cultura Editores.

Dolabela, F. (2000b), *A Vez do Sonho*, São Paulo: Cultura Editores.

Dolabela, F. (2002), *Empreendedorismo. A Viagem do Sonho*, Brasília: AED (Agência de Educaçao para o Desenvolvimento).

Dolabela, F. (2003a), *Empreendedorismo. Uma Forma de Ser*, Brasília: AED.

Dolabela, F. (2003b), *Pedagogia empreendedora*, São Paulo: Cultura Editores.

Dolabela, F. (2004), *A Ponte mágica*, São Paulo: Cultura Editores.

Fayolle, A. (1999), *L'ingénieur entrepreneur français. Contribution à la compréhension des comportements de création et reprise d'entreprise des ingénieurs diplômés*, Paris: L'Harmattan.

Fayolle, A. (2003), *Le métier de créateur d'entreprise. Les motivations, parcours et facteurs clés de succès*, Paris: Éditions d'organisation.

Fayolle, A. (2004), *Entrepreneuriat. Apprendre à entreprendre*, Paris: Dunod.

Fayolle, A., Gailly, B., Kickul, J., Lassas-Clerc, N. and Whitcanack, L. (2005), 'Capturing variations in attitudes and intentions: a longitudinal study to assess the pedagogical effectiveness of entrepreneurship teaching programs', ICSB World Conference, Washington, DC, 15–18 June (published in CD-ROM Conference Proceedings).

Feather, N.T. (ed.) (1982), *Expectations and Actions: Expectancy-Value Models in Psychology*, Hillsdale, NJ: Erlbaum.

Filion, L.J. (1988), 'The strategy of successful entrepreneurs in small business: vision, relationships and anticipatory learning', PhD thesis, University of Lancaster, UK (UMI 8919064).

Filion, L.J. (1989), 'The design of your entrepreneurial learning system: identify a vision and assess your relations system', Third Canadian Conference on Entrepreneurial Studies, University of Calgary, 28–30 September (Best Paper Award of the Conference. Published in J.G.M. McKirdy (ed.) (1989), *Proceedings of the Third Canadian Conference on Entrepreneurial Studies*, pp. 77–90).

Filion, L.J. (1991a), 'Vision and relations: elements for an entrepreneurial metamodel', *International Small Business Journal*, **9** (2), 26–40.

Filion, L.J. (1991b), *Vision et relations: clefs du succès de l'entrepreneur*, Cap Rouge, Quebec: Éditions de l'entrepreneur.

Filion, L.J. (1998), 'Entrepreneurship: entrepreneurs and small business owner-managers', in P.A. Julien (ed.), *The State of the Art in Small Business and Entrepreneurship*, London: Avebury, pp. 117–49, 428–40.

Filion, L.J. (1999), *Self-Space and Vision*, Sixth International Conference of the United Kingdom Systems Society (UKSS), Lincoln, UK, 5–9 July in A.M. Castell et al. (eds) *Synergy Matters*, New York and London: Kluwer Academic/Plenum, pp. 613–18.

Filion, L.J. (2004), 'Operators and visionaries: differences in the entrepreneurial and managerial systems of two types of entrepreneurs', *International Journal of Entrepreneurship and Small Business*, **1** (1), 35–55.

Filion, L.J. (2005), *Pour une vision inspirante en milieu scolaire*, 2nd edn, Cap Rouge, Quebec: Presses Inter Universitaires.

Filion, L.J. and Dolabela, F. (eds) (2000), *Boa Idéia! E Agora? Plano de Negocio, o caminho mais seguro para criar a gerenciar sua empresa*, São Paulo: Cultura Editores.

Fishbein, W. (1981), *Sleep, Dreams, and Memory*, New York: Spectrum Publications Medical and Scientific Books.

Freud, S. (1955), *The Interpretation of Dreams*, New York: Strachey (original German edition, 1900).

Gollwitzer, P.M. (1999), 'Implementation intentions: strong effects of simple plans', *American Psychologist*, **54**, 493–503.

Julien, P.-A. (2005), *Entrepreneuriat régional et économie de la connaissance: une métaphore des romans policiers*, Sainte-Foy, Quebec: Presses de l'Université du Québec.

Kao, R.W.Y., Kao, K.R. and Kao, R.R. (2002), *Entrepreneurism: A Philosophy and a Sensible Alternative for the Market Economy*, London: Imperial College Press.

Kao, R.W.Y., Kao, K.R. and Kao, R.R. (2004), *An Entrepreneurial Approach to Stewardship Accountability*, Singapore: World Scientific Publishing.

Klinger, E. and Cox, W.M. (eds) (2004), *Handbook of Motivational Counseling: Concepts, Approaches and Assessment*, Hoboken, NJ: Wiley.

Lundström, A. and Stevenson, L.A. (2005), *Entrepreneurship Policy: Theory and Practice*, New York: Springer/ISEN.

McClelland, D.C. (1961), *The Achieving Society*, Princeton, NJ: Van Nostrand (also, 2nd edn, 1976, New York: Irvington).

Oetingen, G., Pak, H. and Schneller, K. (2001), 'Self-regulation and goal-setting: turning free fantasies about the future into binding goals', *Journal of Personality and Social Psychology*, **80**, 736–53.

Piaget, J. (1962), *Plays, Dreams and Imitation in Childhood*, New York: Norton.

Rabin, A.I. (ed.) (1981), *Assessment with Projective Techniques: A Concise Introduction*, New York: Springer.

Richardson, A. (1969), *Mental Imagery*, New York: Springer.

Roberts, J. (2004), *The Modern Firm*, Oxford: Oxford University Press.

Say, J.B. (1803), *Traité d'économie politique, ou, simple exposition de la manière dont se forment, se distribuent, et se consomment les richesses (A Treatise on Political Economy; Or the Production, Distribution, and Consumption of Wealth)*, New York: Augustus M. Kelley, 1964 (1st edn, 1827, English translation).

Say, J.B. (1996), *Cours d'économie politique et autres essais*, Paris: GF-Flammarion.

Schmuck, P. and Sheldon, K.M. (eds) (2001), *Life Goals and Well-Being: Towards a Positive Psychology of Human Striving*, Seattle, WA: Hogrefe and Huber.

Schumpeter, J.A. (1934), *The Theory of Economic Development*, Cambridge, MA: Harvard University Press (original German edition, 1912).

Segal, B., Huba, G.J. and Singer, J.L. (1980), *Drugs, Daydreaming, and Personality: A Study of College Youth*, Hillsdale, NJ: Erlbaum.

Semeonoff, B. (1976), *Projective Techniques*, London: Wiley.

Sexton, D.L. and Smilor, R.W. (1997), *Entrepreneurship 2000*, Chicago, IL: Upstart.

Shane, S.A. (ed.) (2002a), *The Foundations of Entrepreneurship*, vol. 1, Cheltenham, UK and Northampton, MA: Edward Elgar.

Shane, S.A. (ed.) (2002b), *The Foundations of Entrepreneurship*, vol. 2, Cheltenham, UK and Northampton, MA: Edward Elgar.

Shane, S.A. (2003), *A General Theory of Entrepreneurship: The Individual-Opportunity Nexus*, Cheltenham, UK and Northampton, MA: Edward Elgar.

Shane, S.A. (2005), *Finding Fertile Ground: Identifying Extraordinary Opportunities for New Ventures*, Upper Saddle River, NJ: Wharton School Publishing.

Singer, J.L. (1973), *The Child's World of Make-Believe: Experimental Studies of Imaginative Play*, New York: Academic Press.

Singer, J.L. (1981), *Daydreaming and Fantasy*, Oxford: Oxford University Press.

Singer, J.L. and Pope, K.S. (1978), *The Power of Human Imagination: New Methods in Psychotherapy*, New York: Plenum Press.

Snyder, C.R. (1994), *The Psychology of Hope: You Can Get There from Here*, New York: Free Press.

Timmons, J.A. (2004), Opportunity recognition, in W.D. Bygrave and A. Zacharakis (eds), *The Portable MBA in Entrepreneurship*, Hoboken, NJ: Wiley.

Van der Horst, R., King-Kauanui, S. and Duffy, S. (eds) (2005), *Keystones of Entrepreneurship Knowledge*, London: Blackwell.

Winget, C. and Kramer, M. (1979), *Dimensions of Dreams*, Gainesville, FL: University Presses of Florida.

Wong, P.T.P. and Fry, P.S. (eds) (1998), *The Human Quest for Meaning: A Handbook of Psychological Research and Clinical Applications*, Mahwah, NJ: Erlbaum.

Appendix 2.1:   *Pedagogia empreendedora* (Author: Fernando Dolabela)
Pedagogia empreendedora (Entrepreneurial pedagogy) describes the Entrepreneurial Pedagogy Methodology developed for Brazilian basic education (nursery school through secondary school – 4 to 17 years of age).

First tested in 2002, the methodology has been used in 121 cities and involved more than 10 000 teachers and 300 000 students – with repercussions for a population of 2.5 million – in the states of Minas Gerais, São Paulo, Paraná and Rio Grande do Sul.

Its challenge? To build new values in Brazilian society, a society marked today by enormous differences of income, power and knowledge. Using the dream as its axis, Entrepreneurial Pedagogy Methodology aims to stimulate the formation of structured dreams and help the dreamer accomplish the dream.

The methodology is based on the concept of social inclusion/social development. It endeavors to promote a liaison between entrepreneurship as venture creation – where it is tied to the restrictive idea of economic growth – and all sectors of human activity. The central theme of the methodology is that entrepreneurship education in Brazil should aim to fight poverty through social development. If it does not, large segments of the population will continue to be denied the possibility of generating income and benefiting from wealth.

140 pages.
Published: August 2003, Cultura Editores.

Appendix 2.2:   *O Segredo de Luísa* (Author: Fernando Dolabela)
Released in June 1999, *O Segredo de Luísa* (Luisa's secret) immediately became a national best-seller. The author wrote the book in novel form because he believes that entrepreneurial content – as a cultural process – must be conveyed differently from purely intellectual knowledge. In a simple and compelling style, the narrative easily carries readers of all ages and education to the story's end. Before they know it, they have been immersed in entrepreneurial culture.

320 pages.
Published: June 1999, Cultura Editores.
Sales: 100 000 copies.
Brazilian national best-seller.

Appendix 2.3:   *A Ponte mágica* (Author: Fernando Dolabela)
A Ponte mágica (The magic bridge) is an educational novel in the style of *O Segredo de Luísa*. It was written as instructional material for elementary-level students 11 to 15 years of age – youth filled with energy and creativity ready to be transformed into reality.

166 pages.
Published: 2004, Cultura Editores.

Appendix 2.4:   Mapa dos Sonhos (Author: Fernando Dolabela, 2002)
Mapa dos Sonhos (Dream map) is the student guide for the entire EPM program. It provides a simple, structured document in which the students describe their dreams and record in detail the paths and strategies they will use to achieve them. The students identify how they will reach their objectives, what they should learn and the resources they will use.

Mapa dos Sonhos has not been commercially published and is available only to schools that use Entrepreneurial Pedagogy Methodology. Designed as an open-ended resource, it can be adapted by the teachers according to their needs.

Appendix 2.5:   Teaching Material: Cadernos (Authors/educators: Cordélia Rodrigues, Sergio Godinho de Oliveira, José Eduardo Vidigal, Sylvia Zanetti, Magda Maria Menezes, Romênia Ayla Moraes, Romilda Rabelo Duarte, Clara Amaral Campos, Fernando Dolabela)
The 'adernos' (notebooks) contain exercises designed to help the teacher apply Entrepreneurial Pedagogy Methodology in the classroom. The exercises seek to develop the support elements proposed by Filion (1991a; 1991b): vision, relations, self-concept, leadership and self-space. They prepare the students to accomplish their dreams.

There are 14 Cadernos, one for each level of basic education. Each contains 40 exercises, one for each week of the program, for a total of 560 exercises in the full series.

The Cadernos provide beginning EPM teachers with a concrete instrument for the classroom. As teachers acquire experience, however, they are invited to develop their own exercises, which would be adapted to a greater degree to the students' reality.

3 The entrepreneurship gender gap in global perspective: implications for entrepreneurship education and programming
Sylvia Maxfield

> To fail to pay attention to women's economic activities is both morally indefensible and economically absurd. (Bradford Morse United Nations Development Program)

Contemporary research highlights the role women play as entrepreneurs in the US, Canada, and to some extent the UK (Carter and Anderson, 2001; Domeisen, 2003; National Foundation of Women Business Owners, 1996). In poorer countries it appears that fewer women participate in entrepreneurial activities, although rates of female entrepreneurship vary dramatically across nations. The entrepreneurship gender gap measures the difference between the number of men and the number of women participating in entrepreneurial activity. The latest data show that among the countries with the largest entrepreneurship gender gaps are nations as varied as Poland, Argentina, Norway, and Greece, while countries with among the lowest gaps include South Africa, Peru, Portugal, and Japan (Minniti et al., 2005). What explains variation across countries in the extent of this entrepreneurship gender gap? What insights might these variations hold for educational organizations and governments around the world that are actively promoting entrepreneurship through a variety of programs and policies.

Entrepreneurship policies and educational programs are often imported from one country to another and rarely differentiate by gender. But if the impetus for entrepreneurial activity varies with gender, national culture, or economic circumstance, similar policies will work well in some situations but not in others. To the extent we can explain variation in the entrepreneurship gender gap, we can better design programs and policies aimed at increasing women's entrepreneurial activity. This chapter identifies and summarizes research on five categories of motivators for female entrepreneurship and briefly surveys how existing programs for women entrepreneurs address these different motivators.

Research on women and entrepreneurship globally
Despite the important role of women among entrepreneurs and small business owners, academic work on entrepreneurship neglects gender. Until the late 1980s most research on entrepreneurial activity was gender 'blind'. Surveys of articles in scholarly journals find fewer than 10 per cent highlight women entrepreneurs in their studies (Baker et al., 1997; Brush and Edelman, 2000; Gatewood et al., 2003). Among articles that do examine or include women in their study of entrepreneurship, thorough review would likely reveal the same geographic bias toward the US and Western Europe found in the general entrepreneurship literature (Audretsch, 2002; Thomas, 2000). For the scholar interested in exploring the interplay of country context, gender and entrepreneurship, the literature is quite meager.

Research conducted in largely Anglo-Saxon countries ranging from the US to Norway and New Zealand suggests that, within the entrepreneurial population, demographics, traits and start-up processes do not vary much by gender (Alsos and Ljunggren, 1998; Brush, 1992; Hisrich, 1986). Other work suggests gender differences may be greater in the case of motivations and success/hindrance factors for entrepreneurial activity. Mueller (2004) concludes that while retrospective studies of entrepreneurship find little gender difference, prospective studies and theories indicate there are gender differences in entrepreneurial motivations and success factors. Mitchell et al. (2000) find that the mental models for evaluating potential entry into the venture creation process are relatively unaffected by differences in national culture but that culture *does* impact the mental models influencing what entrepreneurs actually do once they have decided to create a new venture. Differences in national culture significantly impacted what Mitchell et al. (2000) call 'willingness scripts' and 'ability scripts'. A focus on motivations and correlates of success puts emphasis on factors such as social learning, stereotypes, past experiences and role-modeling that may be culturally dependent, and therefore possibly territorially specific.

Existing scholarship on female entrepreneurship in global context falls into two groups. Country-specific studies of female entrepreneurs typically use surveys and/or interviews to create data about female entrepreneurs (Das, 1999; De Groot, 2001; Hatun and Ozlen, 2001; Hisrich and Fulop, 1994/95; Hisrich and Ozturk, 1999; Izyumov and Razumnova, 2000; Lee, 1997; Lerner et al., 1997; McElwee and Al-Riyami, 2003; Mitchell, 2004; Mroczkowski, 1997; Neaerchou-Ellina and Ioannis, 2004; Scheela and Van Hoa, 2004; Siu and Chu, 1994; Zapalsak, 1997). These studies focus varyingly on identifying demographics of the female entrepreneurial population, rank-ordering motivations for female entrepreneurship from among choice lists that often vary from study to study, and/or gauging the intensity of different success/hindrance factors for female entrepreneurs from more or less open-ended choice sets. Although not designed to allow for statistically significant cross-national comparison, assessing these studies as a group highlights some common themes. One serious shortcoming of these studies is that relatively few try to look for similarities or differences across the population of female and male entrepreneurs.

A second methodology employed in the existing literature draws on a variety of data sources to quantitatively assess patterns of cross-national variation in female entrepreneurship. Because case studies are methodologically useful for hypothesis generation while larger-n studies are useful in hypothesis testing, looking for concordance across these two types of studies helps identify consistent findings, overarching themes, and highlights issues for further study (Rosa et al., 1994, p. 32).

A survey of these two general types of research on gender and entrepreneurship in cross-national perspective highlights five clusters of variables that might shape the entrepreneurship gender gap. These are economic necessity, access to venture finance, the nature of social networks, cognitive traits and national culture.

Economic necessity and the entrepreneurship gender gap
National gross domestic product (GDP) per person, a measure of national economic wealth, clearly shapes the extent of the entrepreneurship gender gap. Across levels of national income, economic necessity is a stronger determinant of entrepreneurial activity

for women than it is for men. Minniti and Arenius (2003) and Minniti et al. (2005) use correlations to describe some of the attributes of female entrepreneurs. These studies focus on female and male entrepreneurial activity as a portion of total entrepreneurial activity. They help demonstrate the U-shaped impact of national income levels on female entrepreneurial activity. Women in middle-income countries, more than in low-income or high-income nations, shy away from entrepreneurial activity. The gender gap in entrepreneurial activity is highest in the middle-income countries and lowest in high-income countries. This replicates other researchers' findings (Verheul et al., 2005).

Across income levels economic necessity is a stronger determinant of entrepreneurial activity for women than it is for men, although this aggregate result is strongly colored by the high levels of necessity entrepreneurship in poor countries. This finding corroborates results of country-specific case studies of female entrepreneurship. In studies of female entrepreneurial activity in Pakistan, Oman, South Africa, Poland and Russia (Izyumov and Razumnova, 2000; McElwee and Al-Riyami, 2003; Mitchell et al., 2000; Ylinenpaa and Chechurina, 2000; Zapalsak, 1997) women chose financial necessity and/or unemployment or underemployment from among a list of factors as strong motivators for entrepreneurial activity. Studies in South Africa and Poland (Mitchell et al., 2000; Zapalsak, 1997) compared female and male populations and support the idea that economic necessity may be a stronger motive for female entrepreneurs than for males.

What we know about economic necessity and the entrepreneurship gender gap defines an important target group for entrepreneurship education and programming among women living in poverty. Until very recently most entrepreneurship education and programming aimed at women occurred in wealthier countries. Starting in the mid-1990s a small number of initiatives helped to encourage female entrepreneurship in poorer countries. The most important force for such initiatives comes from multinational government agencies, often working in conjunction with national governments to implement new initiatives. Within the United Nations (UN) system a variety of organizations are supporting programs for female entrepreneurs. The UN Development Fund for Women (UNIFEM), for example, has several regional program advisors around the world who identify and fund innovative initiatives to reach large numbers of women entrepreneurs. The UN Industrial Develop Organization (UNIDO) also supports female entrepreneurs in industrial sectors. The International Labor Organization and the African Development Bank have a program for women entrepreneurs in three African countries and the Organisation for Economic Co-operation and Development (OECD) also funds and guides a program to develop female entrepreneurship in the Middle East and North Africa. The International Finance Corporation (IFC), the private financing arm of the World Bank, also supports several programs for female entrepreneurs in poorer countries including South Africa. In a speech addressing the Third Millennium Development Goal of Gender Equality in early 2006, World Bank President Paul Wolfowitz showcased a female entrepreneur from Rwanda as he announced his organization's commitment to 'gender mainstreaming', increasing women's access, in infrastructure, energy and transportation sectors.

Venture financing and the entrepreneurship gender gap
Female entrepreneurs use less start-up capital than do male entrepreneurs. The conventional explanation for this gap is that women do not have as much access as men to venture funding (Brush et al., 2003). Women entrepreneurs seek financing but do not find it as

easily or in such great quantity as men. A number of country-based studies examining factors fostering or hindering entrepreneurial success point to this interpretation. Women in studies conducted in Turkey, Cyprus, Hungary and Russia (Hatun and Ozlen, 2001; Hisrich and Fulop, 1994/95; Hisrich and Ozturk, 1999; Izyumov and Razumnova, 2000; Ylinenpaa and Chechurina, 2000) report that difficulty securing finance strongly hinders their success. Across all the country-specific studies covering more than a dozen countries, difficulty securing finance was the hindrance most frequently cited by women in start-ups and established enterprises.

Women also seek less venture funding than men, for several reasons. They fear encountering bias against women in the allocation of start-up financing. This fear appears justified. The UN Industrial Development Organization (UNIDO, 1995) reports 'despite evidence that women's loan repayment rates are higher than men's, women still face more difficulties in obtaining credit, often due to the discriminatory attitudes of banks and lending groups'. An additional part of the financial story behind female entrepreneurship is that female entrepreneurial activity is frequently less capital-intensive than male activity because of the kinds of business sectors that attract female entrepreneurs (for example, small-scale consumer retail, education, and other services). Banks may not have much expertise evaluating the creditworthiness of these types of enterprises. Women also typically have less wealth and therefore less access to collateral to pledge to financing organizations than do men. An additional explanation for the financing gap is that women are more financially risk-averse than men and try to 'do more with less' to avoid increasing their financial obligations (Kickul and Titus, 2005). In poorer countries financing often comes through informal financial networks. In some countries/cultures women may not have strong access to these networks.

The most prolific area of programming for female entrepreneurs in poorer countries is microfinance. Here we find a broad array of actors including multinational organizations, national governments, private enterprises, and non-governmental organizations. A very small percentage of microcredit programming targets women specifically. In 2001, for example, the Venezuelan government founded a women's microfinance institution called Banmujer, a development bank for women. Grameen Bank of Bangladesh is one of the oldest microfinance enterprises serving low- and middle-income countries. Although Grameen does not target women explicitly, females make up the overwhelming majority of microcredit customers. The year 2005 was the International Year of Microcredit – an initiative sponsored by the UN, Visa, ING and Citigroup. There was an implicit focus on women in this initiative called by Nane Annan, lawyer, painter, and wife of the UN Secretary General. 'I hope the International Year of Microcredit,' she said, 'will give even more women access to microfinance services, enabling them to fulfill their hopes and dreams for themselves and their families.' (Annan, 2005) Roughly 60 countries joined the initiative and catalogued their microfinance efforts. Just a few of the 60 countries reported programs aimed specifically at women. Mexico noted its Second Forum on Women's Empowerment. Mauritania and Mauritius reported microcredit promotional activities targeting women laid off from the textile industries in those countries. Monaco emphasized a program to support microfinance for women's cooperatives in the Dakar region. China reported supporting an Asia region conference to explore women's experience with microcredit and Angola highlighted the Ministry of Family and the Promotion of Women's program to finance small-scale commercial, agricultural and fishing activities.

Microfinancing programs for women faces several challenges. Unless programs are mobile and physically reach out to women in rural areas or near their homes in extremely poor neighborhoods, the poorest women will still face financial barriers. Another challenge is supporting growth of women's enterprises. Microfinance rarely generates jobs for others beyond the single female entrepreneur. For this reason a joint program of the International Labor Organization (in 2004) and the African Development Bank is assessing a program targeted specifically to growth-oriented female entrepreneurs in Ethiopia, Tanzania and Zambia. There is increasing call for financial programs that address the 'missing middle' – larger women-owned enterprises capable of providing jobs and contributing to economic growth and diversification.

Governments should work with international organizations to secure financing to support growth-oriented firms as well as the microenterprises supported by microcredit programs. The Global Banking Alliance for Women founded as an outgrowth of an OECD conference in 2000 and housed at the International Finance Corporation of the World Bank in Washington, DC, is well-positioned for this work. Governments could also consider setting targets for loan authorizations by their countries' banks to women entrepreneurs running growth-oriented firms.

In some cases formal and informal gender biases about women's property rights also inhibit women's access to finance. No amount of education or programming will succeed in contexts where women's right to inherit or hold property are questioned, where their mobility is restricted, or where they are not allowed/encouraged to participate in public life by obtaining national identity cards.

Social networks and the entrepreneurship gender gap
Entrepreneurs commonly cite the positive role that networks of other entrepreneurs or related professionals play in their start-up activities. In their large-n quantitative study, Minniti et al. (2005) raises an interesting hypothesis about the role of networks. The Global Entrepreneurship Monitor (GEM) study reports that while quantitative data show that networks of other entrepreneurs are important determinants of both male and female entrepreneurial activity, women's networks are different. The report asserts that this difference between male and female networks is greatest in low-income countries where women's networks are smaller and more geographically concentrated than men's. Minniti et al. (2005) further speculates that in these countries women, more than men, substitute these networks for formal legal contracts.[1]

An interesting twist on the hypothesis that women substitute networks for legal contracts comes from a country-specific case study. Scheela and Hoa (2004) studied female entrepreneurs in Vietnam through open-ended interviews. The study highlights the importance female entrepreneurs attribute to networks of support from government personnel. It concludes that because government institutions are weak, successful female entrepreneurs in Vietnam depend on networks of government officials to help win approvals and support for their enterprises. The authors of the study of female entrepreneurs in Vietnam identify the same underlying problem as Minniti et al. (2005): a weak legal and bureaucratic environment. The interesting question is whether this factor impacts women differently from men. The Vietnam study does not compare female and male populations, so it is difficult to draw conclusions about the possible interplay of gender specific interplay of entrepreneurship and national political circumstances.

The GEM report concludes its discussion of networks by suggesting examination of women's role 'within the larger community' (Minniti et al., 2005, p. 24). This interpretation indicates answers about the entrepreneurship gender gap lie in the realm of social structures.

A number of initiatives for female entrepreneurs in poorer countries focus on women's social environment and network-building. Female entrepreneurs' activities in developing countries frequently differ from men's in their level of integration with household activities. Women whose enterprises are small stores or food processing may intermingle household and business resources. Entrepreneurship programs oriented toward some female populations in poorer countries might help separate household from enterprise by teaching the women to maintain separate accounts. One such program in the Philippines (Seymour, 2001) was highly correlated with entrepreneurial success because women began to take their enterprises more seriously and realized the extent to which they were economically independent of their husbands.

Another aspect of women's social environment is their family obligation (de Groot, 2001). Some case studies of female entrepreneurs point to the role of networks as sources of support for meeting family obligations. While formal childcare programs are out of financial reach for most governments in poorer countries, the time constraints imposed by women's family obligations pose a challenge to female entrepreneurs that sometimes only networks of family and friends can mitigate.

Networks are also important for female entrepreneurs in poorer economic contexts because they can compensate for limited skills and less exposure to travel and the media. The Romanian government has a four-phase program for supporting female entrepreneurs, which began in 2005. The first phase involved 'women entrepreneur days' in seven different Romanian cities and brought together associations of women entrepreneurs, financiers and businesswomen to showcase success stories of female entrepreneurs. A key policy recommendation of a recent OECD study of female entrepreneurship in countries of the Middle East and North Africa is to promote networks as a source of knowledge and tools for female entrepreneurs (Estime, 2005).

Non-governmental organizations (NGOs) also play a role building networks to support female entrepreneurs. One example is Kagider in Turkey. Kagider is a non-profit, non-governmental organization started by 37 prominent Turkish entrepreneurs in 2002. In 2006 it had hundreds of members. Kagider's activities include training, community outreach and mentoring activities. The organization also networks with international organizations of businesswomen and lobbies financial institutions in Turkey to create 'sustainable' credit programs for women entrepreneurs. Another example comes from Africa where UNIDO began work to promote female entrepreneurship in 1994. In Tanzania, UNIDO funds supported creation of the Tanzanian Food Processors Association (TAFOPA) in 1997 as a business network to provide long-term organizational support in business development and marketing for female entrepreneurs. In 2006 it had 220 paying members. Where information technology infrastructure is good, building virtual networks can also help promote female entrepreneurial activity. The Center for Arab Women Training and Research (CAWTAR) in Tunis and funded by the World Bank and the United Nations Development Programme (UNDP) is considering hosting a virtual networking and resource center.

Cognitive traits and the entrepreneurship gender gap

Among results of studies of motivation for female entrepreneurs one of the strongest themes is that women chose entrepreneurship because they seek something better in their lives. This might be personal freedom, job satisfaction, or achievement. For instance, independence, personal freedom and autonomy were strong motivators for women entrepreneurs in many of the country studies, specifically Turkey, Pakistan, Oman, Poland and South Africa (Hatun and Ozlen, 2001; McElwee and Al-Riyami, 2003; Mitchell, 2004; Mroczkowski, 1997). Another study in Poland (Hisrich and Ozturk, 1999) compares female and male entrepreneurs. The study finds that women are more likely than men to feel they cannot achieve their fullest potential as employees and seek entrepreneurial opportunities to remedy this frustration. Achievement was also important in four of the nine country studies.

Another important cognitive factor in research on gender and entrepreneurship is risk-aversion. The literature provides few clear conclusions about gender, risk and entrepreneurship. Because risk-aversion is a well-defined component of national culture that varies across nations, answers to questions about gender and risk-aversion in different national contexts are even more illusive. A study by Kolvereid et al. (1993) compares female and male entrepreneurial populations and yields interesting findings about gendered views of political risk. Overall their study of entrepreneurs in Norway, New Zealand and the UK suggested that country-specific variables had much greater impact on entrepreneurial activity than gender, with one important exception: compared to men, women in all three countries saw much greater political uncertainty in their environment.

Both of these cognitive variables suggest that in entrepreneurship training for women, building a lasting sense of self-efficacy is important. For example, assessment of the separate accounts program mentioned above emphasizes women's realization of their own capacity for financial independence. This realization spurred them to expand their enterprises. Training programs for women range from very basic skills in Afghanistan to new communication and information technologies skills in Morocco. Non-governmental organizations, often working in conjunction with multinational organizations such as the World Bank or the UN are the primary sources of support for these training initiatives. However, as social performance becomes an increasingly important standard for large corporations, they are also funding training programs for female entrepreneurs. In 2005 for example, ExxonMobil launched entrepreneurship training initiatives for women in Indonesia, Kazakhstan and Qatar.

Research on the cognitive factors motivating female entrepreneurs in particular, suggests that training programs explicitly include the objective of building self-efficacy and that assessment of program impact encompass this variable.

Another consideration related to cognitive motivations for female entrepreneurs is whether educational interventions should begin before women reach adulthood. Compared to entrepreneurship education programs for adult women, there are relatively few for girls. One of the few examples come from Uganda where the Ugandan Women Entrepreneurs Association (UWEAL) is training schoolgirls through the UN-supported Girl Entrepreneurship Program (Ssonko, 2004). This program is exceptional because in poorer countries, especially, the first priority is simply facilitating female participation in any kind of schooling – whether entrepreneurship-oriented or not.

National culture and the entrepreneurship gender gap
The cognitive and social factors motivating female entrepreneurship likely interact with aspects of national culture in complex ways. Research on entrepreneurial activity in general draws several conclusions about how national cultures might impact the extent of entrepreneurial activity. Regardless of gender, researchers expect entrepreneurial activity to be higher in more individualistic, less collectivist cultural contexts. Mitchell et al. (2000, p. 894) lays out the connection:

> Entrepreneurs in an individualistic society may have scanning and decision scripts tailored to finding opportunities that they, personally, can take advantage of . . . Entrepreneurs in a collective society may have scanning and decision scripts tailored to opportunities that a group or consortium can take advantage of; these opportunities would involve coordination, collaboration.

Research suggests this conventional wisdom may not hold equally across genders. Mueller (2004) finds that the *more individualist* the national culture, the *larger the gender gap* in entrepreneurial character attributes. In other words, the gender gap in entrepreneurship is lower in countries whose culture exhibits more collectivism than individualism. Mueller uses a broad definition of collectivism. Other researchers (House et al., 2004) narrow the concept of collectivism in two different ways, by focusing on 'family' collectivism and 'distributional' or 'institutional' collectivism. Family collectivism refers to cultures that express pride, loyalty, and cohesiveness in their organizations and families. Distributional collectivism characterizes cultures in which organizational and societal institutions encourage and reward collective action and collective distribution of resources.

Part of the causal story explaining why women find it harder to pursue entrepreneurial activity in cultures exhibiting collectivism may involve women's perceptions of work–family tensions in these cultures. Several country-specific studies, covering Turkey, Cyprus, Poland and Hungary (Hatun and Ozlen, 2001; Hisrich and Fulop, 1994/95; Mroczkowski, 1997; Neaerchou-Ellina and Ioannis, 2004), highlight female entrepreneurs' perceptions that work–family tensions hinder entrepreneurial success.

Evidence from country studies of female entrepreneurship about the leverage women gain from networks of family and friends seemingly contradicts the notion that cultures scoring high in family collectivism create gender-specific tensions that inhibit female entrepreneurial. Tiessen's (1997) work suggests it might be easier to reconcile these contradictory findings if researchers disaggregate behaviors specific to particular phases of the entrepreneurial process. For example, individualism and collectivism promote different aspects of entrepreneurial activity. Opportunity recognition requires individual initiative and creativity but leveraging resources requires collectivism.

Investigations also look at a different dimension of culture called 'uncertainty avoidance', related to the cognitive variable of risk-aversion discussed in the previous section. Cultures that eschew uncertainty do not accept change or admit a variety of opinions as readily as societies where uncertainty is more acceptable. Research (Mitchell et al., 2000) suggests that in societies where uncertainty is accepted in the national culture, women are more likely to be risk-takers in rates equal to those of men. When national culture includes a propensity to avoid uncertainty, women are less likely to go against the cultural grain and engage in entrepreneurial activity.

Mueller's (2004) study includes additional findings that substantiate the broad claim that women are less likely than men to buck dominant cultural values to become entrepreneurs.

The study reports a greater gap in risk-taking between men and women in countries where uncertainty avoidance characterizes the national culture. The Hofstede (1991) index of uncertainty avoidance focuses on the level of tolerance for uncertainty and ambiguity within society. These societies do not accept change or a variety of opinions as readily as societies where uncertainty avoidance is lower. Mueller's research suggests that in societies where risk-taking is embraced in national culture, women are more likely to be risk-takers in rates equal to men. The entrepreneurial gender gap should be lower in those countries. As in the case of collectivism–individualism, this points to the broad suggestion that women find it harder than men to take actions that deviate from the dominant culture. One cognitive level explanation for this macro-level finding comes from the GEM study (Minniti et al., 2005) reporting that female entrepreneurs exhibit fear of failure.

Internal locus of control is another conceptualization of the cognitive variable, self-efficacy, that relates to national cultural contexts. Entrepreneurs tend to feel that they can control the external environment. Mueller finds that women feel more internal control, and are therefore more likely to pursue entrepreneurial behavior, the more masculine the culture. Hofstede's masculinity–femininity measure focuses on the society's reinforcement of stereotypical work models of achievement, control and power. In masculine cultures, according to Hofstede's measures, gender differentiation will be high (Simeon et al., 2001). Here again, compared to men, women are less likely to engage in behavior that goes against the social grain. In societies that do not place such high value on achievement and control, women are less likely than men to pursue entrepreneurial activity. Even though gender differentiation is high, in masculine cultures the value society accords to achievement and control spurs female entrepreneurial activity to a greater extent than male entrepreneurial activity.

Mueller's (2004) findings indicate an overarching suggestion that women are less likely than men to engage in behaviors discordant with national cultural values. This suggestion aligns with cultural dominance theories about entrepreneurial behavior. Studies linking cultural values and entrepreneurial behavior fall into two camps (Uhlaner and Thurik, 2004). Cultural dominance theory holds that entrepreneurial behaviors will be more prevalent in cultures that value entrepreneurial behavior. Using Hofstede's (1991) framework this theory implies that lower power distance, lower uncertainty avoidance, more masculinity and higher individualism engender more entrepreneurial activity. The alternative view is a cognitive dissonance perspective. In this view, entrepreneurial behaviors arise from discord between individual traits and dominant cultural values. In the Hofstede framework, high power distance, more uncertainty avoidance, more femininity, and more collectivism will translate into more entrepreneurial activity. Preliminary research on gender differences in entrepreneurial motivations across different national contexts suggests that female entrepreneurial activity may correspond to a cultural dominance view rather than the theory of cognitive dissonance.

If national cultures demean entrepreneurial activity, women are less likely than men to buck the culture. Programs to support female entrepreneurial activity in such cultures face particularly difficult challenges related to deep-seated aspects of national culture and how these interact with women's cognitive predispositions and social situations.

Changing cultures is not easy, but public media campaigns are an element of entrepreneurship education programs aimed at raising public awareness and acceptance of female entrepreneurship. An extreme example comes from Afghanistan (Roberts, 2005). Mina Sherzoy, an Afghani who returned to her native country in 2002 after 20 years living internationally, speaks and raises funds globally to support initiatives for female entrepreneurs in Afghanistan. She believes that to successfully encourage female entrepreneurship in Afghanistan she must also educate men who would otherwise undermine programming for women.

Conclusion

Interest in entrepreneurship as a way to rekindle or promote new growth is burgeoning around the world, yet relatively little attention is paid to the rapidly growing role of female entrepreneurs. Although scholars have begun documenting and studying female participation in entrepreneurial activity in Anglo countries, female entrepreneurship outside the Anglo world is comparatively understudied. There are good reasons for this. Data collection is challenging, and bridging the individual and national levels of analysis poses methodological hurdles (Verheul et al., 2006). The range of factors contributing to explanations of entrepreneurial activity, including cognitive, cultural and regulatory considerations calls for a breathtaking level of interdisciplinary knowledge.

Fortunately several large new data sets describing entrepreneurial activity and values, including GEM and GLOBE (Global Leadership and Organizational Behavior Effectiveness), are facilitating cross-national research that can complement the small number of country-specific studies dribbling out over the past decade. This chapter has surveyed existing literature on gender and entrepreneurship globally with the goal of synthesizing key findings and framing key questions for future research, using those databases and others. The assumption is that to efficiently inform policy design, theory-building in the field of entrepreneurship must be increasingly contingent. The chapter highlights how finding answers to these key research questions could help guide policy architects concerned with facilitating female entrepreneurial activity, particularly in non-Anglo and lower/middle-income country settings.

Note

1. Economists write extensively on how tax codes, bankruptcy law, shareholder rights and other market institutions might impact entrepreneurial activity. See, for instance, Georgellis and Wall (2004).

References

Alsos, G.A. and Ljunggren, E. (1998), 'Does the business start-up process differ by gender? A longitudinal study of nascent entrepreneurs', *Frontiers of Entrepreneurship Research*, www.babson.edu/entrep/fer/papers98/V/V_A/V_A.html, accessed on 31 November, 2006.

Annan, N. (2005), www.yearofmicrocredit.org/whyayear_quotecollection.asp#naneannan, accessed 31 November 2006.

Audretsch, D. (2002), 'Entrepreneurship policy and the strategic management of places', at www.saturno.lombarida.it/upload/file/369/184535/filename, accessed at 31 November, 2006.

Baker, T., Aldrich, H.E. and Liou, N. (1997), 'Invisible entrepreneurs: the neglect of women business owners by mass media and scholarly journals in the USA', *Entrepreneurship and Regional Development*, 9, 221–38.

Brush, C. (1992), 'Research on women business owners: past trends, a new perspective and future directions', *Entrepreneurship Theory and Practice*, 16 (4), 5–31.

Brush, C.G. and Edelman, L. (2000), 'Women entrepreneurs: opportunities for database research', in J. Katz (ed.), *Databases for the Study of Entrepreneurship*, New York: JAI, pp. 445–84.

Brush, C., de Bruin, A. and Welter, F. (2005), 'Call for papers – special issue: women's entrepreneurship', *Entrepreneurship Theory and Practice*, www.ecsb.org/doc/Call%20for%20papers_womens%20entrepreneurship.pdf.

Brush, C.G., Carter, N.M., Gatewood, E.J., Greene, P.G. and Hart, M.M. (2003), 'Venture capital access: is gender an issue?', in D. Hart (ed.), *The Emergence of Entrepreneurship Policy*, London: Cambridge University Press, pp.141–54.

Carter, S. and Anderson, S. (2001), *On the Move: Women and Men Business Owners in the UK*, Washington, DC: Center for Women's Business Research.

Das, M. (1999), 'Work–family conflicts of Indian women entrepreneurs: a preliminary report', *New England Journal of Entrepreneurship*, **2** (2), 39–47.

De Groot, T. (2001), *Womens' Entrepreneurial Development in Selected African Countries*, Vienna: UNIDO.

Domeisen, N. (2003), 'Canada releases report on women entrepreneurs', *International Trade Forum*, **4** (1), 11–13.

Estime, M.-F. (2005), 'Promoting women's entrepreneurship in the MENA region: background report and policy considerations', MENA-OECD Investment Program.

Gatewood, E.G., Carter, N.M., Brush, C.G., Greene, P.G. and Hart, M.M. (2003), *Women Entrepreneurs, Their Ventures and the Venture Industry*, Stockholm: ESBRI.

Georgellis, Y. and Wall, H.J. (2004), 'Entrepreneurship and the policy environment', Federal Reserve Bank of St Louis, Working Paper Series.

Hatun, U. and Ozlen, O. (2001), 'Interaction between the business and family lives of women entrepreneurs in Turkey', *Journal of Business Ethics*, **31** (2), 95–107.

Hisrich, R.D. (1986), 'The woman entrepreneur: a comparative analysis', *Leadership and Organizational Development Journal*, **7** (2), 8–17.

Hisrich, R.D. and Fulop, G. (1994/95), 'The role of women in Hungary's transition economy', *International Studies of Management and Organization*, **24** (4), 100–18.

Hisrich, R.D. and Ozturk, S.A. (1999), 'Women entrepreneurs in a developing economy', *Journal of Management Development*, **18** (2), 114.

Hofstede, G. (1991), *Culture and Organizations: Software of the Mind*, New York: McGraw-Hill.

House, R.J., Hanges, P.J., Javidan, M., Dorfman, P.W. and Gupta, V. (2004), *Culture, Leadership and Organizations: The GLOBE Study of 62 Societies*, Thousand Oaks, CA: Sage.

Izyumov, A. and Razumnova, I. (2000), 'Women entrepreneurs in Russia: learning to survive the market', *Journal of Development Entrepreneurship*, **5** (1), 1–20.

Kickul, J. and Titus, L. (2005), 'Context for the legitimacy of women entrepreneurs: the role of expert capital', *CGO Working Paper No. 19, Simmons School of Management.*

Kolvereid, L., Scott, S. and Westhead, P. (1993), 'Is it equally difficult for female entrepreneurs to start businesses in all countries?', *Journal of Small Business Management*, **31** (4), 42–52.

Lee, J. (1997), 'The motivation of women entrepreneurs in Singapore', *International Journal of Entrepreneurial Behavior and Research*, **3** (2), 93.

Lerner, M., Brush, C. and Hisrich, R. (1997), 'Israeli women entrepreneurs: an examination of factors affecting performance', *Journal of Business Venturing*, **12** (4), 315–40.

McElwee, G. and Al-Riyami, R. (2003), 'Women entrepreneurs in Oman: some barriers to success', *Career Development*, **8** (7), 339–48.

Minniti, M. and Arenius, P. (2003), 'Women in entrepreneurship', paper prepared for the conference, The Entrepreneurial Advantage of Nations: First Annual Global Entrepreneurship Symposium, United Nations, New York, 29 April.

Minniti, M., Arenius, P. and Langowitz, N. (2005), *Global Entrepreneurship Monitor: 2004 Report on Women and Entrepreneurship*, Babson Park, MA: Center for Women's Leadership at Babson College.

Mitchell, B.C. (2004), 'Motives of entrepreneurs: a case study of South Africa', *Journal of Entrepreneurship*, **13** (2), 167.

Mitchell, R.K., Smith, B., Seawright, K.W. and Morse, E. (2000), 'Cross-cultural cognitions and the venture creation decision', *Academy of Management Journal*, **43** (5), 974–94.

Mroczkowski, T. (1997), 'Women as employees and entrepreneurs in the Polish transformation', *Industrial Relations Journal*, **28** (2), 83–91.

Mueller, S.L. (2004), 'A cross-national study of gender gaps in potential for entrepreneurship', *Journal of Development Entrepreneurship*, **9** (3), 199–221.

National Foundation of Women Business Owners (1995), *Women-Owned Business: Breaking the Boundaries*, Washington, DC: Center for Women's Business Research.

Neaerchou-Ellina, L. and Ioannis, K. (2004), 'Women entrepreneurs in Cyprus: a new dynamic in Cyprus economy', *Women in Management Review*, **19** (6), 325–32.

Roberts, M. (2005), 'Afghan women look to jump-start businesses', *Associated Press State and Local Wire*, 14 January, www.lexis-nexis.com, accessed on 31 November, 2006.

Rosa, P., Hamilton, D., Carter, S. and Burns, H. (1994), 'The impact of gender on small business management: preliminary findings of a British study', *International Small Business Journal*, **12** (3), 25–33.

Scheela, W. and Van Hoa, T.T. (2004), 'Women entrepreneurs in a transition economy: the case of Vietnam', *International Journal of Management and Decision Making*, **5** (1), 1–13.

Seymour, N. (2001), 'Women entrepreneurs in the developing world', Digest No. 01–04, Kaufman Center for Entrepreneurial Leadership Clearinghouse on Entrepreneurship Education, www.celcee.edu., accessed on 31 November, 2006.

Simeon, R., Nicholson, J.D. and Wong, Y.Y. (2001), 'Comparisons of Asian and US workplace gender roles', *Cross Cultural Management*, **8** (2), 47–59.

Siu, W. and Chu, P. (1994), 'Female entrepreneurs in Hong Kong: problems and solutions', *International Journal of Management*, **11** (2), 728–37.

Ssonko, K. (2004), 'Women students go into business', *New Vision* (Uganda), 7 December, www.lexis-nexis.com, accessed 31 January 2006.

Thomas, A. (2000), 'A case for comparative entrepreneurship: assessing the relevance of culture', *Journal of International Business Studies*, **31** (2), 287–304.

Tiessen, J.H. (1997), 'Individualism, collectivism, and entrepreneurship: a framework for international comparative research', *Journal of Business Venturing*, **12** (5), 367–84.

Uhlaner, L. and Thurik, R. (2005), Postmaterialism influencing total entrepreneurial activity across nations, Erasmus University, www.spea.indiana.edu/ids/pdfholder/2005/ISSN%2005-10.doc., accessed 31 November, 2006.

United Nations Industrial Development Organization (UNIDO) (1995), 'Women, industry and entrepreneurship', Women in Industry Series, Vienna: UNIDO.

Verheul, I., van Stel, A. and Thurick, R. (2006), 'Explaining female and male entrepreneurship at the country level', *Entrepreneurship and Regional Development*, **18** (2), 151–69.

Verheul, I., Uhlaner, L. and Thurik, R. (2005), 'Business accomplishments, gender and entrepreneurial self-image', *Journal of Business Venturing*, **20** (4), 485–98.

Ylinenpaa, H. and Chechurina, M. (2000), 'Perceptions of female entrepreneurship in Russia', paper presented at 30th European Small Business Seminar, Ghent, September.

Zapalsak, A. (1997), 'A profile of woman entrepreneurs and enterprises in Poland', *Journal of Small Business Management*, **35** (4), 76–83.

4   Teaching entrepreneurship to non-business students: insights from two Dutch universities
Maryse Brand, Ingrid Wakkee and Marijke van der Veen

4.1   Introduction

Together with a growing appreciation of the relevance of entrepreneurship for society, interest in teaching entrepreneurship has risen significantly. Although some still believe that 'entrepreneurship can't be taught', a wide variety of experiences and studies prove differently. However, there is still a lot of confusion about what it actually entails: teaching entrepreneurship.

Today, entrepreneurship is widely taught at various stages and levels of education (see for some Dutch examples www.lerenondernemen.nl). Although we appreciate the potential value of entrepreneurship education at all levels, in this chapter we focus on entrepreneurship programs at academic institutes. Teaching entrepreneurship at the academic level is particularly relevant for several reasons. First, ventures founded by highly educated entrepreneurs tend to be more innovative, experience higher growth levels and survival rates, and are more often involved in international activities (Ching and Ellis, 2004; The European Observatory for SMEs, 1995). Ergo, stimulating and teaching entrepreneurship among the higher educated has positive consequences for society in general. Second, teaching entrepreneurship at an academic level stimulates entrepreneurship research and raises our knowledge level about entrepreneurship both as a research object and as a career domain. This in turn, leads to improved policy-making and better entrepreneurship curricula at all levels of education.

We argue that entrepreneurship is, and should be, taught following two different approaches: (1) entrepreneurship as a profession, and (2) entrepreneurship as a field of science. Depending on variables such as type of student and educational level, these two approaches should be represented in specific entrepreneurship courses and programs. Building on this dichotomy we may distinguish between several forms of entrepreneurship education in academic institutes:[1]

1.   Majors and PhDs in entrepreneurship, where the focus is on entrepreneurship as a field of science (theory and research) with some attention for entrepreneurship as a profession.
2.   Minors in entrepreneurship directed at business students at the bachelor or masters level, where the focus is on entrepreneurship as a profession with some attention for entrepreneurship as a field of science.
3.   Minors and electives in entrepreneurship targeted at non-business students at the bachelor's, master's and PhD level, again with a focus on entrepreneurship as a profession and some attention for the field of scientific research.

In this chapter, we limit the discussion to this latter form, that is, teaching entrepreneurship minors and electives to non-business bachelor and master students at academic institutes, a subject which is still scarcely researched (Hynes, 1996). Recently, Standish-Kuon and Rice (2002) put forward that introducing engineering and science students to entrepreneurship is still poorly understood, while even less is known about teaching entrepreneurship in non-technical disciplines such as nursing, law and educational sciences.

We examine how entrepreneurship programs can be geared towards stimulating non-business students, in various disciplines, to consider an entrepreneurial career through start-up or intrapreneurial activities. We will scrutinize what essential ingredients should be incorporated in a program catered towards non-business students. To that end, we first briefly describe the history and current state of entrepreneurship education. Next, we present a theoretical model developed by Van der Veen and Wakkee (2004) that depicts entrepreneurship as a process in the pursuit of opportunities. This model allows for a systematic analysis of the entrepreneurial process aimed at the identification of elements to be included in entrepreneurship courses for non-business students. The analysis leads to a framework that can be used as a tool to construct or evaluate entrepreneurship courses or programs.

To illustrate our arguments, we discuss and evaluate the way entrepreneurship has been taught to non-business students at two Dutch academic institutes: one technical university and one classical university. We end this chapter by summarizing our main points and the lessons that can be learned from the experiences in the Netherlands. We also point out some areas in which further research is needed.

4.2 Entrepreneurship education: what we do for non-business students

Since the first entrepreneurship class – supposedly held in the US in 1947 – the academic discipline of entrepreneurship has grown consistently. This is apparent from the number of courses, supplementary infrastructure and publications on the topic, as well as from the increase in endowed positions and dedicated centers (Gorman et al., 1997; Katz, 1991; Kuratko, 2003). Until the early 1990s, entrepreneurship education largely took place in the US, while Europe was lagging behind (The European Observatory for SMEs, 1995). Yet, in the past decade in Europe the number of entrepreneurship courses and other entrepreneurship-related activities has sky-rocketed, and is expected to grow further during the coming years (Cockx et al., 2000; EFMD, 2004). Watkins and Stone (1999), for instance, report that in 1997, 45 per cent of all institutes in the UK offered a complete entrepreneurship program, while 68 per cent of the universities offered at least one course in entrepreneurship. Unfortunately, similar Dutch data are not available. Yet, we know that all 13 Dutch academic universities offer at least one entrepreneurship class, three of which offer one or more complete entrepreneurship programs, two of which will feature as case studies in this chapter. At a recent national meeting on entrepreneurship education (at the Dutch Flemish Entrepreneurship Academy [NVOA], in Utrecht on 7 April 2005), eight of these 13 institutes presented their activities, which at least indicate that entrepreneurship education receives ample attention in a majority of the Dutch universities.

The attention for, and the rising number of, entrepreneurship programs is not surprising considering the attributed role of entrepreneurship in economic growth (Carree and Thurik, 2003; Kuratko, 2003; Ministry of Economic Affairs, 2002; UNIDO, 2005), the creation of jobs (Hynes, 1996) and the strong connection between entrepreneurship and innovation (Jack and Anderson, 1999; Ching and Ellis, 2004). Scholars and practitioners have also pointed towards the increased need for entrepreneurial employees to enable intrapreneurship in established firms (Hornsby et al., 1999; Hornsby et al., 1993; Kuratko et al., 1990). In addition to this scientific evidence, the last decade has shown a growing appreciation of entrepreneurship by the general public and government; in the Netherlands this has been a very striking development (Bosma et al., 2002).

When looking at the current state of the field, it seems that the majority of entrepreneurship programs are being offered at faculties of business administration and economics. As a result most of these programs are targeted at business students and are not open to non-business students (Levie, 1999; NVOA, 2005). A survey conducted several years ago in the UK, showed that only 25 per cent of all students taking entrepreneurship courses were non-business students, even though non-business students comprise almost 90 per cent of the student population (Levie, 1999). Nevertheless, there is strong evidence that more and more programs are now being set up to educate non-business students in the field of entrepreneurship (Cockx et al., 2000; Kuratko, 2003; Standish-Kuon and Rice, 2002; Streeter et al., 2002). For instance, in a European study of Cockx et al. (2000), about two-thirds of the higher education institutes offered entrepreneurship courses to business students, while a third to a half of the institutes offered these courses to non-business students. Moreover, entrepreneurship courses were found to be compulsory for non-business students in 6 to 10 per cent of the institutes. Even considering the fact that the sample was strongly biased towards institutes known for their involvement in entrepreneurial education, these numbers are quite high.

This expansion towards non-business students seems to make good sense. For several reasons, non-business students offer a potentially very interesting target group for entrepreneurship programs. First, non-business students account for the majority of the student-population (Levie, 1999), and as such they are a vast pool of potential entrepreneurs-to-be. Second, non-business students have several entrepreneurship-enhancing characteristics that business students do not have. Most notably they possess domain specific knowledge that is considered important for the recognition of business opportunities (for example, Shane, 2000). We elaborate on the importance of domain specific knowledge in section 3.2. A third factor enhancing the relevance of entrepreneurship education for non-business students is their lack of awareness of the potential for business start-up as a career choice (Birch and Clements, 2004; Hynes, 1996). Awareness is a variable that can be influenced relatively easily through education. Indeed, when being introduced to the field (possibly for a first time) non-business students' intention to start a venture might be affected more strongly than that of business students because they have not considered an entrepreneurial career before (Krueger et al., 2000). Entrepreneurship education also serves to motivate potential entrepreneurs and helps to ensure a critical mass of inflow of ideas and entrepreneurs into the community (Otto, 1999). A study in Sweden found that the number of (actual) entrepreneurs from a university with a three-year undergraduate programme for 'Innovation Engineers' was twice that of other technical universities without such a programme (Andren and Uudelepp, 1996). Finally, non-business students, and especially those with an engineering background, are likely to end up at positions in innovation and new product development. As Charney and Libecap (2000) demonstrate, teaching these individuals how to be entrepreneurial is critical to the innovativeness and growth potential of established organizations.

In the Netherlands the growing attention for teaching entrepreneurship to non-business students seems to be partially caused by the abundance of government-sponsored support and incubation programs such as Technopartner (www.technopartner.nl). These programs are typically directed at professionals or researchers with a non-business background who are interested in starting new ventures in specialized markets that require domain-specific knowledge. Most of these initiatives have sought to establish linkages and relationships with specialists at the universities. This in turn has added to the increased attention for the need to provide entrepreneurship education to non-business students.

We may conclude that a rising number of higher education institutes offer entrepreneurship programs or courses to non-business students, and they have good reasons to do so. Yet, it is still largely unknown what the best approach is. In the next section we propose a theory-based model that could help educators to develop and evaluate such programs.

4.3   Teaching entrepreneurship

When thinking about entrepreneurship programs, our first interest goes to the actual content of the teaching program: what topics are taught and what teaching methods are being used? In addition to this 'development of intellectual content', entrepreneurship departments also put effort in related activities, such as gaining institutional acceptance, engaging students and alumni, building relationships with the business community, and showcasing their successes (Standish-Kuon and Rice, 2002). Although interesting, these other activities are beyond the scope of this chapter.

The field of entrepreneurship is studied and taught by a hetereogeneous group of scholars who unfortunately still lack a common paradigm or integrative framework (cf. Morris et al., 2001; Shane and Venkataraman, 2000). Since the content of an entrepreneurship course will be largely determined by the teacher's perception of what entrepreneurship really means, considerable variation in content exists among entrepreneurship courses (Henry et al., 2003; Sexton and Bowman, 1984). Three main types of entrepreneurship courses may be distinguished. The first deals with the start-up of new business (for example, Gartner, 1985). Such courses will typically use standard textbooks such as Bygrave (1994), Stevenson et al. (1989), Dollinger (2003) and Kuratko and Hodgetts (2001). These books define entrepreneurship as a process, but narrow it down to the sources and discovering of ideas and the process of opportunity evaluation, writing a business plan, accessing resources, start-up, and managing growth. To date, this type of courses is predominant (Cockx et al., 2000; Gnyawali and Fogel, 1994; NVAO, 2005). Yet, in their review of entrepreneurship research, Van der Veen and Wakkee (2004) show that this approach is too limited and perhaps even outdated. Most contemporary theoretical and empirical studies in entrepreneurship take a broader view of entrepreneurship and focus on the pursuit of opportunities rather than on new venture creation as such, and therefore include, for example, intrapreneurship. The second type of courses do focus on entrepreneurship as a process of pursuing opportunities that may take place in different contexts, only one of which is the business start-up (Brush et al., 2003; Hornsby et al., 1999; Hornsby et al., 1993). To our knowledge, none of the widely known textbooks choose this approach. A third category consists of 'entrepreneurship' courses focusing on small business management. Whereas the other two approaches are more concerned with the early stages of the entrepreneurial process, this third approach is more related to managing the existing firm and managing growth. A good example of a book used in this type of course is Scarborough and Zimmerer's 2004 textbook. From the discussions amongst Dutch and Flemish entrepreneurship scholars at the recent meeting of the NVAO (2005) it seems that, at least in the

Netherlands, this broader view of entrepreneurship has not yet filtered through to the bulk of entrepreneurship education.

The few existing entrepreneurship programs that are organized around the pursuit of opportunities are mainly at the PhD level. Several PhD programs in entrepreneurship (largely targeted at business students) have built their curricula on the pursuit of opportunities approach. Examples are the entrepreneurship PhD program offered at the Jönköping International Business School in Sweden (www.jibs.se) and the program described by Brush et al. (2003). Further examples can be found at http://eweb.slu.edu/phdlist.htm. Also, a number of courses directed at PhD students in non-business disciplines reflect the focus on opportunities. An example would be the course 'Science to market' as offered to biomedical PhD students at the Dutch University of Groningen (www.rug.nl/guide/education/generalcourses/courses/sciencemarket). The focus on the pursuit of opportunities at the PhD level is not surprising. It is to be expected that PhD programs are more closely linked to recent developments in the literature than master's and bachelor's programs are (cf. Brush et al., 2003). Moreover, PhD students in engineering and science-related domains will often build on opportunities that they have discovered during their doctoral research. As a result, it is only logical to build on those in the entrepreneurship program.

In addition to being more strongly based in recent literature than the restricted start-up view on entrepreneurship (for example, EFMD, 2004), the opportunity-based view has some other important advantages. These advantages are mainly caused by the fact that the focus is on the *process of entrepreneurship* instead of on the *entrepreneur as a person*. As a result, the pursuit of opportunities approach broadens the domain beyond the formation of new businesses, and allows for the inclusion of entrepreneurial behavior in various settings such as existing commercial companies, universities, and (non-)governmental organizations. Second, by focusing on the process rather than the person, entrepreneurship is no longer seen as something a person has to be born with, but rather as something teachable and thus attainable for a large group of interested individuals (Bygrave, 1994; EFMD, 2004). This perspective on entrepreneurship as (1) a process and (2) broader then just start-ups, is adopted throughout the remainder of this chapter. However, our main argument will also be useful for programs and courses that choose to focus on start-ups only, since the pursuit of opportunities will still be the central process. Entrepreneurship as a pursuit of opportunities process is further explained in the next section.

4.3.1   *The entrepreneurial process*

As discussed above, current entrepreneurship research and textbooks largely agree on defining entrepreneurship as a process aimed at the pursuit of opportunities. In their seminal articles, Shane and Venkataraman (2000; 2001) write about the process of discovering, evaluating and exploiting opportunities. Based on an extensive literature review, Van der Veen and Wakkee (2004) propose somewhat different stages: (1) opportunity recognition (including both discovery and evaluation, and including many feedback loops; see for example De Koning, 1999), (2) preparation for exploitation and (3) opportunity exploitation, which ultimately leads to value creation (see Figure 4.1).

Van der Veen and Wakkee use the label 'opportunity recognition' rather than 'discovery' because this term is dominantly used in the literature (Singh, 2000). During the opportunity recognition process, the entrepreneur develops an initial idea into a viable business opportunity by mentally matching attainable tangible and intangible resources

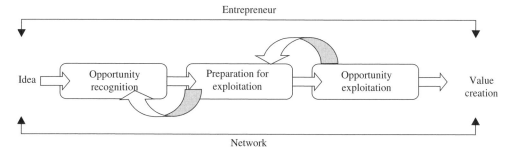

Source: Adapted from Van der Veen and Wakkee (2004).

Figure 4.1 Entrepreneurship as a pursuit of opportunities

such as production facilities, the required knowledge and human resources, with perceived market needs. During the preparation stage, the business opportunity is translated into a concrete business concept that should lead to future exchange with the market. The business concept incorporates all ingredients that are necessary to enable this exchange. One of the most important steps in this process is the development of a resource base (see, for example, Brush et al., 2001; Dollinger, 2003). Also, the creation of a (new) organization (Bruyat and Julien, 2001; Gartner, 1985), the development of a network (for example, Greve, 1995), the development of products, and the development of a business plan have to take place at this stage. When the preparation process has led to the creation of marketable products (goods or services), exchange processes between the firm and its customers begin to take place. At any point during the preparation process, the entrepreneur may realize that an appropriate resource base to exploit the opportunity is not viable. Likewise, the demand for the product or service may turn out to be insufficient for profitable exploitation. In these cases, the business concept may be revised or even abandoned (Herron and Sapienza, 1992).

Throughout the actual opportunity exploitation process the exchange with the market will rise to a higher level. The entrepreneur continues to update the opportunity by adding new or improved goods and services to the market and/or by improving its internal operations. This leads to the creation of value in terms of financial gain, innovation, more choice for customers, increased knowledge, and so on (Autio et al., 2000). The creation of value can be regarded as the outcome of the entrepreneurial process (Zahra and Dess, 2001). During the value-creation process the venture becomes more and more established and day-to-day management activities become increasingly important.

The two large arrows in Figure 4.1 indicate that, although the process appears to be linear and sequential, in fact it is dynamic and iterative (Bygrave and Hofer, 1991; Ropo and Hunt, 1995). It is dynamic in the sense that new ventures evolve over time. As the process unfolds, changing circumstances may require actions to alter or reconsider certain decisions. It is holistic because the course of their evolution is influenced by and sensitive to a system of external variables including the number of competitors, the needs of future customers, and so on that interact to influence outcomes (Bygrave and Hofer, 1991).

To complete the picture, the pursuit-of-opportunities model includes two additional determinants of the entrepreneurial process: the entrepreneur and his or her network. The entrepreneurial process is opportunity based, yet the entrepreneur drives the process: initiating and directing it from the original idea to exploitation. One of the most significant differences between this model and the process presented by Shane and Venkataraman (2000) concerns the addition of the network as a main influencing factor throughout the process. By including this network variable, the model reflects the notion that entrepreneurship does not take place in isolation but is embedded in a social context. In fact, through interactions with the network the pursuit of opportunities is channeled, directed, facilitated and constrained (Aldrich and Zimmer, 1986; Elfring and Hulsink, 2003), and therefore including the network in the model is essential. Throughout the process at different stages, different parts of the network are activated to accommodate different needs (Elfring and Hulsink, 2003; Greve, 1995; Van der Veen and Wakkee, 2004).

In order to successfully complete each of the three stages, an entrepreneur-to-be needs to have a certain level of entrepreneurial awareness and possess entrepreneurial attitudes, skills and knowledge. Awareness of entrepreneurship as a career option is a prerequisite for entrepreneurial behavior (Bosma et al., 2002). As is discussed in more detail in the following sections, awareness also refers to awareness or 'alertness' to opportunities (for example, Kirzner, 1973) and awareness of relevant network partners (Wakkee and Van der Veen, 2004). The development of positive attitudes, knowledge and skills are the main building blocks of professional education (Gorman et al., 1997; Bechard and Toulouse, 1998; Jones-Evans et al., 2000; Wallin, 2003). In the case of entrepreneurship education,[2] attitudes are important as they drive the entrepreneurial process and have proven to be a major predictor of entrepreneurial intentions (Van Gelderen et al., 2003). Knowledge and skills to use knowledge are needed to recognize and exploit the opportunity successfully, by setting up and managing the relevant activities (Bosma et al., 2002). The next subsection discusses the three stages of the pursuit-of-opportunities model in relation to stimulating awareness and teaching relevant entrepreneurial attitudes, knowledge and skills to non-business students. The main points will later be integrated in a framework for evaluating entrepreneurship programs for non-business students.

4.3.2   *Teaching opportunity recognition to non-business students*
Although opportunity recognition is only the first step in the entrepreneurial process, we expect the specific needs of non-business students to be most divergent from the needs of business students in this first and crucial stage. We have two arguments to support this.

First, non-business students possess domain-specific knowledge from their chosen field of education, which directs the type of opportunities they will recognize. While generally all entrepreneurs tap into their personal and everyday life to come up with new ideas, non-business students have the advantage of a specific field of knowledge (related to their education) that may provide innovative ideas for new businesses. For example, engineers (technical non-business students) deal with technological developments and innovation on a daily basis (Drucker, 1985; Fayolle, 1999), giving them a clear advantage over other students. Likewise, non-technical students possess field specific professional expertise that will more or less automatically determine the domain in which they recognize opportunities, for example legal advise for law students or specific translation services for language students. Business students in turn may not be able to recognize opportunities directly from their education; that is, they have no 'logical product or service domain'.

Second, non-business students have no or limited prior knowledge of managerial and business related topics, and of the entrepreneurial process. As a result they might be less or differently aware of their own entrepreneurial possibilities. Also, the choice for a particular study is typically influenced by different personal interests, character traits, cognitive elements, and skills. As a result, non-business students are expected to enter the opportunity recognition process and thus an entrepreneurial career in a specific way (Paffen, 2004).

From the literature we know that the 'search' for a new venture idea can be motivated in roughly two ways (Bhave, 1994; Koller, 1988). First, the wish to start a new (internal) venture may precede the discovery of an idea. As Herron and Sapienza (1992) explain, the motivation to search for opportunities may result from an intolerable level of dissatisfaction arising from, for example, job loss or a lack of money or, in the case of corporate entrepreneurship, an increase in competition. In other words, the entrepreneur actively finds a problem to solve and the new business activities are the answer. Second, the recognition of a gap in the market may precede the entrepreneur's wish to start new venture activities (Bhave, 1994). So, the entrepreneur identifies an opportunity and reacts by providing a solution to an existing need. By choosing a particular education, we can assume that non-business students are more interested in this particular field than in general business. This interest and the accompanying domain knowledge may provide a solid base for specific product/service opportunities. This in turn suggests that for these students, the desire to exploit the specific opportunity (that is, a [technological] discovery by their own hand) might be a stronger motivation than the drive to start a new venture. Business students on the other hand may be more interested in founding a venture per se.

These arguments and the nature of the opportunity recognition process have several implications for teaching. First, in terms of awareness and understanding of the entrepreneurial process, we have to differentiate between compulsory courses offered to all non-business students in a particular program and courses offered as electives for non-business students. Compulsory courses will have to devote ample attention to creating awareness of entrepreneurship as a career alternative. In elective courses, self-selection will lead to a higher level of entrepreneurial awareness to start with. Both groups, however, need to be made aware that entrepreneurship refers to more than starting your own business, and includes recognizing opportunities in other contexts. Second, in relation to opportunity recognition, developing the right attitudes towards entrepreneurship should also be part of the curriculum. After all, discovering an initial idea is not sufficient. Entrepreneurs must be dedicated and motivated enough to continue the development of their idea into a full-fledged business opportunity, which may take considerable time and energy. Having a positive attitude towards entrepreneurship is therefore crucial. Such positive attitudes can be stimulated best by addressing the range of positive effects of entrepreneurship on the individual entrepreneur (such as personal development, potential wealth, freedom, and so on), the company (in case of intrapreneurship) and society (Lucas and Cooper, 2004).

When teaching opportunity recognition to non-business students, educators should realize they may – or even should – build on the domain-specific knowledge that the students have acquired during other courses. However, as knowledge and experience alone are not enough for the recognition of opportunities, educators should also stimulate alertness (Kirzner, 1973) and intentions to discover opportunities. After all, if there is no intention, new pieces of information will be ignored and will not be used to discover opportunities (Bhave, 1994; Wiklund, 1998). Therefore, educators need to train students to link new information to their prior knowledge and experience base in such a way that they will indeed learn to discover new opportunities. Although some authors (for example, Casson, 1982) have argued that this ability is largely innate, we believe this skill can be developed up to a certain level. For instance, Lumpkin et al. (2001), Lucas and Cooper (2004) and Wakkee and Van der Veen (2004) suggest that like creativity, alertness can be enhanced by training (for instance through brainstorming or mind mapping in relation to business courses).

Further, in our view educators need to devote attention to the role of networking in recognizing opportunities. Networks are important for recognizing opportunities in three ways: first, they are the source of new ideas. De Koning (1999) demonstrates that weak ties provide information about new technologies and are thus a source of ideas. Weak ties often operate in other social circles than the entrepreneur and are more likely to possess information that is new and relevant to the entrepreneur (Granovetter, 1973) and therefore lead to new ideas or opportunities. Von Hippel (1988) and Singh (2000) both found that strong ties, for example to customers and suppliers, can also form an important source of ideas. Second they provide feedback and additional information during the development of ideas into opportunities (De Koning, 1999). Both strong and weak ties provide entrepreneurs with access to additional knowledge, feedback, moral and practical support (Birley, 1985; Greve, 1995). Von Hippel (1988) argues that effective innovation derives from active awareness of changing user needs and sometimes from direct user demands or solutions (Moss Kanter, 1988; Rothwell, 1992; Tidd et al., 1997). Therefore using such network contacts smartly, facilitates the development of the opportunity by giving directions in terms of products, applications and markets in the making. Third network contacts provide (moral) support and advice that helps the entrepreneur to continue the process when faced with setbacks and disappointments.

Although networks are equally important to business and non-business students, non-business students are probably less aware of the availability of, for instance, institutional network contacts such as the Chamber of Commerce and Incubator Centers and what these can do for entrepreneurs(-to-be). Also, we expect that many non-business students do not know how they can 'use' domain-specific actors in relation to opportunity recognition. For instance, one of their professors might be able to introduce them to potential lead users, or existing ventures in the market might be willing to provide information that enables them to develop an opportunity further. Therefore, entrepreneurship programs for non-business students should preferably include an introduction to the (institutionalized) support network and trainings to develop network skills.

To summarize the above, in order to facilitate non-business entrepreneurship students to successfully go through the first stage of the pursuit-of-opportunity model, the curriculum should address the following issues: (1) stimulating awareness of entrepreneurship as a career alternative either in new ventures or in established firms; (2) facilitating the development of positive attitudes towards entrepreneurship to increase the desire and commitment to act upon initial ideas and develop these into business opportunities that are exploited later; (3) facilitating the development of the knowledge and skills to use prior domain-specific knowledge to raise entrepreneurial alertness; (4) developing the knowledge and skills for networking to enable opportunity recognition.

4.3.3   Teaching preparation for exploitation to non-business students

At some point during or after the opportunity recognition process, entrepreneurs have to decide whether or not they will try to exploit this opportunity. When the answer is yes, the entrepreneur(s) will have to make commitments to the venture and start preparations for the actual exploitation. We posit that also in this second stage the specific background of non-business students affects how entrepreneurship preparation should be taught.

First, as argued in the previous section, non-business students may not be interested in starting a new venture per se. It is therefore worthwhile to teach non-business students alternative ways to organize the exploitation of their ideas.

Therefore, at this stage, non-business students should be made aware of alternative ways to organize the exploitation of their ideas. These alternative ways include team start-ups (for example, Laukkanen, 2000; Shepherd and Krueger, 2002), corporate venturing (Kuratko and Hodgetts, 2001), and the possibility of taking over existing companies (for example, Bygrave, 1994). Particularly interesting is pointing out the benefits of an entrepreneurial team, for instance the combination of an 'opportunity-motivated' entrepreneur (that is, non-business background) and a 'business ownership-motivated' entrepreneur (that is, business background). Usually such entrepreneurs possess different knowledge and skills and different types of networks that can lead to synergetic combinations that allow for successful venturing. Taking over an existing business (if possible including some of the incumbent management) rather than founding a new venture might be particularly interesting for non-business students. Since they will often lack knowledge of and affinity with management per se, a take-over enables them to set up (domain-related) operations relatively quickly as discussed at length in Bygrave's *Portable MBA in Entrepreneurship* (Bygrave, 1994; Stevenson et al., 1989).

Research shows that in the Netherlands, in the next five years more than 100 000 'older' entrepreneurs (from a total of 640 000 firms with at least one employee) want to sell their existing ventures and retire (CBS www.statline.nl). This means that in the near future, take-over candidates are abundant and affordable (even for starting entrepreneurs who would still need some external funding). Therefore, we argue that entrepreneurship courses should discuss this option seriously.

To create awareness for the different contexts in which the exploitation can be organized, teachers could, for example, bring in entrepreneurs who exploit opportunities through start-ups, team start-ups, corporate venturing, and business take-over to act as role models and tell the students about the benefits and drawbacks of each of these contexts, both in terms of the social and motivational aspects (that is, a team start might be less lonely) and of success rates (Vyakarnam et al., 1997).

Further, while in the opportunity recognition stage domain-specific knowledge is relevant, during the preparation stage, general business and management knowledge gains in importance. Business students will have prior knowledge in these areas through earlier courses when entering an entrepreneurship program, or alternatively they will follow such courses parallel to the entrepreneurship courses. Non-business students will have to obtain and develop such general management and business knowledge as part of their entrepreneurship program. Therefore, entrepreneurship education for non-business students should incorporate relevant fields at an introductory level, the topics including general management, marketing, and finance.

Training of specific skills in relation to identifying and obtaining access to particular relevant resources that are located within or outside the organization should also be a part of the courses in this stage. In the context of team start-ups, corporate venturing or business take-over, team-building skills and skills that enable the non-business student to convince various stakeholders (supervisors, colleagues, banks, and so on) of the value of their opportunities should be part of the curriculum as well. To this end, further training of communication and networking skills will be essential.

Networking helps entrepreneurs in developing the opportunities into marketable products and it may provide the entrepreneur with the required resources. De Koning (1999) suggests that strong ties are particularly important in getting these resources, as strong ties are more motivated to help the entrepreneur than the weak ties and provide entrepreneurs with (access to) resources at a below market price as a result of a stronger relationship. Non-business students might know where to find contacts that help them develop the technical aspects of their products, as these are active in the same professional domain. However, they might be less knowledgeable about potential resource providers and people who help them with the marketing of their product. Also, non-business students might lack negotiating skills needed for gaining access to resources at a (be)low (market) price. Therefore, curricula should focus on how to develop and use a network to gain access to resources. In addition to creating an organization and building a resource base, students should also learn to transform their perceived opportunity into a concrete offering. The offering consists of the products or service in combination with the way it is presented to the market (marketing mix). When dealing with non-business students the focus on the opportunity might lead to extensive research and development (R&D) activities as the 'discoverer-entrepreneur' continues to improve the product rather than bringing it to the market. As a result, such an entrepreneur-to-be may not be able to build the bridge to the market and move into exploitation. Therefore programs directed at technical students need to provide the knowledge and skills to evaluate the extent to which the offering is complete and good enough for the market. Co-development with customers may be a fruitful approach since it forces the entrepreneur to remain problem oriented. Bringing entrepreneurs into the classroom that, for this reason, did not succeed in building the bridge to the market can be a helpful tool in addition to specific case-based assignments on this topic.

In addition to building an organization, creating a resource base and developing the eventual 'offering', at this stage of the entrepreneurial process it is also highly important to convince a wide range of stakeholders of the (potential future) value of the opportunity. A business plan can be an excellent tool for this. This business plan often seems to be positioned as the core topic or assignment of entrepreneurship courses or programs (Karlsson, 2005). This is not surprising considering that it is often the minimal requirement to obtain financing (Kuratko and Hodgetts, 2001). Students typically have to create just one business plan. However, research (for example, Mason and Stark, 2002) shows that, in fact, entrepreneurs should prepare different types of business plans for different audiences, for example, a plan targeted at investors should include sound financial planning, while a business plan directed at lead customers or R&D partners should highlight the functionalities and value of the products-in-the-making. Although it will be unlikely that entrepreneurs indeed create multiple business plans during start-up, we argue that students should at least practice writing plans for specific audiences.

To summarize, we argue that as regards the opportunity preparation stage, entrepreneurship education for non-business students should focus on (1) creating awareness of and positive attitudes towards different contexts (solo-start-up, team start-up, corporate venturing, business take-over) in which organizations can be created for exploiting opportunities; (2) developing the knowledge and skills to build an organization in different contexts including team work, negotiation skills, and networking skills; (3) developing fundamental knowledge and skills of management, marketing, organization and finance and; (4) how to write a business plan targeted at different audiences.

4.3.4   Teaching opportunity exploitation to non-business students

According to a European Foundation for Entrepreneurship Research (EFER) survey (EFER/EFMD, 2004) current entrepreneurship education focuses on business creation (and the development of the business plan) and little on managing and growing an enterprise. As a result, few entrepreneurship programs address the process of exploitation and value creation. Rather, and probably unjustly, these issues are considered part of regular management courses. However, early exploitation and managing growth might be particularly complex for non-business students and thus deserves attention. In this section we examine what kind of awareness, attitudes, knowledge and skills need to be developed in relation to this exploitation stage. Important clues for what might be relevant can be found in examples from small business management courses that are offered at many business schools (in some cases these courses are offered under the label of entrepreneurship courses to business students, for example using Scarborough and Zimmerer's 2004 textbook). Small business management courses usually neglect the recognition of opportunities and the creation of organization but focus on exploitation. Supposing that non-business students are predominantly motivated by the opportunity and less by business ownership, entrepreneurship courses should make students aware of the possibility of hiring management. Newly appointed managers can be made responsible for running the venture on a day-to-day basis, while the founders can focus on their own specialty (that is, develop the domain specific opportunity further).

In addition, the curriculum should focus on making non-business students aware of their advantages in dealing with customers or potential users as compared to business students. Their domain-specific knowledge enables them to better understand the actual needs of the customers. Consequently they can engage in joint product development, they will be better able to recognize when 'technical' or other developments in their field allow for or require updates or improvements of their current offerings and to use customers and suppliers as sources of ideas (Von Hippel, 1988). Making them aware of their potential competitive advantage will add to the non-business students' confidence and thus to the likelihood of entrepreneurial activity.

Recent studies suggest that in the Netherlands there are relatively few high-growth companies in comparison to many other countries. Moreover, the growth rate of the high growth firms is lower than in other countries (Ehrhardt et al., 2004). It seems that this lack of growth is partially due to a lack of growth orientation and even a preference for staying small (Van der Sijde et al., 2002a). As shown by Wiklund (1998), growth is more strongly related to motivation than knowledge. Growth, in its turn has a strong relation to performance. Therefore, it is somewhat surprising to find that very few classes address the issue of firm growth. A desire to stay small does not have to be a problem when it is for the right reasons (less red tape and overhead, control, and so on). However, when lack of growth is due to fear and lack of knowledge, this is regrettable and should be overcome. In our perspective, entrepreneurship courses should address the issue of growth and seek to develop favorable attitudes towards growth. We expect that showing the positive effects of growth in combination with the previously addressed issue of hiring management might be one way of increasing both awareness of and positive attitudes towards growth.

In addition to awareness and having the right attitudes, knowledge and skills remain important during exploitation. Non-business students might have a disadvantage compared to business students in relation to relevant general management knowledge and skills for exploiting the opportunity because of lack of previous education or even lack of interest. Teaching opportunity exploitation to non-business students should therefore focus on managing (ongoing) operations as well as continued awareness of innovation and changes in the market that may create challenges or new opportunities for their venture.

In relation to growth, entrepreneurship courses will have to enhance development of specific knowledge and skills as well. This may include topics related to identifying, obtaining and managing financial investments, human resources, innovation and R&D (Ehrhardt et al., 2004). Further, theoretical knowledge and skills in relation to daily management should also be addressed. Literature study, lectures and practical assignments including traineeships could be useful. Finally, the courses should also address the issue of continued entrepreneurial behavior and remaining alert to new (related or unrelated) opportunities (Churchill and Muzyka, 1994). Topics such as change management and leadership belong in these courses as well. Again, lectures provided by experienced entrepreneurs and assignments and course work may prove useful.

To summarize the above, in relation to teaching exploitation of opportunities a number of issues deserve specific attention: (1) stimulating awareness of the possibilities of hiring external management; (2) enhancing students' awareness of their own competitive advantage, based on their domain-specific knowledge when it comes to dealing with customers; (3) enhancing awareness and a positive attitude towards growth; (4) developing knowledge and skills in relation to identifying and attracting additional resources to enable growth; (5) development of knowledge and skills in relation to the management of small ventures and (6) creating of awareness, knowledge and skills in relation to remaining entrepreneurial, and alert to new opportunities, change management and leadership.

In the following section we present two cases of entrepreneurship minors targeted at non-business students in the Netherlands. We discuss to what extent these programs incorporate the issues discussed above.

4.4   Lessons from experiences in the Netherlands

4.4.1   *Entrepreneurial education in the Dutch context*
In the previous section we presented our view on what entrepreneurship education for non-business students should entail. In the following sections we discuss two cases from the universities of Twente and Groningen that illustrate the current situation in the Netherlands with respect to teaching entrepreneurship to non-business students at the bachelor's level.

As an introduction to these cases, this paragraph provides some general background on the status and level of entrepreneurship in the Netherlands. Table 4.1 shows some numbers,

Table 4.1   Characteristics of Dutch entrepreneurs (percentages are TEA-indexes[1] unless indicated otherwise)

	Netherlands	Other countries
TEA index among total population (2004)	7.9%	EU average 7.9%, US about 11% Highest in study: Peru 40% Lowest in study: Japan about 1%
Average age of people involved in TEA (2004)	39 years	EU average 37.5 years, US 37 years Highest in study: Denmark and UK 40 years Lowest in study: Portugal 32 years

Note: 1.   TEA-index: the percentage of the population involved in setting up a company or leading a company not older then 2.5 years.

Source: Hessels et al. (2005).

using the Total Early-stage Entrepreneurial Activity (TEA) index (the percentage of the population involved in setting up a company or leading a company not older then 2.5 years). The TEA-index in the Netherlands is similar to EU-average; in 2004 7.9 per cent of the Dutch population was involved in entrepreneurial activity, against 7.9 per cent at EU level. The US had an index of just over 11 per cent, and Peru 40 per cent (the highest in this study). The average age of people involved in TEA is rather high as compared to the EU and US (39, 37.5 and 37 respectively). Higher educated people in the Netherlands are about twice as often involved in entrepreneurship as lower educated people, that is TEA-index of 7.2 versus 3.6 per cent (Hessels et al., 2005). During the last decade the appreciation of entrepreneurs and entrepreneurship has risen in the Netherlands and is expected to rise further in the coming years (Bosma et al., 2002; Hessels et al., 2005).

Interestingly, Dutch academic entrepreneurs are very critical of the contribution of their study to their current profession (Bosma et al., 2002). According to them, the educational system is too much focused on theoretical knowledge and transferring knowledge rather than on the development of positive attitudes and skills. This rather negative view might be due to the fact that entrepreneurship education in the Netherlands is fairly recent and that most institutes are still searching for the right balance between academic content and practical use. Although most universities offer courses and programs (NVOA, 2005), and a number of universities have appointed professors in related fields like Small Business Management or have established endowed chairs (such as the Biopartner professors), by the end of 2004, there were still no full professors in entrepreneurship in the Netherlands. Fortunately, the situation is changing rapidly with a growing number of researchers, teachers and PhD students in the area of entrepreneurship. These scholars have taken many initiatives to improve the offer in entrepreneurship programs and courses. Two of these initiatives will be highlighted in the following subsections.

4.4.2   Introduction to two cases

The decision to select the cases from Twente and Groningen is based on two reasons. First, there is the practical reason of gaining access to the data; all authors were involved in one of these cases. Second, considerable variation exists between the cases. In Twente entrepreneurship education is mainly provided to non-business students in technological areas such as electrical engineering and computer science,[3] whereas in Groningen most non-business students enrolling in the entrepreneurship program have a background in alpha and gamma sciences like the social sciences (including psychology, sociology), and arts (*letteren*). Further, the institutional environment of both universities is very different. The University of Twente positions itself as an entrepreneurial university and has an elaborate infrastructure to stimulate academic entrepreneurship. The University of Groningen, on the other hand, presents itself as a classical university and demonstrates little overt support for academic entrepreneurship.

4.4.3   An academic minor for engineering students

The University of Twente is a relatively young university in the eastern part of the Netherlands. It was founded in 1961 to counter the economic decline in the region after the demise of the textile industry. While being mainly a technical university, the University of Twente currently offers programs in both technical areas and non-technical sciences in six different faculties namely: Behavioral Sciences; Business, Public Administration and Technology; Electrical Engineering, Mathematics and Computer Science; Engineering Technology; and Science and Technology. In 2003 approximately 7000 students were enrolled in the university's bachelor's, master's and PhD programs, while almost 2700 employees were working at the university (www.utwente.nl).

Entrepreneurship has been an important element in the policy of the University of Twente since the beginning of the 1980s. This dedication resulted in the creation of the Temporary Entrepreneurship Positions program (TOP) for the support of new ventures created by (former) students and employees from the university (for example, Groen et al., 2004; Van Tilburg et al., 2004), the development of several courses including the course 'Becoming an entrepreneur' at the TSM Business School, and incorporation of the topic in a variety of courses. In 2000 this dedication resulted in the establishment of a minor program in entrepreneurship that is offered by the research institute NIKOS (Dutch Institute for Knowledge Intensive Entrepreneurship) at the faculty of Business, Public Administration and Technology. This minor was set up as an opportunity for non-business students to broaden their scope by getting well acquainted with the subject of entrepreneurship, which is very different from their graduation subject. The curriculum was organized around a three-category framework for describing different aspects of entrepreneurship education: education for, through and about enterprise (Gibb, 1989). Education *for* enterprise seeks to stimulate students to think about starting their own venture as a career option and prepares them for the start-up. Education *through* enterprise concerns developing entrepreneurial (and managerial) competencies in students, and prepares them for the demands of a career in business. Education *about* enterprise aims to inform students about the nature of small enterprise and/in its context and focuses on understanding entrepreneurship and commerce (Van der Sijde and Ridder, 2006).

After only admitting students from a small number of schools in the first two years, in the academic year 2003/04 students from 12 different schools/faculties[4] participated in the program. At this moment, the majority of the students enrolled in the minor are engineering students, yet some students are studying behavioral science (for example, education science and communication). Also, business majors are now being allowed to participate in the entrepreneurship minor as well. Although all students jointly participate in most courses, these business students have to follow an alternative track that is geared towards their advanced theoretical background in relation to business and management.

Theoretical perspective, and outline of the minor in entrepreneurship   In the first four editions of the minor program, 76 students have completed the course (Van der Sijde et al., 2004; Van der Sijde and Ridder, 2006). The opportunity-based process view on entrepreneurship (Van der Veen and Wakkee, 2004) as described above has been adopted widely by the teachers of the minor in entrepreneurship. The consequence of this adoption was that the original textbook by Scarborough and Zimmerer, *Effective Small Business Management* (2004) had to be replaced. In order to give the entrepreneurial process an even more prominent position in the curriculum, the main textbooks became *New Venture Creation: Entrepreneurship for the 21st Century* by Timmons and Spinelli (2004) and (for the marketing course) *The Business Idea: The Early Stages of Entrepreneurship* by Søren Hougaard (2005). It is yet to be evaluated if these books suffice and if they will continue be used in the coming years.

For non-business students the different courses introduce the fundamentals of business management and continues to examine in further detail the theories, concepts, methods and schools of thought in this area. Although the minor does not include separate courses on recognizing opportunities or on entrepreneurial networking, these topics are incorporated implicitly and explicitly in each of the courses. In total the minor has a workload of 560 hours. During the first stage of the program, students are taught the basics of entrepreneurship in a series of six classes. After that the advanced level program *about* entrepreneurship is offered which includes the modules entrepreneurship basics, marketing, finance and business law. In these modules teachers, entrepreneurs and experts present the current schools of thought regarding their application in an entrepreneurship context. In the first four editions these courses were complemented with a course called 'Theoretical aspects of entrepreneurship' (now called 'Entrepreneurship in SMEs'). In this course the emphasis is on 'about' (theory and cases) and 'through' (assignment) entrepreneurship' (Van der Sijde and Ridder, forthcoming). The theoretical topics discussed in this course include innovation, entrepreneurial networking, and entrepreneurial growth. The topics were selected because they were considered as necessary and important for students who are going to work in a company setting; they were not dealt with in the other courses and they provided references for the cases and assignments. The second part of this course is more practical in nature and is taught on the basis of real-life cases from entrepreneurs who present their own experiences with entrepreneurial careers, merger and acquisitions, market introduction of new products and corporate entrepreneurship.

The minor ends with a practical training module that can either be 'Becoming an entrepreneur' or 'Managing an SME'. In the former of these, the ultimate goal is drawing up a realistic business plan. A panel of experts, for example entrepreneurs, accountants and consultants, evaluate the business plans. This approach has multiple functions (Groen et al., 2004):

1. Via the business plan the student shows that the acquired knowledge on entrepreneurship can be put into practice.
2. The business plan is also the instrument to evaluate the student's knowledge on legal issues and financial management. The student has to explicitly address these topics

in his or her business in the plan. The teacher separately grades the legal and financial paragraph in the business plan.

3.   Furthermore, this course provides an opportunity for developing and practicing several skills needed by entrepreneurs, such as sales, negotiation and presentation skills.

In the latter course, students act as personal assistants/consultants for owner-managers of SMEs, who are developing their business plan during this course. This provides a unique opportunity to put theory into practice. Writing a report reflecting on this experience is part of the assessment.

The content of each of these courses addresses the lack of knowledge and experience in the field of business and management and aims at enabling the students to incorporate their previous domain-specific knowledge (based on their major topic) into the assignments (Van der Sijde et al., 2004). Most students did indeed generate their ideas for opportunities from their 'major' subjects as is shown from the overview provided in Table 4.2.

Evaluation of the minor in entrepreneurship   Based on the experiences from the minor in entrepreneurship so far, a number of observations can be made. To begin with, the minor has grown each year in terms of the number of students enrolled. In the first three editions, this growth was mainly driven by the number of faculties that allowed their students to enroll in the minor program. However, in the fourth and fifth years the program continued to grow without an increase in the number of 'participating' faculties. Feedback

Table 4.2   Short indication of business plans produced for 'Becoming an entrepreneur'

Year	Topics business plans	
2000–01	• Animated product with a high educational value • Communication advice • Virtual take away • Consultancy for safety and environment	• Intermediary for Internet services • Efficiency in the catering industry • Student Union shop • Student entrepreneur portal • Personalized products • Radio station
2001–02	• Motorbike taxi service • Mobile ICT consultancy • Delivery service • Technical services at home • Business and IT service	• Examination construction and consultancy • Intermediary for IT services delivered by students
2002–03	• CaRe-mail • Stimulearn • De computer-doctor • The children's bookstore • Grandma cooks dinner • Brocksystems • Networks solutions	• Students solutions Twente • Monito • Automotive consulting • Emocion tuning • Keep IT Simple software • New Vision Solutions

Source: Van der Sijde et al. (2004).

from students suggests this growth is largely caused by word-of-mouth promotion by enthusiastic minor alumni. Further growth is expected during the coming years. The students and faculty members who have participated in the program have been very enthusiastic about the setup of the minor, as has become apparent from the evaluation forms the students have to complete at the end of the course. Further, we agree with the conclusions of Van der Sijde and Ridder (2006) who state that the minor is innovative and potentially successful because it combines the three approaches to entrepreneurship (*for*, *about*, *through*) into one. The course connects education (the actual courses), outreach (interaction with the real business community) and contributes to the research activities of the faculty teaching the minor (see Groen et al., 2004; Nikos, 2005); this is, according to Watkins and Stone (1999), an important prerequisite for a successful and sustainable program (see also Van der Sijde et al., 2002a).

4.4.4 *Alpha and gamma students meet entrepreneurship at the University of Groningen*
The University of Groningen (RuG) is a 'classical' university (founded in 1614) encompassing a broad array of faculties, that is, Management and Organization, Economics, Theology, Arts, Medical Sciences, Behavioral and Social Sciences, Law, Spatial Sciences, Philosophy, and Mathematical and Natural Sciences. In 2003, the university enrolled just over 21 000 students and employed *circa* 6000 staff (annual report RuG, 2003, www.rug.nl). As mentioned previously, the RuG has separate and independent faculties for Economics, and Management and Organization. Generally speaking, however, they both mainly offer what we would label 'business programs'.

During the 1980s and 1990s, both faculties started electives on small business and entrepreneurship. When a local business club sponsored the institution of a special chair in Small Business Management at the Faculty of Economics, a limited offer of non-compulsory courses was developed. These courses paid much attention to entrepreneurial skills; students could write a start-up plan, a business plan, and or start-up a 'real enterprise' within a nationwide project 'mini-enterprises' (cf. Bosma, Stigter and Wennekers, 2002). In 1998, a first coherent small business and entrepreneurship (SB&E) program was developed for graduate students of both faculties. This program was much more an academic program involving the transfer of advanced theoretical knowledge and applying it in various research settings. In the same period, staff research expanded, mainly in the areas of business start-ups and small business management.

In the first period, with only non-compulsory and skills-oriented courses, students from other non-business faculties such as Law incidentally joined these courses, which rendered no major problems. However, as the graduate program was developed and introduced, non-business students encountered difficulties when they were interested in the subject. First, course prerequisites hindered admittance to most courses and, second, the content of the courses became more abstract and research oriented, which was not what these students were looking for. Around that time, the RuG introduced a specific type of undergraduate course, aimed at students from 'foreign' faculties to acquaint students with the topics and scientific habitus of other academic disciplines. When a small subsidy became available for education development, staff responsible for the SB&E program decided to develop a specific course 'Innovative entrepreneurship' to serve interested non-business students. The approach followed was a so-called 'magnet' approach, that is, a university-wide entrepreneurship program offered by a central entrepreneurship group. A study by

Streeter et al. (2002) showed that over 50 per cent of US universities with a university-wide entrepreneurship program follow this model. As will be discussed below, the course has only been taught once, because the faculty board decided to withdraw it after the first year.

Preparation, outline and evaluation of the course   As stated previously, the new course was developed by SB&E staff. Since the extra funds to develop the course were limited, it was decided to make efficient use of elements of existing courses. In order to decide on the actual content and teaching methods, an exploratory, qualitative survey was held among staff, student councilors, and students of all faculties (although some staff denied cooperation, for example at the Medical Faculty[5]). Results indicated that students could be expected mainly from the following fields: law, medicine (dentists, GPs), geography, ICT, and arts (mainly languages). The main objectives of the course were:

- raising awareness of and improving attitude towards entrepreneurship
- providing necessary theoretical foundation of entrepreneurship and management and organization
- developing entrepreneurial skills.

Innovative entrepreneurship became a bachelor elective with a workload of 160 hours. The chosen outline of the course was as follows:

- classes, consisting of both lectures and working groups
- topic specific assignments (individual and small groups)
- developing and writing a business plan (start-up phase)
- presenting the business plan at the 'business challenge' to an outside board
- written theoretical examination.

Following the main program components distinguished earlier in this chapter (awareness, attitude, skills and knowledge) the course can be described as follows. Students from a varied non-business background were taught by a team of SB&E staff complemented with guest lecturers from the business and institutional community. In this way students were confronted with an array of role models, thus stimulating awareness and a positive attitude towards entrepreneurship in general. By showing statistical material about the number of entrepreneurs and the contribution of entrepreneurship to society and individual development, the attitude towards entrepreneurship was further developed. An important role in this was one of the assignments aimed at discovering and appreciating the students' individual entrepreneurial qualities. The remainder of the assignments were aimed at developing the entrepreneurial skills of the students. Focus was on communication skills (within the group, class, teachers and external board) and business plan development and writing skills. Last, but certainly not least, a thorough basis of knowledge about entrepreneurship as a theoretical concept, and its links with business and management theory was included in the course. To this end, the selected book was not a how-to-do-book (which would probably be preferred by some of the students) but a general book with a sound mixture of theory and application. The teaching faculty opted for Kirby's book, *Entrepreneurship* (Kirby, 2003). This book gave a backbone to the course and made it possible to end the program with a serious written examination. Teaching staff used the theoretical lectures to present some examples of recent research in the field, to acquaint the students with the scientific habitus of the business departments.

Evaluation   We will briefly discuss the experiences of both students and staff with the *Innovative entrepreneurship* course. The first year, the course attracted 14 students who were all included in a brief evaluation survey. The students were very enthusiastic about the course. Since they had no background whatsoever in the business field, they felt they were really introduced to a new, interesting, and potentially fruitful area. Being able to use the acquired knowledge in an assignment that required much effort and involved external experts was something most students had not experienced earlier in their studies. Two of the students actually started their own business within months after completing the course. The staff involved were also mainly positive about the course; students were curious and prepared to put in the effort needed to complete the course successfully. However, they also had some points for improvement. First, the background of the students was not as expected. Half the students came from the social sciences (seven), complemented with students who studied languages, biology, and geography. Had this been known, examples and guest lectures would have been better geared towards the actual audience. Furthermore, the limited budget available to develop the course hindered individual staff from putting the desired effort in aligning their contributions. Finally, although students had been working on their business plans enthusiastically, the quality of the plans was mediocre. It was striking to the teaching team that none of the teams made use of its domain-specific knowledge (perhaps with one exception, a group of social sciences students who wanted to open a social club for the elderly). The remaining groups chose safe ideas such as opening an art shop, or developing a website for finding a domestic aid. Although such general opportunities might of course lead to successful ventures, they are easily imitated and not very competitive. After this evaluation, staff had no clear ideas yet how to improve these shortcomings. Unfortunately, the need even to do this disappeared when the faculty board decided to discontinue the course due to the relatively small number of students (in its first year the course did not reach its breakeven point).

In the next section innovative entrepreneurship and the minor in entrepreneurship from Twente will be evaluated more systematically using the process model and guidelines developed in this chapter.

4.4.5   Lessons to be learned

On the basis of the pursuit-of-opportunity model we can draw a number of lessons with regard to the two entrepreneurship programs described above. The lessons can be used to evaluate these and other courses on entrepreneurship as a profession.

Starting at the beginning of the process, the first lesson involves the initial idea and the recognition of opportunities. In Groningen, there is no obligation for students to use domain-specific ideas in their business plans. Although in Twente, students are not obliged to draw on their domain-specific background either, at least they are stimulated to use their domain-specific knowledge in doing their assignments. Despite the fact that students in Twente still call for increased attention to idea generation, the outcomes have shown that most students come up with ideas and opportunities that are related to their major topic.

Regarding preparation for exploitation, both the programs in Groningen and Twente addressed the issue of building resource bases. However, when it comes to the creation of an organization, the focus clearly has been on starting a new venture (either alone or in teams). Based on our model, more attention should be directed at the possibilities of corporate entrepreneurship and taking over existing ventures as a vehicle for exploiting the opportunity. We consider this particularly relevant in the context of teaching entrepreneurship to non-business students because of their limited knowledge and experience in management.

With regards to exploitation, both programs offer basic business management knowledge and skills that are required for running a small venture. In Twente, marketing, finance and business law receive much attention and seem to be considered important areas of knowledge and skills needed to run the new venture. Although these topics may indeed be important, we think that they do not belong to the heart of entrepreneurship and thus should not use up too much time in the entrepreneurship program.

Far less attention seems to be devoted to growth. We concluded that entrepreneurship courses should address the issue of growth more explicitly and should try to develop positive attitudes towards growth and provide students with knowledge and skills that are needed to grow their venture through alternative pathways (cooperation with other ventures, attracting financial investments, hiring management, and so on).

Finally, with respect to networking, the findings indicate that in Groningen there has been no pressure on the students to practice networking to the full. In Twente, networking is stimulated through encouraging the formation of teams for the preparation of the business plans in the course 'Becoming an entrepreneur', and through introducing entrepreneurs as guest lecturers into the classroom who talk extensively about the importance of networking. We argue that by stimulating the formation of teams, a larger share of students might decide to pursue an entrepreneurial career as it can compensate for weaknesses in particular areas and make enterprising a less lonely profession. A focus on networks will enhance the students' confidence in seeking various kinds of support throughout the entrepreneurial process, making them more likely to continue their venture (Elfring and Hulsink, 2003).

The main points that we have made at the end of subsections 3.2 through 3.4 are listed in the first column of Table 4.3. Together they form a framework that can be used to evaluate or develop entrepreneurship programs for non-business students. The framework is applied to the two cases, showing how the different elements (stages and influences) of the process model have been incorporated in the two programs. This overview demonstrates that the Groningen course strongly focuses on stages 1 and 2 of the entrepreneurial process, and puts relatively greater emphasis on knowledge instead of skills. The minor program in Twente, which of course has more room in its curriculum, can be characterized by devoting attention to each of the three stages, but with a stronger focus on preparation and exploitation than on opportunity recognition. In Twente, the academic nature of the program is strictly protected, but knowledge and skills receive almost equal attention. Raising awareness and securing positive attitudes is done both in the entrepreneurship program and at the university level through putting entrepreneurship central to the university's mission.

In addition we can also learn several more general lessons from the illustrative cases. First, the small group of students proved to be beneficiary to the interaction and general

Table 4.3 *A framework for evaluating entrepreneurship programs for non-business students, applied to two Dutch cases*

Framework		Application to two cases	
Stage in the entrepreneurial process	Professional attitudes, skills and knowledge to be taught	Incorporated in minor in entrepreneurship (Case 1: Twente)	Incorporated in innovative entrepreneurship (Case 2: RuG)
1 Opportunity recognition	1. Awareness of entrepreneurship as a career alternative in new ventures or in established firms	1. Yes, mostly for start-ups but increasing attention for intrapreneurship	1. Yes, but only start-ups
	2. Positive attitudes towards entrepreneurship	2. Yes, via guest lecturers, assignments, and lecture content and more generally by including entrepreneurship in the mission of the university and through ample support for entrepreneurs	2. Yes, via lectures, guest lecturers, and assignments
	3. Knowledge and skills to use prior domain specific knowledge to raise entrepreneurial alertness	3. Yes, via guest lecturers and assignments, stimulating teamwork on business plans	3. Limited; business plans lack in this respect
	4. Knowledge and skills for networking	4. Yes, but more attention is needed to actually introduce students in relevant domain-specific and institutional networks	4. Limited; business plans lack in this respect
2 Preparation of opportunity	1. Awareness and positive attitudes towards different contexts (solo-start-up, team start-up, corporate venturing, business take-over)	1. Limited; mostly solo and team	1. No
	2. Knowledge and skills to build an organization in different contexts including team work, negotiation skills, and networking skills	2. Limited through literature and assignment but little practice to develop skills	2. No
	3. Knowledge and skills of management, marketing and finance	3. Knowledge, yes; skills not compulsory, but possibilities for co-operating in 'Becoming an entrepreneur' or to	3. Knowledge in prescribed book, readings, lectures and written exam; no skills

Table 4.3 (continued)

Framework	Application to two cases	
4. How to write a business plan targeted at different audiences.	cooperate with entrepreneurs for the course 'Management of SMEs' 4. Yes, through 'Becoming an Entrepreneur', 'Management of SMEs' and smaller assignments	4. Business plan yes; but only to the audience of potential investors ('outside experts')
3 Exploitation of opportunity		
1. Stimulating awareness of the possibilities of hiring external management	1. Hardly	1. No
2. Enhancing students' awareness of their own competitive advantage, based on their domain-specific knowledge when it comes to dealing with customers	2. Limited as shown from business plans	2. No
3. Enhancing awareness and a positive attitude towards growth	3. Limited in prescribed textbook, readings and lectures	3. Limited in prescribed textbook, readings and lectures
4. Knowledge and skills in relation to identifying and attracting additional resources to enable growth	4. Yes, through assignments and presentations for audiences of institutional network members and other entrepreneurs (business plan competition)	4. No
5. Knowledge and skills in relation to the management of small ventures	5. Yes through 'Financial management in SMEs'; 'Theoretical aspects of entrepreneurship'; 'Marketing oriented entrepreneurship'; 'Legal aspects of management in SMEs'	5. Limited in prescribed textbook, readings and lectures
6. Awareness, knowledge and skills in relation to remaining entrepreneurial, alert to new opportunities, change management and leadership	6. Limited in prescribed textbook, readings and lectures	6. Limited in prescribed textbook, readings and lectures

quality of the classes in both programs. However, contemporary budgeting systems may prevent such courses as long as outside sponsoring is not available, as was shown in the Groningen case.

Second, most students from non-business faculties have no idea of the concept of entrepreneurship, its possibilities for them personally, and the scientific habitus in the business field. In Groningen, most students admitted to having enrolled in the course 'out of curiosity'. This implies that attaining goals such as raising awareness and improving attitude are relatively easily met. However, to create a larger pool of students, it is important that there is sufficient attention for the topic of entrepreneurship throughout the university. In Twente, the initial awareness is likely to be higher as a result of the continuous attention given to entrepreneurship in the university's mission and as a result of the abundance of entrepreneurial support programs such as TOP, the University Student Enterprise Initiative (USE), and presence of successful (former) student entrepreneurs who act as role models

Further, students from non-business faculties have little or no business-related knowledge. Also, they have had little or no contact with outside experts. In order to successfully practice entrepreneurship skills and be able to understand entrepreneurship theory, basic management and strategy knowledge has to be included in the program. At the same time, students should be trained in seeking advice and assistance and in developing cooperation to overcome their lack of knowledge and skills in these areas. In Twente, new teaching cases and experiments involving a variety of regional business cases are expected to further improve and update both teaching methods and examination (Groen et al., 2004). In our view, entrepreneurship minors should keep their focus on topics that are at the heart of entrepreneurship, that is, the pursuit of opportunities. Although understandable, we feel that (too) much attention for topics such as general management and marketing limits the available time for what it is all about: learning to recognize and exploit opportunities.

4.5 Discussion and conclusion

4.5.1 *Discussion*

Entrepreneurship education for non-business students has recently gained increasing attention from educators and policy makers. Yet, so far little is known about how courses and programs should be developed in such a way that non-business students are stimulated to pursue a career in entrepreneurship and to set up and grow successful companies.

We conclude that programs and courses directed at teaching entrepreneurship as a profession to non-business students can be divided into three groups. The first group defines entrepreneurship as starting up new businesses, while the second group has a broader view, that is, entrepreneurship as the pursuit of opportunities. In this chapter, we have argued that the latter approach is to be preferred. To that end, we presented a model of the entrepreneurial process (as developed by Van der Veen and Wakkee, 2004). According to this model, entrepreneurship begins with the development of an idea which needs to be developed into an opportunity for business (opportunity recognition), which in turn needs to be prepared for exploitation, which in the end leads to value creation. This process is driven by the entrepreneur but is strongly affected by the network (Aldrich and Zimmer, 1986; Elfring and Hulsink, 2003). We argue that when such a process view is adopted, it becomes possible to develop or evaluate programs and courses in such a way that all relevant subject areas are covered and that a program is catered towards the specific needs and capabilities of this specific target group.

By adopting the pursuit of opportunities as the central focus, entrepreneurship is no longer limited to business start-ups but expanded to different contexts, including intrapreneurship and entrepreneurship in the non-profit sector. This is important considering that many organizations are in need of entrepreneurial employees to remain innovative (Hornsby et al., 1993; Kuratko et al., 1990). Further, by focusing on the entire process, students will not only learn to found a business – a rather short-term view – but also how to manage, develop and grow their venture. This is especially important considering the limited managerial experience and knowledge of non-business students. Furthermore, growing organizations are generally more beneficial to society than simple start-ups. In the Netherlands data show that firm growth has lagged and should be improved (Ehrhardt et al., 2004).

Finally, by focusing on the opportunity rather than the start-up, students can learn to benefit from their prior knowledge (Shane, 2000). This domain-specific knowledge is highly developed in non-business students through their major subject. This particular prior knowledge is likely to provide them with specific advantages in all three stages of the pursuit-of-opportunities process. Thus, in our opinion, the focus on opportunity will enable non-business students to profit from their competitive advantage.

To illustrate how this model can be used to evaluate existing courses in terms of appropriateness for different groups of students and for teaching entrepreneurship beyond new venture creation, and to what extent these ideas are presently incorporated in entrepreneurship education for non-business students in the Netherlands, we have presented two case examples. These cases from the University of Twente and the University of Groningen were different in several respects. First, the background of the students is different. Whereas most students in Twente have a science and technology background, the students in Groningen are enrolled in alpha and gamma programs. Considering the importance of prior knowledge during the opportunity recognition process, this would suggest that the difference in student background should have implications for the programs in terms of, for instance, the type of guest lecturers that are invited and cases to be discussed in the classroom.

When we compare the programs and their outcomes, the most notable conclusion is that students from the University of Twente seem to be better able to use their prior domain-specific knowledge than those in Groningen. Our explanation is that at Twente there is much more attention at the institutional level for academic entrepreneurship, both in education and in commercialization of research outcomes. As argued, it seems that the presence of highly successful support programs such as USE and TOP have resulted in 'me-too' and 'can-do' attitudes amongst a relatively large group of students. Although a critical mass of successful academic spin-offs and student entrepreneurship may be difficult to achieve, the showcasing of successful entrepreneurial efforts from Groningen might be necessary to develop a similar entrepreneurial spirit there.

Another explanation might be that in Twente opportunity recognition and entrepreneurial networking take a more prominent position in the entrepreneurship education than in Groningen. These concepts are consequently dealt with in most of the courses of the minor by means of articles and textbooks used and by bringing successful entrepreneurs into the classroom. Similar activities might be undertaken in Groningen. For this to work well it is important to know the background of the students; in the Groningen case this background was not as expected. Probably this problem would have diminished if the course had not been withdrawn, and student enrollment would have had the time to stabilize.

With respect to the role of the entrepreneur it is clear that in both programs entrepreneurship is considered a skill or talent that can be developed (up to a certain level) rather than an innate characteristic. Yet, both programs seem to reach only parts of the student population, thus limiting the pool of potential future entrepreneurs. In Twente, male students and students from knowledge-intensive sciences were overrepresented; targeting softer sciences such as communication and educational sciences might lead to a greater influx of female students (Van Hoof, 2004). In Groningen one of the eight non-business faculties (that is, social science) supplied half of the students for the entrepreneurship course.

Finally, we wonder to what extent the students in Groningen and Twente entered the programs with different intentions. It might well be that the large number of (student) entrepreneurs at the campus inspired the students in Twente to really consider entrepreneurship as a career alternative, while for the students in Groningen it might have been mere curiosity. Also the technical background of most students in Twente might have made it easier to come up with ideas for opportunities. It does not seem surprising that it is easier to come up with a 'product' when you have knowledge in the field of computer science than when you are a psychologist. After all there is much more attention given to entrepreneurial activities in the former industry, than in the latter. The abundant examples in the media can create a 'me-too' effect and also provide a starting point in the search for good ideas. Also, the fact that psychologists, lawyers and the like are typically portrayed as professionals, rather than as entrepreneurs will most likely explain why many of them do not perceive of themselves as (potential) entrepreneurs.

4.5.2 *Conclusion and needs for further research*

From previous research, policy demands and the case examples we conclude that it makes good sense to develop entrepreneurship education programs that are directed specifically at non-business students. The reason for this is that these groups have very different knowledge and experiences, and possibly different attitudes towards entrepreneurship, which provides them with different strengths and weaknesses, and thus with different opportunities for entrepreneurship. As argued previously, these differences will be most apparent in the first stage of the entrepreneurial process: opportunity recognition.

We should also recognize that owing to these differences non-business students and business students both have several distinct advantages and disadvantages when it comes to recognizing, preparing and exploiting opportunities. This would suggest that providing an environment that leads to cooperation between business and non-business students could lead to more successful entrepreneurial activities. Even when some courses are developed specifically for non-business students and others developed specifically for business students, joint classroom activities and exercises may not only make both groups of students aware of their own strength and weaknesses, it might also lead to more cooperation between the two groups. Previous research shows that companies founded by teams are more likely to be successful (Bamford et al., 2000; Carter et al., 1996), especially when these teams are heterogeneous in nature.

Second, we conclude that the model of Van der Veen and Wakkee (2004) is very applicable to compare and evaluate entrepreneurship programs in relation to their original goal. By looking at the model, educators can determine to what extent their program covers the different stages of the entrepreneurial process and thus provides the students with sufficient insights to be able to not just become an owner-manager, but also to pursue opportunities from their initial discovery onwards. Clearly, other entrepreneurship models might also be useful; yet, this model is well grounded in the contemporary literature of entrepreneurship research. Further, the model is relatively simple to use and provides a complete overview of the process. As such it can provide the starting point for developing curricula by indicating which subjects and topics should be addressed and how the courses should be adapted to the target group. The fact that exploiting an opportunity (that is, commercializing a 'discovery') is not the same as starting or running a venture should also be incorporated in the design of the courses. This can be achieved by addressing alternative means of exploitation such as taking over existing ventures or hiring managers. By presenting entrepreneurship as a process, teachers can show that it is not limited to a specific context (new businesses) but that entrepreneurship applies to a variety of organizational contexts. Further, this approach assumes that entrepreneurship is teachable rather than innate.

Although the general content of the courses may be the same for students with different non-business backgrounds, by stimulating their students to apply their domain-specific knowledge, teachers may enhance the effectiveness of the program. The use of examples and role models in the form of entrepreneurs from a variety of backgrounds is one way to do this; using literature pointing to the importance of prior knowledge (for example, Shane, 2000) would be another.

Experience from existing entrepreneurship programs in the Netherlands has shown that teaching entrepreneurship to non-business students means setting up special curricula. Non-business students typically need to be made familiar with the field of management in addition to the specific concepts and theories of entrepreneurship, which of course is not necessary for business students. Similarly, non-business students will typically have particular experiences and skills on which the entrepreneurship courses have to build. To enhance this, it seems that creating connections between the entrepreneurship courses and the courses taught in the regular program of the students might add to the value of the curriculum. For instance, not only could the teachers in the entrepreneurship program stimulate students to use their domain-specific knowledge in recognizing opportunities, teachers in the regular (major) program could also stimulate the students in thinking about the entrepreneurial opportunities and implications they can envisage from the knowledge and skills developed in their courses. Setting up some form of coordination between the different programs might therefore be necessary. Yet, when involving too many disciplines such coordination might be difficult, especially if the entrepreneurship course is taught through a maze model (Streeter et al., 2002).

The choice between a maze and a radiant model concerns the issue of where entrepreneurship courses should find their home within academic universities (Streeter et al., 2002). The most common situation in the US (and most likely also in Europe) is the maze model. In this model, which is also applied in Twente and Groningen, entrepreneurship courses are developed and taught by one (central) department or faculty, usually a business school or entrepreneurship center. These courses are then offered to students from all the university's faculties. Alternatively, entrepreneurship courses might also be offered by individual faculties or departments to the students at these particular faculties (radiant model). This model was used in the example of the 'Science to the market' program as is offered at the Biomedical Faculty in Groningen. The maze and radiant models have their own merits and drawbacks and a choice for either one of these models is likely to be influenced by structural factors such as how curricula are financed. The example from Groningen showed that despite enthusiasm from the participating students, the 'Innovative entrepreneurship' program had to be abandoned, as it did not yield sufficient income. Considering the fact that in the Netherlands external sponsoring is not really an option, program directors, teachers and scholars need to come up with alternative means and methods to be able to continue the development of entrepreneurship courses.

4.5.3   Limitations

Non-business students are a large and significant pool of potential entrepreneurs. Nevertheless, so far this group of students has largely been ignored or neglected in studies and debates on entrepreneurship education. Their specific knowledge backgrounds and motivations call for developing programs that are different from the programs for business students. The major contribution of this chapter has been to provide a theory-based tool to develop and compare entrepreneurship programs directed at non-business students.

However, as with any study, our investigation has a number of limitations. First, in the introduction we mentioned that we would focus on subjects and methods that should be included in entrepreneurship programs. We have addressed the subjects that we consider relevant in the form of topics and areas of knowledge. The methods were discussed on the basis of examples of teaching methods such as bringing in guest lecturers to act as role models, the use of outside experts, traineeships and/or cases. Further research into the issue of teaching entrepreneurship to non-business students might also address the more general teaching philosophies behind the different courses and assignments.

In this chapter we have evaluated and discussed two cases of entrepreneurship programs directed at non-business students on the basis of the process model. These cases should be considered only as illustrations and examples of the present situation in the Netherlands and the application of our model. Findings cannot simply be generalized to other programs in the Netherlands or abroad. To enhance the understanding of how entrepreneurship should be taught to non-business students, further research would be necessary. Preferably this research should include a larger sample of courses from different countries and should examine the programs at a more detailed level. Only then can we consider evaluation of specific courses (for example, 'Becoming an entrepreneur'), rather than programs, and of the teaching methods that are being used.

This chapter is not only limited by the extent of the empirical analysis but also in its scope. We have decided to focus specifically on entrepreneurship courses for non-business students at academic universities. Clearly this is not the only level of education where entrepreneurship is being taught. Specifically, in Europe a large number of professional universities offer entrepreneurship courses and programs. A comparison between the academic and professional courses and programs will most likely lead to further insight in how to design the 'optimal' programs.

Notes

1. Higher education institutes (HEI) fall in two categories: academic universities (universities) and professional universities (also called colleges or higher vocational training institutes, or in Dutch 'HBO' institutes).
2. Clearly, when teaching entrepreneurship as a field of research, development of knowledge of entrepreneurship and scientific methodologies for studying entrepreneurial phenomena should be the main focus of the program. Although students of entrepreneurship as a scientific domain should be aware of the importance and roles of certain skills, attitudes and awareness, these students do not necessarily have to develop these.
3. It should be noted that students from communication and education science have also enrolled in the minor program in Twente.
4. Including business information technology; public administration and public policy; civil engineering; chemical engineering; electrical engineering; computer science; industrial engineering and management; applied communication science; telematics; applied physics; educational science and technology; and mechanical engineering.
5. The Medical Faculty has a tradition of independence and acquired an exemption from the student obligation to follow an elective (among which is innovative entrepreneurship) at a 'foreign' faculty. Moreover, this faculty prefers to develop projects in house, for example, it is involved in the PhD course 'Science to the market' which was mentioned in section 3, in which no academic entrepreneurship staff is involved.

References

Aldrich, H.E. and Zimmer, C. (1986), 'Entrepreneurship through social networks', in D.L. Sexton and R.W. Smilor (eds), *The Art and Science of Entrepreneurship*, Cambridge, MA: Ballinger, pp. 3–23.
Andrén, L. and Uudelepp, U. (1996), 'Search for an entrepreneurial education', in H. Klandt, J. Mugler and D. Müller-Böhling (eds), *IntEnt93 – Internationalizing Entrepreneurship Education and Training: Proceedings of the IntEnt93 Conference*, Vienna, 5–7 July, 1993, Köln, Dortmund, pp. 219–28.
Autio, E., Sapienza, H.J. and Almeida, J. (2000), 'Effects of age at entry, knowledge intensity, and limitability of international growth', *Academy of Management Journal*, **43** (5), 909–24.
Bamford, C., Dean, T. and McDougall, P. (2000), 'An examination of the impact of initial founding conditions and decisions upon the performance of new bank start-ups', *Journal of Business Venturing*, **15** (3), 253–77.
Bechard, J. and Toulouse, J.M. (1998), 'Validation of a didactic model for the analysis of training objectives in entrepreneurship', *Journal of Business Venturing*, **13** (4), 317–32.
Bhave, M.P. (1994), 'A process model of venture creation', *Journal of Business Venturing*, **9** (3), 223–42.
Birch, C.J. and Clements, M. (2004), 'Can do, want to do and am going to do! Changing an anti-entrepreneurial culture to enable sustainable economic regeneration', working paper, Staffordshire University, Jacksonville, www.sulc.ac.uk/cjb/pdf/can_do_want_to_do_am_going_to_do.pdf, accessed on 12 April, 2005.
Birley, S. (1985), 'The role of networks in the entrepreneurial process', *Journal of Business Venturing*, **1** (1), 107–17.
Bosma, N., Stigter, H. and Wennekers, S. (2002), 'The long road to the entrepreneurial society', *Global Entrepreneurship Monitor 2001: the Netherlands*, Zoetermeer: EIM Business and Policy Research.
Brush, C.G., Greene, P.G., Hart, M.M. and Haller, H.S. (2001), 'From initial idea to unique advantage: the entrepreneurial challenge of constructing a resource base', *Academy of Management Executive*, **15** (1), 64–78.
Brush, C.G., Duhaime, I., Gartner, W., Stewart, A., Katz, J., Hitt, M., Alvarez, S., Dale Meyer, G. and Venkataraman, S. (2003), 'Doctoral education in the field of entrepreneurship', *Journal of Management*, **29** (3), 309–31.
Bruyat, C. and Julien, P.A. (2001), 'Defining the field of research in entrepreneurship?', *Journal of Business Venturing*, **16** (2), 165–180.
Bygrave, W. (1994), *The Portable MBA in Entrepreneurship*, New York: John Wiley and Sons.
Bygrave, W.D. and Hofer, C.W. (1991), 'Theorizing about entrepreneurship', *Entrepreneurship Theory and Practice*, **16**, 13–22.
Carree, M.A. and Thurik, A.R. (2003), 'The impact of entrepreneurship on economic growth', in D.B. Audretsch and Z.J. Acs (eds), *Handbook of Entrepreneurship Research*, Boston, MA and Dordrecht: Kluwer Academic.
Carter, N., Gartner, W. and Reynolds, P. (1996), 'Exploring startup event sequences', *Journal of Business Venturing*, **11** (3), 151–66.
Casson, M. (1982), *The Entrepreneur: An Economic Theory*, Oxford: Martin Robertson.
Charney, A. and Libecap, G.D. (2000), 'Impact of entrepreneurship education', *Insights: A Kauffman Research Series*, Kauffman Center for Entrepreneurial Leadership, Kansas City.
Ching, H.L. and Ellis, P. (2004), 'Marketing in cyberspace: what factors drive e-commerce adoption?', *Journal of Marketing Management*, **20**, 409–29.

Churchill, N.C. and Muzyka, D.F. (1994), 'Defining and conceptualizing entrepreneurship: a process approach', in G.E. Hills (ed.), *Marketing and Entrepreneurship: Research Ideas and Opportunities*, Westport, CT: Quorum Books, pp. 11–23.

Cockx, R., De Vocht, S., Heylen, J. and Van Bockstaele, T. (2000), *Encouraging Entrepreneurship in Europe: A Comparative Study Focused on Education*, Antwerp: University of Antwerp, Center for Business Administration.

De Koning, A. (1999), 'Conceptualising opportunity formation as a socio-cognitive process', dissertation, INSEAD, Fontainebleau.

Dollinger, M.J. (2003), *Entrepreneurship, Strategies and Resources*, 3rd edn, Upper Saddle River, NJ: Prentice Hall.

Drucker, P.F. (1985), *Innovation and Entrepreneurship: Practice and Principles*, Oxford: Butterworth-Heinemann.

Ehrhardt, J., Van Gelderen, P., De Jong, J., Ten Klooster, H. and Kuipers, J. (2004), *Innovatie en Groei*, Ministerie van Economische Zaken, Den Haag.

Elfring, T. and Hulsink, W. (2003), 'Networks in entrepreneurship: the case of high-technology firms', *Small Business Economics*, **21**, 409–22.

European Foundation for Entrepreneurship Research (EFER/EFMD) (2004), 'Pilot survey on entrepreneurship education at European universities and business schools', retrieved March 2004 from www.efer.nl.

European Foundation for Management Development (EFMD) (2004), 'Entrepreneurship and enterprise education in 'Europe. What must be learned and what can be taught', *EntreNews, the Newsletter of EFMD's Entrepreneurship, Innovation and Small Business Network*, no. 2

Fayolle, A. (1999), *Les ingénieurs entrepreneurs français, Contribution à la compéhension des comportements de creation et de reprise d'entreprise des ingénieurs diplômés*, Paris: L'Harmattan.

Gartner, W. (1985), 'A conceptual framework for describing the phenomenon of new venture creation', *Academy of Management Review*, **10**, 696–706.

Gibb, A.A. (1989), *A Study of the Spirit of Enterprise in Europe: Final Report of the SME Task Force of the European Community*, Brussels: EU.

Gnyawali, D.R. and Fogel, D.S. (1994), 'Environments for entrepreneurship development: key dimensions and research implications', *Entrepreneurship Theory and Practice*, **18** (4), 43–62.

Gorman, G.G., Hanlon, D. and King, W. (1997), 'Some research perspectives on entrepreneurship education, enterprise education and education for small business management: a ten-year literature review', *International Small Business Journal*, **15** (3), 56–77.

Granovetter, M.S. (1973), 'The strength of weak ties', *American Journal of Sociology*, **78** (6), 1360–80.

Greve, A. (1995), 'Networks and entrepreneurship – an analysis of social relations and occupational background, and use of contacts during the establishment process', *Scandinavian Journal of Management*, **11** (1), 1–24.

Groen, A.J., Jenniskens, C.G.M., Van Tilburg, J.J. and Morsink, G.M. (2004), 'Stimulating high tech entrepreneurship in a region: many visible hands creating heterogeneous entrepreneurial networks', in P.C. van der Sijde, A. Ridder and A.J. Groen (eds), *Entrepreneurship and Innovation. Essays in Honour of Wim During*, Enschede: Nikos, pp. 79–94.

Henry, C., Hill, F. and Leitch, C. (2003), *Entrepreneurship Education and Training: The Issue of Effectiveness*, Aldershot: Ashgate.

Herron, L. and Sapienza, H.J. (1992), 'The entrepreneur and the initiation of new venture launch activities', *Entrepreneurship Theory and Practice*, **17** (1), 49–55.

Hessels, J., Bosma, N. and Wennekers, S. (2005), 'Nieuw Ondernemerschap in herstel', *Global Entrepreneurship Monitor 2004, Nederland*, Zoetermeer: EIM Research and Consultancy.

Hornsby, J.S., Kuratko, D.F., and Montagno, R.V. (1999), 'Perception of internal factors for corporate entrepreneurship: a comparison of Canadian and U.S. managers', *Entrepreneurship Theory and Practice*, **24** (2), 9–24.

Hornsby, J.S., Naffziger, D.W., Kuratko, D.F. and Montagno, R.V. (1993), 'An interactive model of the corporate entrepreneurship process', *Entrepreneurship Theory and Practice*, **17** (2), 29–37.

Hougaard, S. (2005), *The Business Idea: The Early Stages of Entrepreneurship*, Berlin and Heidelberg: Springer.

Hynes, B. (1996), 'Example of teaching entrepreneurship to non-business students in Limerick (product design and development)', *Journal of European Industrial Training*, 20/8, 10–17.

Jack, S.L. and Anderson, A.R. (1999), 'Entrepreneurship education within the enterprise culture: producing reflective practitioners', *International Journal of Entrepreneurial Behaviour and Research – Special Edition*, **5** (3), 110–25.

Jones-Evans, D., Williams, W. and Deacon, J. (2000), 'Developing entrepreneurial graduates: an action-learning approach', *Education and Training*, **42** (4/5), 282–8.

Karlsson, T. (2005), *Business Plans in New Ventures, an Institutional Perspective*, JIBS Dissertation Series, Jönköping: Jönköping International Business School.

Katz, J.A. (1991), 'The institute and infrastructure of entrepreneurship', *Entrepreneurship Theory and Practice*, **15** (3), 85–102.

Kirby, D.A. (2003), *Entrepreneurship*, London: McGraw-Hill.

Kirzner, I.M. (1973), *Competition and Entrepreneurship*, Chicago, IL: University of Chicago Press.

Koller, R.H. (1988), 'On the source of entrepreneurial ideas', in B.A. Kirchoff, W. Long, W. McMullan, K.H. Vesper and W.E. Wetzel (eds), *Frontiers Entrepreneurship Research*, Wellesley, MA: Babson, pp. 194–207.

Krueger, N.F., Reilly, M.D. and Carsrud, A.L. (2000), 'Competing models of entrepreneurial intentions', *Journal of Business Venturing*, **15** (5/6), 411–32.

Kuratko, D.F. (2003), *Entrepreneurship Education: Emerging Trends and Challenges for the 21st Century*, Coleman White Paper Series, www.usasbe.org, accessed on 12 April, 2004.

Kuratko, D.F. and Hodgetts, R.M. (2001), *Entrepreneurship: A Contemporary Approach*, 5th edn, Orlando, FL: Harcourt.

Kuratko, D.F., Montagno, R.V. and Hornsby, J.S. (1990), 'Developing an entrepreneurial assessment instrument for an effective corporate entrepreneurial environment', *Strategic Management Journal*, **11**, 49–58.

Laukkanen, M. (2000), 'Exploring alternative approaches in high-level entrepreneurship education: creating micromechanisms for endogenous regional growth', *Entrepreneurship and Regional Development*, **12** (1), 25–47.

Levie, J. (1999), 'Entrepreneurship education in higher education in England: a survey', research report, University of Strathclyde, www.entrepreneur.strath.ac.uk/research/surv.pdf, accessed on 12 June, 2005.

Lucas, W. and Cooper, S. (2004), 'Enhancing self-efficacy to enable entrepreneurship', in *Proceedings 11th High Tech Small Firms Conference Part 1: 263*, 24 May, Enschede, The Netherlands.

Lumpkin, G.T., Hills, G.E. and Schrader, R.C. (2001), 'Opportunity recognition', a CEAE white paper, Coleman Council for Entrepreneurship Awareness and Education (CEAE), www.colemanfoundation.org, accessed on 12 June, 2005.

Mason, C. and Stark, M. (2002), 'What do investors look for in a business plan? A comparison of bankers, venture capitalists and business angels', paper presented at the 25th ISBA National Small Firms Conference: 'Competing perspectives of Small Business and Entrepreneurship', Brighton, UK, 13–15 November.

Ministry of Economic Affairs (2002), *Entrepreneurship Monitor, Spring 2002*, theme issue on entrepreneurship and education, The Hague: Ministry of Economic Affairs.

Morris, M.H., Kuratko, D.F. and Schindehutte, M. (2001), 'Towards integration: understanding entrepreneurship through frameworks', *International Journal of Innovation*, **2** (1), 35–49.

Moss Kanter, R. (1988), 'When a thousand flowers bloom: structural, collective, and social conditions for innovation in organizations', *Research Organizational Behavior*, **10**, 169–211.

Nederlands Vlaamse Academie voor Ondernemerschap (NVAO) (2005), unpublished report and minutes of meeting 7 April, Utrecht.

Nikos (2005), *Progress Report 2001–2005*, Enschede: University of Twente, Nikos.

Otto, J.R.C. (1999), 'Entrepreneurship skills for scientists and engineers: recent European initiatives', *IPTS Report*, **37** (special issue on enhancing human capital), www.jrc.es/pages/iptsreport/vol37/english/ EHC5E376.htm#References, accessed on 12 June, 2005.

Paffen, P. (2004), 'The psychology of the entrepreneur', in A.J. Groen, P.C. van der Sijde and A. Ridder (eds), *Essays in Honor of Wim During*, Enschede: Nikos.

Ropo, A. and Hunt, J.G. (1995), 'Entrepreneurial processes as virtuous and vicious spirals in a changing opportunity structure: a paradoxical perspective', *Entrepreneurship Theory and Practice*, **19** (3), 91–111.

Rothwell, R. (1992), 'Successful industrial innovation: critical factors for the 1990s', *R&D Management*, **22** (3), 221–39.

Scarborough, M.N. and Zimmerer, T.W. (2004), '*Effective Small Business Management*', 4th edn, Englewood Cliffs, NJ: Prentice Hall.

Sexton, D.L. and Bowman, N.B. (1984), 'Entrepreneurship education: suggestions for increasing effectiveness', *Journal of Small Business Management*, **2**, 18–25.

Shane, S. (2000), 'Prior knowledge and the discovery of entrepreneurial opportunities', *Organization Science*, **11** (4), 448–69.

Shane, S. and Venkataraman, S. (2000), 'The promise of entrepreneurship as a field of research', *Academy of Management Review*, **25** (1), 217–26.

Shane, S. and Venkataraman, S. (2001), 'Entrepreneurship as a field of research: a response to Zahra and Dess, Singh, and Erikson', *Academy of Management Review*, **26** (1), 13–16.

Shepherd, D.A. and Krueger, N.F. (2002), 'An intentions-based model of entrepreneurial teams' social cognition', *Entrepreneurship Theory and Practice*, **27** (2), 167–85.

Singh, R.P. (2000), *Entrepreneurial Opportunity Recognition through Social Networks*, New York and London: Garland.

Standish-Kuon, T. and Rice, M.P. (2002), 'Introducing engineering and science students to entrepreneurship: models and influential factors at six American universities', *Journal of Engineering Education*, **91** (1), 33–9.

Stevenson, H., Roberts, M.J. and Grousbeck, H.I. (1989), *New Business Ventures and the Entrepreneur*, Homewood, IL: Irwin Publishing Company.

Streeter, D., Jaquette, P. and Hovis, K. (2002), *University-wide Entrepreneurship Education: Alternative Models and Current Trends*, working paper, March, Cornell University, Ithaca, New York.

The European Observatory for SMEs (1995), report submitted to Directorate-General XXIII of the EU, coordinated by EIM, Small Business Research and Consultancy, Zoetermeer.

Tidd, J., Bessant, J. and Pavitt, K. (1997), *Managing Innovation: Integrating Technological, Organizational and Market Change*, Chichester: John Wiley.

Timmons, J.A. and Spinelli, S. (2004), *New Venture Creation Enterprise for the 21st Century*, 6th edn, McGraw-Hill, Nova Iorque.

UNIDO (2005), *Annual Report 2004*, Vienna, Austria: UNIDO.

Van der Sijde, P.C., Kekale, J. and Goddard, J. (2002a), 'University-region interaction: managing the interface', *Industry and Higher Education*, **16**(2), 73–6.

Van der Sijde, P., Van Karnebeek, S. and Van Benthem, J. (2002b), 'The university–industry relations of an entrepreneurial university: the case of the University of Twente', in F. Schutte and P. van der Sijde (eds), *The University and Its Region: Examples of Regional Development from the European Consortium of Innovative Universities*, Enschede: Twente University Press.

Van der Sijde, P.C. and Ridder, A. (2006), 'Students exploring and experiencing innovation in an entrepreneurship programme', *International Journal of Continuing Engineering Education and Life-Long Learning*, **16** (5), 280–91.

Van der Sijde, P.C., Ridder, A., Brinkman, J.G., Van Benthem, J.W.L., Bliek, P.P., Schoo, J.A. and Rossini, G. (2004), 'Entrepreneurship education for non-business students', in P.C. van der Sijde, A. Ridder and A.J. Groen (eds), *Entrepreneurship and Innovation: Essays in Honour of Wim During*, Enschede: Nikos, pp. 207–19.

Van der Veen, M. and Wakkee, I.A.M. (2004), 'Understanding Entrepreneurship', in D.S. Watkins (ed.), *Annual Review of Progress in Entrepreneurship Research*, vol. 2: 2002–03, Brussels: European Foundation for Management Development, pp. 114–52.

Van Gelderen, M., Brand, M., Van Praag, M., Ombach, M. and Bodewes, W. (2003), 'Some advances in the explanation of entrepreneurial career preferences and expectations', in M. Dowling, J. Schmude and D. zur Knyphausen-Aufsess (eds), *Advances in Interdisciplinary European Entrepreneurship Research*, vol. 3, Münster: LitVerlag.

Van Hoof, J. (2004), *Reflectie op Minor Ondernemerschap 2003–2004*, internal report, Nikos, Universiteit Twente.

Van Tilburg, J.J., Van der Sijde, P.C., Molero, J. and Casado, P. (2004), 'Virtual incubation of research spin-offs', in R. Oakey, W. During and S. Kauser, (eds), *New Technology-based Firms in the New Millennium*, vol. 3, Enschede, The Netherlands: Elsevier.

Von Hippel, E. (1988), *The Sources of Innovation*, New York and Oxford: Oxford University Press.

Vyakarnam, S., Jacobs, R.C. and Handelberg, J. (1997), 'Formation and development of entrepreneurial teams in rapid growth businesses', in P.D. Reynolds (ed.), *Frontiers of Entrepreneurship Research 1997*, Babson College, Wellesley, MA.

Wakkee, I.A.M. and Van der Veen, M. (2004), 'Teaching the entrepreneurial process', *Essays in Honor of Wim During*, in P.C. van der Sijde, A. Ridder and A.J. Groen (eds), Enschede: Nikos.

Wallin, D.L. (2003), 'Motivation and faculty development: a three state study of presidential perceptions of faculty professional development needs', *Community College Journal of Research and Practice*, **27** (4), 317–35.

Watkins, D. and Stone, G. (1999), 'Entrepreneurship education in UK HEIs – origins, developments and trends', *Industry and Higher Education*, **13** (6), 382–9.

Wiklund, J. (1998), *Small Firm Growth and Performance: Entrepreneurship and Beyond*, Jönköping: Jönköping International Business School.

Zahra, S.A. and Dess, G.D. (2001), 'Entrepreneurship as a field of research: encouraging dialogue and debate', *Academy of Management Review*, **26** (1), 8–10.

5 Teaching corporate entrepreneurship the experimental way
Véronique Bouchard

5.1 Introduction

The teaching of corporate entrepreneurship in business schools is far less widespread than that of entrepreneurship. Given the scarcity of empirical research on the topic and the ambiguity of the term 'corporate entrepreneurship', this should hardly come as a surprise. As a result, corporate entrepreneurship cannot be taught relying on tested and solid theoretical, empirical or methodological foundations: it is necessarily a pioneering endeavor.

As all pioneers, those who throw themselves into the adventure have to make choices that can appear arbitrary. They have to take positions on unsettled questions such as 'What is corporate entrepreneurship?', 'Where does corporate entrepreneurship stand vis-à-vis independent entrepreneurship?', 'What is the practical value of corporate entrepreneurship?' They also have to decide what, within a mixed and uneven body of literature, is relevant for future managers. And they have to set objectives, determine contents and select a pedagogy in the absence of tested models.

In these circumstances, it seems prudent to envision the teaching of corporate entrepreneurship as an experimental process, that is, one whose outcomes need to be closely monitored and which is susceptible to be redirected at any moment.

When my colleague Professor Pancho Nunes and I decided to open an elective course in corporate entrepreneurship, we chose to adopt such an experimental posture. This chapter recounts our trajectory, from the moment we took our decision to the most recent edition of the course.

Section 5.2 of the chapter briefly describes and justifies the course's positioning and general orientations. The section 5.3 summarizes the organization and content – to a large extent original – of the course. Section 5.4 describes our pedagogical approach and highlights the benefits of co-teaching. Section 5.5 summarizes what we have learned in the 'experiment' and how we plan to orient our teaching in the future. We conclude with a review of some of the theoretical, pedagogical and managerial implications of what remains in any case a very idiosyncratic process.

5.2 Defining the course's positioning and general orientation

When Pancho Nunes and I decided to propose an elective course in corporate entrepreneurship in 2002, our first impulse was to look for course syllabi on the web. We found almost nothing[1] and quickly realized we would have to build the course from scratch.

We knew the audience we wanted to target. We were both convinced that the students of our part-time MBA program would be ideal participants. They had sufficient work experience – six years on average – to understand the organizational and human issues tied to corporate entrepreneurship and, because of their predominantly technical or scientific background, were particularly concerned by innovation-related topics. Furthermore, many part-time MBAs were personally involved in business development projects and we thought this would contribute to enrich class discussions and, possibly, our database.

Since we had no reference model, we decided early on that the course would be 'experimental', that is, short (12 hours), described as such to the students and the head of the MBA program and carefully assessed with all parties, during and after delivery. If things did not go well, we were willing to radically modify the course, or even call it off. We also established from the start that the course would be highly interactive. We had an audience of managers whose experience and brains we wanted to fully engage and wanted to make sure that, thanks to their continuous feedback, the course's content and pedagogy could be improved in real time. Finally, we thought that being proactive and involved were attitudes required from corporate entrepreneurs and we wanted our course to be a first step in the right direction.

5.3   Defining the contents of the course

When we decided to open a course in corporate entrepreneurship, my colleague and I had been working on the topic for a few years. We had not done joint research but we discussed regularly and had developed some common understanding. We were able to agree on a definition of corporate entrepreneurship which, given the heterogeneity of the concepts subsumed under the heading, was quite an achievement. When we started discussing the objectives of the course, we both agreed that the profile of our audience should guide us. Our part-time MBAs needed to acquire information, concepts and methods they could readily use in their work environment. To reach this outcome, we had to make sure the participants could easily relate to the contents of the course. Finally, concerning the specific concepts and messages we wanted to emphasize, we agreed to disagree: we had different perspectives and wanted to stress different aspects. Our differences and, in some cases, our disagreements would make our teaching more lively.

5.3.1   Defining corporate entrepreneurship

Corporate entrepreneurship is a multifaceted concept that for some refers to a firm-level disposition to strategic daring (Covin and Slevin, 1991; Lumpkin and Dess, 1996; Miller, 1983; Zahra, 1993), for others to the process of new business creation within established companies (Block and MacMillan, 1993; Burgelman, 1984; Vesper, 1985) and for others still, to the adoption of entrepreneurial values and behavior by corporate staff (Pinchot III, 1985; Stevenson and Jarillo, 1990). The literature on corporate entrepreneurship is characterized by a great heterogeneity of purpose and perspective, which stems in part from the multifaceted nature of corporate entrepreneurship but also from the persistence of unsolved 'definitional issues' (Sharma and Chrisman, 1999).

Covering the various facets of corporate entrepreneurship in a 12-hour course destined for practitioners seemed neither feasible nor desirable. It was clear to us that the firm-level literature was too abstract for our audience and that the process literature was much closer to their experience and concerns: we thus decided to limit ourselves to this perspective and agreed to adopt Sharma and Chrisman's (1999, p. 18) definition of corporate entrepreneurship: 'Corporate Entrepreneurship is the process whereby an individual or a group of individuals, in association with an existing organization, create a new organization or instigate renewal or innovation within that organization.'

Table 5.1   Spontaneous versus induced corporate entrepreneurship

Spontaneous corporate entrepreneurship	Induced corporate entrepreneurship
The unplanned process triggered by employees who engage spontaneously in the development of a new activity within an established firm	The programs put in place by companies in order to encourage and support the pursuit of business development projects by employees and their results

5.3.2   Setting the objectives of the course

Because of the profile of our audience, our fundamental objective was to provide the participants with information and models that could help them participate in, elaborate and manage corporate entrepreneurship initiatives.

Corporate entrepreneurship is not only a concept but also a relatively widespread management practice. We thought students should understand how different corporate entrepreneurship programs worked (or not) in reality, and compare and evaluate them.

Self-appraisal was another important objective of the course. We thought the participants should take advantage of the course to position themselves and their company vis-à-vis corporate entrepreneurship. Had they been personally involved in intrapreneurial processes? Did they plan to? Was their company's culture and organization favorable or not to entrepreneurial initiatives? Why? What could be done to improve this situation? This effort of self-appraisal, combined with a knowledge of the structure and dynamics of existing corporate entrepreneurship programs, would constitute, we believed, a solid base for their future involvement.

5.3.3   Key concepts and messages

My research on corporate entrepreneurship case studies (Bouchard, 2001; 2002) had led me to realize the great diversity of realities and processes grouped under this heading. Thus the importance of proper classification tools. The fundamental distinction between *spontaneous* and *induced* corporate entrepreneurship had to be emphasized and would in fact structure the syllabus of the course (see Table 5.1).

The process of spontaneous entrepreneurship has been well explained and described by R.A. Burgelman (1983) and remains remarkably similar in spite of time, space and context differences. It is not difficult to find interesting articles and case studies to nourish reflection and class discussion on the subject.

Induced corporate entrepreneurship, on the contrary, is a heterogeneous phenomenon whose structure and dynamics vary widely according to the context and the originators' intentions. It required, according to us, special attention and a comprehensive set of conceptual tools in order to be correctly apprehended.

5.3.3.1   Spontaneous versus induced corporate entrepreneurship   The study of spontaneous corporate entrepreneurship is important because it makes students aware that all organizations, even the most bureaucratic, are the locus of emergent, bottom-up processes and that strategic renewal depends as much on autonomous strategic initiatives as it does on top-down change programs (cf. Burgelman, 1983).

Another key message is that just as autonomous initiatives 'naturally' emerge, the existing organization – the 'mainstream' to use Kanter and North's terminology (1990) – 'naturally' resists these initiatives and often crushes them unless their initiators manage to avoid conflict and garner appropriate support at each stage of their project. This 'mainstream'/'new-stream' dialectic[2] is well described in a number of articles and business cases (cf. Burgelman, 1983; Dougherty and Hardy, 1996; Hamel, 2000; Hill et al., 1992) that can be analysed and commented on by the students.

The study of induced corporate entrepreneurship is also essential. In effect, over the last three decades, well-known firms such as Eastman Kodak, Xerox Corporation and Lucent Technologies in the United States, SAS, Siemens Nixdorf in Europe, and less known firms, have elaborated and launched their own formal programs destined to encourage and support entrepreneurial initiatives on the part of their employees. A number of well-written cases describe these attempts in detail: Kanter's series on 'entrepreneurial vehicles in established firms' (Kanter and Richardson, 1991; Kanter et al., 1991a; Kanter et al., 1991b), Lerner and Hunt's case (1998) on Xerox's XTV division; Bartlett and Mohammed's case (1995) on 3M; Kanter et al.'s case (1997) on Siemens-Nixdorf; Amabile and Whitney's case (1997) on Procter & Gamble's CNV; Kanter and Heskett's (2000) and Chesbrough and Massaro's cases (2001) on Lucent Technologies NVG; Day et al.'s paper (2001) on Nokia's NVO. Students can pick one of these and, in small work groups, analyse the structure of the program, its functioning and its human and economic impact. They can then compare and rank the various programs in class.

5.3.3.2 A typology of induced corporate entrepreneurship processes The analysis and comparison of corporate entrepreneurship programs reveals a great heterogeneity of purpose and configuration. We therefore propose a two-axis grid to help the students position and compare the various programs. This grid combines categories elaborated by Kanter et al. and Birkinshaw (see Figure 5.1).

In their 'Entrepreneurial Vehicles' series, Kanter et al. (1990) distinguish corporate entrepreneurship programs whose primary goal is *economic* (creating new sources of revenues) from corporate entrepreneurship programs whose primary goal is *cultural* (showing the 'mainstream' how to be more innovative). While some corporate entrepreneurship programs have clearly an economic or a cultural goal, most try to combine both benefits and therefore occupy some intermediary position along the cultural–economic continuum.

Birkinshaw (1997) distinguishes *focused* corporate entrepreneurship from *dispersed* corporate entrepreneurship. Focused corporate entrepreneurship implies the creation of a distinct and autonomous organizational entity whose primary goal is the creation of new business activities. Dispersed corporate entrepreneurship, on the contrary, relies on the assumption that any employee can become an entrepreneur as long as he or she detects an opportunity and is provided with adequate resources and support. In dispersed corporate entrepreneurship, corporate entrepreneurs also belong to the 'mainstream' and, at least initially, continue to perform their regular job and to report to their regular boss.

Combining the two axes, we created a grid that can be used to position corporate entrepreneurship programs. In the classroom, students use it to compare and discuss the position of the different corporate entrepreneurship programs they have to analyse and assess.

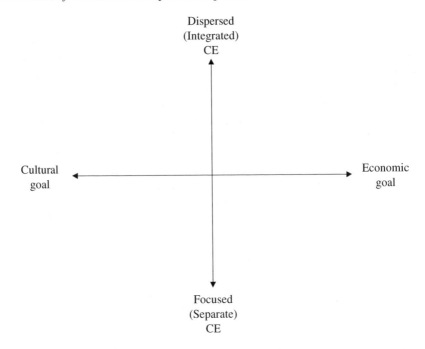

Figure 5.1   Positioning corporate entrepreneurship (CE) programs on a two-axis grid

5.3.3.3   The building blocks of induced corporate entrepreneurship   In spite of the great heterogeneity of corporate entrepreneurship programs, it is possible to find basic similarities in their design principles (Bouchard, 2002). We propose three 'universal' design principles or 'building blocks' (see Figure 5.2).

'*Providing autonomy*' is the first building block we have identified. Individual autonomy, usually restricted in large organizations, is considered by many as the central component of the entrepreneurial orientation (Lumpkin and Dess, 1996) and a basic ingredient of corporate entrepreneurship processes (Burgelman, 1983; Siegel et al., 1988). All the corporate entrepreneurship cases surveyed emphasize the notion of individual autonomy.

Autonomy varies in intensity and kind. At one end of the spectrum, corporate entrepreneurs who belong to a *separate* entity enjoy a great deal of autonomy. They are free to focus entirely on their project and, in between reviews, to use time and available resources as they wish. At the other end of the spectrum, corporate entrepreneurs who remain part of the existing organization have to meet the obligations their regular job entails. However, as their project gains in credibility and acceptance, they are progressively granted autonomy under the form of free time and resources.

The second building block of induced corporate entrepreneurship is '*eliciting personal commitment*'. The promoters of corporate entrepreneurship programs believe that personal involvement can thoroughly modify organizational dynamics, turn low morale into enthusiasm and apathy into innovativeness. In all surveyed corporate entrepreneurship programs, individuals were encouraged to pursue projects to which they identified strongly and personally, and to remain in charge of the projects from inception to completion. Corporate entrepreneurship programs provide different kinds of incentives

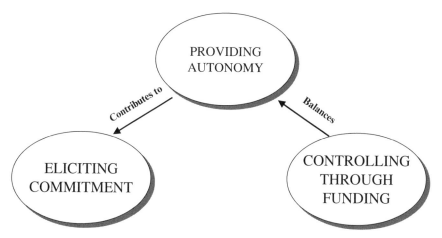

Figure 5.2   The three building blocks of corporate entrepreneurship programs

to would be intrapreneurs, combining intrinsic rewards (such as the excitement and satisfaction deriving from the pursuit of a challenging and creative endeavor) with extrinsic rewards (external visibility, money prizes, prospect of heading one's own activity, 'phantom shares' of the new venture, recognition and career advancement, and so on).

The third building block we identified is '*controlling through funding*'. Most corporate entrepreneurship programs are structured around a stage-by-stage, conditional funding process that disciplines corporate entrepreneurs and balances off their autonomy. Thanks to this process, the accomplishments of corporate entrepreneurs can be periodically reviewed, allowing management to reduce or increase commitment to projects as doubts concerning their potential are removed. The great parsimony with which resources are usually granted to corporate entrepreneurs also contributes to contain the cost and therefore the risk of exploration.

5.3.3.4   A missing building block   My 2002 study confirmed what Kanter et al. stated in their 1990 article, that is, that most corporate entrepreneurship programs faced serious problems at some point of their history, problems that often lead to their demise. Furthermore, similar problems emerged in entirely different settings. Even 3M, so often cited in example in the corporate entrepreneurship literature, faces similar problems albeit in a lighter version (cf. Bartlett and Mohammed, 1997). Though it does not constitute a very positive message, this finding has to be shared with the students and discussed with them. We have observed that the students were neither surprised nor shocked by this negative message since, for the most part, they have directly experienced the tensions at play between the 'mainstream' and the 'newstream', and know that the former usually prevails.

These recurrent problems have multiple causes but we believe that the main one is that the originators and managers of corporate entrepreneurship programs simply ignore the differences between independent entrepreneurship and corporate entrepreneurship and, consequently, neglect the all important process of *interface management*. In effect, contrary to independent entrepreneurs, intrapreneurs are embedded in an existing

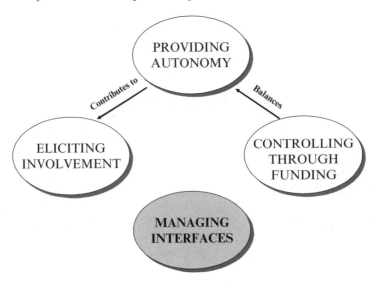

Figure 5.3   The missing building block of corporate entrepreneurship programs

organization and have to constantly negotiate with members of this organization to obtain resources and support, but also to maintain their autonomy.

A key message, therefore, is that 'managing the interface' at the macro level (overall corporate entrepreneurship program/rest of the organization interface), and at the micro level (single intrapreneurial project/rest of the organization interface) constitutes a critical part of any corporate entrepreneurship process: in fact, we view it as the missing fourth 'building block' of corporate entrepreneurship programs (see Figure 5.3).

The practical implications of this fourth block in terms of structure, processes, systems and individual behaviors can be explored and discussed with the students.

In the context of corporate entrepreneurship, *strategic alignment* is definitely a key notion. As Burgelman (1983) has shown, the autonomous initiative/corporation interface is both organizational and strategic in nature. Though many corporate entrepreneurship programs claim they support any intrapreneurial project as long as it is economically viable, one can observe that projects which lie significantly outside the corporate strategic domain have problems of legitimacy and, consequently, tend to receive less support (unless, of course, their promoters are able to modify top management's perception of what constitutes the corporation's strategic domain). Strategic alignment therefore influences the quality and extent of support a project might get from various actors within the corporation; it will also determine whether and how soon a project will be reintegrated in the 'mainstream'. The message we want to pass to the students is that the difficulties faced by intrapreneurs and the risks they take depend, at least in part, on the level of strategic alignment of their project.

5.4   Selecting a pedagogy
Because we considered ourselves students rather than experts in corporate entrepreneurship and because we targeted a professional audience, we wanted student participation to

be a central feature of our pedagogy. Because we shared academic interests and a taste for fun and experimentation, we opted for *co-teaching*. We had no problem obtaining the support of the head of the MBA program, who was receptive to the experimental character of our endeavor and wanted to see us succeed.

5.4.1   Encouraging participation and exchange

We defined most aspects of the syllabus with student's participation in mind. We chose, for example, to limit attendance to 25 participants and to grade students on oral contribution. During most class time, students were active, presenting their work or discussing different topics, our role limiting itself to raising questions and pointing out contradictions.

We dedicated half of the first three-hour module of the course to a roundtable discussion during which all the participants explained what corporate entrepreneurship meant for them and how it related to their present or past work experience. The second module, centered on spontaneous corporate entrepreneurship, was dedicated to the discussion of a business case describing the difficulties faced by a female intrapreneur in a very large corporation (Joline at Polaroid: Hill et al., 1992). This case elicited strong reactions from the students who related emotionally to the story, taking the part of the intrapreneur or, on the contrary, blaming her for the difficulties she was facing. During the third module, dedicated to induced corporate entrepreneurship, student teams presented the structure and dynamics of corporate entrepreneurship programs put in place by well-known companies such as Eastman Kodak, Lucent or 3M. Based on the information contained in the cases, the various teams had to assess the programs and make improvement propositions.

The fourth and last module also involved student participation since it combined final paper presentations with a wrap-up session. Overall, probably less than three hours were dedicated to traditional lecturing.

5.4.2   Co-teaching

My colleague and I had both been doing research on corporate entrepreneurship for a few years when we decided to open our course. We knew that some of our viewpoints were quite different and we thought it would be interesting to confront them in a classroom setting. My colleague was mostly interested by the human and psychological aspects of the intrapreneurial process, while my interest lay more in induced corporate entrepreneurship, more specifically in the interactions between organizational and individual strategies and how they can be turned into win/win games.

Co-teaching has several advantages: it creates a strong class dynamic, it is fun and stimulating and, in an experimental context such as ours, quite comforting. As time went by, we naturally 'specialized', my colleague turning into the spokesman of intrapreneurs, their needs, motivations and doubts, myself into the spokeswoman of effectiveness and performance be it corporate or individual. In a number of situations, we were in clear disagreement, to the great amusement of students. Our heated discussions conveyed an important tacit message: on complex matters, even 'experts' can disagree, but disagreement can be fruitful and stimulating. This teaching mode was very much appreciated by the participants who felt a different, more 'democratic', teacher/student relation had been established as a result of it.

5.5   Teaching corporate entrepreneurship the experimental way

To this day, the course 'Understanding corporate entrepreneurship' has been given three times. As we mentioned, the course initially had been positioned as an experiment and was susceptible to be changed and even discontinued. This did not happen since, fortunately, it was well received by the students from the beginning.

The choice of part-time MBAs as our test audience and the tailoring of the course to their needs and profile was apparently correct if we are to judge by the level of participation and satisfaction we registered. As a result, the objectives, key messages and pedagogy of the course have not changed significantly since we established the first syllabus.

However, because the students and ourselves enjoyed so much the experimental, informal character of the course, we thought it was essential to try and preserve it. To this end, we have decided to introduce and test novelties on a regular basis and we continue to give a lot of importance to students' feedback and input.

In 2005, we added a fifth module and invited a French intrapreneur as guest speaker. His rich and sincere testimony was very much appreciated by the students who recognized many situations and patterns described in class and who did not hesitate to ask our guest very personal questions concerning his motives, expectations and feelings at different stages of the intrapreneurial process. We also changed the format and content of the last module: we asked the students to work in small groups on specific issues, formalize their findings and share them with the rest of the class, respecting strict time constraints. The issues selected – What can trigger an intrapreneurial behavior? What can middle managers do to stimulate and support corporate entrepreneurship? What can top managers do to stimulate and support corporate entrepreneurship? How can one guarantee the strategic alignment of intrapreneurial projects and initiatives? – were concrete but also required a good mastery of the concepts and categories seen in class. The outcomes of this intense teamwork session have been quite interesting and confirmed that students had a good grasp of some of the main organizational, managerial and strategic implications of corporate entrepreneurship (see Figure 5.4).

5.6   Conclusion

When we decided to open an elective in corporate entrepreneurship, my colleague and I were pursuing both individual and collective goals. We wanted, for instance, to contribute to reinforcing EM Lyon's image and positioning as a specialist of entrepreneurship and an innovative business school. Three years later, one has to admit that our contribution to these goals has been rather modest. In effect, our course has only touched a small student population and, because of its experimental nature, has received hardly any publicity beyond word of mouth. In order to further our objectives, we now have to think about diffusing the course to new and broader audiences as well as packaging and circulating its contents.

On top of this institutional objective, we also pursued individual professional goals. For my part I was interested in (1) testing the academic relevance of my research work, (2) feeding my reflection with new questions and data and (3) testing some pedagogical intuitions.

Concerning the first point, the positive reaction and involvement of the students throughout the various editions of the course have confirmed their interest in the topic and the pragmatic and critical perspective we adopt on it. This constitutes a very encouraging

Q4 – Guaranteeing strategic alignment (2005)

- Effective communication of the company's strategic objectives
  - OPS (One Page Strategy)
  - At all levels
- Creation of a formal mentors network
  - Legitimate
  - Supportive of corporate entrepreneurs to
    - critically analyse ideas and projects in view of the company's strategic objectives
    - act as informal counselors and sponsors
- Creation of a project assessment committee
  - Official, properly incentivated group of managers
  - Multidisciplinary to assess
    - the business potential of projects
    - the strategic alignment of projects
- Projects are followed up and supported by the company according to their potential and alignment assessment
    - 'Spin in' project: high potential and alignment
    - 'Spin off' project: high potential and low alignment
    - 'Question mark' project: high potential and uncertain alignment
    - 'NO GO' project: poor potential

V. BOUCHARD | Corporate
P. NUNES | Entrepreneurship

Figure 5.4   Result of a teamwork session on 'How can one guarantee the strategic alignment of intrapreneurial projects and initiatives without killing them?'

signal and a source of renewed motivation. We are aware, however, that the course we propose is incomplete and that there remains space for content development. A longer course of 24 hours – a standard at EM Lyon – should include, in my opinion, the following additional topics: (1) similarities and differences between entrepreneurship and corporate entrepreneurship and (2) corporate entrepreneurship and innovation.

The first topic would greatly benefit from the input of entrepreneurship specialists. The second should help position corporate entrepreneurship vis-à-vis other innovation vehicles (traditional new product development process, management by projects, and so on), indicating its advantages and disadvantages as well as its preferred domain of application. These two additional modules should help the students put corporate entrepreneurship in context, something they usually find quite difficult.

As far as using the course to feed my reflection and research, the results have been somewhat disappointing. We have had access to a few interesting student stories and some of them have made interesting and stimulating points but, overall, the stimulation has worked in the other direction. Several participants have in effect made propositions inspired by the course to their executive committee. In the medium term, a follow-up on these initiatives could produce interesting research data. Generally speaking, it would be interesting to try and measure the impact of this course, if any, on the participants' propensity to act entrepreneurially within or outside their organization.

Finally, concerning my third objective which was to test some pedagogical intuitions, the involvement and satisfaction of all participants, including the teachers, has proved their correctness. The part-time MBA audience was the right target and showed itself eager to learn and contribute. The choice of joint teaching contributed to create a lively and informal climate in which students felt at ease.

We have reached a new stage in the development of our teaching project. We have tested the 'prototype' and we know that it is viable: we now have to both deepen and enlarge the scope of our teaching project. Our ambition is to touch several key audiences of our institution, help them understand what corporate entrepreneurship is, where it stands vis-à-vis other organizational processes and practices, and what its practical value is. In order to do so, we plan to rely on our young experience but also integrate relevant conceptual and empirical findings generated both inside and outside EM Lyon. At this point, executive education constitutes our most natural extension domain. Participants have needs and profiles similar to those of our original audience and we are registering a strong interest for corporate entrepreneurship among our corporate contacts. At the moment, various course designs are being conceived and tested with corporate clients and we hope, in the medium term, to be able to measure their impact not only on participants' satisfaction but also on their propensity to become 'corporate entrepreneurs'.

What matters to us, in any new setting or circumstance, is to be able to maintain a pragmatic and critical perspective on corporate entrepreneurship as well as to create a stimulating learning environment in which all can contribute, develop and enjoy themselves.

Notes

1. The only online syllabi we found at that time were those of the 'Babson Program on Corporate Entrepreneurship', a three-day seminar destined for senior managers and 'Developing Corporate Intrapreneurs', a 14-week open course at the Stevens Institute of Technology (New Jersey). Though it does not mean there were no other courses on corporate entrepreneurship given at the time, it does indicate a scarce offer.
2. The 'mainstream'/'newstream' dialectic refers to the conflict of interests and the profound differences that oppose the part of the organization that is involved in reproducing, administrating, optimizing and controlling (the 'mainstream') and the part of the organization that is involved in experimenting and creating (the 'newstream'). Importance of short-term results, attitude towards risk and acceptance of errors, respect of rules and procedures, reliance on informal networks are all dimensions on which the 'mainstream' and the 'newstream' are radically opposed. The frictions thus generated, amplified by turf wars, lead to open or masked conflicts which generally end to the detriment of the weaker 'newstream'.

References

Amabile, T. and Whitney, D. (1997), 'Corporate New Ventures at Procter & Gamble', *Harvard Business School Case*, 9-897-088.
Bartlett, C.A. and Mohammed, A. (1995), '3M: profile of an innovating company', *Harvard Business School Case*, 9-395-016, 1–20.
Birkinshaw, J. (1997), 'Entrepreneurship in multinational corporations: the characteristics of subsidiary initiatives', *Strategic Management Journal*, **18** (3), 207–29.
Block, Z. and MacMillan, I.C. (1993), *Corporate Venturing: Creating New Businesses within the Firm*, Boston, MA: Harvard Business School Press.
Bouchard, V. (2001), 'Exploring corporate entrepreneurship: a corporate strategy perspective', *Cahiers de Recherche d'EMLYON, N° 2001/12*.
Bouchard, V. (2002), 'Corporate entrepreneurship: lessons from the field, blind spots and beyond . . .', *Cahiers de la Recherche d'EMLYON, N° 2002/08*.
Burgelman, R.A. (1983), 'A process model of internal corporate venturing in the diversified major firm', *Administrative Science Quarterly*, **28** (2), 223–44.

Burgelman, R.A. (1984), 'Designs for corporate entrepreneurship in established firms', *California Management Review*, **26** (3), 154–66.

Chesbrough, H.W. and Massaro, A. (2001), 'Lucent Technologies: the future of the New Ventures Group', *Harvard Business School Case*, 9-601-102, 1–19.

Covin, J.G. and Slevin, D.P. (1991), 'A conceptual model of entrepreneurship as firm behavior', *Entrepreneurship Theory and Practice*, **16** (1), 7–25.

Day, J.D., Mang, P.Y., Richter, A. and Roberts, J. (2001), 'The innovative organization: why new ventures need more than a room of their own', *McKinsey Quarterly*, **2**, 21–31.

Dougherty, D. and Hardy, C. (1996), 'Sustained product innovation in large, mature organizations; overcoming innovation-to-organization problems', *Academy of Management Journal*, **39** (5), 1120–53.

Hamel, G. (2000), 'Waking up IBM: how a gang of unlikely rebels transformed Big Blue', *Harvard Business Review*, **78** (4), 137–48.

Hill, L.A., Kamprath, N.A. and Conrad, M.B. (1992), 'Joline Godfrey and the Polaroid Corporation (A)', *Harvard Business School Case*, 9-492-037, 1–15.

Kanter, R.M. and Heskett, M. (2000), 'Lucent Technologies New Ventures Group', *Harvard Business School Case*, 9-300-085, 1–16.

Kanter, R.M. and Richardson, L. (1991), 'Engines of progress: designing and running entrepreneurial vehicles in established companies; the Enter-prize program at Ohio Bell, 1985–1990', *Journal of Business Venturing*, **6** (3), 209–29.

Kanter, R.M., McGuire, J.F. and Mohammed, A. (1997), 'The Change Agent Program at Siemens Nixdorf', *Harvard Business School Case*, 9-396-203, 1–17.

Kanter, R.M., North, J., Piaget Bernstein, A. and Williamson, A. (1990), 'Engines of progress: designing and running entrepreneurial vehicles in established companies', *Journal of Business Venturing*, **5** (6), 415–30.

Kanter, R.M., North, J., Richardson, L., Ingols, C. and Zolner, J. (1991a), 'Engines of progress: designing and running entrepreneurial vehicles in established companies: Raytheon's New Product Center, 1969–1989', *Journal of Business Venturing*, **6** (2), 145–63.

Kanter, R.M., Richardson, L., North, J. and Morgan, E. (1991b), 'Engines of progress: designing and running entrepreneurial vehicles in established companies; the New Venture Process at Eastman Kodak, 1983–1989', *Journal of Business Venturing*, **6** (1), 63.

Lerner, J. and Hunt, B. (1998), 'Xerox technology ventures: March 1995', *Harvard Business School Case*, 9-295-127, 1–12.

Lumpkin, V. and Dess, V. (1996), 'Clarifying the entrepreneurial orientation construct and linking it to performance', *Academy of Management Review*, **21** (3), 135–72.

Miller, D. (1983), 'The correlates of entrepreneurship in three types of firms', *Management Science*, **29** (7), 770–91.

Pinchot III, G. (1985), *Intrapreneuring: Why You Don't Have to Leave the Corporation to Become an Entrepreneur*, New York: Harper and Row.

Sharma, P. and Chrisman, J.J. (1999), 'Toward a reconciliation of the definitional issues in the field of corporate entrepreneurship', *Entrepreneurship Theory and Practice*, **23** (3), 11–28.

Siegel, R., Siegel, E. and MacMillan, I.C. (1988), 'Corporate venture capitalists: autonomy, obstacles and performance', *Journal of Business Venturing*, **3** (3), 233–47.

Stevenson, H.H. and Jarillo, J.C. (1990), 'A paradigm of entrepreneurship: entrepreneurial management', *Strategic Management Journal*, **11**, special issue, 17–27.

Vesper, K.H. (1985), 'A new direction or just a new label?', in J. Kao and H. Stevenson (eds), *Entrepreneurship: What It Is and How to Teach It*, Boston, MA: Harvard Business School Press.

Zahra, S.A. (1993), 'A conceptual model of entrepreneurship as firm behavior: a critique and extension', *Entrepreneurship Theory and Practice*, **17** (4), 5–21.

PART II

INSTITUTIONAL CONTEXT

6 From theoretical production to the design of entrepreneurship study programmes: a French case

Thierry Verstraete and Martine Hlady-Rispal

Introduction

Two principal issues seem to justify the increase in teaching in entrepreneurship. The first consists of accepting the idea that entrepreneurship is, among others, a question of culture. Consequently, the education system has a role to play in spreading what hereafter everybody agrees to call an enterprising spirit, in particular in regard to a public that does not sufficiently profit, in their circle of relationships, from entrepreneur[1] models. But the insertion of entrepreneurship into training programmes is not exactly easy in contexts where, like that of France, we had to convince that a teaching programme does not consist solely of the diffusion of techniques via a univocal pedagogy of the information transmission – reception type. According to Saint-Onge (1996), it is advisable to discuss certain pedagogical precepts that insidiously let us believe, among other things, that any subject is interesting enough to capture the attention of the students, so that they can take in a one-hour continuous flood of information, that listening is sufficient to enable them to learn, and that the students can translate what they hear into action, and so on. The idea is not so much to radically refute the preceding assertions than to discuss them. If the objective is to make the students on a university campus aware of the setting up of companies and to make them take part in a seminar (which one will suppose is non-compulsory), we gain more by stimulating their curiosity beforehand than to believe in their spontaneous interest. Guided by the concepts, the teaching of entrepreneurship requires the creation of situations in which the student will be able to mobilize these concepts. Teaching in entrepreneurship is generally not confined within the perimeter of a classroom. It sends the students into practical training situations where concepts will guide them, will speak to them and will clarify the contexts of their actions.

The second issue relates to the socio-economic dynamics of national and regional development. Within this framework, it is almost usual to insist on the contribution of the creation or the buyout of a company by private individuals to the enrichment of a region, whether it has to do with the renewal of the industrial fabric, employment creation or other types of value, from which the stakeholders will draw benefit. Entrepreneurship is then reduced, certainly, to its most fundamental demonstrations. Furthermore, we should not forget the contribution of all the established firms, in particular the small and medium-sized enterprises, which in normal conditions, need to be entrepreneurial. To react to this matter, it is not unreasonable to send recruiters, trained individuals, or at least those who have been made aware of the initiative taking process or the carrying of a project, or more basically, entrepreneurship. It is not a question of confusing all sorts of initiatives or projects with entrepreneurship. Moreover, we would like to point out a difficulty here, because to discuss the teaching of entrepreneurship, it is still necessary to agree on what entrepreneurship is. Our conception, presented in the first section, falls under the paradigm of the creation of an organization. Any teaching gains from emerging out of a relatively circumscribed conception (which does not mean being totally confined); first, in order to help the students with determining the field for which the programme is conceived, and, then, to help them with holding the train of thought on which he or she can load the sum total of the general principles acquired. In other words, the programmes we give comprise a part of the 'understanding'.

The other part, presented in the second section, aims at 'acting'. It consists of putting the students into action so that they can assimilate certain dimensions that cannot be obtained through a class that one would describe as more 'traditional', except by preparing them by presenting the process they are about to undertake.

Finally, to connect the four poles of the typology of Bertrand (1995),[2] this chapter does not enter two opposing debates: on the one hand, the question of nature versus nurture and, on the other hand, the question of technique and art. Certain individuals have predispositions, others have gaps to be filled and, in any case, solutions exist that reveal students' potential. As for the less entrepreneurial, a course in entrepreneurship shows them that they need entrepreneurs while making them, especially the students of the artistic, literary or scientific fields, aware of the realities of the economic world. Any programme needs to be set up according to the following minimum contingencies:

- The intervention level (for example, secondary teaching, higher level, university or postgraduate education).
- The objective of the programme (for example, to make aware, to train, to accompany).
- The type of public (for example, original training and/or night classes, engineers, decision managers, students of artistic or scientific culture) and professional objectives of the students.
- The amount of time granted by the person in charge for the training (conference, seminar, diploma granting module or training dedicated to entrepreneurship).

The third section of this chapter delivers our conception of various programmes relative to these contingencies. The remarks from the first two sections relating to our conception of the entrepreneurial phenomenon (section 6.1) and to the related process and serving the setting in motion of the students (section 6.2), deliver the fundamental bases of these programmes.

6.1   To understand: three levels of analysis illuminating the relationship binding the entrepreneur to the organization which he or she runs

According to the Fiet's point of view (2000a; 2000b) the theory dimension is very important in entrepreneurship teaching. A theory-based approach in teaching entrepreneurship must be in line with a clear definition of entrepreneurship as a field of teaching. That is the main reason why we propose in the next section our view on these questions.

Without accepting that a definition can constrain the multiple dimensions to which the entrepreneurial phenomenon refers, one can reasonably agree to see this as:

> An initiative carried out by one or several individuals to create or seize a business opportunity (at least what is considered or evaluated as such), of which the profit is not inevitably of a monetary

order, by the impulse of an organization able to give birth to one or more entities, and to create new value (greater in the case of an innovation) for stakeholders to whom the project is addressed. (Verstraete and Fayolle, 2005)

The matter gathers four dominant paradigms of the field: the creation of an organization, the business opportunity, innovation and the creation of value. Our approach falls under the paradigm of the creation of an organization, completely complementary and nonexclusive of the other paradigms. Indeed, when it comes to taking advantage of an opportunity (discovered or initiated), or creating value by innovating (in this last case, as Bruyat, 1993, specifies, the contribution of new value is then significant), in all cases the entrepreneur must consequently organize the various resources that he or she needs for the undertaking. We will see later that the programmes we coordinate aim precisely at provoking the training inherent in this organization. Knowing how to make it tangible leads the student to understand the concept of opportunity like that of creation of value, in particular when he or she must convince the owners of resources to adhere to the project and become stakeholders.[3] The organization is dynamic, in that when the students are sent to collect information, to interact with the environment of their business project, their impetus causes their vision of the business to become reality. The result of this dynamic leads, or should lead, to the creation of one or several entities which, when registered legally (that is, at the Chamber of Commerce), fulfil the criteria of property and responsibility. This allows them to protect and assert their rights and obliges them to respect those of others. Both the dynamic and the resulting entities call for the efficient management of the united, allocated resources.

Without entering here into the detail of the different theories guiding our teaching programmes,[4] the following summary gives the conceptual base, in which three levels clarify the comprehension of the entrepreneurial phenomenon binding an entrepreneur (single or plural) to the organization that he runs. It should be understood that the theories guiding our programmes fall under the paradigm of the creation of an organization, and it is the relationship of the individual to the organization he or she runs that is necessary for us to teach to the student. Three levels, and their interactions, clarify this relation. As a whole, five elements make up the equation then lead to the entrepreneurial phenomenon (PhE):

$$\text{PhE} = F[(C \times P \times S) \subset (E \times O)] \qquad (6.1)$$

C (cognitive level), S (structural level) and P (praxeological level) are irreducible for analysis requirements, but are inextricable on a practical level; their interactions (the '$\times$' in the model) also constitute research levels of analysis in entrepreneurship. To take an example that binds the cognitive level and the structural level in order to better understand the process of entrepreneurial socialization, it is possible to resort to culturalist theses to a limited degree as well as to theories such as that of conventions or that of social representations, which may constitute a relevant analysis prism when these theories are articulated with those of the identity.

Thus, the research contribution on the phenomenon relies on: the comprehension of the entrepreneur's knowledge leading him or her to undertake (C); the singularity of the actions called upon by the act (P); the structure of the contexts in which the phenomenon emerges (S); the entrepreneur (E) as an individual, in particular his or her background and other general aspects (dispositions, affectivity, emotions, and so on) allowing us to better know him; the organization (O). In other words, a research programme in entrepreneurship aims to bring knowledge on each dimension C, P, and S, on their interactions, and the relationships to which they apply, namely, the entrepreneur (or entrepreneurs) and the organization (E and O).

It is not difficult to imagine the importance of making the students aware of the elements of this theory, according to which, to understand and represent the entrepreneurial phenomenon, it is possible to consider more precisely:

- A cognitive level (C). This is, obviously, the major-part in the design of a teaching programme, since it aims at contributing knowledge that should serve both in controlling the entrepreneurial phenomenon as well as the undertaking of the candidates wanting to set up the company. This corresponds to the cognitive state that leads an individual to act, the entrepreneur's knowledge and all that contributed to bring them this knowledge and to forge this cognitive state (including their intentions and attitudes). This results from a permanent reflexive exercise, learning situations in which they were placed and from the strategic vision that they have of their business. When there are several individuals who join together to undertake a project, problems relating to conflicts which one could describe as 'cognitive' are likely to emerge and, for some, can take them as far as the courts. Conversely, the confrontation of various representations can be enriching, benefiting the project as much as the protagonists (but only when these divergences do not harm the constructive interaction of those responsible for the project).
- A structural level (S). This corresponds to the context structure surrounding the acting entrepreneur. Without eliminating too easily the influence of the individuals, one should not neglect the weight of the structures on the other levels of the model. It is important to understand the structural basics of the system, whether they be the rules, conventions, representations, or institutions with which the entrepreneur must manoeuvre to win the commitment of the stakeholders and to perpetuate the organization (at least, when that is the objective of the entrepreneur). Obviously, the entrepreneur can set up a conventional system in which the stakeholders will detect favourable conditions of exchange.
- A praxeological level (P). This integrates the fundamental actions undertaken. These emanate, on the one hand, from the multiple positioning of the entrepreneur and the organization with respect to competitors and the various stakeholders and, on the other hand, from the configuration formed in order to produce the elements, which will allow the exchange, durable if possible, with these actors. Within this framework, the policies put in place (financial policies, political wage, and so on) aim to optimize the exchange relationships between the stakeholders. From the pedagogical point of view, the praxeological level sends us back to the process arranging the tasks and activities to be undertaken. Thus, the link is made with the process presented in section 6.2.

As for the relationship (E × O) which makes it possible to explain the preceding levels and their interactions, it requires a true symbiosis[5] between one or more undertaking individuals:

- The entrepreneur(s) (E). Their personality (locus of control, tolerance to ambiguity, lifestyle, and so on), their motivations (in which one will discuss the logics of push or pull entrepreneurship), their leadership, their biography (origin, training, experience, and so on) have to be considered to understand the singularity of entrepreneurship. In an entrepreneurship training programme, 'to know' the entrepreneur allows those responsible for the project to identify with, and to project themselves into, this role that they are considering endorsing. Other actors of the environment interested in the entrepreneurship venture (for example, advisers, bankers, and so on), need to understand these undertaking individuals with whom they will have working relationships. In particular, the advisers, in their adequacy evaluation of the entrepreneurs and their creation project, will have to endorse the candidates whom they will support on the basis of the knowledge they have on this subject.
- Organization (O). The creation of an organization results in having to anticipate at the same time its future (in other words its strategy since, as the maxim of Sénèque says so well, 'there is no favourable wind for him who does not know where he wants to go!') and the resources that have to be obtained (and organized) to arrive at the desired future. It is then advisable for the entrepreneur to position him or herself with respect to resources owners who have to be convinced to become shareholders and to assemble the organizational structure making best use of these resources through the implementation of policies (purchase, wage, marketing, financial policies, and so on) aimed at the optimization of the value exchange relationships. The organization is thus not only the entities emerging from the entrepreneurial phenomenon, but also all related organizational dynamics.

The theory summarized here is used as a common theme for the conceptual training of the students, and the third section of this chapter presents some illustrations. In this generic apprehension of the entrepreneurial phenomenon, the model considers time as a contextual variable (the concept of window of opportunity could be called upon here as an example). When it is a question of putting the students into action, by our use of the praxeological level of the model, the recourse to the concept of process places time as a contingent and experiential structuring variable.

6.2   To act: a process to mark out entrepreneurial training – from the idea to the business plan

The process presented to the students begins with the idea and leads to the business plan (Figure 6.1). This is not to say that the entrepreneurial process is strictly marked out, at its beginning, by the idea and, at its end, by the business plan. The process presented here is a guide for the teacher and the student, or the adviser and the entrepreneur, in the construction and the development of the business. It constitutes the teaching aid.

For each stage, it is a question of positioning oneself in multiple environments to collect information, to establish a network, to act, to convince, and so on, and to organize the resources collected to think, to build, to realize, to manage, and so on.

On the time axis, the sinusoidal shape of the course in Figure 6.1 testifies to a back and forth thought process between the stages. The representation of this figure in three dimensions could be compared with a screw, which, when it turns in a direction seals the object which it formalizes, and, in reverse, releases this object either to give the necessary play or

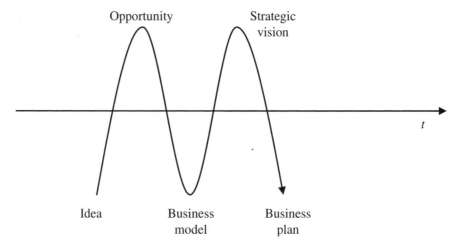

Figure 6.1   The entrepreneurial process

to release it completely (that is abandon it). The axis of time turns more or less quickly; time is a relative variable in such a process. It can also, to some extent, move backwards, even if the clock and the calendar advance unrelentingly. In other words, the process is not linear. For example, the development of the business model often results in working the idea over again.

Certain potential creators experience the desire to do something before even having an idea capable of being used as a basis for a business model. Others are persuaded that they have had the ideas before everyone else. Who has never heard 'I told you so'. An idea alone is nothing, since it is not exploitable when delivered in its rough state, and when it is not exploited, it is forgotten. So that the project can be tangible, the idea must reveal a true business opportunity, which we will define as the conjunction between an idea and a socio-economic reality. It is from this opportunity that the business model can be formalized. It becomes indispensable when it is a question of approaching the resource owners to trans-form them into stakeholders. The corresponding exercise of convincing then requires a document to be prepared that would be used to sell to all the stakeholders the vision that the creator has of the project (the first of them being him or herself), a document which we call the business plan.

The approach, as presented here, is linear. An idea must be tested to verify that an opportunity is worth exploiting, then, that the business model can be built and the business plan will emerge from the strategic vision. It is more a question of suggesting a procedure to follow than of presenting the exact reproduction of a reality which offers, as we might imagine, approaches that are much less linear: for example, the case of an entrepreneur who reaches a market without having thought about it too much, then creates an organization for this purpose, a step during which ideas and new sources of opportunities are revealed to him or her, from which other initiatives are considered.

In a more detailed way, let us now see the essential elements on which our students are called to work, in a summarized presentation of the remarks made to these apprentices, and which might appear somewhat unexceptional to the reader of this chapter.

The idea

It is astonishing to note, very regularly, the great discretion the carriers of projects show with their idea. If their prudence in this field seems comprehensible, how many times have we heard speak about the same ideas, put forward by various people, each one being persuaded of its originality and the exclusiveness of his or her source: we should wonder whether our ideas are really our own.

Information is exchanged more and more quickly. The Internet, the multiplication of the media, the internationalization of the exchanges of any type, are some of the factors that support the nearly simultaneous appearance of identical ideas in various parts of the world, in various minds. What is true on the international level is not less true at the national, even regional, level, because of the factors that bring individuals together such as being of the same culture or in close geographical proximity.

Rather than believing in the spontaneous generation of brilliant ideas, appearing instantaneously in the mind of their inventors, it is better to consider more reasonably that an idea of company creation must be conceptualized, that is, built, starting from a vague notion. It must be intellectualized to become a more precise object, but at the same time remain sufficiently simple in order to be quickly communicated and quickly understood by the stakeholders (during the drafting of the business plan, this idea must be written in a paragraph of one, two or three sentences, maximum). It is only when this first work is accomplished that one can think of protecting the idea, even if this is more complicated than it appears at first sight. The protection of an idea can be very complicated and expensive. An idea can be more or less easy to protect. Protection requires in any event a specific treatment that exceeds the framework of this chapter, and the inventor will approach specialized organizations, which will be able to help it in this task.[6] Among the guidance lavished on students, is that one should not fall into the paranoiac behaviour of those who fear that at any minute their idea might be stolen from them, especially as the development of an idea has to be discussed: to approach the Valorization Cell for Research or the incubators in their establishment when their project is of an innovative nature; to consider the relevance of protection by patent; to mobilize the techniques truly allowing the idea to be developed. On this last point, there are often proposed some methods generally gathered under the name of 'methods of creativity'. Creativity is not a usual step, although it maintains a close relationship with innovation. The methods soliciting creativity can be mobilized by the company creator and his or her team. Let us think about the analysis known as 'defectuologic', whose principle is to inventory the functions of a product in order to systematically criticize them: with the MLI (for more or less interesting), they consist of becoming aware of the advantages (more) and the disadvantages (less) of a question or a proposal while trying to relegate preconceived ideas, to then study the aspects requiring additional exploration (it would be interesting to know . . .); to a nominal group, particularly effective as a team preoccupied with a problem, which invites the participants to state, then to treat on a hierarchical basis, concepts relating to the question or the subject; and so on, all these methods allow the updating or the refinement of new ideas. The methods of creativity are invaluable tools even for a company that will have gained in maturity. They can be also used to reformulate an idea, when its evaluation on the market does not reveal a business opportunity, or when it is not possible to mobilize the resources necessary for the development of the business model.

Opportunity
A true business opportunity cannot be seen, detected, raised or built, unless the price of confrontation is paid between the starting business idea and the socio-economic reality within which the resources must be mobilized to concretize this opportunity. The concept 'fit' is at the heart of our meaning of opportunity.

In a more pragmatic way, the creator of the company will have to test the idea, in as much as this is possible, to verify that an opportunity really exists or can be exploited. During this stage, the techniques and the tools from the marketing field are an invaluable help, if they are adapted to the case of the company creation. The market is indeed one of the first sub-sets of socio-economic reality with which the idea must be compared. The company creator will try to identify the factors apparently expected by the context in which he or she is to operate; identifying these factors, called here 'key factors of success' (KFSs)[7] and 'strategic risk factors' (SRFs),[8] will allow him or her to approach the following stages of the plan with more confidence.

The evaluation of an opportunity, that is, the measurement of the aptitude of an idea to satisfy the stakeholders (initially the customers) on an ongoing basis is not easy for the novice. As a first approach, one could consider that the existence of a prospective customer, that is, a customer who has ordered the product or the service, proves the business opportunity. Indeed, how many people can confirm an idea is well founded and incite the individual to launch out in business if they are not, themselves, open to acquire the object proposed in the exchange? Consequently, to carry out a sale would confirm the business occasion. However, is this sufficient? Does one swallow make it spring?

Conversely, does a broad market study from which a positive evaluation is produced of the idea to launch out in business, does this guarantee the success of the project being undertaken? The problems posed by the bringing together of company creation and marketing remove any hope for the precision of the estimations. The lack of a past, from which projections are sometimes possible, also impairs definitive calculations. In addition, how, on a practical level, can we test an idea to appreciate the business opportunity that it claims it can become?

Ideally, it would be necessary to appreciate the potential of an idea, to confront it with the types of values it can bring to the various stakeholders. Such an evaluation would suppose the meeting of each type of resources owner likely to acquire the status of stakeholder. But this would be taking a great step, since often the only effective way to proceed with this evaluation is to actually create the company, in the most traditional sense of the term. Since we are by definition upstream of this effective creation, the principal point likely to interest the stakeholders in the company's potential is the capacity of the latter to interest a sufficient number of customers. Consequently, it is not unreasonable to consider that a business opportunity exists only when the elements are measured making it possible to appreciate its capacity to interest this sufficient number. This comparison with the market is obviously progressive, and becomes explicit throughout the process of the company creation, from the original interview of a simple presumption of opportunity until the achievement of the final sales turnover. In other words, at the beginning, opportunity is generally revealed approximately, then is confirmed little by little thanks to the methods implemented for, in particular, delimiting the market. It will be verified by the effective launching of the business, therefore always a posteriori, unfortunately for those who like certainty.

The business model

At this stage of his plan, the company creator, reassured as to the existence of a business opportunity and knowing that he or she holds the resources and competence necessary to seize the opportunity, can be tempted to take a pen, and without waiting longer, write in the rules of the business plan in order to share his or her conviction with any person useful to the initiative. However, an additional effort of conceptualization is required of the creator, what one calls a business model: it is a question of showing the stakeholders what makes up the heart of the business, so that they agree to recognize that it is a good way of increasing its value, which initially necessitates by the achievement of a sales turnover; but at the same time these stakeholders will know better, at the end of this demonstration, what the true business of the company is. The business model is seen here as a conceptualization of the business, the whole picture showing, at the same time, in a concrete way, how the money will come in and, in a more abstract way, how the exchange relations with the stakeholders will take place. One cannot ignore that this additional task requested of the entrepreneur is closely related to the blossoming of the start-ups born from the new economy (Jouison, 2005). If its use were spread and not reduced to the lone qualification of the companies based on the Internet, it would exceed a simple fashion effect and bring a considerable amount of additional information on a great number of company creation projects. Again, we still need to deliver our meaning of the business model, which we thus share with the students.

We stress that to convince a resource owner to become a stakeholder, a company creator must show the resource owner the value that he or she can draw from the project. This exercise of convincing can be better understood with recourse to the theory of conventions that we have already mobilized to show that the entrepreneur must convince while making the resource owners adhere to the conventional register of business which the creator proposes. The theory of the conventions, briefly summarized, articulates the individual and the collective by the cognition of a symbolic universe laying down the rules of the economic game; this universe constitutes a place of shared representations, making it possible to set up standards of economic and social behaviour. If we situate the business model within this theoretical framework, the entrepreneur has the choice of two options: either to convince them that his or her business model can become a new business convention, or justify that his or her model respects the conventions in power and that the market makes it possible for it to make a place for itself there. If it is a question of modifying the rules (in particular within the framework of an innovation) or of respecting them, the model must show the stakeholders the value that they will be able to draw from it. Two well-identified stakeholders are on the front line when it comes to carrying their convictions:

- the company creator (or rather the entrepreneurial team here), because this stakeholder must inspire confidence and he or she is the designer of the business model
- customers, because their presence ensures recognition of the estimated value of the project, when these customers pay the value for what they consume or when this value is compensated for by other channels (for example, by Internet connections or television publicity).

In other words, the business model, seen as a conventional register, must, on the one hand, convince of the potential sales turnover and specify the channels by which the remuneration of the value brought will reach certain categories of shareholders, and, on the other hand, explain how the other stakeholders will be able to benefit from the value that they draw from the exchange relationship. Formulated in a synthetic way, the business model objective consists of starting from the idea to show that it constitutes a real business opportunity, and conceptualizing the offer by showing at the same time what it is and how it is remunerated.

It is then possible to mobilize what the strategists call the supply system, which determines the resources able to be mobilized by a pivotal firm and which explains how the collective action requires coordination of not just the management of resources already in its possession, but more widely that of available resources. Consequently, it seems useful to show how the company that is being created acquires the resources, and in particular how it moves them through its network. One sees, besides, that these problems exceed the framework of the Internet start-ups and relate to any firm being created, and even more any organization aiming to achieve a common goal of efficiency. From a strategic point of view, business models also call on the concepts of strategic intention, resources and competencies. The definition of the business model presupposes knowing where one wants to go (that is, having a goal, or at least an intention), and knowing the available distinctive resources in order to offer the stakeholders a value on which they will speculate, and then invest in.

In short, discussing a business model can be easier if one refers to the diagram in Figure 6.2. The figure that we propose can be read from the bottom up or from the top down, the business model (BM) being the junction between upper part and the lower part.

Starting from the top, the idea must meet a socio-economic reality so that the creation can be carried out or a market exploited, without which, in the absence of a business opportunity, the process goes back to square one. In fact, it is not always a question of a step backwards because confrontation with reality very often provides interesting training. However, to conceive the BM, that is, also to model the offer, it is still necessary to reunite and exploit the required resources and, even more so, competencies. These are mobilizable, when they are possessed by the organization or by partners of the offer system. Without these competencies, the system cannot offer what is perceived as the expectation and two possibilities then emerge. The first is to go back to the opportunity to redefine its parameters, even if that must sometimes impose new work on the idea. The second requires patience while trying to develop or acquire the needed competencies (for example, those necessary for the development of a prototype), but not forgetting that an opportunity has a temporal window and thus will not remain an opportunity forever.

Nevertheless, understanding a BM will not be possible without an ascending reading of Figure 6.2. Resource owners must perceive the value of the BM, that is to say, believe in its potential to garner sufficient sales turnover. A resource owner cannot change into a stakeholder if he or she does not think that meeting with the customers' demands is possible. However, even if the resource owner thinks that this *is* possible, it is still not sufficient, because it is still necessary to agree on the compensation of the value produced on the market. A required first measure consists of convincing the resource owner that the financial resources indeed will move through the channel planned in the model. The second corresponds to the sharing of this remuneration, since what interests the resource owners who are interested in becoming stakeholders, is how much they will profit in supporting the project. In short, resource owners not perceiving the value of the BM will lose

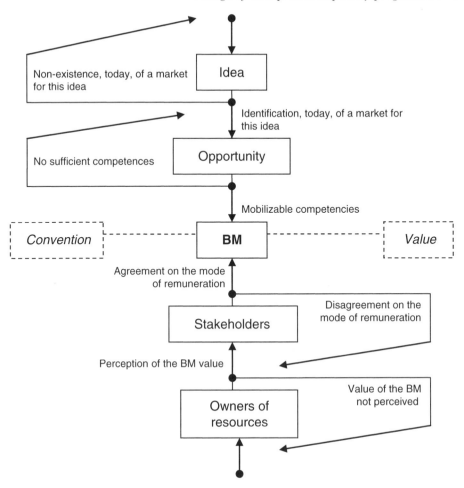

Non-existence, today, of a market for this idea

Idea

Identification, today, of a market for this idea

No sufficient competences

Opportunity

Mobilizable competencies

Convention

BM

Value

Agreement on the mode of remuneration

Disagreement on the mode of remuneration

Stakeholders

Perception of the BM value

Value of the BM not perceived

Owners of resources

Source: Verstraete and Jouison (2006).

Figure 6.2   The business model

interest here, and the stakeholders that are not in agreement with the remuneration of the value (of the BM but also of the value that they bring) do not take part in designing the BM, which then loses its stakeholders. In this way, the resource owners, even more those who became stakeholders, influence the offer, and therefore the BM. To use a metaphor, they take part in the receipt of the cake that they perceive as appetizing and plentiful, while wishing to see it grow larger, and, in return for what they bring, they negotiate a share of that cake.

Respectively on the right and on the left of the BM (dotted lines) are two already evoked concepts, value and convention, which intervene with each stage of this modeling process. Retaking the descending reading, the move from the idea to the opportunity can be conceptualized as recognition, at the same time, of the value of this idea and the existence of a market. The move from the opportunity to the BM, for this part of the figure, supposes having the resources that can be proliferated (one of the criteria of the strategic management of resources approach), the convention expressing itself by their coordination. In an ascending reading, any resource owner can become a stakeholder only after being convinced by the creator's exercise of persuasion, that is, the clarification of the business convention that he or she proposes. This exercise of persuasion will relate, on the one hand, to the value of the BM and, on the other hand, to the sharing of this value (the agreement on the mode of remuneration, as much as the channel and the sharing). These efforts on behalf of the creator call for an oral performance, that is, a meeting with the resource owners in order to transform them into stakeholders, accompanied by a written document, since a convention is evidenced in the business world by the attainment of a business plan.

Strategic vision
The development of a predictive model of performance remains a perilous exercise and to provide potential business creators or those considering consultancy with automatic receipts of success can fall within the caricature. Nevertheless, research highlights the central role of the entrepreneur and his or her vision is of great importance. Whatever the contingencies influencing the success of the project, the representation its carrier forges is a variable that is not only constant, but also one that many firms agree is a major factor. When we ask the question about the knowledge necessary for an adequate conception of the project, it is not unreasonable to consider this project as non-existent, at the origin, only in the immateriality of thought of the creator wishing to accomplish it. On the practical level, the challenge is then to identify the generic components of a good vision, in order then to be able to implement them in a concrete project.

Two principal dimensions of this vision are extracted from the modeling of the entrepreneurial phenomenon presented in the first section of this chapter: the praxeological dimension of this model insists, on the one hand, on multiple *positionings* leading to exchanges with a number of stakeholders and, on the other hand, on the *organizational configuration* optimizing the organization of the business, in particular by a variation in functional policies of the company's strategy. These two central aspects constitute for us the base on which the company creator's vision is built.

As a question of multiple environments in which the entrepreneur and the organization position themselves, we can call again on the traditional distinction consisting of breaking down this environment into, on the one hand, a macro-environment, composed of socio-economic, institutional, technological, ecological and cultural dimensions, and, on the other hand, a closer micro-environment composed of activities and markets, competitors and stakeholders.

In talking about the organizational configuration, the manufacturing of the products or the offering of a service, the corresponding processes requires thought. Moreover, the entrepreneur must configure the organization so that the functional policies making it possible to optimize the value exchange relations with the stakeholders, be put into action (purchase policy being a question of the exchange of value with the suppliers, wage policy as regards the employees, marketing policy for the customers, and so on). For this, he or she will have divided (thus organized) the resources assembled to steer the project he or she has embarked on.

Each of these stakeholders evaluates, according to its own criteria, the *performance* of the company. The entrepreneur wishing to control the organization which he or she created

Figure 6.3   Essential generic elements of a strategic vision

will take care to be kept informed of these criteria by the use of a control system, without forgetting to include the follow-up of the key factors of success. Among these factors, the entrepreneurial contexts raise certain personal characteristics of the individual undertaking to the level of true competencies, and the creator will draw up an assessment of his or her own *strengths and weaknesses* in relation to the adventure which he or she has launched. To compensate for his or her weaknesses, but more largely to learn the art of entrepreneurship, he or she must be open to the large amount of training during the first years of the company. This *training* can benefit from advice from tutors, trainers or consultants, or others having the knowledge or ability to overcome a difficulty, that is, having the means to support the evolution of the company.[9] It is then time to bring the entrepreneur's vision into reality using tools that for the majority are marked by the singularity of entrepreneurial situations. Synthetically, six points deserve some attention within the framework of a strategic honing of the entrepreneurial project, as Figure 6.3 suggests.

Business plan
The interest given to the business plan should not make one lose sight of its subordinate position relative to the quality of the carrier(s) of the project. This is to say to which point, beyond the elements presented by Figure 6.1, that the project carrier is important. For the tutors or guides, all work then consists in appreciating the adequacy between the project and its carrier(s). Beyond this difficult to bypass criterion, the business plan must convince that the business model deserves support, thanks to the relevance of the strategic vision delivered in the details to the potential or effective stakeholders. Gumpert (1996) compares the business plan to a selling document used to sell the business under consideration to the stakeholders, and not just the potential financers. The creator is the first interested party and the appeal to his or her critical sense guarantees an honest and perspicacious construction of a negotiation document evoking his or her vision of the

business. Obviously, the knowledge of the financers and their decision criteria influence the drafting of the plan. The last developments of this section propose a standard structure suggested for students.

The writing of a business plan should not be considered as a constraint, but as an occasion to specify one's strategic vision. It is transversal by nature. It combines dimensions concerned with marketing, finance, law, and so on that need to be articulated, coordinated and managed. For this reason, the development of the business plan has a formative character, initially by confronting the creator with the managerial competencies he or she will need to have, then by obliging him or her to anticipate the evolution that he or she will need to manage. For this reason, we consider that the carrier of the project must be the author of the document, even if he or she is assisted by an expert (chartered accountant or the adviser from a specialized agency in the accompaniment of creators).

Within the framework of a company creation, the written statement of a strategic vision presents as much an obligatory nature as a necessary one. The obligation is posed by stakeholders wishing, when in possession of the supporting details, to measure the degree of analysis relating to the project. The business plan shows, and the verb is not fortuitous, that a strategy 'exists' and that the creator has a clear vision, because it is easily communicable and elaborated. We propose the following definition: the business plan is the written form of the convincing exercise which communicates the strategic vision of the project carrier(s) and which shows that the model considered can generate sufficient shareable value to be supported by the parties to which the document is addressed, and whose resources are expected. It registers the project in time by the clarification of the required and employed resources to achieve the goals and, thus, to accomplish the vision. Each element of this definition corresponds to key elements explained in the teaching programme (in a more or less detailed way according to the volume of the programme). For example, owing to the fact that the exercise is written, we explain to the students that the oral form would not be enough to convince certain stakeholders. If close friends or parents agree to lend or invest financially without any guarantees other than the emotional relationship, other resource owners, possibly already stakeholders when again requested, require the delivery of a file allowing them to acquaint themselves with the details of the finalized project. The document is not thick. If the complexity of the project causes the number of pages to exceed 40, the reader will likely become weary. This remark does not apply to the business plan completed for a complex new project for a large company, for example relating to the establishment of a new factory abroad, or even for specific operations but of a large scale (for example, as Richard Stutely, 2002, remarks, with the organization of the Olympic games) whose documents can reach a few hundred pages. Models for business plans are available on the Internet, and we are satisfied to propose to our students a standard structure, which uses the basic given rules in the realms of company creation. For this reason, venture (risk) capital experts give their point of view on concrete business plans and deliver their methods of analysis not so that the students thwart the possible mistrust of the investors, but so that they prepare a business plan without omitting the expected essential elements.

6.3   Teaching: combining understanding and action into teaching programmes

As Figure 6.1 suggests, and as has been said from the very beginning of the chapter, the entrepreneurial process, including that of the company creation, is not linear and the constitutive activities of each stage actually serve several stages. The development, just like the back and forth movement between the elements of this figure are frequent. We have tested this presentation, whose relevance has little by little been affirmed, during many pedagogical experiments, in the service of more or less long modules. By also taking into account the type and level of the students, we worked out a certain number of teaching programmes, all tested, during which colleagues with different specialties in various disciplines or specialities intervene, as well as professionals from other areas of business life (for example, capital risk investors). The version of the entrepreneurial process that we propose makes it possible to improve the effectiveness of the programme, by interspersing the interventions in a judicious way along the process schematized by Figure 6.1. For example, we preferably invite the specialists in marketing during the time between the idea and opportunity in Figure 6.1, and ask them to deploy the tools allowing them, if not to test the idea, at least to approach the most reasonable interpretation possible of what the market can be. This, without forgetting that the process is not linear, but as with writing, teaching programmes require a beginning and an end.

The teaching programmes that we propose depend on the theroretical model delivered in the first section associated with the process as schematized by the second section. The model serves as a global and distant comprehension of the phenomenon, the process primarily aims at training through action. The complementarity of the two approaches constitutes the key factors of success of a high-level pedagogical programme. However, in the short training programmes (for example, an awareness seminar) we highlight the process in order to put the students into action quickly, and they often produce something concrete and active after years of 'immobile' training. This highlight does not want to imply that the model is forgotten. In fact, it serves as principal reading grid to students following long and specialized training, such as a master's degree in Entrepreneurship. These students then regard time as a contingent element, the process constitutes the guideline on which stages put the components of the model in relation to each other. In other words, the stages combine with time, either to try to accelerate it, to slow it down, or to reverse it. Each stage links a carrier(s) (E) with an organization (O) that he or she runs and make things concrete by which knowledge (C) serves and flows from an action (P) happening in a structure (S) composed of actors (competitors, stakeholders, the authorities, and so on) acting with the conventions (legal, cultural, representational, and so on) and with the social representations composing this structure (the levels S of the model can theoretically be read by a conventional approach or an institutional approach). In the specialized high-level training, this diagram (see equation 6.1) serves to help comprehension of the actors and the entrepreneurial contexts. The students often strive to become specialists in entrepreneurship in general, and in the creation or buy-out of companies in particular. They are carriers of a project, or are considering a career as an entrepreneur without yet having the business idea; sometimes they wish to be involved in the field of entrepreneurship (for example, consultancy, which is generally the case for students who carried out a training course in a consultancy organization and can easily move into the corresponding profession), or to follow a specialization perceived as advantageous to their basic profession (for example bankers and, sometimes, chartered accountants). It is then a question of presenting the relevance of the analysis to the students, by showing them each component of the model and how these interact. For example, when looking at the cognitive level ('C' of the model on page 101), the highlight is on the levels and the elements of the training which any entrepreneur must undertake. It would be possible to mobilize Argyris and Schon's (1978) theory, distinguishing training in single loop and double loop, sufficiently well known that we need not delay on it here, to understand what the term 'levels' means here.[10] As it is difficult to understand how one thinks, therefore also how one learns, without forcing oneself to a certain extent to know who one is and, in particular, to update our aspirations, the 'E' of the model is an invitation to discuss the question of an approach based on one's 'innate traits' and an approach based on 'acquired' character traits (behaviourist approach), the motivations of the entrepreneur, the career of entrepreneur, and so on. It is also a question of confronting the student[11] with a particularly committing life project, and asking property ownership and social responsibility questions (which also sends one back to the interactions between the C and the S of the model). If these problems exist for any type of professional project, the frequent intimacy that this maintains with the personal life of an entrepreneur delivers a batch of constraints for which the student must be prepared (he or she then deduces much better the needs for enriching his or her knowledge, therefore the 'C' of the model). Any entrepreneur also knows that it is more difficult for him or her to leave the organization he or she set up, especially if he or she is the owner, than for an employee, whose competence is recognized, to change organizations (that is, employers). The training aims to better serve future actions, the student endorsing in the programme the role of an entrepreneur, led to anticipate their actions. It is then a question of helping the individual to picture his or her desired future, a strategic vision. The concepts are of cardinal importance here, when they are used in case studies in comparison with the duration of the programmes (Hlady-Rispal, 2002). Besides, psychologists regard vision as conceptual knowledge. In other words, the concepts constitute elements of knowledge serving the action. Seemingly trivial, the example conveyed by Weil-Barais (1999) is explicit. If an individual has to distribute 28 sweets to four children, two types of conceptual knowledge can be required. The first is the concept of distribution, consisting of giving the sweets one by one to each child until none of the 28 parts remain. The second is that of division, where the individual implements an arithmetic equation to directly give each child the result of the calculation, that is to say $28 \div 4 = 7$. These two types of knowledge are put to the test by the facts of an effective distribution of sweets to the children and can lead to adjustments (this brings us closer to the concept of reflexivity). For the strategist who must become the entrepreneur, it is the same, that is, it is advisable to inculcate in him or her the strategic concepts appropriate to the situations that he or she is likely to face in the accomplishment of the project so that he or she can at least be prepared to build the strategic vision.

According to the training course (level, public, and so on), the teaching programme combines the readings (from press to academic articles), the intervention of specialists (risk capital investors, advisers, creator, and so on), presentations, roundtables, the organization of demonstrations, case studies, a project of creation going either until the 'sale' of a business model (short training), or until the presentation of a business plan. Within the framework of a short module, it is reasonable to stop with the business model, because the realization of a business plan generally provides simple documents. This does not mean that the students do not have to hand in a document. This document then comprises the first headings of an executive summary, that is:

- a paragraph to describe the idea
- two paragraphs to show that the idea constitutes a real business opportunity, by citing the legitimate and reliable sources that have served such an interpretation

- two paragraphs to convince one of the business model, by showing how it is built (the ingredients of the 'cake', let us say its recipe, to which stakeholders, through their requirements, take part in, then recover a share).

Two additional pages are required, in which the students deliver mainly their sources, the difficulties and the people they met, and the deployed methods.

The students work in teams and defend their business model in front of teachers who make up a panel of judges for this purpose. The teachers offer one or more appointments of about 15 minutes to the groups of students to help them progress further.

Within the framework of a long programme, this brief (but demanding in terms of conviction and quality factors) presentation is replaced by the business plan in its entirety. The business model is defended all the same in front of the teacher in charge of the programme (for a detailed presentation of our conception of the business model and the linked pedagogy, see Verstraete and Jouison, 2006), but in the middle of the programme, whereas at the end, the defence of the business plan takes place in front of consultants, advisors, investors, resource contributors and business managers who make up the panel of judges. In other words, within the framework of a long module or a course leading to a diploma, the business plan constitutes the result of know-how assessed by the professional world, to which it is naturally presented for evaluation. The students can, during the year, profit from the advice and recommendations of the teaching staff.

The students of a specialized master's degree also write a dissertation on a theme related to entrepreneurship in order to show the relevance of an academic and distant approach of the studied phenomenon (with an empirical phase generally done through interviews or case studies). This dissertation, taking as a starting point the academic style, is short (by about 30 pages) but the quality factor required is high.

We finish this chapter with a table of some training programmes given in the Bordeaux context with a short description of a recent teaching programme within a specialized programme in entrepreneurship (Table 6.1).

A teaching programme linking theoretical production with field research has been recently developed for the master's degree in Entrepreneurship in Bordeaux, France. The students attend a seminar on research methodology, then choose a specific case illustrating an entrepreneurship phenomenon, for example, a creation project, a buyout, a specific entrepreneurship strategy, a group of entrepreneurial firms, and so on. For six months, the students carry out their case study, progressively defining the frontiers of the case, using theoretical concepts such as: the 'hypo firm', a concept developed by Michel Marchesnay for those entrepreneurs who desire not to grow because they have a unique competitive advantage requiring this choice; describing the context – the entrepreneur family and shareholders for instance; and sampling – collecting specific data in relation with a problem they progressively discover. The future entrepreneurs learn how to be selective with data, how to choose the entrepreneurship concepts that can help them to understand the phenomenon under study, how to describe the reality they observe and how to analyse qualitative data they collect through observation, interviews and written information. A tutor meets each student twice during the field research period. The meeting has to be prepared by the student (specific questions he or she will ask, pre-analysed data, first interpretations, and so on). E-mail communication can also take place.

Table 6.1   Some example programmes

Type of programme	Teaching contents	Work to be turned in
Awareness seminar of approximately 12 hours, divided into three half-days and a 15-minute defence panel two months later. This seminar can be deployed in a school of engineers, in the first year of business schools, in two-year vocational course	The contents are primarily based on the process. This is presented in the first half-day, then the students work in teams on a case study where each stage of the process, up to the business model, is analysed. The last two hours of the seminar are based on the theoretical model to approach the singularity of entrepreneurship and to talk about entrepreneurs, the contexts, the action types, without forgetting to come to a conclusion about the adequacy carrier-project by making links with the studied process	The business model (BM) is defended two months after the seminar in front of a jury made up of teachers. The students profit from one to three appointments with teachers during these two months. A case study is analysed at the time of the seminar and a report is returned to the teacher
Entrepreneurship training courses for carriers of projects, sometimes under development, of about 30 hours distributed over several weeks	Near to the preceding contents. After a generic presentation of the processes, different lecturers specialized in marketing, financing of projects, etc., the discussions deepen on the stages and through a concrete case	According to the organization by which the training is given, required work is identical to the preceding programme or no work is required
Entrepreneurship training course within a non-dedicated context training given to scientific students, literary students, to schools of engineers, etc. to university level programmes	Close to the preceding contents, but the initial work of a business model is required this time. The classes are given by various lecturers	BM in front of a jury and various case studies. Possible written examination
Entrepreneurship training course in a general training programme that may comprise a dedicated specific option (e.g., in first	The course is of an academic nature, it is based on the theoretical model of the first section to approach the singularity of entrepreneurship and its various expressions, and each component of this	Written examination, possible BM in front of a jury if part of a specialized option of a programme

Table 6.1   (continued)

Type of programme	Teaching contents	Work to be turned in
year of a master's degree)	model goes back to contingent elements. The process is then presented as a prosaic expression of the praxeological (P) component of the model. Links with the essential subjects to know in management are pointed out	
Entrepreneurship training course in a Specialized Training Programme, aiming at making students experts in entrepreneurship. The dedicated volume of hours of the master's degree in Bordeaux is 350 hours	See the details on the site of University Montesquieu Bordeaux IV, or consult www.adreg.net	Written examination, case studies, presentations, concrete achievements (e.g., a newspaper), business plan, dissertation, internships/placements

6.3   Conclusion

The generic model (section 6.1) as well as the process (section 6.2) leads to combining, for the majority, research and teaching from the start. This can partly be explained by the fact that the teaching staff essentially comprise members of a research team in the field of entrepreneurship (the others are entrepreneurs, business angels, and so on). Doctorates are actually prepared which are connected with these models. For example, a doctoral work concerns the business model, and aims to answer the following problem.[12]

The entrepreneur's main problem is to convince stakeholders to adhere to his or her project. We can explain this crucial point for the success of the future business through the entrepreneur's powers of persuasion aimed at obtaining resource holders' support: to 'transform' them into stakeholders, making them adhere to the business convention he or she proposes is necessary. The problem can be turned into a theoretical problem combining two corpuses: the conventions theory and the stakeholders theory. The theoretical problem helps with understanding the exercise of persuasion that causes resource holders to adhere to the proposed business model. This theoretical combination is useful to conceptualize the notion of business model and may help entrepreneurs expose clearly their business model in order to 'sell' their business to stakeholders.

This doctoral work illustrates the theoretical, pedagogical and practical interests of the conception given here. From a practical point of view, the methodological protocol is an action research that places the PhD candidate in the situation of coaching entrepreneurs to create their company. Indeed, it seems important to us to have coherent operational frameworks with the goals of the research programs. This calls for a discussion on research methodologies for entrepreneurship, but that is another 'story'.

Notes

1. The children of entrepreneurs seem more inclined to become entrepreneurs. A process of socialization as well as the accessibility of the model of the entrepreneur via their parents play a role not discussed here. More generally, Minniti and Bygrave (1999) consider that the simple fact of observing around oneself, a behaviour similar to that which one is considering adopting, exerts a positive influence in favour of this behaviour, and can bring adhesion, in spite of the original reserves, if the number of the behaviours observed exceeds a certain threshold. From this observation, drawn from the theory of riots, by the American sociologist Mark Granovetter, the demonstration can be continued by taking the case of the decision to create a company. Their work is an original attempt at explaining the difference in rates of entrepreneurship in different areas (countries or regions). The theory of the conventions, combined with the theory of the social representations, provides another possible analysis framework for the increase in entrepreneurial behaviours (Verstraete, 2005).
2. We quote here this typology, used in the paper of Béchard and Grégoire (2005), where four poles give a frame to the theories of education: one focuses on the content (academic theories), another focuses on the individual (personalist and spiritualist/ethical theorie), the third focuses on the interface with society (social/economic theories), the last focuses on the interaction of these poles (psycho-cognitive theories, social-cognitive theories, technological theories).
3. An owner of resources agrees to become a stakeholder only once convinced of the value of the project and more still by the exchange (of value) that should be established.
4. For that, the reader should refer to Verstraete (2002; 2005).
5. Three types of relationship are possible: the symbiotic, the commensal, and the parasite. Remember that a commensal lives with its host by diverting some of the latter's resources, whereas the parasite infects the host and can cause its death. The inverse is so with the symbiotic relationship; the protagonists benefit mutually from the other.
6. In France: the INPI (see www.inpi.fr), which examines the requests and delivers industrial property titles that it publishes in the Bopi (official bulletin of the industrial property); the APP is interested in protection of the computer programmes (see HTTP://applegalis.net); the Company of the Men of Letters was created in 1838 by famous writers (Honoré de Balzac, Victor Hugo, Alexandre Dumas, George Sand) and its mission is to protect the interests of the authors of writings and intellectual creations, and it can offer assistance (see http://sdgl.org).
7. A KFS is regarded here as one of several factors essential to the success of a business. Not controlling a KFS will lead to failure (for example, the time period necessary for a pizza delivery company to deliver a pizza).
8. An SRF is as significant for the evolution of the business as a KFS, but it is not directly controllable. To counter its possibly harmful influence, it is advisable to deploy retreat strategies (for example, for an agricultural company, to envisage the infrastructures for possible bad weather conditions by putting the crops in greenhouses or by draining the ground, and so on).
9. The concept of authorized capital of the sociologist Pierre Bourdieu can be used here.
10. See the detail of the level training in Verstraete (2005).
11. Should the student have a project to create a business or become a consultancy specialist therein.
12. This work is realized by Estèle Jouison.

References

Argyris, C. and Schon, P.A. (1978), *Organizational Learning: A Theory of Action Approach*, Massachusetts: Addison Wesley.
Béchard, J.-P. and Grégoire, D. (2005), 'Entrepreneurship education research revisited: the case of higher education', *Academy of Management Learning and Education*, **4** (1), 23–43.
Bertrand, Y. (1995), *Contemporary Theories and Practices in Education*, Madison, WI: Atwood.
Bruyat, C. (1993), 'Création d'entreprise: contributions épistémologiques et modélisation', thèse pour le Doctorat de Sciences de Gestion, ESA – Université Grenoble II.
Fiet, J.O. (2000a), 'The theoretical side of teaching entrepreneurship', *Journal of Business Venturing*, **16** (1), 1–25.
Fiet, J.O. (2000b), 'The pedagogical side of entrepreneurship theory', *Journal of Business Venturing*, **16** (2), 101–18.
Gumpert, D.E. (1996), *How to Really Start Your Own Business*, Boston: Inc magazine and Goldhirsh Group.
Hlady-Rispal, M. (2002), *La méthode des cas: application à la recherche en gestion*, collection Perspectives Marketing, Bruselles: De Boeck.

Jouison, E. (2005), 'Délimitation théorique du Business Model', Conférence International de Management Stratégique, Caen.

Minniti, M. and Bygrave, W. (1999), 'The microfoundations of entrepreneurship', *Entrepreneurship Theory and Practice*, **23** (4), 41–52.

Saint-Onge, M. (1996), *Moi j'enseigne, mais eux apprennent-ils?*, Laval, Québec Editions Beauchemin.

Stutely, R. (2002), *Business Plan – to Conceive an Effective Business Plan*, Paris: Echoes Edition.

Verstraete, T. (2002), 'Essay on the singularity of entrepreneurship as a research domain', Les Editions de l'ADREG, May, www.editions-adreg.net, accessed in 2000, reprinted in D. Watkins *ARPENT – Annual Review of Progress in Entrepreneurship Research*, vol. 1, Brussels: European Foundation for Management Development, 2002.

Verstraete, T. (2005), 'Proposal for a theoretical framework for research in entrepreneurship', Les Editions de l'ADREG, April, www.editions-adreg.net, accessed 2000.

Verstraete, T. and Fayolle, A. (2005), 'Quatre paradigmes pour cerner le domaine de l'entrepreneuriat', *Revue de l'Entrepreneuriat*, **4** (1), www.revue-entrepreneuriat.com, accessed 2001.

Verstraete, T. and Jouison, E. (2006), 'Connecting stakeholders theory and conventions theory to highlight the adhesion of stakeholders to the business model of a start-up', International Council for Small Business 51st world conference, Melbourne, Australia, June.

Weil-Barais, A. (1999), *L'homme cognitif*, Paris: Presses Universitaires de France.

7 The impact of tertiary education courses on entrepreneurial goals and intentions
Michael T. Schaper and Gian Casimir

Introduction

During the last 20 years, there has been a substantial international expansion in the number of small business courses and entrepreneurship courses offered within tertiary institutions (Ulrich, 1997). Once a relatively esoteric research area, many business schools now offer programmes in the area of small business and entrepreneurship; many in fact also offer degree majors or specializations in the area (De Faoite et al., 2003; Vesper and Gartner, 1999). In part, this growth has been driven by student demand, but it has also been led by the perception amongst educators that entrepreneurship courses create more entrepreneurial students, which in turn leads ultimately to a greater number of students willing to start their own business ventures. This approach has also been encouraged by government policy-makers, who have recognized that the creation of new businesses plays an important role in both regional and national economies (Lean, 1998).

Accompanying this growth in teaching has been a substantial increase in the research literature dedicated to entrepreneurial pedagogy (Béchard and Grégoire, 2005). Major studies have now been conducted into such issues as the different modes of teaching, ways of mixing practical skills with research-based evidence, and the integration of entrepreneurship into the broader business curriculum (Garavan and O'Cinneide, 1994).

Central to this endeavour has been the notion that teaching entrepreneurship and entrepreneurship-related topics (such as business planning, new venture creation, small business management, and/or family-based business management) is a useful way of producing more entrepreneurs. However, the validity of this argument has rarely been tested. Few studies have set out to explicitly determine if undertaking an entrepreneurship course actually leads to more entrepreneurs. Little evidence exists to prove (or disprove) the notion that entrepreneurship programs are a useful way of producing a new generation of business founders.

Research in this area is important to those educators who are concerned with the practical application of their teaching. To what extent, for example, do formal entrepreneurship courses actually alter the subsequent behaviour of students? Does tertiary-level instruction actually make any significant difference in an individual's inclination to start a business?

The impact of tertiary courses is also a significant issue for government, since public funds provide the bulk of university funding within many countries. Budgetary support for business schools is premised on the assumption that their courses (and, ultimately, their degrees) enhance the overall level of commercial skills. But is this really the case? Empirical data that evaluates changes in student skills and knowledge is often limited.

Finally, the effectiveness of entrepreneurship courses is also important to society as a whole. The notion of an 'enterprising society' has become increasingly popular in recent years, and implies the development of communities that are more willing to innovate, accept risk and undertake new challenges. Education is often seen as a key tool in building such communities. At its most basic level, entrepreneurship courses should ideally help create such outcomes by producing graduates who are more willing to launch their own commercial ventures.

Overall, there is still much that needs to be known about the actual impact of formal educational courses on entrepreneurial activity. To what extent do tertiary business school courses actually raise the level of student knowledge about entrepreneurship, the entrepreneurial process, and the issues involved in enterprise formation? Do such courses actually influence the desire of students to want to launch their own ventures? And are there particular types of students who are more likely to want to form their own business than others? All these issues are important to entrepreneurship educators, government and policy-makers.

The objective of the study outlined in this chapter was to examine one of the most common forms of university entrepreneurship education – the 'stand alone' semester-long course. Such programmes are now found in many business schools, and are provided to give students an introduction to the core basic aspects of entrepreneurship and new venture creation. Typically, such programmes introduce the concept of entrepreneurship, discuss the process of new business idea generation and feasibility testing, examine the process of launching and growing the venture, and conclude by looking at how to terminate the venture. The research project attempted to answer the following questions:

1. Does completing an entrepreneurship course affect one's self-reported level of knowledge about entrepreneurship?
2. Does studying an entrepreneurship course actually affect a person's inclination to start a new business venture?
3. Does an improvement in the level of knowledge lead to an increased propensity to launch one's entrepreneurial venture?
4. Are there any other broad-based, easily identifiable characteristics that might also be used to predict a student's likelihood of launching a new business venture?

Background: literature review

There is often a presumption amongst policy-makers, educators and business people that the creation of entrepreneurship courses has led to an improvement in entrepreneurial outputs – most typically in the form of new business ventures launched. For example, Sexton and Kasarda (1991) have argued that whilst the two most important goals of business education programmes are to prepare people for career success and to increase their capacity for learning, the ultimate measure of success for entrepreneurship education and training is whether it cultivates aspirations of entrepreneurship and leads to new business ventures.

Gorman et al. (1997, p. 56) have claimed that the 'propensity or inclination towards entrepreneurship and small business is commonly associated with several personal characteristics that might be expected to be influenced by a formal program of education'. These include attitudes, personal goals, creativity, risk-taking propensity and locus of control. Dyer (1994) concluded that participating in entrepreneurship education may increase one's likelihood of becoming an entrepreneur, because such education provides access to entrepreneurial role models who make entrepreneurship appear more attractive to participants as a result of a socialization process in which entrepreneurship is presented as a viable career path. Similarly, Scott and Twomey (1988) looked at the career aspirations of participants towards self-employment and identified three factors that influence entrepreneurial aspirations. These aspirational factors were predisposing, triggering and possessing an idea. They concluded that these factors, particularly triggering factors and possessing an idea, could be shaped by appropriate education.

It would therefore seem reasonable to hypothesize:

H_1: Undertaking an entrepreneurship course increases a student's self-reported level of knowledge about entrepreneurship.

There is some evidence that studying an entrepreneurship course leads to a greater stated desire to start one's own business (Lean, 1998), and there is some research which has focused directly on whether participation in entrepreneurship courses leads to the start-up of more new businesses. For example, Webb et al. (1982) found that students who participated in entrepreneurship programmes at Babson College, a US tertiary institution with a strong focus on entrepreneurship, were more likely to start their own businesses than were a control group. In another study, Garnier and Gasse (1990) found that many respondents taking training programmes delivered through newspapers and television started their own businesses. Additionally, Kolvereid and Moen (1997) found that graduates with an entrepreneurship major were more likely to start new businesses and had stronger entrepreneurial intentions than other graduates.

Overall, however, the level of evidence to show that entrepreneurship education directly leads to more entrepreneurs is weak. Garavan and O'Cinneide (1994, p. 3) maintain that 'there is a lack of evidence how entrepreneurship education learning strategies influence the development of entrepreneurial competence and how these competences transfer into new project/venture formation'. This argument is echoed by Falk and Alberti (2000), who reviewed the state of entrepreneurship education over 20 years and concluded that there was still a need for more research into the effectiveness of entrepreneurship courses, and the actual impact of these courses on the process of new venture creation.

These two conflicting views suggest that the following hypothesis needs to be examined:

H_2: Undertaking an entrepreneurship course increases a student's inclination to start a new business venture.

Effective enterprise education is about more than just the mere acquisition of knowledge about the entrepreneurial process. To be truly meaningful, such extra knowledge should also ideally lead to an increased number of business start-ups amongst students. Such an argument has been put forward by Bandura (1986), who claims that education can serve a preparatory function in relation to new venture initiation or start-up, whereby the transfer of additional knowledge and the acquisition and development of skills should be expected to increase domain-specific self-efficacy. Is this really the case?

A contrasting perspective is provided by Jones and English (2004), who have argued that whilst the traditional focus of most university-level enterprise programmes has been on raising entrepreneurial skills and knowledge, it is by no means clear that the mere development of such knowledge is sufficient to lead to increased business formation by students. They contend that other factors, such as external environmental risk, may still be too great to offset the increase in knowledge. Whilst such an argument appears plausible, it still needs to be tested:

H_3: *An increased level of knowledge leads to an increased propensity to launch one's own business venture.*

Finally, there also appears to be some evidence that entrepreneurial intentions amongst students can vary according to demographic factors such as gender and age. Wilson et al. (2004), for example, found that women tended to be less inclined to start a new venture than males, whilst a study of gender differences in entrepreneurial intentions amongst secondary school students concluded that females were less inclined to start a new venture than their male counterparts (Kourilsky and Walstad, 1998). A similar pattern has been found amongst MBA students, where women were less likely to undertake entrepreneurial endeavours than their male counterparts (Thandi and Sharma, 2004).

Age is also a factor in many entrepreneurial endeavours (Thandi and Sharma, 2004). Many researchers argue that younger individuals are more likely to start a new venture than older persons (Thandi and Sharma, 2004), although this is by no means always the case. Weber and Schaper (2004) have argued, for example, that in some circumstances older persons may in fact be more likely to start a new venture than their younger counterparts, since they have accrued greater levels of technical and commercial skill, have larger financial resources to support the venture, and a wider range of business networks.

The role of these demographic characteristics can be assessed by testing the following hypothesis:

H_4: *Age and gender of students can predict the likelihood of launching one's own business venture.*

Method

The participants in this study were students undertaking an introductory entrepreneurship unit within their undergraduate degree, at one of two major Australian university business schools. In this study, a 'unit' refers to a semester-long course of study undertaken within an Australian university business school. This sampling frame included a wide variety of students, including those enrolled in an entrepreneurship major, others studying the unit as an option (that is, studying for another major, but voluntarily choosing to supplement their core work with some studies in this field), and those obliged to undertake such a course as a requisite unit in their own major from another business discipline.

Measuring the level of knowledge is a problematic issue. There are a number of different ways of evaluating just how much students learn from a course. As both Ticehurst and Veal (2000) and Heiman (2001) have pointed out, measuring effects and outcomes is often difficult, and often self-measured responses are just as valid as objective measures. Conventional entrepreneurship teaching relies heavily on external assessment (such as examinations and assignments) to judge the level of learning obtained. However, such methods are not perfect (one examiner's fail, for example, may be another's pass), and some assessment items only examine part of the body of knowledge obtained (essays, for example, are very convenient in assessing formal writing and research skills, but less appropriate in evaluating other learning). Moreover, such instruments can only be used towards the end of a semester of instruction; any tools administered at the beginning are almost inevitably bound to produce poor scores. For these reasons, external objective indicators of entrepreneurship knowledge are often flawed indicators.

In contrast, self-reported perceptions of what one knows are (in many respects) more important than any objective evaluation of knowledge levels, since individuals more frequently act upon their perceptions than they respond to an objective reality (c.f. Hunt, 1991). In other words, students' self-reported perceptions of their own levels of knowledge are important in understanding the effects that entrepreneurial courses have on outcomes, and should not be regarded as an epiphenomenon. This process of measuring levels of entrepreneurial knowledge is broadly analogous to Johannisson's (1991) 'know what' content level of entrepreneurial knowledge.

For the purposes of this research study, it was decided to rely on the student's self-reported level of knowledge as the most valid construct of learning. Following the guidelines suggested by Heiman (2001), students in this study were asked to rate their own level of knowledge on a five-point Likert scale (ranging from 1 = very low level of knowledge through to 5 = very high).

To gauge the entrepreneurial intentions of students, all participants were asked if they intended to start their own new business within the next five years. Setting too short a time frame would artificially exclude some students who might otherwise be inclined to launch a business venture in the medium term, whilst setting a longer time frame was seen as unrealistic.

Participants were also asked a number of supplementary questions, including their age, gender, whether or not they were already involved in a business venture, and whether or not they participated in an existing family-based business venture.

Data were collected through a simple one-page questionnaire at the commencement of the first class of the semester, and the same instrument was applied again at the end of the final class of the same semester. The questionnaire was administered by one of the authors, and completed *in situ*. Participants were also asked to provide their student numbers on each questionnaire, so that their completed responses could be matched, thus providing the researchers with a complete set of matched-pairs samples.

Results and discussion
A total of 180 participants provided usable questionnaires. Of these, 42 respondents were excluded from the study because they either already owned a business (n = 15), or else their family owned a business which they were already involved in the management of (n = 27). These participants were deemed ineligible for the study, since the main objective was to examine the effect of entrepreneurship courses on one's inclination to start a new business venture.

The mean age of the remaining 138 participants was 25.5 years (s.d. = 9.3) at the start of the semester. Actual ages of students varied widely, ranging from 18 years to 66 years. In terms of gender composition, the respondent set comprised 75 males (54 per cent) and 63 females (46 per cent). Interestingly, the female students were significantly older than the males (t = 3.3, p < .01): the mean age of the females was 28.4 years (s.d. = 11.3) whilst the mean age of male respondents was only 23.1 years (s.d. = 6.4).

Twenty-three students (17 per cent) were undertaking an entrepreneurship unit as part of an entrepreneurial degree major, whilst 74 (54 per cent) had enrolled in the unit as an option. The remaining 41 (30 per cent) were studying the unit as a required course in another, non-entrepreneurship degree major program.

H_1: Undertaking an entrepreneurship course increases a student's self-reported level of knowledge about entrepreneurship
Students were first asked to what extent they agreed with the proposition 'Do you believe you have the business knowledge needed to run your own business?' (wherein 1 = very little/none and 5 = a lot/very much). The mean response for students at the start of semester was 3.1 (s.d. = 0.9) out of a possible maximum of 5, whilst the end-semester mean score was 3.8 (s.d. = 0.9).

A correlated t-test was then conducted to examine the differences between start-semester and end-semester scores, and indicated that the increase in self-reported knowledge was statistically significant (t = 7.6, p < .001). Clearly, participants believed that they had the business knowledge necessary to run their own business more strongly at the end of semester than they did at the commencement of their course. This upholds the findings previously reported by Thandi and Sharma (2004), and others, that entrepreneurship courses can indeed raise the level of student knowledge about entrepreneurial activity.

H_2: Undertaking an entrepreneurship course increases a student's inclination to start a new business venture
Participants were also asked if they intended to begin a new business venture within the next five years.

At the beginning of semester, 34 of the 138 (25 per cent) students planned to start a business, 44 (32 per cent) did not, and 60 (43 per cent) were uncertain about their intentions. By the end of semester, these figures had changed only slightly: 34 (25 per cent) still planned to start up, 49 (35 per cent) did not, and 55 (40 per cent) remained unsure of their future entrepreneurial intentions (see Table 7.1). At first glance, these figures seem to confirm the null hypothesis that entrepreneurship courses do not affect a student's intention to operate their own business.

Close inspection of Table 7.1 reveals that despite the consistency between the start-semester and end-semester overall intentions, significant proportions of students from each category changed their intention to start their own business (x^2 = 56.9, df = 4, p < .001). Specifically, of the 34 students who stated initially that they intended to start

Table 7.1   Start-semester and end-semester intentions to start own business

	End-semester			
Start-semester	Yes	No	Uncertain	Total
Yes	22	1	11	34
No	3	29	12	44
Uncertain	9	19	32	60
Total	34	49	55	138

their own business, more than one-third (that is, 12) changed their intention by the end of semester. Similarly, of the 44 students who stated initially that they would not be starting their own business, 15 (34 per cent) changed to being uncertain or intended to start their own business. Finally, of the 60 students who were initially uncertain about starting their own business, 19 (32 per cent) reported at the end of semester that they would not start their own business whilst nine (15 per cent) reported that they intended to start their own business. These findings are interesting because they reveal that 40 per cent (that is, 55 out of 138) of the students changed their intention to start a new business.

To some extent, these findings support the arguments of Garavan and O'Cinneide (1994) that education and/or training can influence the development of the entrepreneurial role. However, such influence can be a two-way street: some students become more inclined to launch a venture, whilst others are dissuaded. More specifically, the results of the current study indicate that education does not always produce a predictable, one-directional outcome – more entrepreneurship education does not always lead to students becoming more entrepreneurially inclined.

H_3: An increased level of student knowledge leads to an increased propensity by students to launch their own business venture

A one-way between-subjects analysis of variance (ANOVA) was conducted to test the differences at start-semester between the three intention groups (that is, Yes, No, and Uncertain) on their belief that they had sufficient knowledge to run their own business. Table 7.2 contains the means for the three groups. The ANOVA revealed a significant main effect {$F (2, 135) = 5.8$, $p < .01$}. Fisher's least significant difference post-hoc analyses revealed that students who intended to start their own business were more likely to believe they had sufficient knowledge to run their own business than students who were uncertain or not going to start their own business. The difference between the No and Uncertain groups was not significant.

A one-way between-subjects analysis of variance (ANOVA) was conducted to test the differences at end-semester between the three intention groups (that is, Yes, No, and Uncertain) on their belief that they had sufficient knowledge to run their own business. Table 7.2 contains the means for the three groups. The ANOVA revealed a significant main

Table 7.2   *Post-hoc results and mean (s.d.) scores for intention-to-start-own-business groups on belief that one has sufficient knowledge to run one's own business*

	Start-semester intention to start own business			End-semester intention to start own business		
	Yes[a]	No[b]	Uncertain[c]	Yes[a]	No[b]	Uncertain[c]
Knowledge	3.5 (0.8)***	2.8 (1.0)	3.9 (0.7)	3.0 (0.8)*	3.9 (0.9)*	3.5 (1.0)**
N	34	44	60	34	49	55

Notes:
[a] Indicators of statistically significant differences between the Yes and No groups.
[b] Indicators of statistically significant differences between the No and Uncertain groups.
[c] Indicators of statistically significant differences between the Uncertain and Yes groups.
* $p < .05$, ** $p < .01$, *** $p < .001$.

effect {F (2, 135) = 4.2, p < .05}. Fisher's least significant difference post-hoc analyses revealed that students who did not intend to start their own business were less likely to believe they had sufficient knowledge to run their own business than both students who intended to start their own business and students who were uncertain about starting their own business. The difference between the Yes and Uncertain groups was not significant.

The findings from the two ANOVAs indicate that intention to start one's own business is related to one's belief that one has sufficient knowledge to do so. Specifically, at both the start and the end of the semester, those students who intended to start their own business had a significantly higher belief in their knowledge to start their own business than those students who did not intend to start their own business. It is noteworthy that, at the end of the semester, those students who were uncertain about starting their own business did not differ significantly from those students who intended to start their own business in terms of their belief about having sufficient knowledge to run their own business.

These findings indicate that many more factors other than just business knowledge influence intentions to start one's own business. This is not surprising since variables such as personality, the nature of the business opportunity, and external factors have all been shown to play a moderating role in the propensity to commence a new business venture (Schaper and Volery, 2004).

H_4: Age and gender of students can predict the likelihood of launching one's own business venture
The data did not indicate any linkage between age or gender and future entrepreneurial plans. Age did not correlate significantly with intention to start one's own business at start-semester (r = −.15, p > .05) or at end-semester (r = −.07, p > .05). At the start of the semester, males (mean = 2.4, s.d. = 0.7) were more likely than females (mean = 2.0, s.d. = 0.9) to report that they intended to start their own business (t = 2.6, p < .05), but by the end of the semester there was a non-significant gender difference in intention to start one's own business (t = 1.2, p > .05) between males (mean = 2.2, s.d. = 0.7) and females (mean = 2.1, s.d. = 0.9). These results indicate that neither the age nor the gender of students is a significant factor regarding propensity to launch one's own business after completing the course and contradict the findings of previous researchers such as Wilson et al. (2004), Kourilsky and Walstad (1998), and Thandi and Sharma (2004).

A final issue to bear in mind when considering these results are the limitations inherent in the methodological approach employed. For example, the study was limited to under-graduate business school students in two particular Australian universities, and no attempt has been made to claim that these are necessarily fully representative of all students in entrepreneurship courses. The current study is also limited by virtue of the fact that it did not measure the long-term impact of the course; it has only sought to assess the immediate (that is, end of term) impact of the course on participants' self-reported levels of knowledge and propensity to launch a new business.

Conclusion
As this study shows, entrepreneurship education produces a mixed bag of results. On the one hand, it clearly leads to an improvement in the levels of student knowledge about how to launch and manage a new business venture. On the other hand, it does not appear to change the overall proportion of students who want to run their own enterprise, though

this belies the changes that it can cause within a cohort; some students become more confirmed in their opinions, others previously enthusiastic are dissuaded, some doubters are convinced that it is possible after all, and those who were uncertain to begin with tend to have their anxieties confirmed.

These results have some clear implications for educators:

- *Not all students will become entrepreneurs.* As the respondents in this study indicate, the majority of students do not plan to begin their own business in the foreseeable future. Accordingly, programmes need to be written and delivered not only for those who want to start their own business, but also with a view to simply providing more information for those who will never venture down the self-employment path.
- *Uncertainty is a given.* Entrepreneurship courses, as the findings discussed above show, sometimes create more anxiety and ambiguity for students. Some participants may find, for example, that their previously optimistic ideas need far more work, or that their projections are unrealistic and cannot be guaranteed. Entrepreneurship is not a 'black and white' subject; there is no one way to assured success, and both students and teachers need to be careful to avoid the problem of assuming that there are magic answers.
- *Just who is an entrepreneur is a guessing game.* Individual students are likely to move from one perspective to another over the course of a semester, and those at the start who seem most enthusiastic may not be the ones at the end who are actually planning to launch a venture. Educators should therefore avoid focusing their attention on 'the most likely' students within a class, since many of them may in fact become the least likely by semester's end.

This is an issue that clearly requires more examination, and there is a need for more testing to confirm the initial findings of this one study. A first priority would be perhaps to replicate the research with a greater sample size and covering more introductory entrepreneurship courses at different universities, in order to determine if these original results are reliable and generalizable across a larger cohort of students.

An additional field of useful enquiry might be to employ a longitudinal research design that also involves control groups (that is, non-participants) so as to better understand the long-term impact of entrepreneurship programs on participants (Garavan and O'Cinneide, 1994). It might be the case, for example, that an entrepreneurship programme plants a seed in some participants that will not germinate for many years to come, owing to their need to further develop certain requisite skills and resources before they are able to launch a new business venture.

Finally, on a more philosophical note, it might also be worth asking: should entrepreneurship programmes endeavour to create entrepreneurs anyway? It is commonly recognized that not all people are, or will become, entrepreneurs. Such individuals are, in fact, relatively rare, and not everyone aspires to be one. It would be overly simplistic to argue that an entrepreneurship programme is a failure if it does not generate more entrepreneurs than would otherwise be the case. The role of education is, after all, to inform, and there are many people who work alongside entrepreneurs (such as banks, business advisers and policy-makers) who will never aspire to be one themselves, but whose decisions will still be tempered by what they know about entrepreneurs and the entrepreneurial process. For them, an entrepreneurship course will not be a wasted programme, even though they do not become entrepreneurs themselves.

References

Bandura, A. (1986), *Social Foundations of Thought and Action*, Englewood Cliffs, NJ: Prentice Hall.

Béchard, J.P. and Grégoire, D. (2005), 'Entrepreneurship education research revisited: the case of higher education', *Academy of Management Journal*, **4** (1), 22–43.

De Faoite, D., Henry, C., Johnston, K. and Van der Sijde, P. (2003), 'Education and training for entrepreneurs: a consideration of initiatives in Ireland and the Netherlands', *Education + Training*, **45** (8/9), 430–8.

Dyer, W.G. (1994), 'Toward a theory of entrepreneurial careers', *Entrepreneurship Theory and Practice*, **19** (2), 7–21.

Falk, J. and Alberti, F. (2000), 'The assessment of entrepreneurship education', *Industry and Higher Education*, **14** (2), 101–9.

Garavan, T.N. and O'Cinneide, B. (1994), 'Entrepreneurship education and training programmes: a review and evaluation', *Journal of European Industrial Training*, **18** (8), 3–12.

Garnier, B. and Gasse, Y. (1990), 'Training entrepreneurs through newspapers', *Journal of Small Business Management*, **28** (1), 70–73.

Gorman, G., Hanlon, D. and King, W. (1997), 'Some research perspectives on entrepreneurship education, enterprise education, and education for small business management: a ten-year literature review', *International Small Business Journal*, **15** (3), 56–77.

Heiman, G. (2001), *Understanding Research Methods and Statistics: An Integrated Introduction for Psychology*, New York: Houghton Mifflin.

Hunt, J.G. (1991), *Leadership: A New Synthesis*, London: Sage.

Johannisson, B. (1991), 'University training for entrepreneurship: a Swedish approach', *Entrepreneurship and Regional Development*, **3** (1), 67–82.

Jones, C. and English, J. (2004), 'A contemporary approach to entrepreneurship education', *Education and Training*, **46** (8–9), 416–23.

Kolvereid, L. and Moen, O. (1997), 'Entrepreneurship among business graduates: does a major in entrepreneurship make a difference?', *Journal of European Industrial Training*, **21** (4), 154–60.

Kourilsky, M.L. and Walstad, W.B. (1998), 'Entrepreneurship and female youth: knowledge, attitudes, gender differences, and educational practices', *Journal of Business Venturing*, **13** (1), 77–89.

Lean, J. (1998), 'Training and business development support for micro businesses in a peripheral area', *Journal of European Industrial Training*, **22** (6), 231–6.

Schaper, M. and Volery, T. (2004), *Entrepreneurship and Small Business: A Pacific Rim Perspective*, Brisbane: John Wiley & Sons.

Scott, M.G. and Twomey, D.F. (1988), 'The long-term supply of entrepreneurs: students' career aspirations in relation to entrepreneurship', *Journal of Small Business Management*, **26** (4), 5–14.

Sexton, D.L. and Kasarda, J.D. (1991), *The State of the Art of Entrepreneurship*, Boston, MA: P.W. Kent.

Thandi, H. and Sharma, R. (2004), 'MBA students' preparedness for entrepreneurial efforts', *Tertiary Education and Management*, (10), 209–26.

Ticehurst, G.W. and Veal, A.J. (2000), *Business Research Methods: A Managerial Approach*, Sydney: Longman.

Ulrich, T. (1997), 'An empirical approach to entrepreneurial-learning styles', paper presented at the Internationalising Entrepreneurship Education and Training Conference, IneEnt97, California, 25–27 June.

Vesper, K.H. and Gartner, W.B. (1999), University entrepreneurship programs, Lloyd Greif Center for Entrepreneurial Studies, Marshall School of Business, University of Southern California, Los Angeles, CA.

Webb, T., Quince, T. and Wathers, D. (1982), *Small Business Research: The Development of Entrepreneurs*, Aldershot: Gower.

Weber, P. and Schaper, M. (2004), 'Understanding the grey entrepreneur', *Journal of Enterprising Culture*, **12** (2), 147–64.

Wilson, F., Marlino, D. and Kickul, J. (2004), 'Our entrepreneurial future: examining the diverse attitudes and motivations of teens across gender and ethnic identity', *Journal of Developmental Entrepreneurship*, **9** (3), 177–98.

8 Operating an entrepreneurship center in a large and multidisciplinary university: addressing the right issues

Cécile Clergeau and Nathalie Schieb-Bienfait

Since the late 1990s, French higher education establishments have taken a very much closer interest in entrepreneurship, as demonstrated by the inclusion of entrepreneurial training on the curricula and the setting up of entrepreneurial-focused mechanisms. Such initiatives have encountered support from both the governing bodies and public and private institutional partners. Indeed, the development and the concrete implementation of these projects have given rise to challenges and raise various questions pertaining both to the pedagogy and the means of implementation, as well as to the analysis, all of which are the focus of this study. This study draws on the experience that the authors had throughout the setting up of an entrepreneurship resource center in a large French university. This experience was a pioneer in the implementation of such programs in large French universities. It was acknowledged by the French government, and was distinguished as 'House of Entrepreneurship' in July 2004.

There is no common agreement over what constitutes entrepreneurship education or how it is taught (Kirby, 2003), and this lack of consensus, widely described in the current literature (Scott et al., 1998; Vesper, 1982), is one of the first difficulties encountered during the implementation of such a program. This innovative project requires a process of convergence and mutual adjustment concerning its missions and objectives. Researchers, teachers, students and external partners, such as the Chambers of Commerce and Regional Councils, have to be associated with this process, each having its own objectives, its own perception of what is entrepreneurship, its own expectations. Moreover, the success of this process of negotiation depends on the ability of the participants to build the legitimacy of the project. In other words, the particular context of a French university, which is large and multidisciplinary, whose culture is far from entrepreneurship, constrains negotiation not only with people and institutions, but also with cultures, habits and work methods.

After a short description of the context and the historical implementation process, we explicitly acknowledge the realities of the organization surrounding the entrepreneurship center. In other words, the explicit consideration of the organizational mission, priorities, audiences and constraints are seemingly prerequisites when implementing subsequent entrepreneurship education in order to enhance the process of legitimization for entrepreneurship education on the university curricula.

The chapter then goes on to appraise the choices made and what forms of entrepreneurship education seem to match the specific framework of higher education.

The remainder of this chapter focuses on building an analysis and identifying both educational, political issues and the tensions surrounding the implementation of an entrepreneurship education throughout the university. This discussion can help to improve models of good practice in order to develop similar centers and programs.

8.1 The context in which the project emerged

The project emerged in a favorable setting where the many participants had fostered an initial awareness of the interest in enhancing scientific, technical and human potential in the university environment. In practical terms, this meant the appearance of certain isolated initiatives in the different university departments. However, the path leading to the creation of an entrepreneurship resource facility would have been extremely long had it not been for several internal and external factors combining so that such a project could take shape.

8.1.1 A favorable national context

In the late 1990s, a number of new dispositions made the French context more favorable for incubating initiatives within the university environment. In 1998, the Ministry of Education, Research and Technology called on the doctorate academies to implement additional training courses with a view to preparing the future doctors for their professional lives. From this point on, it has been the responsibility of these schools to help diffuse information concerning the sectors of economic activity, to raise corporate awareness and to set up facilities which will make their students' professional futures easier.

One year later, the passing of the Innovation Law reiterated the government's support for entrepreneurship and, above all, provided a legal setting for enhancing university research through venture creation which would now also include researchers/professors.

During the same period, the launch of the French 'Académie de l'Entrepreneuriat' along with the setting up of studies and symposiums (Fayolle and Livian, 1995; Saporta and Verstraete, 1999; Schieb-Bienfait, 2004) provided clarity to the practices and aimed to increase the number of meetings between the various parties involved in the different projects. These meetings could be in the environment of the university or the postgraduate schools, and could stimulate exchange as well as the cross-fertilization of ideas. Along with the creation of an observatory for the pedagogy relating to entrepreneurship oriented practices (OPPE), the observation of the relevant mechanisms became a systemized activity and finally made it possible to contemplate a comparative analysis such as those proposed by Karl Vesper (1985; 1993; Vesper and Gartner, 1994; 1997; 2000).

8.1.2 The local context: a few isolated initiatives within a composite university

The University of Nantes is a multidisciplinary university which comprises 35 000 students and 1500 professors/researchers. It is made up of five parts of different sizes: Human Science and Arts hosts around 1300 students, the Faculty of Science 5600, the Health unit 4200, the Law/Economics/Management house 6300 students and higher institute of technology 3200 students. The university therefore comprises 13 departments, two higher institutes of technology, and an engineering school. There are 73 official research teams and 58 of these have gained recognition from the relevant bodies overseeing research.

8.1.2.1 A composite university
The CRÉACTIV'NANTES project came with the observation that students, teachers and/or researchers were both lacking in access or had unequal access to the entrepreneurial world and its culture. It had been noticed very early on that there was a gap between the training and research units in engineering or the life sciences and the other sciences (social and human sciences, medicine, and so on). As a consequence, it was mainly the doctorate schools in the life science and engineering

science disciplines who held awareness-raising days. Likewise, the engineering school or the higher institutes of technology introduced programs onto the curricula based on raising awareness about entrepreneurship or entrepreneurship courses.

Within the economics/management domain, the Business Administration Institute set up two master's degree courses in collaboration with the science park in order to study the creation of corporate ventures and the development of new products, as well as specific training directed towards the creators of innovative firms.

No training or awareness-raising sessions were put forward for the Departments of Law, Sociology, Modern Languages, Arts, History/Geography, Philosophy, and so on.

This combination of actions was not coordinated at the university level which left the initiative to each component. In addition, the actions were part of a diploma conferring logic; there was no systematic awareness-raising procedure and large parts of the student population were disregarded (notably the undergraduates).

8.1.2.2   The first initiatives   During the course of 1998–99, certain transversal initiatives were undertaken, that is, a grant was attributed to venture-implementing projects targeting the whole student and /or researcher population of every part of the university. The reasons were to provide the expression, the enhancement and perhaps the materialization of ideas and research projects. The proposal was that the people concerned work for several months with teams of students of management, who would help them to carry out feasibility studies prior to the construction of their projects.

Such an initiative got a favorable feedback from university head office. It pointed to a greater opportunity for proposing the setting up of a university center helping both venture creation and the development of activities.

This idea was subsequently chosen by the university authorities and became part of its development strategy which was formalized by its master plan of 1999–2003. This endowed the project with greater clarity and helped to inscribe it within the external political sphere. However, the implementation met with a number of difficulties which were to considerably hamper it.

First, while it was being integrated into a procedure to make it accessible to the socio-economic environment of the university, the project required partnerships, for example, with participants from the various economic spheres or other higher education establishments and in particular the Post Graduate School of Management. Naturally, this project was designed and firmed up under supervision. Nevertheless, it got weighed down by the negotiation and definition of the lines of cooperation that could be envisaged with local participants. This meant that the university did not give any prior thought to the contents, the objectives or the program organization. In fact, it intended to define them as negotiations with its partners progressed. As a consequence, this approach helped spark problems owing to conflicting ideas, cultural differences and conflicts of interest. In addition, misinterpretations were underscored by a certain sluggishness which jeopardized the laying down of the operational features of the project.

Secondly, the project forged *in situ* links among several groups of participants: on the one hand, university people, members of the university board in charge of these negotiations and, on the other hand, the architects and the conveyors of actions already underway that were fostering the entrepreneurship development. The first group were put in charge of the negotiations with the institutional partners, given the 'political' character that this contractual multi-partner project was beginning to assume. The second group, that is, teachers/researchers, masterminded this entrepreneurship initiative and wished to be involved in its definition and implementation. In fact, the bargaining had got underway before the project was really defined. It was therefore the political negotiation that was to give it substance. In other words, the project initiators – who will probably be in charge in the future – were not involved in the definition process. Such a situation led to a certain amount of confusion both in the university and among its partners, and it equally demotivated the keenest teachers.

Faced therefore with a project that was in the process of stalling, the president of the university entrusted the overseeing of the project to a single teacher/researcher who, once having internally and externally sounded out the expectancies of both the university people and the partners, would accomplish the mission of setting up an entrepreneurship resource center that was suitable for the university. By associating the project with one person, the previous situation could now be cleared up, and it above all marked the university's eagerness to avail itself of a clear and original structure.

8.1.3   *The decisive support of the external partners*

In no time at all, CRÉACTIV'NANTES became a strategic project for the university because it was a productive vehicle for the relationship with its socio-economic environment. It got a very warm reception, particularly from the Chamber of Commerce and Industry (CCI) and the Regional Council, and this it equally reciprocated. For the former, it was an opportunity to tighten the links with a key player in the world of higher education and it meant targeting a mixed public. For the latter, this action was a part of the general economic policy on area development and on research enhancement (Henriquez et al., 2001). The Regional Council wanted CRÉACTIV'NANTES to be a pilot scheme that could be diffused to other universities around the region. Several contracts were negotiated and signed with the CCI and the Regional Council in which the setting up of an entrepreneurship resource center featured as a scheduled action.

The commitment of these partners provided the project with sterling advantages. On the one hand, it provided a solution to the problem of mobilizing resources. As a result, the CCI was going to make a mission supervisor available to the resource center, who was specialized in assisting venture creators. On the other hand, this commitment made it possible to build up the network of partners and to move closer to intermediary organizations, firms, entrepreneurs and other players in the economic sector. Getting into already existing networks appeared as a key factor in the center's development. Added to this was the acknowledgement of awareness-raising and teaching operations that it proposed to set in motion. Finally, this commitment made it possible to benefit from the experience of professionals who assisted corporate undertakings. These were part of a committee whose main missions were to define the actions that were undertaken and to pilot the center.

8.2   What to provide for what objectives: nurturing an entrepreneurial culture at university

In September 2002, CRÉACTIV'NANTES came into being. Its main thrust was defining the missions of the center, which were laid down using the three key principles – awareness-raising, training and assisting (Fayolle, 2003; Fayolle and Degeorge, 2003; Sexton and Bowman, 1988; Vesper, 1971). The methods of action were appraised in minute detail, given that making a mission statement in a university setting means taking the constraints and its culture into consideration. Consequently, a number of questions referred more broadly to the missions and modus operandi of a French university.

8.2.1   The underlying paradigms

During the course of 2001–02, an assessment was made on the raising of entrepreneurship awareness and teaching programs. The findings showed a common view, shared among the initiators, that of an entrepreneurship that would uniquely concern:

- the creation of a private firm
- the creation of new technology.

These training schemes perfectly fit into the first of the reference paradigms analysed by Béchard (1994) and Béchard and Toulouse (1998), in order to define entrepreneurship teaching.

This first paradigm relates to business economics (Drucker, 1985). It considers the phenomenon of entrepreneurship from an economic standpoint and, more particularly, from the venture creation standpoint. In practice, this means having curricula that privilege a highly restrictive approach to entrepreneurship. Teaching entrepreneurship is restricted to venture-creating training courses. In addition, the training of creators only refers to the heroic and stereotyped figure of the Schumpeter entrepreneur who creates wealth by seizing new opportunities.

The second paradigm of an entrepreneur society encompasses a wider vision of the entrepreneur by looking at the economic forces of innovation that are being produced discontinuously. It equally includes the psychological and cultural forces that make innovation behaviors and social change possible, and finally considers the organizational forces which are being spun through the networks of exchange. At this point, the socialized entrepreneur takes center stage (Boutillier and Uzunidis, 1999a; 1999b; Granovetter, 1985), and he/she possesses a social capital based on three financial, cognitive and relational domains. This paradigm paves the way for other entrepreneurship teaching objectives.

8.2.2   The underlying debates: missions and realities

Before the idea of creating an entrepreneurship center got the go-ahead and above all before it was internally relayed, it appeared necessary for us to take on board each reservation and query in order to define our subject and our missions.

The diversity of the relevant participants and components (university departments, laboratories, institutes) did not lend itself to either any obvious understanding or any unanimous approval of the project. The issue that underpinned the debates was about the interest in teaching entrepreneurship and about the university's right as a de facto framework for enhancing entrepreneurial behavior. Such an issue fuelled many a debate. For example, some people felt that these missions do not fall within the scope of the education system, mainly because this system would face certain limitations, especially when it promoted the autonomy and creativity that are required with entrepreneurship. They considered that the institutionalization of education means that the spirit of enterprise is impractical in a university setting. In the Departments of Human and Social Science some teachers were not forthcoming in their appreciation of a project which bore such a likeness to economic and even business-related concerns. A plethora of questions concerned the suitability of the missions that the CRÉACTIV'NANTES center had set itself and the provision of services it proposed. Moreover it questioned the predominance of economic logic in the method, that is, training students in the shortest time so that they created ventures. The diversity of the missions in the pipeline had to be more explicit so as to be presented and above all understood by our interlocutors.

At this juncture, it became clear that there was a need to include items in the center missions such as the students' orientations and their professional aims (the wage earning path versus the entrepreneurial path), the matter of employability (intrapreneurship) and, finally, the backing up of projects likely to lead to undertaking ventures (associations, and so on). In addition, it appeared judicious to us that the means of intervention proposed by the center should not just be limited to an economic vocation being linked to venture creation. It should equally endeavor to make a large number of students appreciate the importance of entrepreneurs (Saporta and Verstraete, 1999), notably by enhancing the status that entrepreneurial activities enjoy (Filion, 1990; 1991; Gasse, 1985; 1992). As a matter of fact, to favor an entrepreneurial education is first and foremost to arouse intention and afterward to seek the passing from intention to the entrepreneurial act.

8.3   Orientations and choices made

By extending the objectives pursued, the question was raised about the training provision segmentation. This made it possible to match the diversity of the public to the needs observed within the different components of the university. The main idea that was chosen was to design a program of actions and interventions comprising different levels. This would familiarize the students with this subject and allow them to discover entrepreneurial models in order to boost their will to undertake the program.

The general schemes were declined in such a way as to fit the specific backgrounds and professional orientations, that is, researcher/entrepreneur, law student or psychology student, the self-employed, the pharmacy student/pharmacist, and so on. Parallel to this, it seemed advisable to our minds to conceive the means likely to foster the development of the students' entrepreneurial capacities.

Entrepreneurial teaching generally follows two main objectives: acting on intention and acting on action. As regards this type of teaching, the CRÉACTIV'NANTES project aims at enriching the students' interest. On the one hand, this bears in mind the youthful age of the mainly student public, of whom only a small number will supposedly launch into a venture at the end of their university studies. On the other hand, considering the cultural gap that exists between the world of university and that surrounding a venture undertaking, the objectives focus more on entrepreneurial culture than on the implementation of an entrepreneurial project. This leaves the task of assisting the relevant projects to the specialized organizations. The objective therefore is not the creation of entrepreneurs nor the inception of new ventures, but the development of the students' willingness to become entrepreneurs or intrapreneurs within any type of organizations, public, private or association (Saporta and Verstraete, 1999).

8.3.1   *An original positioning: a resource center at the service of all the participants*
Given that the route towards entrepreneurship is often a privileged one due to an access to an entrepreneurial culture via family agencies[1] or friends, or by previous personal

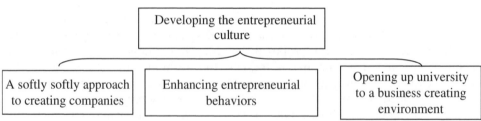

Figure 8.1   The lines of development of the entrepreneurial culture

ventures, CRÉACTIV'NANTES operates by pursuing its prime objective of incorpo-
rating entrepreneurship into both the culture and outlook of students and teachers/
researchers. This objective is divided into sub-objectives as in Figure 8.1.

The multidisciplinarity of the university was a definite asset right from the moment the
CRÉACTIV'NANTES project was conceived. In fact, it made it necessary to consider the
cultural diversity, the diversity of the ideas and common conceptions, and it enhanced
the need for adaptation. CRÉACTIV'NANTES must be a service that is common to the
whole university but must be tailored to the multiplicity of the teaching, the research, the
culture and the background. This means being constantly receptive to the expectancies of
teachers, researchers and students when designing such a program.

8.3.2   What CRÉACTIV'NANTES offers
CRÉACTIV'NANTES strives to make its activities available to all members of the university, identical for each and everyone but suited to all. These activities are all developed
in association with the CCI, which provides a logistic and educational backup as well as
bringing in its knowledge of the entrepreneurial environment.

8.3.2.1   Roundtable discussions   CRÉACTIV'NANTES holds roundtable sessions
between university people (students, teachers and researchers) and entrepreneurs with a
view to creating a type of osmosis between both worlds. Our aim in this is to acculturate
students in respect to entrepreneurial culture (Drucker, 1985; Fayolle, 2003; Gasse, 1985).
These encounters take place with the agreement, and more often at the request, of teachers who teach a small number of students in a particular year of study. Another objective
is to get in speakers who are legitimate participants in the students' view. In addition, every
effort is made to invite entrepreneurs who have had university training and possibly in the
same subject as the students and teachers who are attending.

The stage is not set so much therefore for a conference as for an exchange. This has the
major advantage in that students are entitled to ask personal questions 'Do you really
have the time to drop your children off at school?', 'Do you have the feeling you work too
hard?', 'What does your husband think when you tell him your plans?', 'Why didn't your
first venture come to anything?', 'Where did you get the money to get going? Banks don't
really trust young people like us.' Such questions make it possible to break down the
stereotyped image of a heroic entrepreneur being totally aloof and inaccessible. The
encounters help the student to get bearings notably on the function of the entrepreneur
but also on the world of work. These meetings represent real places of exchange between
individuals who come from different worlds and who do not know each other.

Such meetings equally develop students' self awareness, that is, the way in which they perceive themselves and their awareness of relating to the models to which they have identified themselves (Filion, 1994; 1990). In this way, the entrepreneur models from which students can draw their inspiration probably play a paramount role, and the sooner the face-to-face encounter takes place on the course, the more time the student can lend thought to what he or she wants to do and to therefore envisage his or her future.

Finally, such meetings can make the students aware, and even change their conceptions, of the relationship between the firm and themselves. When the students discover that being an entrepreneur can forge their professional paths and is accessible to them, they may contemplate this alternative to being a wage earner. In this perspective, we can distinguish 'self-enterprise' on one side, and 'entrepreneurs for their own lives', on the other side.

As the project has developed, the active participation of teachers as well as their support system have become a cornerstone of the project, and this is framed with an objective of enrichment and cultural development, given the weight of authority that the teachers' opinions being to bear on a pending issue. More generally, it has seemed indispensable that the university environment should play this role of promoter in order to make others aware that 'being an entrepreneur' is a path that can be followed and by basing itself on the diffusion of models of local entrepreneurs. The university had every interest in subscribing to such a method. Apart from the aim of downplaying the procedure for starting a business by helping both students and researchers to broaden their horizons when they meet entrepreneurs of 'that ilk', such encounters also help the university to integrate better with its environment. The entrepreneurs readily fall in with this situation and uncover an aspect of the university and the world of teaching that they were previously unaware of. They therefore came over as more open and more dynamic, but these meetings demonstrate above all that the university possesses resources, know-how and skills which can equally be assets for the companies themselves.

8.3.2.2 The workshops   A second main feature of the CRÉACTIV'NANTES project is the workshops, that is, 12-hour sessions (suggestion boxes) or 21-hour sessions (tool boxes), during which the students and researchers assess their entrepreneurial capabilities, their professional paths and the place such a project has in them (Table 8.1). In the tool box sessions, they learn about the fundamental elements that carry through both the venture-creating project and the drafting of a business plan.

The choice was made at first to enhance the multidisciplinarity of the university:

- The groups comprise 15 people, students and researchers from different backgrounds. As a result, an engineering student liaises with a management student and a sociology lecturer.
- All kinds of projects are considered, ranging from the creation of a small private venture to a student service association.

Naturally, attendance at these workshops is voluntary, although a training attendance certificate is delivered at the end of the session, at the students' request.

Initially, these workshops were reserved only for students or teachers with an idea for a project. This did not mean studying the project with them, but assisting them upstream in their appraisals. Having come to an agreement with the project partners, particularly

Table 8.1   CRÉACTIV'NANTES workshop schedule

Suggestion box: 4 discovery modules	Tool box: 7 operational modules
• Different ways of being an entrepreneur • My entrepreneurial capabilities: knowing myself better to start a business more efficiently • To approach idea research idea techniques • The project method	• Methodologies and project implementation tools • Knowing one's economic environment and the market • The economic viability of one's project • Finding the financial backing • Laying down one's commercial approach • Choosing one's status and the administrative procedures • Presenting one's business plan

in the CCI and science park, each bearer of a defined project would be directed towards an ad hoc help structure. In fact, it was more a question of pre-incubating the project than actually providing help to achieve it.

Since 2004, suggestion box meetings have been held to bring in people who do not have a project but who are asking themselves questions, 'fairly tempted by this adventure' without 'really knowing why'.

8.3.2.3   Entrepreneurship Day   Entrepreneurship Day provides a meeting place for entrepreneurs, their advisors, students and teachers/researchers. This event is hosted in collaboration with the Chamber of Commerce and Industry who call on their own network of entrepreneurs to attend.

There are three themes running through the conferences: research enhancement via the creation of firms, the creation and acquisition of firms and the creation of social economic firms.

The game-like aspect which attracts the students comes from the activities surrounding the different subjects, ranging from the analysis of one's entrepreneurial capabilities to the mastering of a brainstorming session via talking-head forums. What is striking is the theme that has most interested the students in all these workshops is 'my capabilities of undertaking a venture': a hundred or so of them took turns to meet a psychologist, took tests, or became involved in discussions related to the notions of entrepreneurial capabilities. The interest aroused by this workshop shows that the creation of a firm is actually perceived by the students as being first and foremost a personal adventure. The 'technical' aspects involved in undertaking a venture continue to be tools at the service of this personal adventure.

8.3.2.4   A personalized reception   CRÉACTIV'NANTES is situated in the middle of the main university campus. The consular project leader is on duty there on a part-time basis and can meet students who present their projects to him, and inform him of their doubts, while benefiting from his advice. This leader had never seen any students in the CCI before, and the fact that he has an office on site allows students to overcome any reservations they may have, that is, the students feel less intimidated and they do not feel compelled to come up with a result nor even have to implement the project in order to benefit

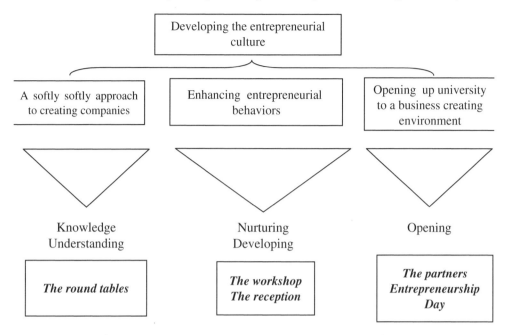

Figure 8.2   CRÉACTIV'NANTES program

from this advice. Geographical proximity thus creates social proximity. The project leader learns about the university world as he goes out to meet teachers/researchers, organizes workshops for students who see him on campus and see his name on the programs. In fact, he closely contributes to a process of mutual provision that will gradually break down barriers and draw in an increasing number of students seeking advice.

8.3.2.5 Synthesis   Figure 8.2 synthesizes the CRÉACTIV'NANTES educational program.

8.4   Teaching, questioning and outlook
CRÉACTIV'NANTES is a relevant example of an entrepreneurial project being developed within a large public body. This was initially handled by a few isolated teachers/researchers and depended on different components. It was necessary to think out the structuring of this ground-breaking project, and to prepare the conditions for implementing it. In addition it was necessary to clearly define its missions and objectives and, above all, to share them out. Such steps are time-consuming as the project falls within an area of tension linked to the relatively antagonistic nature of the administrative university's system and the entrepreneurial actions. As a matter of fact, this CRÉACTIV'NANTES project requires a certain degree of autonomy, a propensity to innovate, to seek out new directions, and a feel for action. It also exhibits an experimental approach, whereas the university always naturally acts in a system of cultivation (March, 1988). As a result, there is a marked confrontation of attributable conditions (allotting existing resources, arbitration between projects, between components and the choice of functioning) and creative conditions (project development, new behaviors, the search for new resources).

What is more, as the project uses existing training facilities and operating procedures, it disrupts the current budgetary and administrative rulings and thus calls for new regulations (Reynaud, 1989).

Finally CRÉACTIV'NANTES is part of the dynamics surrounding a network of players. It was initiated by a group of teachers who had already tested out pedagogical projects related to entrepreneurship and who therefore maintain a relationship with the network such as corporate undertaking assistance structures.[2] It is part of a university action program and as such is discussed and negotiated with the institutional partners of the university. CRÉACTIV'NANTES will therefore be discussed, negotiated and designed among the university and its partners at different levels, that is, between the various departments at university head office in the same way as the more or less decentralized units and departments. The innovative, experimental and reticular nature of the project has subjected it to tensions which have surfaced in the operational aspects surrounding the implementation and the questioning of the educational issues.

8.4.1   A reticular negotiation

As happens with the numerous innovations that are undertaken within a large organization, there have been many areas of negotiation for the project from the outset and these function according to their own rules (cf. Figure 8.3).

The first area of negotiation occurred between the teachers masterminding the project and university head office. The teachers sought to extend and institutionalize their initiatives. While head office recognized the interest in having an entrepreneurship center, it felt

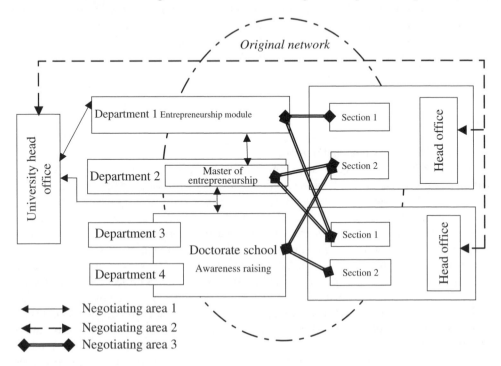

Figure 8.3   The project negotiation areas

that the initiating teachers lacked the legitimacy required to run what should be a real common service in relation to their colleagues from other university departments. Despite an acknowledgement of the aptitudes of the project initiators as regards entrepreneurship, the university feared that they were illegitimately turning what it considered to be a common project into an establishment project status. This area of negotiation belongs to internal politics. All the renegotiating that takes place within it revolves around the power-sharing associated with an innovation and to the spheres of uncertainty that it creates. This was according to the analysis made in organizational sociology (Crozier and Friedberg, 1977; Friedberg, 1995).

A second area of negotiation opened up between university head office and its institutional partners (the CCI and the Regional Council): the university is very keen to be part of a strong dynamics of collaboration with these partners. In fact, it suffers from being seen as a little out of step due to the thousand years in which it has traditionally created and spread culture and knowledge as opposed to the modern need for professionalizing its students. It also lives in a world of budget squeezing and encounters difficulties in initiating original programs by itself (Musselin, 2001). In addition, the university was then involved in an establishment project process which it was finding hard both to develop and implement. As for the institutional partners, each had its own line of thought. The Regional Council and the CCI saw venture creation as an important tool for local economic development, the utility of which was proportionate to the rate of unemployment. The Regional Council already pursues actions in favor of PhD students and is eager that new professional horizons will be opened for these students. In addition, it endeavors to enhance all initiatives in favor of technological development. The CCI sees the university as a cultivator of future venture creators whom they will consult. This area of negotiation therefore comprises external politics.

A third area of negotiation is already open: this concerns the teachers in charge of up and running entrepreneurship programs as well as the institutional partners with whom they were working. In this way, the area of negotiation may be described as one containing the original network of the CRÉACTIV'NANTES project. This area of negotiation is also that of the intrapreneurs, that is, all the teachers/researchers whom it mobilizes who have masterminded entrepreneurial programs. Within this area, the participants know each other well and there is an atmosphere of trust. Certain teachers wish for the institutionalization of, a sometimes, already longstanding cooperation and are eager to play a key role in the process. Others do not wish to commit themselves and consider that the decentralized programs that they have already developed are enough in themselves. All of them are well aware that everything will be worked out 'at the higher levels', and this probably explains the qualms that certain people express about investing themselves in the general program. The relations between participants in this third area of negotiation and their hierarchies have little in common. The employees of the institutional partners display a greater coherence while those of the university advance in a dispersed way.

In a three-dimensional negotiating process (see Figure 8.3), there is an obvious risk of the project being bogged down if the three networks remain impenetrable. The multiplicity of the participants, the levels and the rationale behind the actions require both a mobilization of the three networks around a single project and that everyone's aspirations converge. The project leader here fulfils a real intrapreneurship function as described by Breton and Wintrobe (1982), which means network mobilization and confidence boosting that will facilitate transactions. The project leader plays the role of arbitrator (Pettigrew, 1987) and this implies a firm influential base in the university in general and among the network of the concerned participants in particular.

Legitimacy is a key factor in the confidence and success of any negotiating process. The extremely feeble legitimacy of the university had been observed when it was a matter of entrepreneurial issues. As a result, the partners held doubts about its capacity to implement a relevant and viable program of this type. The university is too often considered to be a complete stranger to any economic realities (Musselin, 2001). It was therefore necessary to initiate a process of entrepreneurial legitimation for a university (Bourgeois and Nizet, 1995). Bearing this in mind, the personal social networks of the university people already involved in entrepreneurial programs and those of the project leader exerted a discrete but decisive influence. For example, such programs led to interaction with business chiefs or management representatives whose backing in the fine tuning of the action programs and/or whose personal commitment to directly involve themselves in the project to monitor students or feature in seminars helped create credibility, confidence and legitimation.

8.4.2   *A tension-filled program*
The CRÉACTIV'NANTES project construction process bears all the characteristics of political decision-making, that is, a process of convergence and mutual adjustments among players who possess different sets of values, as well as relative autonomy and their own power (Monnier, 1987). In the same way, CRÉACTIV'NANTES is more the result than the prior condition for the implementation process, a compromise between the different types of logic of action, interests and sets of value whose stability and development depend on its regulation.

CRÉACTIV'NANTES tries to strike a balance between the various tensions that are outlined in Figure 8.4, that is, tensions inside the logic of action (economic versus educational), the conceptions of the entrepreneur, political maneuvering, bankrolling, the debates surrounding the university's missions and the respective know-how from the different parties involved.

Such a balance is intrinsically unstable and requires that those piloting the project furnish a substantial investment in an almost never-ending process of adaptation and optimization. The joint regulation, symbolized by a piloting committee pooling the three main project partners aims to be the selected method of adaptation and compromise.

8.4.3   *Constructing legitimacy*
As remarkably emphasized by Reynaud (1989) in his theory of social regulation, in ground-breaking processes the dynamics of adjustment hinges on the capability of the participants to build legitimacy, an external legitimacy in relation to the result and an internal legitimacy in connection to the group that it is helping to train.

Constructing the legitimacy of CRÉACTIV'NANTES calls various aspects into question:

1.   What are the results that one can hope to attain? What priorities must the center give itself? As a result, it appears necessary to set out the priorities, to avail oneself of a clear and shared strategy with precise objectives that are fixed annually (the master

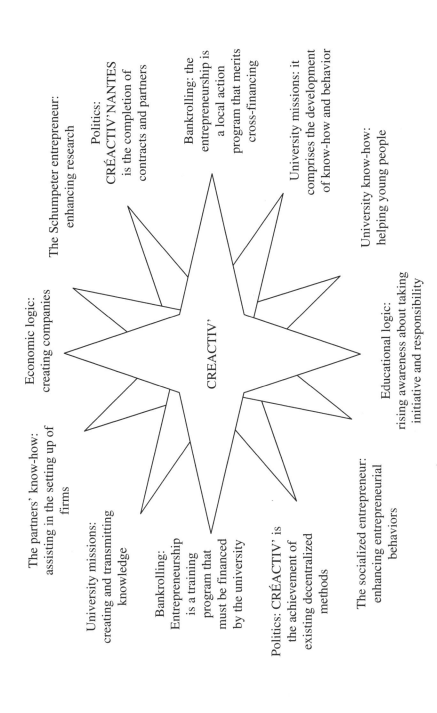

The partners' know-how:
assisting in the setting up of
firms

University missions:
creating and transmitting
knowledge

Bankrolling:
Entrepreneurship
is a training
program that
must be financed
by the university

Politics: CRÉACTIV' is
the achievement of
existing decentralized
methods

The socialized entrepreneur:
enhancing entrepreneurial
behaviors

Economic logic:
creating companies

CREACTIV'

Educational logic:
rising awareness about taking
initiative and responsibility

The Schumpeter entrepreneur:
enhancing research

Politics:
CRÉACTIV'NANTES
is the completion of
contracts and partners

Bankrolling: the
entrepreneurship is
a local action
program that merits
cross-financing

University missions: it
comprises the development
of know-how and behavior

University know-how:
helping young people

Figure 8.4   The tensions imparted to the CRÉACTIV'NANTES project

plan) in order to have an accurate knowledge of the actions undertaken and their effectiveness. Such a question refers to the activity pointers (students having being contacted or firms set up). These prove extremely painstaking, as they imply a long-term vision from the partners that may exceed their own work cycles. This question of results directly impacts the educational questions. According to the set targets, the pedagogics that will be developed are more or less directed to the awareness-raising and the enhancement of responsibility and initiative behaviors. On the other hand, the pedagogics will be oriented towards the technical feature involved in setting up a company. This will then make it possible to target the means towards the really motivated students and researchers who have projects that deserve due consideration.

2.   What role does the center play in a system assisting venture creation? Is it situated far upstream in order to attract this university component of the 1.6 million French people who say that they dream about starting a business one day? Is it more downstream and focused on students and researchers who have projects, with the risk of having to painstakingly share skills with partners originally assisting in the venture creation?

3.   What role does the center have in the university? As an experimental process, CRÉACTIV'NANTES went a whole year without any legal or accountable status. As the project had been accepted, the university decided to place it within an 'economics-management' section of the university. This confers it with many advantages but it could nevertheless deprive it of its legitimacy as a common service. It forces the center to boost its efforts towards the teachers with their aforementioned strategic role in the diffusion of an entrepreneurial culture.

4.   What motivations have the project bearers got? Does the university legitimate this choice of activity? It is common knowledge that the civil service is a huge machine which discourages intrapreneurship (Clergeau, 1994). Given the administrative cumbersomeness, the complete lack of professional acknowledgement of the commitments, and the paucity of means, piloting such projects requires a heavy internal influence and an abundance of energy from the operational team. Apart from the pioneering spirit or vocation, the timelessness of such projects means that mechanisms are put in place so that the team sees its commitment being recognized and legitimated, compared with the career prospects offered by the university system.

8.5   Conclusion
Apart from sharing the experiences, this study pursued the objective of analysing the rationale and tensions underlying the definition and then the operation of an entrepreneurship center within a large university. The growth in the number of facilities of this type in France and the encouragement that they get from the government (with the setting up of a 'House of Entrepreneurship') will rapidly prompt questions pertaining to assessment. Indeed, to our minds, understanding the rationale of the participants and the underlying tensions which accompanied the implementation is already a necessary step towards assessment.

This chapter owes more to action research than to case studies because the authors were also involved in the project. And here lie the interest and the drawbacks in this. Given that they were full participants in the CRÉACTIV'NANTES project, the authors pinpointed the tensions from its earliest stages and were compelled to negotiate in a framework with different systems. Nevertheless, such action taken within a studied reality makes any generalization of the analyses difficult.

French university culture was previously hardly open to this type of project which was at variance with the overriding interpretation of missions conducted at the university. Considering the strategic position of teachers in the innovation diffusion process in education and training and of the diversity of the possible explicative paradigms,[3] their associating themselves with the project is a sine qua non condition for its success. For this reason, the commitment by the university is a prerequisite for launching a transversal project of entrepreneurship awareness-raising.

However, university supervision also brings administrative cumbersomeness which does not fit with the organization of the project team at the center. This is the final tension at CRÉACTIV'NANTES, that is, speaking about entrepreneurship, raising awareness about assuming responsibility and running an innovative project within a centralized and bureaucratic structure. Such a project requires flexibility and autonomy to meet the constraints of project management in an open network. For this reason the setting up of a 'House of Entrepreneurship' has made it possible to overturn certain routines and hesitations, and is seemingly, to our minds, a significant vehicle for the development of university structures.

For Timmons (1989), entrepreneurship is the ability to create and build something from practically nothing. It is initiating, doing, achieving, and building . . . rather than watching, analyzing or describing. It is the ability to sense an opportunity where others see chaos, contradiction and confusion (Timmons, 1989). According to this consensual definition of entrepreneurship, entrepreneurship education requires teaching methods more concerned with practice and more oriented towards action (Hills and Morris, 1998). Nurturing entrepreneurial culture at the university requires organizations that encourage cooperation and coordination, networking, teamwork and creativity. This means creating learning contexts which are more flexible, less structured, and more real-world orientated. Surprisingly, these new educating approaches have been supported by both our external partners and our colleagues. The need for educational flexibility meets the need for flexibility in the negotiation process. It becomes an opportunity to make the project legitimate and to consolidate its evolution.

Nevertheless, this nurturing orientation provokes questions about the program's evaluation. Educational programs have to be results oriented at different temporal levels, in order to take into account the partners' own evaluation procedures. For instance, political partners are more short-term oriented than the university. Moreover, outcome measures should be introduced at the individual, organizational and regional levels. Our experience calls for a more in-depth research in this area.

In July 2004, CRÉACTIV'NANTES was designated the title of 'House of Entrepreneurship' by the ministry in charge of research. Such acknowledgement by the government is the final step in the legitimation process that has been in progress for several months. The success of educational initiatives, albeit scattered, had highlighted the opportunity for such a project. Above all, it allowed CRÉACTIV'NANTES to be firmly anchored in an institutional network that was also an efficient participant. A significant advantage was created by the university governing board becoming aware of the need to develop an entrepreneurial culture and the inclusion of CRÉACTIV'NANTES into the establishment project process. This, therefore, could be used to implement the internal process of legitimation.

Notes

1. Bygrave (1997) states that in Babson College (US), more than half the entrepreneurship students come from families who run their own businesses.
2. Science park, foundations, venture networking, confederations of industries, young entrepreneurs associations.
3. Epidemiological model, social interactionism model, institutionalization model and action research model.

References

Béchard, J.P. (1994), 'Les grandes questions de recherche en entrepreneurship et éducation', *Cahier de recherche HEC Montréal*, n°94–11–02.
Béchard, J.-P. and Toulouse, J.-M. (1998), 'Validation of a didactic model for the analysis of training objectives in entrepreneurship', *Journal of Business Venturing*, **13**, 317–32.
Bourgeois, E. and Nizet, J. (1995), *Pression et légitimation*, Paris: PUF.
Boutillier, S. and Uzunidis, D. (1999a), 'Entrepreneur, esprit d'entreprise et économie: un enseignement supérieur basé sur le tryptique Structures-Comportements-Performances', *Actes du premier congrès, Académie de l'entrepreneuriat*, Lille.
Boutillier, S. and Uzunidis, D. (1999b), *La légende de l'entrepreneur*, Paris: La découverte, Syros.
Breton, A. and Wintrobe, R. (1982), *The Logic of Bureaucratic Conduct*, New York: Cambridge University Press.
Bygrave, W.D. (1997), 'The entrepreneurial process', in W.D. Bygrave (ed.), *The Portable MBA in Entrepreneurship*, New York: John Wiley and Sons.
Clergeau, C. (1994), Bureaucraties publiques et innovation, éléments d'une analyse économique, thèse pour le Doctorat en Sciences Economiques, Université de Nantes.
Crozier, M. and Friedberg, E. (1977), *L'acteur et le système*, Paris: Le Seuil, coll Points.
Drucker, P.F. (1985), *Innovation and Entrepreneurship: Practices and Principles*, New-York: Harper and Row.
Fayolle, A. (2003), 'Using the theory of planned behaviour in assessing entrepreneurship teaching program: exploratory research approach', *13th IntEnt Conference Proceedings*, Grenoble, 7–10 September.
Fayolle, A. and Degeorge, J.-G. (2003), 'Role of entrepreneurship teaching on some entrepreneurial intention determinants: exploratory study', *13th IntEnt Conference Proceedings*, Grenoble, 7–10 September.
Fayolle, A. and Livian, Y.F. (1995), 'Entrepreneurial behavior of French engineers: an exploratory study', in S. Birley and I. MacMillan (eds), *International Entrepreneurship*, London: Routledge, pp. 202–28.
Filion, L.J. (1990), 'Vision and relations: elements for an entrepreneurial metamodel', in Neil C. Churchill et al. (eds), *Frontiers of entrepreneurship research*, Wellesley, MA: Babson College, pp. 57–71.
Filion, L.J. (1991), 'L'éducation en entrepreneuriat. Sur quoi devrions nous mettre l'accent: le médium ou le message?', *Revue Organization*, **1** (1), Autumn.
Filion, L.J. (1994), 'Compétences à concevoir et espace de soi: éléments de soutien au système d'activité entrepreneuriale', *Cahier de recherche*, n°94–10–02.
Friedberg, E. (1995), *Le pouvoir et la règle*, Paris: Le Seuil, coll. Points.
Gasse, Y. (1985), 'A strategy for the promotion and identification of potential entrepreneurs at the secondary school level', *Frontiers of Entrepreneurship Research*, Wellesley, MA: Babson College, pp. 538–59.
Gasse, Y. (1992), 'Pour une éducation plus entrepreneuriale: quelques voies et moyens', *Colloque l'éducation et l'entrepreneuriat*, centre entrepreneuriat, Québec, Trois Rivières.
Granovetter, M. (1985), 'Economic action and social structure: the problem of embeddedness', *American of Journal of Sociology*, **91**, 481–510.
Henriquez, C., Verheul, I., Van der Knaap, I. and Bischoff, C. (2001), 'Determinants of entrepreneurship in France: policies, institutions and culture', Institute for Development Strategies Indiana University, available at www.spea.indiana.edu/ids/pdfholder/ISSN-01-4.pdf, accessed in March 2005.
Hills, G.E. and Morris, M.H. (1998), 'Entrepreneurship education, a conceptual model and review', in M.G. Scott, P. Rosa and H. Klandt (eds), *Educating Entrepreneurs for Wealth Creation*, Aldershot: Ashgate.
Kirby, D.A. (2003), *Entrepreneurship*, Maidenhead: McGraw-Hill.
March, J.G. (1988), *Decisions and Organizations*, New York: Blackwell.
Monnier, E. (1987), *Evaluation de l'action des pouvoirs publics*, Paris: Economica.
Musselin, C. (2001), *La longue marche des universités françaises*, Paris: PUF.
Pettigrew, A. (1987), 'Context and action in the transformation of the firm', *Journal of Management Studies*, **24** (6), 649–70.
Reynaud, J.D. (1989), *Les règles du jeu. L'action collective et la régulation sociale*, Paris: Armand Collin.
Saporta, B. and Verstraete, T. (1999), 'Réflexions pour une pédagogie de l'entrepreneuriat dans les composantes en sciences de gestion des Universités françaises', *Actes du premier congrès de l'Académie de l'Entrepreneuriat*, Lille.
Schieb-Bienfait, N. (2004), 'A real world project driven approach, a pilot experience in a graduate enterprise programme: ten years on', *International Journal of Entrepreneurship and Small Business*, **1** (1/2), 176–91.

Scott, M.G., Rosa, P. and Klandt, H. (eds) (1998), *Educating Entrepreneurs for Wealth Creation*, Aldershot: Ashgate.

Sexton, D.L. and Bowman, N.B. (1988), 'Validation of an innovative teaching approach for entrepreneurship courses', *American Journal of Small Business*, **12** (3), 11–18.

Timmons, J.A. (1989), *The Entrepreneurial Mind: Winning Strategies For Starting, Renewing and Harvesting New and Existing Ventures*, Andover, MA: Brick House.

Vesper, K.H. (1971), 'Venture initiation courses in U.S. business schools', *Academy of Management Journal*, **6**, 14–19.

Vesper, K.H. (1982), 'Research on education for entrepreneurship', in C. Kent, D. Sexton and K. Vesper (eds), *Encyclopedia of Entrepreneurship*, Englewood Cliffs, NJ: Prentice-Hall.

Vesper, K.H. (1985), *Entrepreneurship Education*, Wellesley, MA: Babson College.

Vesper, K.H. (1993), *Entrepreneurship Education*, Washington: University of Washington.

Vesper, K.H. and Gartner, W.B. (1994), 'Experiments in entrepreneurship education: successes and failures', *Journal of Business Venturing*, **9**, 179–87.

Vesper, K.H. and Gartner, W.B. (1997), 'Measuring progress in entrepreneurship education', *Journal of Business Venturing*, **12**, 403–21.

Vesper, K.H. and Gartner, W.B. (2000), *University Entrepreneurship Programs – 1999*, University of Southern California, Marshall School of Business, Lloyd Greif Center for Entrepreneurial Studies, Los Angeles.

9 Interdisciplinary approaches in entrepreneurship education programs
Frank Janssen, Valérie Eeckhout and Benoît Gailly

Introduction

The last 30 years have seen a growing interest from the scientific community in entrepreneurship, driven by the increasing dynamic role of small and medium-sized enterprises (SMEs) in job creation and innovation, and boosted by the emergence of new business environments, new technology and globalization (Fiet, 2000a). In parallel, a growing number of entrepreneurship education programs (EEPs) have appeared, first in the United States where, today, more than 2200 courses are offered at over 1600 schools (Katz, 2003; Kuratko, 2005), and then, more recently, in Europe, where most programs have been created in the last decade (Klandt, 2004).

This late reaction from the European educational system, in particular its universities, can be explained by the relative absence of entrepreneurial culture in Europe (Commission of the European Communities, 2003), where entrepreneurial careers are often not perceived by students as an attractive path. Indeed, most (academic) programs tend to promote low-risk professional tracks and therefore scare students away from career choices where failure risks are perceived as significant. Moreover, many in the academic world still believe that entrepreneurs are born 'gifted' and therefore, that entrepreneurship cannot be taught. Yet numerous studies have demonstrated that entrepreneurship involves skills and abilities that can be developed and learnt (Gorman et al., 1997). Finally, EEPs are sometimes perceived as not being grounded in a solid theoretical basis and therefore not 'scientific' enough to be taught in universities.

Despite those obstacles to the emergence of academic EEP, the educational system and, in particular, universities now play a significant role in the emergence and diffusion of entrepreneurial culture (Fayolle, 2000). It strongly influences how students are able to detect, evaluate and capture attractive value-creation opportunities. Education is therefore a core element of entrepreneurial spirit and initiatives. This, coupled with the growing importance of SMEs in their socio-economic environment, has pushed a growing number of European universities to develop EEPs.

Today, entrepreneurship tends to be recognized as an academic field (Bruyat and Julien, 2000; Cooper, 2003). It has an important scientific community that has produced a significant body of research (Acs and Audretsch, 2003; McGrath, 2003). To convince oneself of this, one should look at the numerous conferences organized throughout the world, as well as at the 44 Anglophone academic journals dedicated to entrepreneurship (Katz, 2003). Because of unclear boundaries with other fields and a certain lack of consensus about a shared paradigm (Bruyat and Julien, 2003), some authors tend to think that it is a blossoming field that cuts across different disciplines (Acs and Audretsch, 2003). It can also be argued that the field is inclusive and eclectic (Low, 2001) and that it is too heterogeneous to be reduced to a single definition (Verstraete and Fayolle, 2004). It is certainly larger than the single 'business creation' perspective. It also includes opportunity seeking, risk-taking, value creation, innovation aspects. Kuratko (2005, p. 578) argues that ' "an entrepreneurial perspective" can be developed in individuals. This perspective can be exhibited inside or outside an organization, in profit or not-for-profit enterprises, and in business or nonbusiness activities for the purpose of bringing forth creative ideas.' From an educational point of view, this means that entrepreneurship education cannot limit itself to firm creation, but has to be broadened to the development of an entrepreneurial spirit which consists of, in business or in any other human activity, identifying opportunities and gathering different resources in order to create richness which meets a solvable demand (Albert and Marion, 1998).

Nascent or mature, entrepreneurship as an academic field is by nature interdisciplinary, and therefore requires adapted teaching methods. Several universities have tried to develop such educational approaches, dedicated to the specific objectives and requirements of their EEP. However, only a few universities appear to have adopted educational approaches that are truly interdisciplinary. Indeed, universities are often locked into their disciplinary structures while entrepreneurship classes are school-specific and only offered to students from one or, sometimes, two disciplines. In this context, the aim of this chapter will be to discuss the link between entrepreneurship and interdisciplinary teaching approaches, through the case analysis of a cross-faculty EEP run since 1997 in the Université catholique de Louvain. Hence this chapter tries to contribute to an answer to one of the criticisms towards entrepreneurship education literature recently stressed by Béchard and Grégoire (2005). Because this literature very seldom borrows concepts or theories from disciplines other than management (Gorman et al., 1997), these authors underline the necessity to develop research and expertise at the intersection between entrepreneurship and education science.

We discuss in the next section the potential learning objectives of EEP and the corresponding teaching strategies involved. We then review, on the basis of Rege Colet's conceptual framework, the link between entrepreneurship and the interdisciplinary approaches it involves. We discuss this aspect through the analysis of an existing EEP and in particular its interdisciplinary features. We conclude with a discussion of the entrepreneurial impact of the interdisciplinary EEP.

9.1 Objectives of EEP and corresponding teaching and learning strategies

Entrepreneurship education programs have been the subject of academic research for more than a decade (Gartner and Vesper, 1994; Johannisson, 1991), with results differing according to the specific objectives of each EEP (Gibb, 1992). Fayolle (1999) classifies EEPs into three categories, corresponding to distinct types of objectives in terms of student impact.

The first category relates to *mobilization* programs. These EEPs target the general student population and aim at increasing their entrepreneurial spirit and culture, as well as exposing them to entrepreneurial experiences and opportunities. They are often run in management and technology schools, mostly at undergraduate level.

The second category relates to *entrepreneurial training* programs. These EEPs target students who aspire, or have the intention, to launch entrepreneurial activities, but who have not yet identified a specific business opportunity. Entrepreneurship education programs in that category aim at providing students with the specific skills and abilities of entrepreneurship, in order to allow them to develop their entrepreneurial attitude and aptitude, and later to be prepared to create or buy a new business or to develop new activities within an existing firm.

The last category relates to *entrepreneurial support* programs. These EEPs target students who have already identified a potential business opportunity, and who are looking for targeted and/or personalized assistance and advice to help them capture that specific opportunity. They tend to involve older, more experienced, students and typically involve some kind of upfront selections of the project, or students, that will be supported.

An adapted educational approach corresponds to each of these categories. Mobilization programs are mostly taught through traditional teaching methods, where teachers 'tell' students about entrepreneurship. Such programs typically involve learning about the models, concepts and theories that have been developed in that field, with the level of conceptualization and theory which is a prerequisite of any university-based approach (Fiet, 2000b). Beyond those, such EEP can help students to discover what launching a business means, and whether it could be a potential career option for them (Fayolle, 1999). As a consequence, such EEP also typically involve case studies and testimonies of entrepreneurs.

Entrepreneurial training programs, while also involving the models, concepts and theories of entrepreneurship, must go beyond traditional knowledge 'transmission-reception' teaching approaches. Indeed they must confront students with reality in order to develop their entrepreneurial attitudes and abilities (Saporta and Verstraete, 2000). Those 'student centered methods' can be derived either from the nature of the entrepreneurship theory or from its interdisciplinary dimension, and it is difficult to identify which of these two factors plays the most important role. Active involvement of the students and 'problem-based learning' approaches appear adequate in such EEPs in order to achieve the right confrontation between theoretical concepts and practical business problems. Those confrontations might involve real-life problem solving, direct implications with entrepreneurs and business leaders, or virtual business simulation games. Such educational tools allow students to learn, exchange, debate and negotiate around business challenges as well as to make decisions and to take initiatives in high-uncertainty, fast-moving and limited information environments. Finally, such programs, like any learner-centered program, tend to involve more important teaching resources and/or smaller groups of students than traditional academic programs.

The third category of EEP, support programs, typically involves a more individualized approach, fine-tuned to the specific characteristics of the business opportunity identified by each student or team and involving a significant amount of coaching, networking and ad hoc data-gathering. This type of learning experience can, for example, be achieved in the context of a student's thesis, a business plan competition or through the provision of personalized coaching.

While these three categories involve different objectives and means, in all three cases students must face issues related to fields ranging from economics, management and law to psychology, sociology and, in some cases, technology. The corresponding educational approaches, while different in nature and scope in the three categories, must therefore in all cases involve a strong interdisciplinary dimension. They must do so not only addressing in parallel each of those fields, but also confronting them transversally, in the same way that the different facets of a business must simultaneously be managed by real-life entrepreneurs. In the next section we review a conceptual model of such an interdisciplinary approach in the context of EEPs.

9.2 Interdisciplinary approach and EEP

We consider here an interdisciplinary teaching approach as 'the implementation of a learning experience where disciplinary skills and knowledge are confronted to a specific situation or problem defined in a non-disciplinary way, in order to foster the acquisition of an integrated body of knowledge' (Rege Colet, 2002, p. 11). While multidisciplinary approaches only consider the juxtaposition of several disciplines, an interdisciplinary pedagogy involves the integration of those disciplines. This arises from the 'discipline paradox' (Petrie, 1992), where the existence of scientific disciplines drives the necessity of interdisciplinary approaches to tackle real-life problems and escape disciplinary ethnocentrism (Campbell, 1969), while any interdisciplinary approach has to rely upon the disciplines in order to ground its credibility.

Integration, collaboration and *synthesis* are the three basic elements of the interdisciplinary teaching approach model (Rege Colet, 2002), which is presented in Figure 9.1. The integration principle defines the interrelation and relative importance of the respective disciplinary bodies of knowledge. The collaboration principle addresses how the stakeholders of the interdisciplinary project interact and manage work processes together. Finally, the synthesis principle covers the confrontation of the two first principles, and the resulting learning experience and impact. Those three principles can be related to the three axes of the pedagogical triangle of Houssaye (1993), which defines the three-way relations between the teacher, the learner and the knowledge, and the processes that connect them: teach, learn, train and manage (the latter being conceived at a more organizational level). Let us stress that Rege Colet's model allows us to reconsider the links between disciplines, be it from an institutional point of view (academic structures), a portfolio point of view (programs offered to the students) or an educational point of view (teaching methods).

The cognitive objective of an interdisciplinary teaching approach is mainly to lead students to change their perspective and disciplinary point of view. If we consider that a disciplinary point of view can be linked to a disciplinary culture, interdisciplinary teaching approaches therefore involve an education to intercultural dimensions (Rege Colet, 2002). Moreover the construction of an integrated knowledge involves a learning experience and cognitive processes of the highest level in the reference taxonomy: analysis, synthesis and evaluation (Bloom, 1979). To reach that level, learning activities and working methods become more significant than content. The interdisciplinary approach becomes instrumental, the various disciplines involved converging to address the situation/problem at hand. This convergence process allows the discipline to go beyond the classification and simplified representation of the complexity of reality to the generation of significant learning experience grounded in genuine problems or situations (Rege Colet, 2002). In that sense, one can say that it can be considered as a heuristic method (Bayad et al., 2002). The results are not central anymore, but the process is – the purpose being to build coherence between the aims and the means mobilized to find a solution, not an optimal one, but a satisfying one. The project cannot be separated from its environment and, as a result, from an educational point of view, an interdisciplinary approach becomes necessary (Bayad et al., 2002).

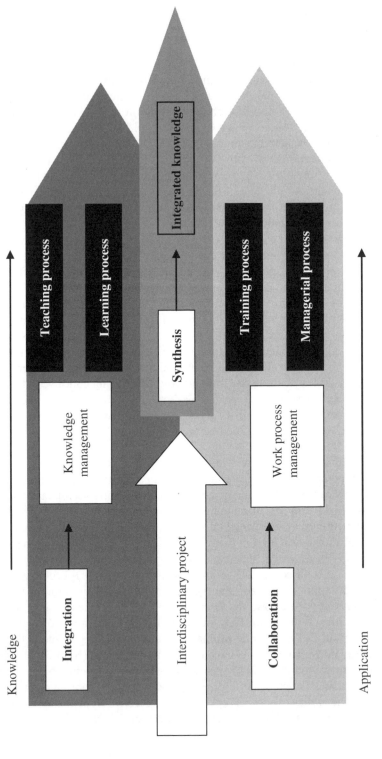

Knowledge

Application

Integration

Teaching process

Learning process

Knowledge management

Integrated knowledge

Synthesis

Interdisciplinary project

Training process

Managerial process

Work process management

Collaboration

Source: Rege Colet (2004).

Figure 9.1   A conceptual model of the interdisciplinary teaching approach

Project and problem-based learning approaches appear therefore to provide an answer to the requirement of interdisciplinarity. Hence they appear to be the natural choice for EEP, not only because of the 'real-life' dimension of entrepreneurship, but also because of its interdisciplinarity. We illustrate this close link between interdisciplinary teaching approaches and entrepreneurship in the next section, where we analyse the case of a cross-faculty EEP developed in Belgium by the Université catholique de Louvain (UCL) since 1997.

9.3   An interdisciplinary EEP: the UCL experience

We will present in this section the EEP that has been developed in Belgium by the Université catholique de Louvain, its objectives, target audience, format and content, teaching approaches, and then discuss in particular its interdisciplinary dimension.

9.3.1   EEP

The objective of the academic authorities at the launch of the program was to stimulate new business creation and entrepreneurship, in particular within its local socio-economic environment. Indeed, the local region (the 'Région Wallonne', the southern part of Belgium) had been identified by the Global Entrepreneurship Monitor (GEM, 2002; 2003)[1] as a poor performer in terms of entrepreneurship and several of the leading local industries (steel, textile, and so on) had experienced a steep decline since the early 1980s. Contributing to 'boost entrepreneurship' in its environment was therefore perceived as a valuable objective by the university in the context of its mission of service to society.

The EEP's initial stated objective was 'to train students to deal with the issues related to new business creation', and 'to provide potential student-entrepreneurs with the analysis and problem solving tools and concepts that will help them along their process of new business creation'. Since then, the objective of the EEP has actually been enlarged in order to include entrepreneurship skills and activities in their widest sense (business buyout, intrapreneurship, spin-offs, not-for-profit start-ups, and so on).

The target audience of the EEP are students in the process of completing the second year of a bachelor university degree in law, management, biosciences or engineering. They are selected through a written application and interviews on the basis of their motivation and likely ability to develop an entrepreneurial activity in the future. The EEP is not in itself a separate master degree but consists of a coherent set of dedicated elective classes that are integrated in the corresponding law, management, biosciences or engineering bachelor and master degrees completed by the students, in close collaborations with the faculty managing those degrees.

In terms of format and content, the program is spread over the last three years of its 'parent' bachelor and master degrees, and leads to a master thesis project addressing the creation of a new business activity. About 30 students are selected each year, leading to a total number of about 80 students over the three cohorts of students, taking into account those who have failed or left the EEP. The first year electives total 135 hours (equivalent to 20 ECTS (European Credit Transfer System)) and cover the legal, financial and managerial aspects of SME management and creation. The second year electives cover 100 hours (15 ECTS) and address entrepreneurship itself as well as the management and development of new business activities. This second year combines interventions from academic experts, SME specialists and entrepreneurs, case studies, fieldwork and a virtual new business creation game. The final (third) year is mainly devoted to the completion of the master thesis project and to a 30-hour class addressing business planning methodologies (five ECTS). The master thesis project must be completed by interdisciplinary groups consisting of three students from three different faculties.

In terms of the educational approaches adapted to entrepreneurship (Dilts and Fowler, 1999), the program focuses on problem-based learning and intense interactions among students and teachers. The settings of the program (schedule, facilities, equipment, and so on) have been specifically designed in order to foster students' autonomy, responsibilities and professional approach. The classes are given in a dedicated building in the evening and students have an exclusive 24 hours a day access to the program facilities, including computer and telecommunication equipment, team room, logistic support, and so on. Those facilities are managed by the students themselves, with the three cohorts sharing responsibilities. This collaboration and the access to an exclusive space generate a 'club' effect among students, who develop their own learning community cutting across the three cohorts and across their original disciplinary affiliation. Moreover, sharing a physical space fosters the exchange of knowledge and experience among students and creates a bonding effect, providing a sense of security. This helps students in their attempt to face the challenges and uncertainties of entrepreneurship.

In terms of learning objectives, the EEP targets both training and support objectives, overlapping the second and third categories of EEPs as described in the first section of this chapter. It adopts the corresponding educational approaches. Indeed the first two years correspond rather to the second category of EEP, providing students with the specific skills and abilities of entrepreneurship through the review of the relevant concepts and tools, and problem-based learning activities, combining interventions from academic experts and entrepreneurs, case studies, fieldwork and a virtual new business creation game. The third year relates more to the third category of EEPs, where students receive dedicated coaching and support for the completion of their master thesis project addressing the creation of a new business activity. Along those two objectives, the program addresses both cognitive (integration principle) and non-cognitive (collaboration principle) abilities. In particular in non-cognitive terms this academic EEP also aims at developing autonomous and responsible citizens as well as collaborative leaders.

9.3.2   Interdisciplinary aspects of program design
In terms of interdisciplinary teaching design, the students must first complete throughout the EEP numerous group projects, including their master thesis project, involving students from distinct disciplinary affiliations. But the interdisciplinary dimension of the program design is much deeper, in terms of target audience, governance and learning experience. Those aspects will be discussed hereafter.

First, in terms of target audience, as mentioned above, the aspiring entrepreneurs are selected from within four different schools (management, law, engineering and biosciences) early in their program (at the end of the second year of their bachelor degree). This allows students to be trained in parallel with their disciplinary specialization, rather than subsequently. This feature distinguishes this EEP from other experiences which rely on entrepreneurial education offered in the context of postgraduate, lifelong learning or executive education programs.

Second, in terms of governance, the program is managed by a scientific committee including academic representatives from the four faculties involved. Moreover, the program structure and content have been validated by each of these faculties and are recognized as an integral part of their respective bachelor and master degrees. This full recognition is demonstrated by the fact that the master thesis project of the EEP, although managed by the interfaculty scientific committee of the EEP, actually replaces the master thesis project required in each of the disciplinary master degree programs.

It should be noted that this strong integration of the EEP within the respective disciplinary programs, both in terms of student audience and governance, is unique given the deep and old disciplinary tradition of most universities. It provides a fertile ground for the emergence of a truly interdisciplinary teaching and learning experience.

Finally, beyond being rooted within the disciplinary structures and processes of the university, it is through its educational approach that the EEP aims at being truly interdisciplinary. The team of teachers and coaches, the student projects, the learning and assessment activities as well as the examination and master thesis jury all feature a strong interdisciplinary dimension. The sequence of learning activities and content is designed to drive students to progressively free themselves from their disciplinary point of view and adopt a wider perspective allowing them to apprehend entrepreneurship as an integrated body of knowledge. The initial classes start with the basic disciplines (management, law, and so on) to rapidly bring the students to address real-life problems. This early exposure to real-life problems forces students to test their ability to leverage their disciplinary knowledge as well as to appreciate how those disciplines interact and overlap in a business context.

This transition from disciplinary concepts to real-life problems relies upon a progressive intensification of students' involvement and interactions. While the first classes typically involve teachers sharing with students specific issues, concepts and tools (teaching process), they are followed by more interactive sessions where the teachers limit their intervention to the presentation of business problems that students have to collectively address within a given cognitive context (framing process). Finally, through the joint development of their new business project, students must identify, analyse, combine and develop on their own the relevant specific knowledge (learning process). This growing autonomy of the students goes hand in hand with coaching and support that is increasingly personalized around the specific expectations, objectives and abilities of the student groups. The involvement of the teachers becomes in itself entrepreneurial, having to respond to changing demands, deal with projects with uncertain prospects and sometimes explore uncharted territories.

9.3.3   *Interdisciplinary aspects of program objectives and assessment*

In terms of professional development objectives, the EEP ultimately aims to contribute to the launch of interdisciplinary entrepreneurial teams, as student groups consist of future professionals who should be able to combine their respective expertise, learn to adopt each other's point of view and use each other's language. This process of intercultural learning across multiple disciplines is a key element of the EEP, frequently stressed by the students and by the teachers. This again reinforces the interdisciplinary dimension of the EEP. The exposure to real-life business projects that could ultimately lead to entrepreneurial career opportunities for the students also contribute to this dimension, as students are forced to adopt interdisciplinary perspectives if they want to be able to deal with the complexity of real business problems. Doing this as an entrepreneurial team requires students to learn how to, on the one hand, reach a sufficient level of autonomy and professionalism and, on the other hand, trust, leverage and recognize the specialized skills of each member of the group. The entrepreneurial projects that are progressively shaped by the students along the EEP therefore constitute a cornerstone of the professional development objectives of the program.

For the initiators and sponsors of the EEP, the new business activities to be created should contribute to regional economic development, which is one of the initial stated objectives of the creation of the EEP. For the teachers and program managers, these projects constitute the core or trunk around which the contributions of each discipline can be combined and integrated as the different facets of entrepreneurship. This project also generates a stronger commitment by the students to achieve concrete results, leading them to engage more proactively in the learning process.

Let us stress again that the learning process per se can be considered as more important than the end product, as significant learning can be extracted even if the entrepreneurial project does not ultimately succeed. Through this active learning process students will have, during three years, apprehended and confronted the various aspects of entrepreneurship and its diversity of tools, semantics and perspectives by testing, exploring, challenging, assessing and ultimately validating (or not) their entrepreneurial project. This is achieved with the help of the tools and concepts provided and through interactions with their learning peers. Let us note that project-based learning is indeed a natural choice for EEP because the notion of project is common to all types of entrepreneurial activities (Bayad et al., 2002).

On the other hand, like any teaching program that goes beyond the simple acquisitions of disciplinary concepts and tools, the assessment of the EEP is by nature difficult to implement, be it in terms of the definition or of the measurement of evaluation criteria. As an academic program integrated in the university bachelor and master degrees, it must however include a formal assessment of the students that must be consistent with the requirements of the respective disciplines, and recognized as such by the respective academic authorities.

This interdisciplinary assessment of the student's learning represents a particular challenge given that the respective disciplines tend to rely on different assessment criteria, measurement methods, scale or philosophy. This assessment must therefore take into account not only the integration principle of the EEP (assessment of the acquisition of an integrated body of knowledge) but also its collaboration principle. It must aim at also assessing how well tasks, responsibilities and deliverables were shared and coordinated among the members of each entrepreneurial team. Both principles are often intertwined, as each member tends to take responsibility for the issues related to his or her disciplinary affiliation, but also for the implications of those issues and their resolution on the other dimensions of the projects and for the resulting interactions with the other team members.

Depending on the characteristics of the entrepreneurial projects, the tasks and issues at hand might be strongly unbalanced towards the disciplinary expertise of some of the team members (for example, in a high-tech project, unbalanced towards engineering, or in a service business involving complex contractual agreements, unbalanced towards legal aspects). It is, however, the collective work and results of the students that is valorized, meaning that all team members are assessed based upon the collective quality of the teamwork. This leaves the responsibility for the balance of workload and quality of deliverables to the team members themselves. Individual assessment is therefore used only for an assessment of the disciplinary skills involved in the EEP and of the students' ongoing participation to the learning activities. Moreover, it is the quality of the group work that is evaluated, not the economic potential of their entrepreneurial project. Indeed, a group might do a good job by correctly concluding that the entrepreneurial opportunity they had considered had no or limited potential, given its features, resources requirements, competitive environment or market. The result of the project in itself cannot be the only assessment criterion. It is the ability of the team to reach this conclusion, to argument and to synthesize it that will be assessed, as it reflects their ability to adopt the integrated point of view required in an entrepreneurial context.

The master thesis project students have to complete at the end of the program provides a good illustration of this collective interdisciplinary assessment and its complexity. As each group includes members from different disciplines, they will be mentored by a team of academics including members of the corresponding faculties. These typically involve three thesis directors (instead of one in traditional projects), from three different schools of the university. This multi-headed structure, with which academics are sometimes uncomfortable, can generate negative side effects that might affect the principle of collaboration underpinning the EEP. Indeed, each director can feel that his or her contribution is diluted or underrepresented in the project, and therefore may not contribute significantly enough to its success. On the contrary, one of the thesis directors can try to bias the project towards his or her own disciplinary interest or assessment criteria, threatening the overall balance and coherence of the entrepreneurial project. It is the EEP manager's responsibility to ensure that those potential pitfalls are avoided across the portfolio of projects that is generated each year.

Detailed and quantifiable assessment criteria are therefore difficult to define and/or implement, and the assessment of each project tends to be consensus based, the program manager balancing the opinions of each of the thesis directors involved. While this approach appears relatively pragmatic, let us stress that it generates some discomfort as students are faced with an assessment process that sometimes appears arbitrary or at least that lacks transparency. This assessment issue is frequently raised in the feedback provided by the students, although it does not affect their overall (positive) perception of the EEP itself. This issue of the evaluation of the impact of the EEP itself, by the students and from an entrepreneurial point of view, is discussed next.

9.4 Evaluation and impact of the interdisciplinary EEP

The impact of the EEP has been or is currently evaluated along three axes: students' satisfaction, level of interdisciplinarity and entrepreneurial impact. The students' satisfaction was evaluated through annual surveys completed since 2000. The level of interdisciplinarity was evaluated using an assessment grid (Rege Colet, 2002). Finally, the entrepreneurial impact is evaluated with respect to the initial objective of the EEP to contribute to the regional development through the creation of new business activities. These three evaluations are presented hereafter.

9.4.1   Students' satisfaction
In order to assess the students' satisfaction, a first qualitative survey (including open and semi-open questions) was sent to the first three promotions of students, having completed the programs in 2000, 2001 and 2002. Based on this preliminary survey, a questionnaire with 57 closed questions and three open questions (related respectively to the key strengths of the program, its key limitations and some suggestions) was defined and sent by post to the 2003 and 2004 promotions. All the students completed the first survey, and 54 per cent replied to the postal questionnaire.

The surveys provide very encouraging results: they indicate that 98 per cent of the students are 'quite satisfied' or 'very satisfied' with the EEP as a whole. The two main positive motivations stated by the students relate, on the one hand, to the interdisciplinary approach of the program and, on the other hand, to the high level of interactivity of the learning process. Those two features of the EEP also appear as the main driver of student satisfaction a posteriori, indicating that their expectations regarding interdisciplinary approach and interactivity have been met.

Compared to traditional courses, the EEP requires additional efforts from these students who have to dedicate two evenings to their entrepreneurship classes during three years and to provide a lot of additional work for their different assignments. This means that these students are probably more motivated, but also probably more demanding than 'regular' students. In terms of evaluation, we can assume that the process is more similar to adult education programs, grouping people with different backgrounds and expectations, than to traditional disciplinary student evaluation. However, compared to adult education evaluation, the fact that the students have different educational backgrounds is not perceived as a problem, because interdisciplinarity is at the core of the program. As result, students are not dissatisfied because of different initial levels of knowledge among their peers.

Regarding factors that could be improved, students mention, first, the coordination among the teachers and, second, the assessment process. They report that the links between the different classes should be made more explicit, indicating that the integration between the various classes could be improved. They also tend to perceive that the collective assessment process lacks transparency and is somewhat unfair. In particular, as mentioned above, a small weight is attached to the individual contributions relative to the collective results of the group. Furthermore, the interdisciplinary dimension of the program makes it difficult to select detailed and explicit assessment criteria and thresholds that would cope with the diversity of the student projects in terms of scope, content and disciplinary knowledge mobilized. In particular the respective expectations of the teachers coming from various disciplines, and how they are combined towards a consensus, appear sometimes unclear to the students, or at least are not communicated clearly enough. The weakness of the program thus seems to appear in the collaboration principle. However, let us remember that the interdisciplinary dimension is present at the level of the program content, the teaching team, the student groups, the guest speakers and the assessment jury. These multiple sources of interdisciplinarity probably partially explain their relative dissatisfaction.

9.4.2   Interdisciplinary dimension
In parallel with the students survey mentioned above, we have evaluated the EEP, adapting an assessment tool of the interdisciplinary dimension, developed by Rege Colet

(2002). This tool, approved by the original author, evaluates the level of integration, collaboration and synthesis involved in an interdisciplinary learning process, based on Likert-scale surveys. This approach validates the balance between, on the one hand, the structure of the knowledge contents (integration principle) and, on the other hand, the work processes organizations (collaboration principle).

In this approach, the integration principle is declined along four indicators: the type and level of content integration, the problem-based learning processes and, finally, the assessment. The collaboration principle is declined along four other indicators: teacher cooperation, students' cooperation, student–teacher interactions and course settings. Those eight indicators are each covered by several items along which the questionnaire tests the level of agreement of the students (completely agree, and so on). Finally, an interdisciplinary index is defined as the ratio of the scores along the integration and collaboration dimensions. A truly interdisciplinary program should be balanced along those two dimensions, that is, achieve an interdisciplinary index of 1 (Rege Colet, 2002).

This test, conducted with the first-, second- and third-year students' cohorts in April and December 2004, confirmed that the EEP was quite interdisciplinary, with interdisciplinary indices of respectively 1.08, 1.17 and 0.99 for the three years of the program. The balance between the structure of the contents and of the work organization of the programs during the three years appears, therefore, well perceived by the students.

The test also provides detailed information regarding the perceived strengths and weaknesses of the program in terms of coherence of the teaching strategy. These results were consistent with the students' satisfaction surveys mentioned in the previous section. Again, room for improvement was identified in terms of collaborations between the teachers and in terms of clarity of the student assessment process. As highlighted above, collaboration between teachers and consensus about the assessment process are contingent to the willingness and ability of teachers and speakers from distinct disciplines to work together, exchange information and experience as well as communicate and act as a team – all things that are not common and do not tend to emerge spontaneously from an academic environment.

Let us stress that both evaluations were built and conducted with the intention to provide the teachers and the program managers with feedback that could be used to valorize and regulate the quality of this complex interdisciplinary program.

Given that the first students only graduated in 2000, further investigations will be required regarding the assessment of the program in terms of short- and medium-term professional development. In particular, the professional development objective of the EEP to help the students in their process of creation of a new business activity cannot yet be fully tested. We discuss this issue of the entrepreneurial impact of the EEP in the next section.

9.4.3 Entrepreneurial impact

In the early stages of the EEP, at least from a formal point of view, its aim was limited to entrepreneurship in its most restrictive meaning, that is, new firm creation. In this perspective, such a program could only be targeted to potential firm creators and would be conditioned by a success imperative: the number of new firms created (Schmitt, 2003). This approach is largely predominant within university entrepreneurship courses and/or programs. Under the simultaneous influence of students and professors, the purpose of this EEP has actually been broadened beyond firm creation in a restrictive sense, to include intrapreneurship, working for an SME, not-for-profit creation, spin-offs, and so on. Entrepreneurial intentions (Fayolle, 2003; 2005; Fayolle et al., 2005) and perceptions, such as self-efficacy (Ehrlich et al., 2000) can indeed also be demonstrated through the development of new business activities in existing organizations, an involvement in a young SME or a not-for-profit activity. In particular, any young graduate joining a start-up could in a way be considered as entrepreneurial, even if he or she did not create the firm himself or herself.

Among alumni of the EEP, some have launched their own business, developed a not-for-profit association or joined a start-up or a university spin-off.[2] The entrepreneurial impact of the EEP overall can from that point of view be considered quite positive, when taking into account entrepreneurial activities in their widest sense, beyond the immediate creation or buyout of a new business. There is, however, a significant number of alumni of the EEP that have made 'traditional' career choices, joining large corporations or organizations. Those choices correspond in general to their disciplinary affiliation. Over time, we have identified various potential explanations of this apparent misfit, in terms of delayed effects, selection bias, technology intensity or lack of entrepreneurial culture. We discuss these next.

Delayed effects can derive from the fact that the EEP has actually taught students to apprehend an entrepreneurial career with care and caution, highlighting the pitfalls of naïve 'dot-com type' projects. Some students with strong entrepreneurial aspirations could therefore decide to first learn about 'the business' in a traditional organization before trying to launch their own venture. For those students the entrepreneurial impact of the EEP in terms of future intentions (Kolvereid and Moen, 1997; Noel, 2001) is not yet visible, and can only be observed from a long-term perspective. This 'cautious patience' from the students and 'observation delay' of the EEP's impact is consistent with several empirical studies that have shown that a strong functional or sector-based professional experience from an entrepreneur actually improves the subsequent survival prospects and increase the growth potential of his or her venture (Dahlqvist et al., 1999; Dunkelberg and Cooper, 1982; Hambrick and Mason, 1984; Storey, 1994; Westhead and Birley, 1995). The entrepreneurial impact of an EEP can therefore only be assessed several years after its launch (Block and Stumpf, 1992). Informal studies quoted by Vesper and Gartner (1997) have indicated a strong correlation between the participation in an entrepreneurial course and the likelihood of launching one's own business in the future. This should also be the case when considering students attending complete EEP rather than only one course.

A selection bias in the students attending the EEP, diverging from the new business creation objective, could be another potential mitigating factor of the entrepreneurial impact of the program. Indeed, anecdotal evidence suggests that some students apply for the program not because they want to become entrepreneurs, but because they perceive that attending this program would boost their perceived value on the job market, either because of its interdisciplinary dimension or because of the positive perception often associated by recruiters with entrepreneurship. These 'resume-driven' students would probably never create a new business activity, whatever entrepreneurial training would be offered to them. Dealing with this selection bias would require the EEP managers to be able to better select up front the students with the right entrepreneurial aptitudes.

A survey of the academic research (Brenner et al., 1991; Chen et al., 1998; Chell et al., 1991; Filion, 1997) identifies several factors that can be associated a priori with entrepreneurial aptitudes: individual characteristics (independence, result-orientation, internal locus of control, flexibility, leadership), motivations (self-realization, search of autonomy) and external factors (socio-cultural environment, family context, education). Similarly, typologies of entrepreneurs have been suggested. However, the entrepreneurial process remains multifaceted and contingent, and cannot be reduced to a predefined model that can be used to identify a priori future entrepreneurs. Indeed, some psychological tests or typology that had been developed to 'spot' entrepreneurs have been severely criticized (Chell, 1985). If the elements mentioned above can contribute to improve the design and implementation of the selection process (that is, the format and content of the written application and interview), the entrepreneurial aptitudes of a student remain very difficult to assess a priori in a systematic manner. However, even this audience of 'resume-driven' students can play a role in the diffusion of an entrepreneurial culture within their future organizations or within society at large and therefore contribute to the objectives of the EEP. Indeed, the promotion of an entrepreneurial culture should also involve the education of students whose career will have indirect entrepreneurial features (Saporta and Verstraete, 2000). Such students will be involved with entrepreneurs as managers and consultants, or can contribute to the emergence of a more entrepreneurial environment.

The 'technology intensity' of the program could also have mitigated its entrepreneurial impact so far, as technology-oriented start-ups such as university spin-offs were probably overrepresented in the first editions of the program. Indeed, as part of the interdisciplinary requirements all project groups had initially to include a student from the engineering faculty. As a consequence most of the master thesis projects had a strong technology orientation. In particular, a large proportion of those projects related to the valorization of intellectual property and technologies developed within the university. This technology bias excluded de facto a wide range of entrepreneurial opportunities, for example in the retail or service sectors, that could otherwise have been pursued in the context of the EEP. To deal with this 'technology' issue, the rules defining the structure of the master thesis groups have since been made more flexible. Students are now allowed to develop their own project even if it involves no or limited technology and therefore offers limited room for an in-depth contribution from an engineering student. Yet all groups must remain interdisciplinary, that is, include students from at least two different schools.

The last element that could explain the limitation of the entrepreneurial impact of the EEP relates to the relatively low level of entrepreneurial culture in the education system as a whole in Europe in general and in Belgium in particular. This issue, however, goes far beyond the scope and reach of the EEP considered here, and should probably be tackled through other 'mobilization' EEPs, as defined earlier in this chapter, aimed at introducing a more entrepreneurial culture during the first years of university education or even at an earlier stage.

9.5   Conclusions

Entrepreneurship is a domain of choice for universities wanting to develop new educational interdisciplinary approaches, be it because entrepreneurship as a theoretical body of knowledge is by nature an interdisciplinary field or because entrepreneurship education is well suited to the teaching approaches related to interdisciplinary content. However, as discussed above, the interdisciplinary dimension of entrepreneurship education programs also generates specific challenges in an academic environment, such as the lack of readiness of academics to collaborate across their respective disciplinary fields or the difficulty of defining and applying common assessment criteria and methods.

Moreover, the case study of a university EEP presented in this chapter illustrates how interdisciplinary university programs can at bachelor or master degree level already help students to build bridges between academia and the 'real' world, as well as between themselves and their future professional development. It allows students to be exposed not only to interdisciplinary content and problems but also to interdisciplinary teamwork, managed in the case of the EEP around their entrepreneurial master thesis project. Programs like this interdisciplinary EEP provide fertile grounds for the development by teachers of new educational approaches and skills that can spill over to other (disciplinary) programs of the university. This reinforces interdisciplinarity as one of the core assets of the university, where various experience, theories and knowledge can confront and feed each other. As Schumpeter stressed decades ago, most innovations do emerge from the creative combination of existing knowledge.

On the other hand, and as stressed by the students, the interactive and embedded learning approaches developed in interdisciplinary programs such as the EEP presented here are one of their most attractive features. Those approaches are now being reinforced within academic institutions and are developed throughout the university as a way to address new problems within their respective contexts. As a paradox, this could lead to a decreasing interest of the students for the EEP, as its original features in terms of educational approaches can now be found in many other programs. However, in a retroactive movement, the generalization of active and contextualized teaching methods could lead more students to be attracted by interdisciplinary programs like the UCL EEP, because they would already have become accustomed to its methods.

In their introduction to the special *Academy of Management Learning and Education* issue on entrepreneurship education, Greene et al. (2004) stress the fact that entrepreneurship classes have often been training grounds for teaching methods which tend to be generalized today within traditional business courses, such as computer simulations, practitioners' testimonies and interdisciplinary teaching. We believe that this generalization can be considered a success for the university as a whole, and for entrepreneurship programs in particular, because these could serve as role models.

Finally, the intrinsic interdisciplinary dimension of the EEP should be considered in the light of its overall objectives. Those objectives should definitely not only relate to the number of start-ups created in the short-term, but also be considered in terms of entrepreneurial activities, intention and attitudes in their widest sense. This includes new business development, involvement in SMEs and all the activities directly or indirectly related to entrepreneurship. The objectives of an EEP should therefore also be conceived from a cultural perspective, as a contributor to the emergence of an environment that stimulates and values entrepreneurship. In other words, as David Birch declared in a recent interview (Aronsson, 2004), the role of entrepreneurship education is to stress the social and economic role and importance of entrepreneurship, as well as to make the public and the political leaders aware of it in order to generate a favorable environment. Among all mechanisms contributing to this cultural objective, university programs are 'entrepreneurial socialization spaces' (Vaudelin and Levy, 2003, p. 5). Universities can play an active role in the creation and development of entrepreneurial aptitudes, intentions and attitudes, as illustrated by the multiple initiatives launched by universities with the support of public authorities and private organizations across Europe. But, while this often meets an explicit demand from the students, the university cannot play this educational role alone. Earlier initiatives, before students reach the university, are probably necessary.

In terms of further research developments, we are currently trying to assess more accurately the impact of the analysed EEP on entrepreneurial intentions and on entrepreneurial career paths through longitudinal surveys on our students and through a survey conducted among our alumni. Another interesting research avenue would be to compare the skills students develop through such an interdisciplinary EEP with those developed by students with a similar disciplinary background, but through entrepreneurship classes taught within their school only. Such a study could help answer the following question: is interdisciplinarity only one pedagogical mean among others to teach entrepreneurship, or is it intrinsically bound to EEPs and a distinctive feature of the academic field of entrepreneurship and of its teaching?

Notes

1. These are the only two reports specifically analysing Wallonia. Although the data for 2003 show some improvement, later reports about Belgium as a whole conclude that the situation is still worrying.
2. We are currently conducting research about the EEP's entrepreneurial impact in terms of careers paths. Our current knowledge of our former students' entrepreneurial activities rests on informal information.

References

Acs, Z.J. and Audretsch, D.B. (2003), 'Introduction to the Handbook of Entrepreneurship Research', in Z.J. Acs and D.B. Audrestch (eds), *Handbook of Entrepreneurship Research*, Boston, MA, Dordrecht and London: Kluwer Academic, pp. 3–20.

Albert, P. and Marion, S. (1998), 'Ouvrir l'enseignement à l'esprit d'entreprendre', in S. Birley and D. Muzyka (eds), *L'art d'entreprendre*, Paris: Village Mondial, pp. 28–30.

Aronsson, M. (2004), 'Education matters – but does entrepreneurship education. An interview with David Birch', *Academy of Management Learning and Education*, **3** (3), 289–92.

Bayad, M., Schmitt, C. and Grandhaye, J.-P. (2002), 'Pédagogie par projet et entrepreneuriat: réflexions autour d'une démarche et de différentes expériences', *Actes du 2ème Congrès de l'Académie de l'Entrepreneuriat*, Bordeaux, April.

Béchard, J.-P. and Grégoire, D. (2005), 'Entrepreneurship education research revisited: the case of higher education', *Academy of Management Learning and Education*, **4** (1), 22–43.

Block, Z. and Stumpf, S.A. (1992), 'Entrepreneurship education research: experience and challenge', in D.L. Sexton and J.M. Kasarda (eds), *The State of the Art of Entrepreneurship*, Boston, MA: PWS-Kent, pp. 17–45.

Bloom, B.S. (1979), *Taxonomy of Educational Objectives: The Classification of Educational Goals*, London: Longman.

Brenner, O.C., Pringle, C.D. and Greenhaus, J.H. (1991), 'Perceived fulfilment of organizational employment versus entrepreneurship: work values and career intentions of business college graduates', *Journal of Small Business Management*, **29** (3), 62–74.

Bruyat, C. and Julien, P.-A. (2000), 'Defining the field of research in entrepreneurship', *Journal of Business Venturing*, **16**, 165–80.

Campbell, D.T. (1969), 'Ethnocentrism of disciplines and the fish-scale model of omniscience', in M. Sherif and C. Sherif (eds), *Interdisciplinary Relationships in Social Sciences*, Chicago, IL: Aldine.

Chell, E. (1985), 'The entrepreneurial personality: a few ghosts laid to rest?' *International Small Business Journal*, **3** (3), 43–54.

Chell, E., Haworth, J. and Brearley, S. (1991), *The Entrepreneurial Personality: Concepts, Cases and Categories*, London: Routledge.

Chen, C.C., Greene, P.G. and Crick, A. (1998), 'Does entrepreneurial self-efficacy distinguish entrepreneurs from managers?', *Journal of Business Venturing*, **13** (4), 295–316.

Commission of the European Communities (2003), *Green Paper: Entrepreneurship in Europe*, COM (2003) 27 final, Brussels, 21 March.

Cooper, A. (2003), 'Entrepreneurship: the past, the present and the future', in Z.J. Acs and D.B. Audrestch (eds), *Handbook of Entrepreneurship Research*, Boston, MA, Dordrecht and London: Kluwer Academic, pp. 21–34.

Dahlqvist, J., Davidsson, P. and Wiklund, J. (1999), 'Initial conditions as predictors of new venture performance: a replication and extension of the Cooper et al. study', paper presented at the 44th World Conference of the International Council for Small Business, Naples, 20–23 June.

Dilts, J.C. and Fowler, S.M. (1999), 'Internships: preparing students for an entrepreneurial career', *Journal of Business and Entrepreneurship*, 11 (1), 51–63.

Dunkelberg, W.G. and Cooper, A.C. (1982), 'Patterns of small business growth', *Academy of Management Proceedings*, 409–13.

Ehrlich, S.B., De Noble, A.F., Jung, D. and Pearson, D. (2000), 'The impact of entrepreneurship training programs on an individual's entrepreneurial self-efficacy', *Frontiers of Entrepreneurship Research*, Babson Conference Proceedings, www.babson.edu/entrep/fer, accessed May 2006.

Fayolle, A. (1999), 'Orientation entrepreneuriale des étudiants et évaluation de l'impact des programmes d'enseignement de l'entrepreneuriat sur les comportements entrepreneuriaux des étudiants des grandes écoles de gestion françaises: étude exploratoire', in *Actes du premier Congrès de l'Académie de l'Entrepreneuriat*, Lille, November, pp. 180–91.

Fayolle, A. (2000), 'Editorial du dossier sur l'enseignement de l'entrepreneuriat', *Revue Gestion 2000*, 17 (3), 74–5.

Fayolle, A. (2003), 'Using the theory of planned behaviour in assessing entrepreneurship teaching program', *IntEnt 2003 Conference*, September, Grenoble.

Fayolle, A. (2005), 'Evaluation of entrepreneurship education: behaviour performing or intention increasing?', *International Journal of Entrepreneurship and Small Business*, 2 (1), 89–98.

Fayolle, A., Gailly B. and Lassas-Clerc N. (2005), 'The long-term effect of entrepreneurship teaching programmes on entrepreneurial intention', *RENT XIX – Research in Entrepreneurship and Small Business Naples*, 17–18 November.

Fiet, J.O. (2000a), 'The pedagogical side of teaching entrepreneurship', *Journal of Business Venturing*, 16, 101–17.

Fiet, J.O. (2000b), 'The theoretical side of teaching entrepreneurship', *Journal of Business Venturing*, 16, 1–24.

Filion, L.J. (1997), 'Le champ de l'entrepreneuriat: historique, évolutions et tendances', *Revue Internationale P.M.E.*, 10 (2), 129–72.

Gartner, W.B. and Vesper, K.H. (1994), 'Experiments in entrepreneurship education: successes and failures', *Journal of Business Venturing*, 9 (2), 179–87.

Gibb, A. (1992), 'The enterprise culture and education: understanding enterprise education and its links with small business, entrepreneurial and wider education goals', *International Small Business Journal*, 11 (3), 11–35.

Global Entrepreneurship Monitor (GEM) (2002), *The Global Entrepreneurship Monitor: Rapport Régional sur la Wallonie*, www.gemconsortium.org/, May 2006.

Global Entrepreneurship Monitor (GEM) (2003), *The Global Entrepreneurship Monitor: Rapport Régional sur la Wallonie*, www.gemconsortium.org/, May 2006.

Gorman, G., Hanlon, D. and King, W. (1997), 'Some research perspectives on entrepreneurship education, enterprise education and education for small business management: a ten-year literature review', *International Small Business Journal*, 15, 56–77.

Greene, P., Katz, J. and Johannisson, B. (2004), 'From the guest co-editors: entrepreneurship Education', *Academy of Management Learning and Education*, 3 (3), 238–41.

Hambrick, D.C. and Mason, P.A. (1984), 'Upper-echelons: the organization as a reflection of its top managers', *Academy of Management Review*, 9 (2), 193–206.

Houssaye, J. (1993), 'Le triangle pédagogique, ou comment comprendre la situation pédagogique', in J. Houssaye (ed.), *La pédagogie: une encyclopédie pour aujourd'hui*, Paris: ESF éditeur.

Johannisson, B. (1991), 'University training for entrepreneurship: a Swedish approach', *Entrepreneurship and Regional Development*, 3 (1), 67–82.

Katz, J.A. (2003), 'The chronology and intellectual trajectory of American entrepreneurship education: 1876–1999', *Journal of Business Venturing*, 18, 283–300.

Klandt, H. (2004), 'Entrepreneurship education and research in German-speaking Europe', *Academy of Management Learning and Education*, 3 (3), 293–301.

Kolvereid, L. and Moen, O. (1997), 'Entrepreneurship among business graduates: does a major in entrepreneurship make a difference?', *Journal of European Industrial Training*, 21 (4), 154–60.

Kuratko, D.F. (2005), 'The emergence of entrepreneurship education: development, trends and challenges', *Entrepreneurship Theory and Practice*, 29 (5), 577–97.

Low, M.B. (2001), 'The adolescence of entrepreneurship research: specification of purpose', *Entrepreneurship Theory and Practice*, 25 (4), 17–27.

McGrath, R.G. (2003), 'Connecting the study of entrepreneurship and theories of capitalist progress: an epilogue', in Z.J. Acs and D.B. Audrestch (eds), *Handbook of Entrepreneurship Research*, Boston, MA, Dordrecht and London: Kluwer Academic, pp. 515–31.

Noel, T.W. (2001), 'Effects of entrepreneurial education on intent to open a business', *Frontiers of Entrepreneurship Research*, Babson Conference Proceedings, www.babson.edu/entrep/fer, May 2006.

Petrie, H.G. (1992), 'Interdisciplinary education: are we faced with insurmountable opportunities?', *Review of Research Education*, **18**, 299–333.

Rege Colet, N. (2002), *Enseignement universitaire et interdisciplinarité: un cadre pour analyser, agir et évaluer*, Bruxelles, De Boeck Université.

Rege Colet, N. (2004), 'Plenary conference of the Chaire de Pédagogie Universitaire', *Enseignement interdisciplinaire: le défi de la cohérence pédagogique*, UCL, Louvain-la-Neuve, February.

Saporta, B. and Verstraete, T. (2000), 'Réflexions sur l'enseignement de l'entrepreneuriat dans les composantes en sciences de gestion des universités françaises', *Revue Gestion 2000*, **17** (3), 97–121.

Schmitt, C. (2003), 'De la formation à l'entrepreneuriat à la formation en entrepreneuriat: le rôle de la complexité', Grand Atelier MCX-APC, *La formation au défi de la ccomplexité: interoger et modéliser les interventions de formation en situations complexes*, Lille, September.

Storey, D.J. (1994), *Understanding the Small Business Sector*, London and Boston, MA: International Thomson Business Press.

Vaudelin, J.-P. and Levy, T. (2003), 'L'entrepreneuriat est-il énonçable et enseignable', in AIREPME, *L'entrepreneur en actions: contextes et pratiques*, Agadir, October.

Verstraete, T. and Fayolle, A. (2004), 'Quatre paradigmes pour cerner le domaine de recherche en entrepreneuriat', *Proceedings of the 7ème Congrès International Francophone en Entrepreneuriat et PME*, October, Montpellier.

Vesper, K.H. and Gartner, W.B. (1997), 'Measuring progress in entrepreneurship education', *Journal of Business Venturing*, **12** (5), 403–21.

Westhead, P. and Birley, S. (1995), 'Employment growth in new independent owner-managed firms in Great Britain', *International Small Business Journal*, **13** (3), 11–34.

PART III

NATIONAL CONTEXT

10 Entrepreneurship and education in Belgium: findings and implications from the Global Entrepreneurship Monitor
Dirk De Clercq and Hans Crijns

Introduction

The objective of this chapter is to provide the empirical findings from a research project with regard to the role of entrepreneurship and education in Belgium. More specifically, we highlight the findings with respect to the role of education in fostering, or inhibiting, entrepreneurial activity in Belgium as found by the Global Entrepreneurship Monitor.[1] Our study fits into an increasing awareness of policy makers and educators across the world that the level and success of entrepreneurial activity within a country is to an important extent related to the quality and focus of its educational programs (Acs et al., 2005; Minniti et al., 2006; Reynolds et al., 2004).

Several reasons have been given for why a country's educational system may be important for stimulating entrepreneurship (Reynolds et al., 1999; Verheul et al., 2002). For instance, education may provide individuals with a feeling of autonomy, independence or self-confidence, which are all characteristics potentially important when starting a new business. Furthermore, education broadens the horizons of individuals, thereby making people better equipped to perceive new business opportunities. However, it has also been suggested that a distinction needs to be made between 'general' education on the one hand, and more 'specific' education focusing on the promotion of entrepreneurship and the stimulation of entrepreneurial skills and knowledge on the other. For instance, the educational system can be used specifically for the encouragement of commercial awareness, and for the development of necessary entrepreneurial skills such as negotiations and opportunity recognition (Gavron et al., 1998).

Overall this chapter provides empirical evidence with regard to the role of education in stimulating entrepreneurship. The chapter is structured as follows. First, a short presentation is given of the Global Entrepreneurship Monitor (GEM) project and its main objectives as pertaining to the relationship between entrepreneurship and economic growth, and the role of education in fostering entrepreneurship. Second, a short overview is given of the academic literature on entrepreneurship and education, as pertaining to the definition of 'entrepreneurship education' and the role of education (and human capital) for entrepreneurs' success. Third, the methodology of the study is presented, and a description is given of the data collection mechanisms used. Fourth, the empirical findings from the study are presented, and a distinction is made hereby between the quantitative and qualitative results. Fifth, some specific implications are formulated in terms of how education can further encourage entrepreneurship. Finally, some overall conclusions are formulated.

10.1   Global Entrepreneurship Monitor

In the last decade, the concept of entrepreneurship has received increasing emphasis internationally. A shift in thinking has placed entrepreneurship at the center of the forces that drive economic growth – as distinct from previous emphases on large established firms (Wennekers and Thurik, 1999). It is now widely accepted that entrepreneurial capability is a necessary ingredient in a country's capacity to sustain economic growth (Thurik and Wennekers, 2002). The question of what determines the level of entrepreneurial activity, and how such activity should be promoted, is therefore important to both academics and policy makers. Consequently, a considerable body of recent research has sought to understand the factors that determine the supply of entrepreneurial activity, and hence the creation of new ventures (for example, Brock and Evans, 1989; Gavron et al., 1998; Grilo and Thurik, 2004; Storey, 1999; Thurik and Wennekers, 2002).

The Global Entrepreneurship Monitor project fills an important gap in the international entrepreneurship research as it devotes in-depth attention to the strength and influence of the entrepreneurial sector of the economy, that is, new firm creation and growth. The Global Entrepreneurship Monitor is a collaborative project led by Babson College and London Business School, and carried out by multiple national teams across the world (for example, Acs et al., 2005; Minniti et al., 2006; Reynolds et al., 2004; Reynolds et al., 2005). Over the years more than 40 countries have participated in the study.[2] The main objectives of GEM is to create an annual assessment of (1) the levels and nature of entrepreneurial activity across countries, (2) the factors within countries that give rise to systematic differences in entrepreneurship rates, and (3) national outcomes of entrepreneurship. In this chapter we address the broader question of how entrepreneurial activity can be stimulated within a country, and we focus in particular on the role of *education* in promoting, or inhibiting, entrepreneurship.

The overall GEM model is presented in Figure 10.1 (Reynolds et al., 2005). The model provides a framework for assessing key empirical relationships between entrepreneurship and economic growth. The central argument of the model is that national economic growth is a function of two parallel sets of interrelated activities: (a) those associated with established firms, and (b) those related directly to the entrepreneurial process.

The role of larger established firms is shown in the top half of Figure 10.1. Large firms, often competing on a global scale, clearly make a major contribution to economic growth and prosperity. Furthermore, these large corporations foster the development of smaller existing firms (that is, SMEs) through a wide range of cooperative agreements (for example, R&D partnerships, supplier–customer relationships, and so on). The success of the established firms is determined in part by the national context in which these firms operate, which is represented in the model by the 'General national framework conditions' (for example, nature of the labor market, efficiency of financial markets).

The role of start-ups and entrepreneurship is shown in the bottom half of Figure 10.1. Prior work has suggested that transactional activity among large firms explains only a portion of the variation in economic growth (Wennekers and Thurik, 1999). More specifically, the entrepreneurial process also accounts for a significant proportion of the differences in economic prosperity between countries. Entrepreneurial activity is driven by the perception of entrepreneurial opportunities combined with the capacity (that is, skills and motivation) to exploit these opportunities. When opportunities are combined effectively with individuals' skills and motivation, the outcome is the creation of new firms and, consequently, economic growth.

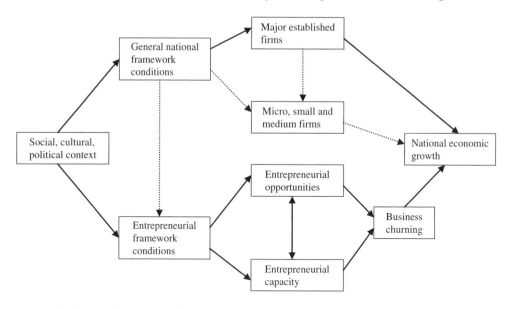

Figure 10.1   GEM conceptual model

The dynamic transactions presented in the bottom half of Figure 10.1 occur within a particular context, which is referred to in the GEM model as 'Entrepreneurial framework Conditions' (Reynolds et al., 2005). These include key variables such as government policies and programs designed to support start-ups, or the development of an *educational system* that stimulates entrepreneurship. We focus on this last point: how can a country's educational system promote, or discourage, entrepreneurial behavior among its residents?

The results that are presented in this chapter pertain to one particular country, that is, Belgium. While it could be interesting to make a comparative study of educational efforts towards entrepreneurship across countries, such an approach does not fall within the scope of this chapter. However, although we provide results for one particular country, we believe that the insights from the reported study can to a great extent be extrapolated to many other (European Union – EU) countries. Moreover, the fact that Belgium has a relatively high level of overall educational attainment (as reported in section 10.4.2.1) compared to other EU countries makes it an interesting case in respect of the specific issue of 'entrepreneurship' education.

10.2   Academic research on entrepreneurship and education

Academics and policy makers agree that the realization of an entrepreneurial society is largely related to the extent to which entrepreneurship education is incorporated at all levels of the educational system, from primary and secondary schools to universities and business schools. We first offer some insights into what prior research has understood by the term 'entrepreneurship education'. Second, we provide some theoretical foundations for why education is such a key factor affecting the level of entrepreneurship within a country, and we rely hereby on prior academic research that has emphasized the role of education, and *human capital* in general, in fostering new venture activities.

10.2.1   Definition of entrepreneurship education
Some researchers have defined 'entrepreneurship education' as the process of providing individuals with the concepts and skills necessary to recognize new business opportunities, and to provide self-confidence to enact upon such opportunities (McIntyre and Roche, 1999; Verheul et al., 2002). Important aspects that may be included in this type of education, in addition to opportunity recognition, are the marshaling of resources in the face of risk, the actual initiation of a business venture, the development of the business plan, capital development, and cash flow analysis. Furthermore, there is a debate in the literature on whether entrepreneurial qualities can be taught (Gibb, 1993), and this debate is related to the question of what the scope of entrepreneurship education should be.

In fact, there is no consensus among entrepreneurship scholars with respect to the exact definition of entrepreneurship education. Some researchers have pointed to the existence of two streams in terms of the nature of entrepreneurship education: one stream advocates a focus on small business management and the other emphasizes start-ups and growth (Solomon et al., 1994; Zeithaml and Rice, 1987). A common theme among these two streams is that entrepreneurship education programs should provide a breadth of creative managerial skills and knowledge. The differences between the two types of educational approaches are linked to a difference in the ultimate objective to be achieved: whereas small business management courses aim at providing students with solid foundations in the management and operation of existing companies, 'pure' entrepreneurship courses focus on the activities involved in originating and developing new growth ventures. In this study, we concur with the second approach, and emphasize that entrepreneurship education should be directed towards potential starters who seek rapid growth, high profits, and a possible quick sellout with a large capital gain.

10.2.2   Human capital and entrepreneurship
An important concept pertaining to the role of education in fostering entrepreneurship is the notion of 'human capital'. The term 'human capital' refers to the knowledge and skills acquired by, and embedded in, individuals (Becker, 1975). An important source of human capital lies in the nature of individuals' formal education and training. Prior research suggests that human capital has important and beneficial effects at the societal level. For example, Maskell and Malmberg (1999) argued that the overall stock of skills in a country affects what type of business activities are undertaken, and therefore influences the country's overall competitiveness. Similarly, Cannon (2000) argued that human capital raises overall productivity at the societal level through its effect on where physical and intellectual efforts are invested. Prais (1995) examined how a country's education and training system may foster overall productivity, and he emphasized the need to have the right balance of educational resources devoted to general academic issues versus matters directly connected to professional life. Also, Dakhli and De Clercq (2004) showed that a country's level of human capital (which is partly based on citizens' educational attainment) is positively related to its level of innovation.

Prior researchers have made a distinction between different types of human capital (Florin et al., 2003), which can be categorized as 'general' human capital and 'specific' human capital. General human capital pertains to knowledge and skills that are applicable to a broad range of activities, whereas specific human capital pertains to skills relevant to particular activities, for example, entrepreneurship and new venture creation. It has been argued that the level of specific human capital in a society has a positive relationship with the likelihood that individuals decide to engage in entrepreneurial activity (De Clercq and Arenius, 2006). The rationale for this positive relationship is partly based on the idea of self-efficacy.

The term 'self-efficacy' pertains to one's confidence in his or her skills and ability to successfully undertake career-related activities (Bandura, 1978). The effect of self-efficacy on an individual's behavior is related to the role of learning in that self-efficacy pertains to the belief that one has the necessary knowledge to successfully perform a particular task. Prior research has, for instance, found a positive relationship between self-efficacy and performance (for example, Bandura, 1978; Locke et al., 1984). However, self-efficacy does not only have direct performance effects but also drives individuals' choices and behavior. It has indeed been argued that the cognitive perception about one's skills and abilities has an important effect on where efforts are undertaken and how one persists in these efforts when obstacles arise (Bandura, 1978). Further, the belief in one's own abilities may be an important mechanism through which individuals set goals for future actions (Locke et al., 1984). For instance, individuals may be more inclined to choose for a career as entrepreneur if they believe to have the knowledge required to be successful in this choice (Boyd and Vozikis, 1994; Krueger et al., 2000).

In summary, given the importance of human capital at all levels of activity, it can be reasoned that a country's level of entrepreneurship-specific human capital (partly realized through the educational system) will influence the creation of start-ups within its borders. Individuals likely have different endowments of entrepreneurial abilities based on their training or education. Consequently, they have varying levels of confidence in their ability to successfully undertake start-up activities. In the context of new venture creation, the human capital resides to a great extent in the skills and capabilities of the founding entrepreneur (Davidsson and Honig, 2003). These skills may to a great extent depend on the educational background of the entrepreneur. Someone who has been exposed to entrepreneurship-related issues in his or her training may be more likely to engage in entrepreneurial activity because he or she will have the necessary training and background to successfully perform the start-up activity.

10.3 Methodology of the study

In order to assess the educational system in Belgium in terms of the stimulation of entrepreneurship, information has been collected through the Global Entrepreneurship Monitor in the period 2000–2004. More specifically, important insights were collected from the input provided by a myriad of 'country experts'. These are individuals who hold particular knowledge about entrepreneurship resulting from their experiences.

The following steps were used in the selection of the country experts: (1) the use of formal and informal networks and search media coverage about entrepreneurship, economic and business development in order to create a list of potential experts, (2) the investigation of each potential expert's background to establish his or her knowledge and experience relative to entrepreneurship, and (3) the insurance that a broad range of experts over differing status, gender and geographic locations were included.

In essence two types of people were contacted and interviewed, that is, professionals and entrepreneurs. *Professionals* included venture capitalists, academics, bankers, consultants, politicians and other people who are involved in entrepreneurial ventures in

Table 10.1   Three standard questions asked during face-to-face interviews

Strengths	In your opinion, what are the most significant factors pertaining to education that contribute to entrepreneurship in Belgium?
Weaknesses	In your opinion, what are the most significant factors pertaining to education that limit entrepreneurship in Belgium?
Recommendations	Can you give recommendations about what can be done in terms of education in order to increase entrepreneurship in Belgium?

addition to their full-time professional activity. *Entrepreneurs* are individuals with a history of practical entrepreneurial activity in their country (for example, founders of companies, or people who work in areas related to company development). A minimum of 36 experts have participated annually in the study since 2000.

The data from the experts were gathered through two data collection mechanisms, that is, face-to-face interviews and the expert questionnaire. The face-to-face interviews were semi-structured and basically had the objective to identify *qualitative* information about factors contributing to or limiting the development of entrepreneurship in Belgium. Furthermore, throughout the interviews the experts were probed about recommendations in terms of how entrepreneurship can be stimulated. The corresponding questions that were used as anchors during the interviews are shown in Table 10.1.

The objective of the expert questionnaire was to gather *quantitative* information on several environmental conditions that influence entrepreneurship in Belgium. An important part of the questionnaire pertained to the role of the educational system in fostering, or inhibiting, entrepreneurial behavior. Table 10.2 gives an overview of the six questions pertaining to the role of entrepreneurship education. The experts had to mention to what extent they agreed with six statements on a one-to-five point Likert scale.

10.4   Empirical findings
We first provide the results from the quantitative part of the data collection (that is, the expert questionnaire), and then turn our attention to the qualitative findings from the face-to-face interviews.

10.4.1   Quantitative findings
In the GEM study the role of education refers to the extent to which the educational and training systems at all levels (from primary and secondary school to university and business school) deal with the creation and managing of independent new or growing business.

As indicated above, the Belgian experts who participated in the GEM study were asked over the years about how (in)effective the *educational system* in Belgium is in preparing young people for a career as entrepreneur. The detailed results are shown in Table 10.3. More specifically, we show the results for Belgium spanning the 2000–2004 period, and we also compare the Belgian scores with the average scores in 2004 for the 12 EU countries that participated in the GEM study in 2004.[3]

In general, when we compare the longitudinal figures of the past five years it can be seen that there is relatively low variation in the answers about education. The stability is rather logical given that the educational system in a country, and in particular people's

Table 10.2   Six standard questions included in the expert questionnaire

Standard questions	Answers						
Teaching in primary and secondary education encourages creativity, self-sufficiency, and personal initiative.	1	2	3	4	5	K	NA
Teaching in primary and secondary education provides adequate instruction in market economic principles.	1	2	3	4	5	K	NA
Teaching in primary and secondary education provides adequate attention to entrepreneurship and new firm creation.	1	2	3	4	5	K	NA
Universities and other higher education institutions have enough courses and programs on entrepreneurship.	1	2	3	4	5	K	NA
Level of business and management education is truly world-class.	1	2	3	4	5	K	NA
Vocational, professional, and continuing education systems provide good preparation for self-employment.	1	2	3	4	5	K	NA

Note: 1: Completely false; 2: Somewhat false; 3: Neither true nor false; 4: Somewhat true; 5: Completely true; K: Don't know; NA: Not applicable.

perception about the system, does not change substantially from year to year. Furthermore, the consistency of the results is an indication of the robustness of the GEM methodology.

The first three statements in Table 10.3 pertain to the attention that is paid to entrepreneurship-related issues in *primary and secondary* education. It can be seen that the (entrepreneurial) educational situation at the primary and secondary school level is one of the problem areas in Belgium. More specifically, as regards the primary and secondary educational system, the Belgian scores have continued to be very low over time, *and* the Belgian 2004 scores are lower than the EU averages in terms of (1) the encouragement of creativity, self-sufficiency, and personal initiative, (2) the provision of adequate instruction in market economic principles, and (3) the provision of adequate attention to entrepreneurship and new firm creation. In short, the scores in terms of the efforts in primary and secondary education for the stimulation of entrepreneurship have been shown to remain weak and are somewhat lower than the EU averages.

Furthermore, whereas the scores for the statements regarding the *post-secondary and continuing* education are somewhat better than the scores for the primary and secondary education system and are also a little higher compared to the EU averages, the figures have also kept being relatively low over time. Also, there has been a decrease in 2004 compared to the peaks that were obtained in 2002. In other words, further efforts are needed to stimulate entrepreneurship in the higher education system in terms of (1) universities and other higher education institutions having enough courses and programs on entrepreneurship, (2) the world-class level of the business and management education, and (3) the preparation for a career as entrepreneur through the vocational, professional, and continuing education systems.

Table 10.3   Opinion of Belgian key informants with respect to education (scale from 1 to 5)

	Belgium					EU
	2004	2003	2002	2001	2000	2004
Teaching in primary and secondary education encourages creativity, self-sufficiency, and personal initiative.	2.12	2.08	1.95	2.17	2.02	2.27
Teaching in primary and secondary education provides adequate instruction in market economic principles.	2.08	2.13	1.87	2.26	2.15	2.14
Teaching in primary and secondary education provides adequate attention to entrepreneurship and new firm creation.	1.62	1.59	1.68	1.66	1.52	1.76
Universities and other higher institutions have enough courses and programs on entrepreneurship.	2.49	2.41	2.58	2.47	2.20	2.45
Level of business and management education is truly world class.	3.04	3.37	3.82	3.32	2.95	2.93
Vocational, professional, and continuing education systems provide good preparation for self-employment.	2.86	2.78	n/a	n/a	n/a	2.62

Note: EU: European Union; n/a: not applicable.

As a summary of the quantitative results pertaining to the role of education in entrepreneurship, we compare the composite score for the six education questions for Belgium in 2004 with the other EU countries (Figure 10.2). In the following section, the quantitative findings discussed above are complemented with the qualitative results from the face-to-face interviews.

10.4.2   Qualitative findings
During the face-to-face interviews the experts were asked to point to (1) education-related factors contributing to entrepreneurship, (2) education-related factors limiting entrepreneurship, and (3) recommendations about how entrepreneurship can be stimulated. Below we give an overview of the findings pertaining to points one and two; in the final section we discuss some recommendations.

10.4.2.1   Strengths of the educational system   Many key informants felt that the educational level of Belgian students is rather high compared to the level of foreign students, for example, students who come to Belgium to participate in the Erasmus exchange program. There was also a notion that Belgian students studying abroad often get relatively high marks compared to their international counterparts. A further positive note is the willingness of Belgian students to be persistent in their post-secondary studies. Technical and business training is of an excellent level, and people do not bother to study for a long time. However, the last point may also be thanks to the cheap cost of the Belgian education system.

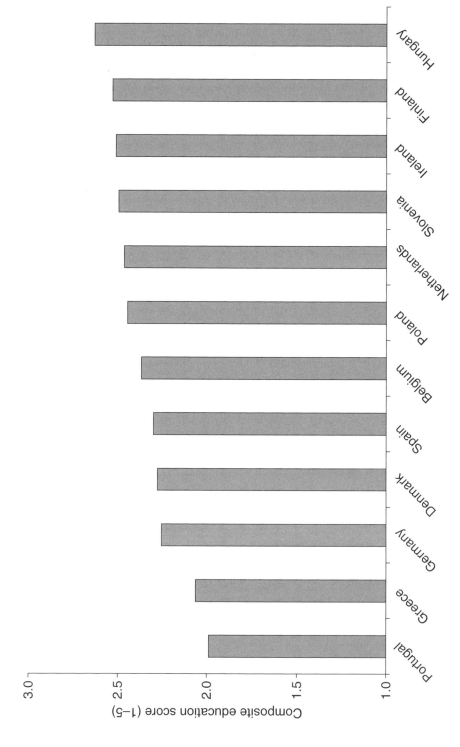

Figure 10.2   Comparison of the strength of the educational system in terms of entrepreneurship across several EU countries (data pertaining to 2004)

It also appears that several positive actions have been undertaken in the past years in Belgium in terms of the attention devoted to entrepreneurship. One example of good practice is the 'mini-enterprise' project and the 'DREAM' project in secondary education. In these projects students set up an own enterprise and need to make decisions similar to the decisions real-life entrepreneurs are confronted with. Enterprise can be associated with a set of attributes, skills and attitudes that enable people to create and thrive on change. Enterprise education enables pupils to develop confidence, self-reliance and willingness to embrace change. Through participation in mini-enterprises pupils can practice risk management, learning from mistakes and being innovative.

Another positive aspect is that the number of entrepreneurship courses at the university level and in other post-secondary education has been growing and the enrollment for these courses has been increasing steadily. For instance, most universities have decided that, with the introduction of the new 'Bachelor – Master' structure (following from the Bologna agreement), an entrepreneurship course will be mandatory for all students. Universities and post-secondary education (such as Vlerick Leuven Gent Management School, Ghent University, KU Leuven, ULG Liège, ULB, UCL and Solvay Business School) indeed offer more and more courses in entrepreneurship, business planning, and so on. However, it was also indicated that there is a need for a formal inventory system in Belgium with respect to the educational initiatives that have been taken in the area of entrepreneurship.

An interesting initiative in terms of the stimulation of entrepreneurship education in the French-speaking part of Belgium is the 'FREE foundation', which stimulates entrepreneurship at various stages of the educational system. One objective of this initiative is the provision of more entrepreneurship courses at the university and other levels, and a more extended outreach of educational institutions towards entrepreneurs (for example, in terms of educational and support programs).

Furthermore, business plan competitions are organized at the regional and national levels with the aim of increasing the entrepreneurial objective of students. For instance, the national 'Enterprize' competition was launched for the first time in 2003, with great success. Over 180 projects were registered, exceeding the enrolment objectives by 50 per cent. The 'Bizidee' project, which partners the 'EnterPrize' competition, has a mission in stimulating the entrepreneurial spirit in Flanders among the youth. Another partner in the EnterPrize competition is the Network for Teaching Entrepreneurship in Belgium (NFTE), who through entrepreneurship education helps young people from low-income communities build skills and unlock their entrepreneurial creativity. In order to do so, the NFTE trains its own certified entrepreneurship teachers.

Also, according to the key informants, professional and inter-professional organizations increasingly pay attention to the role of education in stimulating entrepreneurship. Another good initiative that was brought up pertains to the Regional Technological Centers, which have been charged with facilitating collaboration between schools and the business community and providing teachers with opportunities for practical training in companies. Also, there is an intention to further reorganize 'the teaching of teachers' so as to train future teachers in the competences required to teach entrepreneurship.

10.4.2.2   Weaknesses of the educational system   Despite the increasing attention to entrepreneurship in the Belgian educational system, it is acknowledged that there are serious barriers that hinder the implementation of entrepreneurial education in schools and universities.

In general, Belgian experts viewed their educational system as not satisfactory for enhancing entrepreneurial attitudes. Consistent with the quantitative results, there was a general perception that whereas the level of business and management education is of good quality, there is a negative feeling in terms of stimulating entrepreneurial behavior in primary and secondary education. It was often mentioned that the training system at these lower levels does not inspire creativity, independence and personal initiative, all necessary characteristics for future entrepreneurs. Furthermore, the contact with entrepreneurship comes at too late a stage. The schools often take too few efforts to let young people know more about assessing rational economic risks and taking economic responsibility.

An important problem, according to the experts, pertains to the curriculum. If schools intend to introduce entrepreneurial elements in their curriculum, these elements will necessarily replace other subjects which are currently being taught. As a result, certain teachers will stand to lose a part of their assignment and will naturally oppose the change. A policy aim to embed entrepreneurship in the final attainment levels for primary education and in the cross-disciplinary final attainment levels for secondary education would be very welcome, according to the experts. This would constitute a major breakthrough.

Furthermore, there is a concern about the methodology used in the educational system. Entrepreneurship is arguably one of the most difficult topics to teach. It involves the introduction of entrepreneurial attitudes and entrepreneurial skills. To succeed as an entrepreneur, one not only needs to master basic business skills, such as accounting, finance, strategic business planning and business law, but this knowledge input must be accompanied by the more difficult process of acquiring more general and fundamental skills and insights. Many experts thought that students must receive training in more subtle issues, such as people management skills, opportunity recognition, organizing skills, business ethics and negotiating skills. At the same time, entrepreneurial attitudes such as creativity, risk-taking, initiative and self-guidance must be emphasized in the courses. According to the experts, a methodology adapted to the needs of every level of education is needed. The experts recommended making an inventory of available good practices on case-study teaching, business-plan writing or business games for primary and secondary school levels in Belgium and in other countries. It was also suggested that a subsidy scheme for pilot projects developing new learning methods to incorporate entrepreneurial elements in the curriculum could be installed. Fortunately, the concept of project-driven education, which is now active in some Belgian schools, already allows for the introduction of an entrepreneurial project.

An additional critical point which was often referred to is the role of the teachers. According to the experts, the teachers teaching entrepreneurship face a very difficult task for which they are often not prepared. The experts often thought that teachers are ill-prepared for this task. There is a barrier between the business world and educational institutions, especially at the secondary level. Many teachers do not know an entrepreneur or do not have any contact with the business community and therefore tend to skip over concepts such as 'company' or 'economics' in their classes. Teachers should be stimulated to visit companies, or even work in these companies for some time in an internship.

A final issue, of a more general nature, is the experts' perception that many people in society are against the idea of focusing on business needs and requirements in education.

These people fear that the educational program would pay too much attention to practical issues, which would then be detrimental for the general education level. According to the experts, it is therefore imperative to demonstrate that the benefits of entrepreneurial education are complementary with other educational goals. A related concern of the key experts pertained to the narrow-minded ideas many youngsters have about entrepreneurship. For them, a company is still synonymous with greed, bribery and cheating. Therefore, it is the duty of the teachers at all levels of the educational system to change this way of thinking.

10.5   Implications

Based on the findings reported above, some recommendations can be drawn. The focus is on how the educational system can prepare students for entrepreneurial behavior. We believe that the recommendations mentioned below are not only applicable to Belgium but also to many other countries faced with a similar cultural, economic or political context.

Overall, we recommend that entrepreneurial attitudes in general and the development/implementation of business ideas in particular, should be integrated more extensively in the education system. More attention is required in primary, secondary and post-secondary education in terms of creating an awareness of self-employment, independence, creativity and entrepreneurial orientation. As important as accounting, finance, law, marketing and so on, is the provision of training in issues such as opportunity recognition, negotiating skills, business ethics and people management skills. Although various government bodies have launched various initiatives on these 'entrepreneurship' topics (for example, the 'Greenbook of Entrepreneurship' in the EU), this seems not (yet) to be the case throughout the different levels of education.

In the following paragraphs, we give some specific indications of how changes in education could promote entrepreneurship. We make a distinction between issues pertaining to the general educational system on the one hand, and issues pertaining to the inclusion of entrepreneurship-specific topics on the other.

10.5.1   *General education*

Traditionally, the Belgian educational system has been – and often still is – teacher- and content-oriented. To some extent, this inhibits the development of an entrepreneurial spirit. The results included in this chapter indicate the need for further changes if the objective is to stimulate entrepreneurial behavior. An educational system that focuses more on creativity and communication could improve the entrepreneurial skills of students. Children and students are to learn how to think systematically and to develop a critical attitude. This prepares people to become knowledgeable citizens and well-equipped potential entrepreneurs who can and will contribute to economic growth and prosperity. In other words, more emphasis should be put on stimulating independence, creativity, risk-taking and initiative, and to help individuals to become more independent and enterprising. The current educational system is not very interactive: subjects are often taught *ex cathedra*, without any interaction with the students. Students should be encouraged to be more curious to discover new things. The current information and communication technology (ICT) possibilities have changed the relationship between the teacher and student. For instance, thanks to the Internet, students may know more about a certain theme than the teacher, and therefore, the teacher's role has to change from being a mere provider of information to becoming a facilitator of creative information processing.

Furthermore, entrepreneurial activity could be encouraged by closing the wide gap between the educational system and the business world. On the one hand, schools could focus more on how people cope with (business) problems and on how to find creative solutions to these problems based on effective information gathering. On the other hand, companies should also better understand that not everything can be taught at school and that training cannot remain up to date forever, that is, there is a need for continuous learning. A more active cooperation between companies and schools can be realized when companies clearly define their educational needs and when schools become aware of and adequately respond to these needs. For instance, teachers should be given the opportunity to follow company courses.

In short, an entrepreneurial attitude calls for drive, creativity and persistence. Considering that both personality and management skills are key elements for success, general personal skills relevant to entrepreneurship should be taught from an early stage and be maintained up to university level, where management capacity can also be developed. From childhood on, people are often educated *not* to discover and develop their own talents in a creative way. However, children should be educated in a way that they have the opportunity to develop their own talents. Creativity should be presented in a positive way, and much earlier in the stage of a person's life (at primary school).

10.5.2 *Entrepreneurship education*

Education about entrepreneurship should start early. Today, this kind of education is too limited: it is only in some particular cases taught during the last two years of secondary school and then only to a limited number of students. It is very necessary, however, to motivate young people about pursuing an entrepreneurial career because the roots of entrepreneurship can often be traced back to the childhood of the entrepreneur (most entrepreneurs are inspired by their parents or other role models). The education system can provide both skills and exposure as a contribution to fostering entrepreneurship. Therefore, entrepreneurship training should be part of a school's curriculum, entrepreneurs should be invited into the classroom, apprenticeships for students to work with experienced entrepreneurs should be installed, and so on.

Within universities and business schools, there is also a need for more training in entrepreneurship. Entrepreneurship training should not only be for MBA students, it should be available for students in other fields; for example, in technical colleges it may contribute to matching entrepreneurial and technological potential.

Interestingly, our findings showed that, at all levels of education, there is a gap in terms of teaching competence. Because of its multidisciplinary nature, entrepreneurship is a specific topic to 'teach' and needs a specific interdisciplinary approach. It is surprising that in the myriad of emerging training programs, there are limited entrepreneurship 'train-the-trainers' programs in Belgium. As educational programs should be more focused on stimulating creativity, teachers also need to learn how they can better teach entrepreneurship. Some potential initiatives are to make use of ambulant teachers who mainly concentrate on entrepreneurial topics or to let existing teachers become acquainted with entrepreneurial life.

Below we mention some additional specific initiatives that could be taken to promote entrepreneurship in the educational system. The focus here is on students at the university level:

- Local entrepreneurs are an important source of practical wisdom for students. They could provide a 'window' of experience through mentoring students while setting up an own venture.
- Internships and consulting opportunities could allow students to apply entrepreneurial skills. Universities could offer existing entrepreneurs the opportunity to have their businesses 'evaluated' by students and/or teachers at little or negligible cost.
- Educational institutions could develop innovative ways to ensure that students 'stretch' their entrepreneurial muscles and become aware of the true risk–reward nature of entrepreneurship. For instance, students could be asked to develop a business plan and be provided with seed capital to start a business. The coursework could then guide the students in planning, launching, and managing a for-profit venture. The businesses could be liquidated at the end of the school year, and the profits could be used to fund a charitable project.
- In order to help students better understand the investor's perspective, they could be put in the 'investor's seat'. More specifically, students could be put in charge of operating a private equity investment fund under the guidance of seasoned venture capitalists.
- Chairs of Entrepreneurship could be established with a mandate for risk-taking and innovation, and with the support of university leaders. The objectives of these chairs should be to create greater depth to the existing entrepreneurship program, greater visibility across campus, and a greater connection between the classroom and the business community.

10.6   Conclusion
In this chapter we have provided some recommendations on how the educational system in Belgium could encourage entrepreneurship among students at all levels of development. We acknowledge that although our findings may be applicable to many other countries (especially other EU countries), a limitation of this study was its focus on only one particular country. Future research efforts should therefore benefit from comparing perceptions about entrepreneurship education across a wide variety of countries. Such a comparison could allow for the transfer of best practices across countries. Notwithstanding the limited geographical focus of our study's findings, we believe that its conclusions have external validity for other geographical areas. More specifically, we conclude that three important goals may need to be achieved when considering how entrepreneurial education needs to be developed.

A first goal is to enhance general awareness for the importance of entrepreneurship and its contribution to society and economic welfare. Although for most people lifetime employment in the same company is no longer a given fact, the educational system does not adequately reflect this trend, as it is generally geared towards preparing people for employment and less towards preparing them for a career as an entrepreneur. In order to encourage a reversal of this trend, students must be made aware of the opportunities offered by self-employment as a serious alternative to working as an employee. A second goal is to stimulate a positive attitude towards entrepreneurship among the young (and the population at large), and to encourage and develop their entrepreneurial attitudes. These entrepreneurial attitudes refer to personal characteristics such as creativity, risk-taking, initiative and goal-setting. An important notion is that entrepreneurship can be developed, even though these entrepreneurial attitudes seem to be closely connected with personal identity and personality. Therefore the entrepreneurial spirit should be developed at an early age, in primary and secondary schools, when a person's character is being developed. A final goal is to train students in certain entrepreneurial skills, such as general management skills, financial management and drawing up a business plan. Teaching these skills can be seen as preparing students to become entrepreneurs themselves.

From the above, it should be clear then that many countries, such as Belgium, could benefit economically from the fact that young adults graduate from school with a high sense of entrepreneurial spirit. We hope then that this chapter can serve as a stepping-stone to further investigation and measures of how a country's educational system can stimulate entrepreneurial activity within its borders, and hence also contribute to economic growth.

Notes

1. More specific information about the objective and content of the Global Entrepreneurship Monitor is given in section 2 of this chapter.
2. The countries that have participated in GEM include Argentina, Australia, Belgium, Brazil, Canada, Chile, China, Croatia, Denmark, Ecuador, Finland, France, Germany, Greece, Hong Kong, Hungary, Iceland, India, Ireland, Israel, Italy, Japan, Jordan, Korea, Mexico, Netherlands, New Zealand, Norway, Peru, Poland, Portugal, Russia, Singapore, Slovenia, South Africa, Spain, Sweden, Switzerland, Taiwan, Thailand, Uganda, the United Kingdom, the United States, and Venezuela.
3. The EU countries that participated in GEM 2004 include Belgium, Denmark, Finland, Germany, Greece, Hungary, Ireland, Netherlands, Poland, Portugal, Slovenia, and Spain.

References

Acs, Z., Arenius, P., Hay, M. and Minniti, M. (2005), *2004 Global Entrepreneurship Monitor*, London and Babson Park, MA: London Business School and Babson College.
Bandura, A. (1978), 'Reflections on self-efficacy', *Advances in Behavioral Research and Therapy*, **1**, 237–69.
Becker, G. (1975), *Human Capital*, New York: National Bureau of Economic Research.
Boyd, N.G. and Vozikis, G.S. (1994), 'The influences of self-efficacy on the development of entrepreneurial intentions and actions', *Entrepreneurial Theory and Practice*, **18**, 63–90.
Brock, W.A. and Evans, D.S. (1989), 'Small business economics', *Small Business Economics*, **1** (1), 7–20.
Cannon, E. (2000), 'Human capital: level versus growth effects', *Oxford Economic Papers*, **52**, 670–77.
Dakhli, M. and De Clercq, D. (2004), 'Human capital, social capital and innovation: a multi-country study', *Entrepreneurship and Regional Development*, **16**, 107–28.
Davidsson, P. and Honig, B. (2003), 'The role of social and human capital among nascent entrepreneurs', *Journal of Business Venturing*, **18**, 301–30.
De Clercq, D. and Arenius, P. (2006), 'The role of knowledge in business start-up activity', *International Small Business Journal*, **24** (4), 339–58.
Florin, J., Lubatkin, M. and Schultze, W. (2003), 'A social capital model of high-growth ventures', *Academy of Management Journal*, **46** (3), 374–84.
Gavron, R., Cowling, M., Holtham, G. and Westall, A. (1998), *The Entrepreneurial Society*, London: Institute for Public Policy Research.
Gibb, A.A. (1993), 'The enterprise culture and education: understanding enterprise education and its links with small business, entrepreneurship and wider educational goals', *International Business Journal*, **11** (3), 11–34.
Grilo, I. and Thurik, A.R. (2004), 'Determinants of entrepreneurship in Europe', working paper, ERIM Report Series Research in Management (ERS-2004-106-ORG).
Krueger, N.F., Reilly, M.D. and Carsrud, A.L. (2000), 'Competing models of entrepreneurial intentions', *Journal of Business Venturing*, **15**, 411–32.

Locke, E.A., Frederick, E., Lee, C. and Bobko, P. (1984), 'The effect of self-efficacy, goals, and task strategies on task performance', *Journal of Applied Psychology*, **69**, 241–51.

Maskell, P. and Malmberg, A. (1999), 'Localized learning and industrial competitiveness', *Cambridge Journal of Economics*, **23**, 167–85.

McIntyre, J.R. and Roche, M. (1999), University education for entrepreneurs in the United States: a critical and retrospective analysis of trends in the 1990s, working paper, Georgia Institute of Technology.

Minniti, M., Bygrave, W.D. and Autio, E. (2006), *Global Entrepreneurship Monitor: 2005 Executive Report*, London and Babson Park, MA: London Business School and Babson College.

Prais, S.J. (1995), *Productivity, Education and Training: An International Perspective*, Cambridge: Cambridge University Press.

Reynolds, P., Bosma, N., Autio, E., Hunt, S., De Bono, N., Sevais, I., Lopez-Garcia, P. and Chin, N. (2005), 'Global Entrepreneurship Monitor: data collection design and implementation 1998–2003', *Small Business Economics*, **24** (3), 205–31.

Reynolds, P.D., Bygrave, W.D., Autio, E. (2004), *Global Entrepreneurship Monitor: 2003 Global Report*, Wellesley, MA: Babson College.

Reynolds, P.D., Hay, M. and Camp, S.M. (1999), *Global Entrepreneurship Monitor: 1999 Executive Report*, Wellesley, MA: Babson College.

Solomon, G.T., Weaver, K.M. and Fernald, L.W. (1994), 'A historical examination of small business management and entrepreneurship pedagogy', *Simulation and Gaming*, **25** (3), 338–52.

Storey, D.J. (1999), 'Six steps to heaven: evaluating the impact of public policies to support small business in developed economies', in D.L. Sexton and H. Landström (eds), *Handbook of Entrepreneurship*, Oxford: Blackwell, pp. 176–94.

Thurik, A.R. and Wennekers, A.R.M. (2002), 'Entrepreneurship, small business and economic growth', *Journal of Small Business and Enterprise Development*, **11** (1), 140–49.

Verheul, I., Wennekers, A.R.M., Audretsch, D.B. and Thurik, A.R. (2002), 'An eclectic theory of entrepreneurship', in D.B. Audretsch, A.R. Thurik, I. Verheul and A.R.M. Wennekers (eds), *Entrepreneurship: Determinants and Policy in a European–US Comparison*, Boston, MA and Dordrecht: Kluwer Academic, pp. 11–81.

Wennekers, A.R.M. and Thurik, A.R. (1999), 'Linking entrepreneurship and economic growth', *Small Business Economics*, **13**, 27–55.

Zeithaml, C.O. and Rice, G.H. (1987), 'Entrepreneurship/small business education in American universities', *Journal of Small Business Management*, **25**, 44–50

11 Building Aboriginal economic development capacity: the Council for the Advancement of Native Development Officers[1]

Robert Anderson, Scott MacAulay, Warren Weir and Wanda Wuttunee

Introduction

The experience of Aboriginal peoples in North America with globalization (or at least something very like it) is not simply a feature of the current era. It began some five centuries ago, upon first contact with Europeans. The negative impact has been well documented: socially cohesive communities have suffered severe dislocation. What receives less attention, but is more important, is the degree of cohesion that remains and the burning desire among Aboriginal people to rebuild their communities on this foundation. Remarkably, they intend to do this by participating in the global economy, but on their own terms. Business development (that is, entrepreneurship) and participation in the workforce lie at the heart of their approach to this participation.

One organization, the Council for the Advancement of Native Development Officers (CANDO), is playing a key role in the development of the entrepreneurial capacity that is essential to successful participation in the global economy. This chapter describes the activities of CANDO, in particular its development of a national training and professional certification program for economic development officers working for Aboriginal communities and organizations. It places CANDO's success in the latest thinking on capacity-building.

The material that follows is presented in three sections. The first sets out the context in which Aboriginal economic development activities are taking place. It does so by briefly describing the current socio-economic circumstances of Aboriginal people and their response to these circumstances – participation in the global economy through business development. The second section consists of a brief overview of development theory as it has evolved (albeit with considerable delay) in response to the emergence of the global economy. Of particular significance is the role of entrepreneurship and capacity-building as the vehicle for effective participation in the global economy. The second section closes with a shift to things Aboriginal as we consider ways in which Aboriginal people can manage the development process and its essential institutions and activities in order to obtain their objectives. The final section looks at the emergence of one Aboriginal institution – the Council for the Advancement of Native Development Officers – and its activities in support of Aboriginal entrepreneurship and economic development.

Context

The current economic circumstances of Aboriginal people in Canada are abysmal. For example, according to 1991[2] census data 42 per cent of Aboriginal people living on reserve received social welfare, while only 8 per cent of other Canadians did. Unemployment among Aboriginal people stood at 24.6 per cent, almost two and a half times the national rate of 10.2 per cent. The on-reserve rate was even higher; often well above 30 per cent and approaching 90 per cent in isolated communities. Housing conditions tell a similar story with 65 per cent of on-reserve and 49 per cent of off-reserve people living in substandard housing.

Aboriginal people in Canada are not standing idly by and accepting these circumstances. They are pursuing a strategy of economic development. Their objectives include (1) greater control of activities on their traditional lands, (2) an end to dependency through economic self-sufficiency, (3) the preservation and strengthening of traditional values and their application in economic development and business activities, and (4) improved socio-economic circumstances for individuals, families, and communities. The process emerging to meet these objectives involves creating and operating businesses that can compete effectively over the long run in the global economy. Opportunity identification and entrepreneurship, alliances among themselves and with non-Aboriginal partners, and capacity-building through education, institution-building, and the realization of Aboriginal rights to land and resources are key elements of the process.[3]

Theoretical basis
The modernization and dependency perspectives dominated development thinking throughout the middle decades of the twentieth century. Even as modified in the later decades of the century (So, 1990) to take into account events in the Far East and Latin America, the two perspectives continue to present conflicting and incompatible views of the relationship between a 'developing' community/region (Aboriginal or any other) and the 'developed' world. Typical of those commenting on this conflict, Stuart Corbridge says

> The changing contours of global production are no more accessible to accounts of modernization theory and neoclassical economics than they are to MDS [Marxist development studies]: indeed, a metatheoretical commitment to the logic of diffusion or to freely functioning markets is even less fitted to the task than is faith in the development of underdevelopment. (Corbridge, 1989, p. 624; see also Schuurman, 1993)

Many have concluded that both perspectives are incomplete, with each describing a possible, but not inevitable, outcome of interaction between a developing region and the global economy. Instead, Corbridge and these others argue that the outcome experienced at a particular time and in a particular place is contingent on a variety of factors, many of which are at least partially under the control of the people in the developing region. In this vein, Corbridge says there is a powerful trend 'towards theories of capitalist development which emphasize contingency . . . a new emphasis on human agency and the provisional and highly skilled task of reproducing social relations' (1989, p. 633). Regulation theory, the post-imperial perspective, and alternative/Indigenous development approaches are three of the contingent approaches to economic development that are emerging from the impasse between the modernization and dependency perspectives.

Common to these three contingent perspectives[4] is the view that economic activity in a particular region, while it is and must be integrated into the global economy, can exhibit characteristics unique to that region and serve the particular needs of its people. For example, Dicken emphasizes that successful participation in the global economic system 'is created and sustained through a highly localized process' and that 'economic structures, values, cultures, institutions and histories contribute profoundly to that success' (1992, p. 307). According to Scott, the result is a 'very specific articulation of local social conditions with wider coordinates of capitalist development in general' (1988, p. 108). The strategy adopted by Aboriginal people is an example of this 'highly localized process' of development involving participation in the global economy. At least at the abstract theoretical level, the Aboriginal approach to development seems sound. It could succeed.

Broad theory aside, the question is, How do people participate successfully in the global economic system and in doing so build an economy? The answer is through the process of entrepreneurship; not the entrepreneurship that is narrowly conceived of as a small business operated and/or a new business created by an entrepreneur, but the entrepreneurship that is broadly conceived of as an economy-building process. Michael Morris in his book *Entrepreneurial Intensity: Sustainable Advantages for Individuals, Organizations and Societies* (1998) captures the broad nature of this process saying, 'entrepreneurship is a universal construct that is applicable to any person, organization (private or public, large or small), or nation'. He goes on to argue that an 'entrepreneurial orientation is critical for the survival and growth of companies as well as the economic prosperity of nations' (1998, p. 2). Ken Blawatt takes a similarly broad view of the nature of entrepreneurship and the relationship between it and the economy saying: 'Entrepreneurship is a series of skills, but more so an anthology of developed principles that have origins in humankind's earliest evolution. Entrepreneurship itself is the genesis of business activity. More importantly, it forms the basis of an economy and, by some standards, is the economy of a nation' (1998, p. xii).

In accepting Morris's and Blawatt's views of the universality of entrepreneurship, we wish to stress that 'entrepreneurship' can be and is shaped by cultural context (Corbridge, 1989; Dicken, 1992; Scott, 1988) and can serve a variety of purposes extending from the narrow objective of creating a society of individual profit-seekers to the broader objective of creating a network of social entrepreneurs and institutions whose objective is to enhance social cohesion and socio-economic development. Aboriginal people have adopted this latter broad objective (Basso and Johnstone, 1999).

Accepting what has been said about the contingent nature of the outcome of participation in the global economy and the role of entrepreneurship in this the process, a final question remains. How can Aboriginal people manage the development process and its essential institutions and businesses in order to attain their broad objectives? We will use David Newhouse's (2000b) work as a starting point in addressing this question.

Newhouse says management of the development process in an Aboriginal context involves a series of tensions that need to be resolved. These tensions can be thought of as occurring on two dimensions. The first tension is between economic objectives on the one hand and broader social objectives on the other. The second involves tensions between modern and traditional management values, principles and practices.

These tensions do not necessarily produce a set of mutually exclusive alternatives. In fact, it is often possible to resolve a tension by addressing the underlying issue in a way that satisfies what at first appear to be competing objectives. Take for example the desire to respect and use traditional Aboriginal values when managing organizations. It is commonly believed that there is a tension or conflict between this desire and the need to manage in a 'business-like fashion', but theory tells us that this need not be so.

Collective societies reflect a lower tolerance for power-distance[5] than is accepted in individualistic societies. This is certainly true for Aboriginal societies and is reflected in their traditional views relating to (1) division of labour, (2) leadership, and (3) decision-making. With respect to the division of labour, Redpath and Nielsen say Aboriginal societies 'have been nonhierarchical and had a division of labour based on expertise and responsibility'. While regarding leadership, they say: 'leaders did not seek power but were informally chosen or recognized by the community, not only for their exceptional skills, but also for the example they set in terms of their lifestyle and values . . . the leader must have the support of the group to remain in his or her position'. Finally, with respect to decision-making they observe that 'consensual decision-making prevailed' (Redpath and Nielsen, 1997, p. 331). These views are not unique to Redpath and Nielsen. They are widely accepted as true in the literature about Aboriginal people in Canada, and Indigenous (traditional) societies around the world.

Far from conflicting with modern management theory's views on the division of labour, leaders and leadership and decision-making, these traditional values and practices fall well within the mainstream. In fact, it can be argued that they are at the leading edge. There is no conflict; the tension can be resolved. Similar ideas need to be explored about traditional organization structures, methods of compensation, human resource policies, forms of ownership and the like. There is an Aboriginal approach to management in the same sense that there is a Japanese approach, an American approach, a Spanish approach, and so on. It is an approach that is modified to fit the circumstances of individual Aboriginal businesses in contemporary society.

Going beyond management, Newhouse talks explicitly about 'capitalism with a red face' which reflects efforts to adapt capitalism and 'to make it work in accordance with aboriginal belief systems' (2000a, p. 56). Newhouse suggests a number of ways that the practice of capitalist economic development could be (and is being) modified to suit Aboriginal values. We highlight three that seem especially relevant to our discussion here.

First, 'development will be seen as a joint effort between the individual and the collective and its institution' (Newhouse, 2000a, p. 59). Second, 'the development effort will emphasize human capital investment rather than individual capital accumulation. This focus on the human aspects of development will cause developers to explicitly consider the effects of their activities upon the quality of life which includes the environment and which affect development choices' (ibid.). Third, there will be 'a whole range of secondary economic support institutions such as development agencies, management advisory groups, loan funds, etc., whose primary function is not economic activity itself but the increasing efficiency of [and capacity within] the economy' (ibid., pp. 59–60). More broadly, according to Wein, the Aboriginal development process involves in part 'the building of institutional capacities within aboriginal communities which could then begin to deal with the various problems and issues of aboriginal life' (Wein, 1999, p. 61). One such institution is the Council for the Advancement of Native Development Officers.

Council for the Advancement of Native Development Officers
In 1990, Aboriginal economic development officers from across Canada founded the Council for the Advancement of Native Development Officers (CANDO). The Council was federally incorporated as a non-profit association in May 1991. Over the past 15 years, CANDO has become the premier national organization devoted to the promotion

of a high standard of economic development activities in Aboriginal communities across Canada. As of January 2006, CANDO had 321 members coming from every province and territory of Canada.

A key accomplishment for CANDO has been its development of a national training and professional certification program for economic development officers (EDOs) working for Aboriginal communities and organizations. The next two sub-sections contain a description of the activities of CANDO over its 15 years of existence.

Introduction to CANDO
Starting in the late 1970s, the delivery of economic development services has been increasingly devolved from senior Canadian governments to the community level. This devolution resulted in the creation of economic development delivery mechanisms in many Aboriginal communities. Typically, these local initiatives included the creation of economic development officers who worked with community members to encourage the development of successful community-based business ventures. In addition, other Aboriginal institutions began employing EDOs to work at the district, tribal and provincial/regional levels.

With this devolution came a number of challenges and opportunities for Aboriginal communities. Economic development officers created CANDO, in part, to provide for a systematic and organized way to deal with these challenges and opportunities. Initially, members envisaged CANDO as an organization that would help its members to perform more effectively at the local level by facilitating the ongoing development of their EDO skills and abilities. This was reflected in the 1990 mission statement of CANDO that was to 'actively promote and provide professional development and networking opportunities for economic developers working to strengthen Native communities across Canada'.

Flowing from this mission, the founding members of CANDO developed five overarching goals to guide the strategic activities of their organization. These were to:

1. provide a forum for the membership to exchange ideas, share information and solve problems of mutual concern. In many communities, the EDO is a sole practitioner and, thus, needs a means of establishing and maintaining contact with EDOs who work in similar situations;
2. build the capacity of economic development officers through ongoing training and education;
3. research key economic issues to assist the Native community from a policy development/advocacy perspective;
4. establish effective management capacity, a capable delivery mechanism and a sound financial and administrative structure to assure that overall objectives are realized, and;
5. encourage community-based business development and employment.

In order to achieve these goals CANDO embarked on several initiatives, including newsletters and bulletins, regional workshops for EDOs, a national journal for Aboriginal economic development practitioners, a national directory of EDOs, a workbook on conducting a human resource development assessment, a facilitator's guide to assist in the community-based strategic planning process, a database of reference materials for EDOs, and the collection of information about over 150 educational institutions in Canada offering specialized courses or program relating to Aboriginal community and economic and business development.

The Council's mission and goals have evolved over its 15-year life. Its mission statement is now 'Building capacity to strengthen Aboriginal communities' and its goals are to:

1. provide mechanisms for professional development and capacity-building for EDOs;
2. promote public education and awareness of Aboriginal community and economic issues;
3. assist in stabilizing community environments so economic development can flourish;
4. foster partnerships and alliances for Aboriginal community and economic development; and
5. have accountable, quality, effective operations.

In pursuit of it goals, one of CANDO's important and ongoing accomplishments has been the development and implementation of a national training and professional certification program for economic development officers working in and with Aboriginal communities and organizations. This professional certification is the first of its kind in the world. The development of this program is the subject of the next sub-section.

National Training and Professional Certification Program
The idea for the certification of economic development officers working in an Aboriginal context emerged in 1993 with the CANDO report *Training Needs Analysis of Economic Development Officers* (Price Waterhouse, 1993). The findings in the report were based on an analysis of 165 telephone surveys completed by economic development officers from across Canada. The survey results indicated, 'EDOs are less knowledgeable about the business and economic aspects of economic development than about their communities and government'. The survey results also indicated 'strong support for a special training program for economic development officers in Native communities'. The authors of the report concluded that CANDO could play a role in developing and administering such a program, and that this role could take one of two forms.

Under the first alternative, CANDO would design, develop and deliver a new training program tailored to meet the needs of Aboriginal community EDOs. The second approach involved CANDO evaluating and accrediting existing courses and programs offered in Canadian colleges and universities. In the report authors' opinion, the first option suffered from two problems. It would be costly and CANDO was not set up to be a training institution. On the positive side, under the first option the program content could be tailored to the specific needs of EDOs working in Aboriginal communities and/or for Aboriginal organizations. Conversely, the second option would be far less costly and would not require that CANDO develop the capacity to operate as an education institution. The problem with the second option was program content. Do existing programs address the knowledge and skill requirements of EDOs working in an Aboriginal context?

The Council's decision was to adopt the second approach but with the proviso that only those programs with content specific to the Aboriginal context would be accredited. It was clear that before being able to accredit programs/courses, CANDO would have to develop a set of occupational standards or guidelines. These would indicate the nature of the challenges faced by EDOs working in an Aboriginal context and the skills and knowledge they need to meet such challenges. Only then could the appropriateness of existing courses and programs be evaluated. In 1994 CANDO's Board created a Standing Committee on Education, Training and Employment.[6] This committee was mandated 'to develop and facilitate the delivery of a relevant, accessible, affordable and accredited curriculum for native EDOs, through research and consultation with members'.

In order to begin this work on a solid base, the committee held two three-day workshops to develop a DACUM (Developing a Curriculum) chart. Twenty-four volunteer EDOs from rural and urban settings participated in the sessions. The resulting DACUM chart provided CANDO with a comprehensive profile of the job of an EDO working in the Aboriginal context. It was to serve two purposes – accreditation and the professional certification. In the first instance, accreditation, the information was to be used to ensure that the content of a particular university or college program was relevant to the field of Aboriginal economic development. In the second instance, it was to be used to assess the level of competency of individuals seeking professional certification.

From 1994 to 1996, CANDO continued to develop the professional certification program. In 1996, the Standing Committee on Education, Training and Employment in a report to the CANDO Board proposed 10 principles to be followed by CANDO in its certification of Aboriginal EDOs. These were:

1. The process of certification should be established, directed and controlled by CANDO.
2. The certification upon fulfillment of the requirements should be issued by CANDO.
3. The standards for EDO certification should be established by CANDO.
4. The standards for EDO certification should be based upon the EDO competency profile chart completed in 1996.
5. The method of delivery of training and education for individuals seeking CANDO certification should be consistent with the CANDO recommendations to the Royal Commission on Aboriginal Peoples (RCAP), namely that it be:
   (a) delivered by Aboriginal-controlled institutions;
   (b) modular in nature;
   (c) accredited by post-secondary education institutions for certificate, diploma or degree programs.
6. Individuals should be able to meet the certification requirements through a combination of two methods:
   (a) accredited courses from post-secondary education institutions, and
   (b) experience as evaluated by a prior learning assessment (PLA)[7] process
   Candidates for certification should also have significant practical experience.
7. Individuals who qualify for and receive the CANDO certification may use a registered professional designation.
8. Individuals who receive the CANDO designation will be expected to participate in on-going professional development activities in order to retain their certification.
9. Individuals receiving the CANDO designation will be expected to conduct themselves in accordance with the CANDO code of ethics adopted August, 1994.
10. Individuals must be members in good standing of CANDO in order to retain their designation.

On Tuesday, 29 October 1996 at CANDO's Third Annual Conference in Saskatoon, the Honourable Ethel Blondin Andrew (Secretary of State: Training and Youth) announced that the federal government was going to help fund the certification/accreditation project in the amount of $436 000. With this financial assistance CANDO and the Standing Committee on Education were able to begin the implementation of the certified Aboriginal economic development program. The Standing Committee on Education was made up of professors from academic institutions across the country and community members who worked on establishing this program. They brought considerable expertise and commitment to meeting a standard of excellence that is unparalleled in this area. They worked closely with a supportive board to develop a useful tool.

The remainder of this section is a description of the program itself. Candidates must satisfy the requirements of the first or 'technician' level of the program before proceeding to the second, or 'professional', level. The technician level consists of 16 core competencies (gleaned from the 1994 DACUM results). They include

1.   the nature, structure functioning and development of economies,
2.   community economic development philosophy and theory,
3.   community economic development practices,
4.   community and political processes,
5.   the nature, structure, and functioning of organizations,
6.   the context of Aboriginal economic development,
7.   contemporary Aboriginal development approaches and issues,
8.   financial accounting,
9.   managerial accounting,
10. community impact analysis and assessment,
11. introductory marketing,
12. new enterprise development,
13. community-based research methods,
14. Aboriginal business law and policies,
15. written and oral communications, and
16. computer applications.

Candidates can use one of three methods to demonstrate competency in the 16 areas listed above. They can complete a program offered at a college or university that CANDO has accredited as meeting all 16 requirements. Alternatively, they can apply to have courses they have taken evaluated on a course-by-course basis. For example, the successful completion of an introductory economics course will suffice as demonstration of competency 1: the nature, structure, functioning and development of economies. Finally, they can use 'prior learning assessment' techniques to demonstrate the completion of any of the technician level competency requirements.

The second or professional level requirements include (1) participation in and completion of CANDO's professional development course, (2) completion of two years of experience in Aboriginal economic development, and (3) the completion and acceptance of a paper or case study related to Aboriginal economic development.

The professional development course – Integrating knowledge and experience – represents the capstone course of the professional level of the certification program.

During the intensive five-day course, participants are asked to integrate knowledge learned in previous sections of the certification program, discuss their experiences, and share ideas on three overriding themes: ethics, communication, and leadership. The course is structured to encourage participation and the open and forthright discussion of professional standards, the CANDO Code of Ethics (CED), and other current and pressing CED issues. By the end of the week participants develop and present outlines of their required paper or case study on Aboriginal economic development. To date the Professional Development Course (PDC) has been developed and piloted twice. In 1999 CANDO delivered the PDC in partnership with Chemainus Native College in British Columbia. The course focused on ethics, leadership, communications, and current topics/issues. The Council for the Advancement of Native Development Officers offered the PDC for a second time in 2001 at the Cape Breton University in Sydney, Nova Scotia.

The certification continues to be one of the primary focuses of the CANDO Board of Directors. In their 1999–2002 work plan, Goal 1 is 'to provide mechanisms for professional development and capacity building of Economic Development Officers'. The work plan lists three activities for the three-year period, including (1) promoting the program to its member EDOs and Aboriginal leaders as a new career path for youth/students, (2) promoting the program to universities and colleges and encourage them to seek accreditation, and (3) updating the certification materials on the CANDO web page. There have also been requests from Indigenous EDOs and educational institutions in Central and South America to have access to the program and training in Spanish.

The program has been well received to date. Interest and participation by individuals and education institutions has been encouraging. As of July 2004, there were a total of 195 candidates in the certification process and 34 technician-level graduates. The breakdown of candidates and technician graduates by province is shown in Table 11.1.

By the same date, there were five accredited programs: Nicola Valley Institute of Technology, British Columbia; Nunavut Arctic College, Nunavut; University College of Cape Breton, Nova Scotia; Aurora College, Yukon; and Algoma University College,

Table 11.1   Participants in certification program by province and territory

Province	Candidates	Technicians
Yukon	16	0
Nunavut	26	0
Northwest Territories	4	0
British Columbia	41	21
Alberta	16	4
Saskatchewan	23	0
Manitoba	9	2
Ontario	10	1
Quebec	7	2
New Brunswick	17	0
Nova Scotia	22	4
Prince Edward Island	2	0
Newfoundland	2	0

Ontario. The Council will continually work with post-secondary institutions towards accredited programs for the Aboriginal Economic Developer Process.

Concluding comments

The Council's efforts with respect to certification (and its other activities) are an example of effective institution-building in support of entrepreneurship and economic development. The professional certification program was born of the need to increase the effectiveness of individuals playing a prominent role in economic development in Aboriginal communities and organizations. Economic development officers are at the forefront of the entrepreneurial process that is the key to the implementation of the Aboriginal approach to economic development. They must be able to do their job effectively if the Aboriginal approach to development is to emerge as a successful 'articulation of local social conditions with the wider coordinates of capitalist development' (Scott, 1988, p. 108) to which Aboriginal 'values, cultures, institutions and histories contribute profoundly' (Dicken, 1992, p. 307).

Notes

1. A brief version of this paper was presented at the 2001 Conference of the Canadian Council for Small Business and Entrepreneurship in Quebec City.
2. Data for 1991 is used because the Royal Commission on Aboriginal People (1996) used the same census for its 'baseline' data.
3. See Anderson and Giberson (2002, p. 3) for a more in-depth description of this approach including evidence that it is being implemented.
4. See Anderson and Bone (1995) and Anderson (1997; 2002) for an in-depth discussion of these perspectives and an argument that they can be combined into a 'contingency perspective' on economic development.
5. Based on Hofstede (1980).
6. The authors of this chapter are all long-standing members of this committee.
7. Prior learning assessment is based on the idea that valuable learning is not limited to a formal education setting, but also occurs in many other settings. Many practicing EDOs have already mastered many of the core competencies described in level one, and the PLA process acknowledges and credits this experience.

References

Anderson R.B. (1997), 'First nations economic development: the role of corporate Aboriginal partnerships', *World Development*, **25** (9), 1483–503.
Anderson, R.B. (2002), *Aboriginal Entrepreneurship and Business Development*, North York: Captus Press.
Anderson R.B. and Bone, R.M. (1995), 'First nations economic development: a contingency perspective', *The Canadian Geographer*, **39** (2), 120–30.
Anderson, R.B. and Giberson, R.J. (2002), 'Aboriginal economic development: theory and practise', paper presented at the 2002 Babson Kauffman Entrepreneurship Research Conference, Boulder, CO: BKERC.
Anderson, R.B. and Giberson, R. (2003), 'Aboriginal economic development in Canada: thoughts on current theory and practise', in C. Stile and C. Galbraith (eds), *Ethnic Entrepreneurship: Structure and Process*, Oxford: JAI Press/Elsevier, pp. 141–67.
Basso, G. and Johnstone, H. (1999), 'Social entrepreneurs and community development', paper presented at the Atlantic Schools of Business 1999 Conference, Halifax, Nova Scotia.
Blawatt, K. (1998), *Entrepreneurship: Process and Management*, Scarborough: Prentice Hall, Canada.
Corbridge, S. (1989), 'Post-Marxism and development studies: beyond the impasse', *World Development*, **8** (5), 623–39.
Dicken, P. (1992), 'International production in a volatile regulatory environment', *Geoforum*, **23** (3), 303–16.
Hofstede, G.H. (1980), *Culture's Consequences: International Differences in Work-related Values*, Beverly Hills, CA: Sage Publications.
Morris, D. (1996), 'Communities: building authority, responsibility and capacity', in J. Mander and E. Goldsmith (eds), *The Case against the Global Economy: And for a Turn toward the Local*, San Francisco, CA: Sierra Club Books.

Morris, M. (1998), *Entrepreneurial Intensity: Sustainable Advantages for Individuals, Organizations and Societies*, Westport, CT: Quorom Books.

Newhouse, D. (2000a), 'Modern Aboriginal economies: capitalism with a red face', *Journal of Aboriginal Economic Development*, **1** (2), 55–61.

Newhouse, D. (2000b), 'Review of community development around the world: practice, theory, research and training', H. Campfens (ed.), *Journal of Aboriginal Economic Development*, **1** (2), 65–6.

Price Waterhouse (1993), *Training Needs Analysis of Economic Development Officers*, Edmonton: Price Waterhouse.

Redpath, L. and Nielsen, M. (1997), 'A comparison of native culture, non-native culture and new management ideology', *Canadian Journal of Administrative Sciences*, **14** (3), 327–39.

Royal Commission on Aboriginal Peoples (1996), *Report of the Royal Commission on Aboriginal Peoples*, Ottawa: Royal Commission on Aboriginal Peoples.

Schuurman, F.J. (ed.) (1993), *Beyond the Impasse: New Directions in Development Theory*. London: Zed Books.

Scott, A.J. (1988), *New Industrial Spaces: Flexible Production Organization and Regional Development in North America and Western Europe*, London: Pion Ltd.

So, A. (1990), *Social Change and Development: Modernization, Dependency, and World-System Theories*, Newbury Park, CA: Sage Publications.

Wein, F. (1999), 'The Royal Commission report: nine steps to rebuild Aboriginal economies', *Journal of Aboriginal Economic Development*, **1** (1), 102–19.

12 New Zealand graduates in entrepreneurship: toward a paradigm of interdependence

Léo-Paul Dana

Introduction and methodology

WHAT do students do after they graduate university? This chapter is the result of research about graduates of the University of Canterbury in Christchurch, New Zealand. Christchurch is the largest city on New Zealand's South Island and opportunities for careers with government or with large firms are limited here.

Methodology involved seven focus groups conducted with former students of the University of Canterbury. Those who have opted to get involved in entrepreneurship, rather than seek employment, were invited for open-ended interviews.

In contrast to the American stereotype of the entrepreneur, who is individualistic and seeks independence, interviewed graduates tended to seek co-operation in networks. This was manifested in two forms: (1) an attraction to becoming franchisees, and (2) active participation in existing networks.

Much literature discusses networks that are created along ethnic lines, as entrepreneurs are comfortable doing business with like-minded people, whom they understand, and with whom they get along. Rather than using ethnicity as the basis for networking, respondents of this study have been networking with others who share the same techno-culture.

The following sections discuss this techno-culture, and then review the literature relating to education and entrepreneurship. This is followed by a literature review of the classic independent entrepreneur, revealing that interviewees do not fit this traditional image. A literature review of networking and an introduction to New Zealand are followed by a discussion of techno-culture networking in New Zealand. Franchising is shown to be one form of networking. The chapter concludes with a discussion of implications and suggestions for future research.

Techno-culture

Even before globalization affected society at large, the elite of one country often mixed with the elite of another. Although the peasantry of England had little – if any – contact with that of the Continent, the royalty corresponded with, intermingled with, and even married with the aristocracy in Europe. While the English commoner had little in common with any Prussian, Victoria and Albert shared a regal culture that transcended national boundaries. Queen Victoria had more in common with her German-speaking husband than with the working class of East London or the herder of the Highlands. In other words, the elite shared a trans-national culture that transcended national boundaries.

In today's world, the traditional factors of production have given way to knowledge as the driving force behind wealth creation. An educated class of people has created a new trans-national culture around new technologies, and people who adhere to it gravitate to one another. Dana et al. (2002) refer to this as techno-culture. This chapter identifies techno-culture in New Zealand, and examines networking linked to it. Once again, birds of a feather flock together. Findings indicate that connecting with other graduates, in a techno-culture network, is enhancing opportunity for co-operation and profit in entrepreneurship. Findings also reveal, that for less technical ideas, graduates are attracted to franchise business systems.

Education and entrepreneurship
Cooper and Dunkelberg (1987) found that entrepreneurs had more education than non-entrepreneurs. It makes sense, then, to investigate entrepreneurship among graduates.

There has been scepticism, however, as to whether universities actually contribute to entrepreneurship. According to Knight (1987), potential entrepreneurs can be encouraged by schools, but he argued that business school graduates become entrepreneurs in spite of the educational system, rather than because of it. Kao (1988) went as far as to say that many people lose their entrepreneurial sprit because of an educational system that does not encourage non-conformity. Consistent with this view, Castro et al. (1988) reported that universities of North America contribute a minute fraction of new ventures formed. Fleming (1988) investigated whether universities contributed to the formation of entrepreneurs in Australia, and found only 16 per cent of her sample considered there to be any value in the contributions of academia.

Nevertheless, empirical research has shown that increased education correlates positively with increased likelihood of becoming self-employed. Robinson and Sexton (1994) found a positive correlation between education and self-employment. Their study estimated that each year of education increases the likelihood of self-employment by 0.8 per cent, and annual income by US$1208. The authors concluded that 'The net result is that although education is important for wage and salaried workers, it is even more important to the success of the self-employed' (Robinson and Sexton, 1994, p. 152).

Light and Rosenstein (1995) agreed that there is a positive correlation between education and self-employment. Their study estimated that each year of education increases the likelihood of self-employment by 0.7 per cent.

The study upon which this chapter is based found that graduates in New Zealand are benefiting from networking with other educated graduates interested in techno-culture. Respondents indicate that networking with other graduates is enhancing opportunities for co-operation and profit in entrepreneurship. While the traditional entrepreneur in the literature is an individualist non-conformist, New Zealand graduates appear to be willing to conform to like-minded graduates in techno-culture networks.

The independent entrepreneur
The traditional focus of entrepreneurship literature was on personal qualities of the entrepreneur. Cantillon (1755) was the first to discuss entrepreneurs as risk-takers. Say (1803; 1815) and Mill (1848) also linked entrepreneurship to risk. Ely and Hess defined entrepreneurs as 'the ultimate owners of business enterprises, those who make the final decision and assume the risks involved in such decisions' (1893, p. 95). Knight (1921) described the entrepreneur as a taker of *non-quantifiable risks*, and profits as a reward that owner-managers receive for bearing risk. Oxenfeldt (1943) recognized the centrality of risk in entrepreneurship. Cole (1959) also examined the risk of uncertainty. Cochran (1968) discussed risk as a distinguishing attribute of the entrepreneur. Shapero found that

in 'almost all the definitions of entrepreneurship, there is agreement that we are talking about a kind of behavior that includes . . . the acceptance of risk' (1975, p. 87).

Considerable research has been done on the personality of the entrepreneur. Examples include Begley and Boyd (1987), Brockhaus (1982), Brockhaus and Horwitz (1986), Gasse (1977; 1985), Kets de Vries (1977), Sexton and Bowman (1985), Sexton and Bowman Upton (1990), and Timmons et al. (1985). Whereas much of this literature suggests the entrepreneur usually has certain characteristics that are innate, others including Gibb (1986) and Knight (1987) showed that entrepreneurial behaviour might also be enhanced through training.

While there is no unique, universally accepted definition of what is an entrepreneur, researchers agree that entrepreneurs are individuals with unique traits.

Individualism and a desire for independence have traditionally been listed among these traits.

Networks

While the stereotypical entrepreneur is individualistic with a desire for independence, a rich sociological literature focuses on entrepreneurs who benefit from reduction of risk, brought about from networks. Networking involves calling upon a web of contacts for information, support and assistance. Reciprocal preferential treatment reduces transaction costs.

Aldrich and Zimmer (1986) integrated social network theory into the study of entrepreneurship, and investigated the impact of social networks on self-employment; they concluded that networking might be an essential requirement for entrepreneurial success. Carsrud et al. (1986) also found networks important to the understanding of new venture development.

Aldrich et al. (1987) studied the impact of social networks on profit, as well as on business creation; they found network accessibility significant in predicting new venture creation. Likewise, Dubini and Aldrich (1991) found networks central to entrepreneurship. Gomes-Casseres (1996) focused on the alliance strategies of small firms. Anderson (1995), Dunning (1995), Holm et al. (1997), and Johanson and Associates (1994) studied the effect of business networks on internationalization of firms.

Other studies that have found networks to be central to entrepreneurial activity include: Aldrich (1989); Birley (1985); Johannisson (1987); Olm et al. (1988); and Shaver and Scott (1991).

Networking often takes place among entrepreneurs of similar cultural or ethnic affinities. Aldrich et al. (1984) focused on networks between immigrant entrepreneurs and their country of origin. Analysing Asian entrepreneurs in Britain, their study found that Asian entrepreneurs benefit from 'certain advantages denied non-ethnic competitors' (Aldrich et al., 1984, p. 193). They identified a strong internal solidarity in the ethnic enclave. Werbner (1984) likewise examined networking among Pakistani entrepreneurs in the United Kingdom. Given that the possibility of exploiting opportunities appears to be linked to the internal organizing capacity of a group, such as creating an ethnic network, Auster and Aldrich (1984) concluded that the ethnic enclave reduces the vulnerability of small firms, by providing an ethnic market and also general social and economic support, including credit.

In their study of Koreans in Atlanta, Min and Jaret (1985), found their networks to be a source of personnel for entrepreneurs. Aldrich and Zimmer (1986) likewise found ethnic networks in England to be effective.

Boissevain and Grotenbreg (1987), in their study of the Surinamese in Amsterdam, suggested that access to a network of contacts is an important resource for entrepreneurs. They noted, for instance, that networks could provide introductions to wholesalers and warnings of government inspections, and they showed that small firms in Amsterdam succeed within a social support network of like-minded people. Iyer and Shapiro (1999) demonstrated how expatriate ethnic entrepreneurs leverage their membership in local ethnic networks, in the countries to which they had emigrated, to import from their country of ethnic origin; these business people thus infused international activity into the supply and value chains of the social/ethnic networks in both countries.

Other contributions to the literature on ethnic enterprise include Aldrich et al. (1984); Aldrich and Waldinger (1990); Cummings (1980); Dana (1995); Jenkins (1984); Light (1972; 1980; 1984); Light and Bonacich (1988); Min (1984; 1986–87; 1987); Min and Jaret (1985); Portes and Bach (1985); Portes and Jensen (1987; 1989; 1992); Sanders and Nee (1987); Waldinger (1984; 1986a; 1986b); Waldinger and Aldrich (1990); Waldinger et al. (1990a); Waldinger, McEvoy and Aldrich (1990b); Ward (1987); Ward and Jenkins (1984); Wong (1987); and Wu (1983). It is clear that in Europe, in the Americas, and in Asia, there are entrepreneurs who have traditionally sought business support from ethnic networks, consisting of people of similar ethnicity.

In contrast, the empirical research upon which this chapter is based suggests that New Zealand graduates are not actively seeking to limit their networks along ethnic lines. Instead, they are networking among people who share their techno-culture.

New Zealand
New Zealand, today, has one of the world's most open economies, with one of the most deregulated business sectors. Given this deregulated environment, and the small size of the domestic market, it is becoming increasingly difficult for independent, small firms in New Zealand to thrive on their own. Considering that New Zealand is regarded as a nation of small enterprises (Linowes and Dixon, 1992), this is an important problem, potentially affecting a large percentage of the population in this country. Cameron et al. (1997) calculated that 85 per cent of all New Zealand firms employed five persons or less. McGregor and Gomes (1999) reported that SMEs employed 60 per cent of the New Zealand workforce at the time. Fletcher (1999) noted that out of a total of 250 000 firms in New Zealand, only 1300 employed more than 100 people.

Interest in New Zealand's small firms has been on the rise. Levine and Levine (1983) focused on small enterprises on Stewart Island. Levine (1985) conducted an ethnographic study of self-employed fishermen on Stewart Island, and their effects on the social organization of the community. Taylor (1993) found that small firms in New Zealand were less market-orientated than larger ones. Likewise, in their study of 427 respondents (from a list, of 1250 organizations, supplied by the New Zealand Department of Statistics), Taylor and Brooksbank (1995) found significant differences between small and large firms.

Combining in-depth case research and a mail survey, Coviello and Munro (1995) obtained data from 25 computer software firms based in New Zealand. Their study found that foreign market selection and entry initiatives came from opportunities created through formal and informal network contacts. Network relationships facilitated rapid growth and actively influenced the growth pattern and internationalization process. It was concluded that small New Zealand software firms relied on network relationships for marketing-related activities in foreign markets.

In their qualitative study of the causal processes of exporting in 12 owner-controlled New Zealand manufacturers, Chetty and Hamilton (1996) found support for Reid's (1981) stage model and concept of psychic distance. That study also revealed other causal factors influencing the exporting process; these included relative technological sophistication, firm size, and the domestic market environment.

Carlsson (1996) conducted an international comparison of manufacturing firms in Europe, New Zealand, and the United States. This study found a unique scenario in New Zealand. While the economy declined, the number of manufacturing establishments grew rapidly, but manufacturing employment fell. Therefore, the average manufacturer declined in size, from 30.9 in 1978 to 11.5 employees in 1993.

Coviello and Munro (1997) examined the internationalization process of four software firms in New Zealand. They found the establishment chain to be rapid and compressed into only three stages, and characterized by externalization of market development activities, through investment in network relationships. The authors suggested that internationalization patterns could be better understood by integrating the models of incremental internationalization with the network perspective.

Dean et al. (1998) focused on manufacturing firms in the Province of Canterbury. In their examination of export development, they identified two types of barriers to export: those that were stable across stages of development and those that changed, in their level of importance. Berg and Hamilton (1998) focused on internationalization efforts of New Zealand firms, and found that joint ventures tended to result in failures. Sadler and Chetty (2000) found New Zealand exporters influenced by business networks.

Techno-culture networking in New Zealand

Every week, in Christchurch, like-minded graduates – interested in science and technology – get together at what appears to be an informal barbecue. This event, called the Tech BBQ (barbecue), was initially hosted by individuals who were involved in the local incubator programme. Nowadays, entrepreneurs and innovators who represent a variety of businesses and technologies attend it regularly. At this function, the graduates socialize, network and strike deals.

The purpose of the incubator programme was to nurture entrepreneurship, and stimulate exports. Yet, it was felt that the incubator itself was poorly promoted. To raise community awareness, and create an opportunity to meet like-minded graduates, its participants opted for the Tech BBQ. Outsiders also took interest in this event, and it has since become a local institution of techno-culture, albeit an informal one. It brings together technology developers, industries, investors, and even artists, whose complementary skills help each other's business. In the words of Mary Wilson, presenter of *Newztel News*, 'There is a bit more cooking than the sausages.'

The Tech BBQ is attended by a wide range of innovation leaders. These include: Colin Chapman, founder of Invensys Energy (formerly known as Swichtec); John Hamilton of the Canterbury Innovation Incubator; Christine More, Word Engineer; and Warwick Schaeffer, the entrepreneur behind Boulevard Web Systems. The branding and logos for Boulevard Web Systems are designed by a local artist, whom Mr Shaeffer met at the Tech BBQ. Mr Shaeffer has found an investor, as well as seed customers, at this networking function. Likewise, David Lane, a self-employed open source software expert who develops the functionality of websites, gets new clients through the weekly event; some of his projects have involved graphic designers whom he met at the BBQ.

Hugo Kristinsson summarized the benefits he has obtained from these events: legal issues; insurance issues; distributor agreements; finding office space; finance issues, social issues, packaging issues, and employment issues. Rob Glassey elaborated, 'Many contacts have been made outside the more familiar "techy" environment that most tech company people already know. For example, finding contacts for PR, graphics design, accounting, legal work, marketing and distribution.'

In addition, the BBQ allows its participants an opportunity to share experiences, to discuss problems, and to learn from one another. This includes business strategy as well as technology. Simultaneously, successful entrepreneurs become mentors or role models for aspiring businesspeople, and self-confidence is boosted. Deborah Sharplin, formerly Vice President for Export Institute Canterbury, added, 'in reality export is based on relationships . . . '

Reciprocal preferential treatment among participants does indeed reduce transaction costs. The entrepreneurs are willing to give up some of their independence, to benefit from the advantages of *interdependence*. In the words of Christine More, 'This is a community. It supports . . . '

Franchising
While informal techno-culture networking has been effective for some graduates, other graduates have expressed a preference for greater structure and formality, as offered by franchising – a method of distribution of goods and services, whereby a franchiser expands by means of a network of franchisees. The franchise network is bound together by a contractual agreement between a relatively large franchiser, and smaller franchisees. Franchising thus creates networks of small firms, distributing a proven product and/or service on behalf of a larger enterprise.

For franchisers, franchising is a means to rapid market penetration. For the franchisees, it is a way to buy into an existing business network. Franchising helps both – franchisers and franchisees – to obtain economies of scale. Given that it is increasingly difficult for independent, small firms to thrive on their own unless they are globally competitive, franchising is becoming an increasingly popular means of co-operation among firms in New Zealand.

For recent graduates, franchising has appeal, because the franchiser provides a marketing programme to a smaller-scale entrepreneur. This includes a brand name and logo, trademarks, products, service standards, technical expertise, advertising and methods of operation. The advantages of franchising, from the franchisee's perspective, include commitment from the franchiser, which involves a support system. The franchisee is assisted with location selection, design start-up, operations and advertising. The franchiser provides the product, and the service quality. The franchisee obtains access to economies of scale, thanks to the franchiser's network. The franchiser also provides access to expertise, experience, training and marketing. What this means for the recent graduate is a higher chance of success, thanks to a shorter learning curve and an established trademark/servicemark provided by the franchiser. Also, bank financing often favours franchised businesses. Such arrangements allow franchisees to achieve economies of scale, by integrating into the networks of the larger franchisers. For the franchiser, franchising provides an inexpensive source of capital for expansion, while offering greater control than would a strategic alliance. New symbiotic relationships are thus created, allowing firms to achieve the expanded reach and efficiencies associated with internationalization – more rapidly and effectively than they could on their own.

Until recently, in New Zealand, other types of collaborative arrangements between small firms and large firms were transaction-based; in other words, they could be terminated at the will of either party – usually the larger one. Franchising is characterized instead by interdependence, with each party relying on the other in a sustained, ongoing manner. In a truly symbiotic relationship, franchisers cannot operate without franchisees.

Franchising allows firms to achieve symbiotic relationships in which franchisers and franchisees rely on each other to attain world-class competitiveness for their entire network. The resulting increase in efficiency enables the network as a whole to compete more effectively and to gain market share globally. Young graduates can draw upon the pooled capabilities and knowledge stock of their entire network, instead of developing the required knowledge themselves.

Implications

Whereas the entrepreneur was traditionally portrayed as an independent risk-taker, there is currently a trend toward *interdependent networking* in New Zealand. This is quite a shift from the traditional literature. In contrast to the ethnic networks prevalent elsewhere, this chapter has focused on networking among individuals who share a techno-culture. This is quite a new phenomenon, with a gap among existing theories.

Nowadays, it is no longer simple for graduates in New Zealand to become independent entrepreneurs, as the environment is no longer a protected one. Networks now compete for global market share.

This leads to pedagogical implications. To work in networks, entrepreneurs will need more people skills than ever before. They will need to learn to interact effectively with other entrepreneurs in the same network and with other networks.

There are also practical implications. Building upon knowledge networks is a new strategic competence that is bound to challenge managers, especially those still orientated toward fully independent operations. There are far-reaching consequences of this paradigm shift from independence toward interdependence. The implications largely contradict conventional thinking about the independent growth and management of small enterprises. The global environment calls for new strategies, often involving a trade-off between independence and profit.

Symbiotic networking is leading to interdependence in business; we are moving beyond a focus on the firm – toward a focus on relationships with networks. Power and control is divided among New Zealand graduates who co-operate voluntarily for increased efficiency and profit.

Toward future research

Traditional entrepreneurship research has focused on the individual entrepreneur. This may no longer be sufficient. If entrepreneurs work in networks, then perhaps the unit of interest should be the network.

Future research might compare the situation in New Zealand with that elsewhere. Is networking become universal or is it simply a necessity in an environment of economic malaise?

References

Aldrich, H.E. (1989), 'Networking among women entrepreneurs', in O. Hagen, C. Rivehum and D.L. Sexton (eds), *Women-Owned Businesses*, New York: Praeger, pp. 103–32.

Aldrich, H.E. and Waldinger, R.D. (1990), 'Ethnicity and entrepreneurship', in W. Scott and J. Blake (eds), *Annual Review of Sociology*, **16**, 111–35.

Aldrich, H.E. and Zimmer, C. (1986), 'Entrepreneurship through social networks', in D.L. Sexton and R.W. Smilor (eds), *The Art and Science of Entrepreneurship*, Cambridge, MA: Ballinger, pp. 3–24.

Aldrich, H.E., Jones, T.P. and McEvoy, D. (1984), 'Ethnic advantage and minority business development', in R. Ward and R. Jenkins (eds), *Ethnic Communities in Business: Strategies for Economic Survival*, Cambridge: Cambridge University Press.

Aldrich, H.E., Rosen, B. and Woodward, W. (1987), 'The impact of social networks on business foundings and profit in a longitudinal study', *Frontiers of Entrepreneurship Research*, Wellesley, MA: Babson College, pp. 154–68.

Anderson, P.H. (1995), *Collaborative Internationalisation of Small and Medium-Sized Enterprises*, Copenhagen: DJOF.

Auster, E. and Aldrich, H.E. (1984), 'Small business vulnerability, ethnic enclaves and ethnic enterprise', in R. Ward and R. Jenkins (eds), *Ethnic Communities in Business: Strategies for Economic Survival*, Cambridge: Cambridge University Press, pp. 39–54.

Begley, T.M. and Boyd, D.P. (1987), 'Psychological characteristics associated with performance in entrepreneurial firms and smaller businesses', *Journal of Business Venturing*, **2**, 79–93.

Berg, J.N. and Hamilton, R.T. (1998), 'Born to fail? International strategic alliances experiences of New Zealand companies', *Journal of International Business and Entrepreneurship*, **6** (1 and 2), 63–76.

Birley, S. (1985), 'The role of networks in the entrepreneurial process', *Frontiers of Entrepreneurship Research*, Wellesley, MA: Babson College, pp. 325–37.

Boissevain, J. and Grotenbreg, H. (1987), 'Ethnic enterprise in the Netherlands: the Surinamese of Amsterdam', in R. Goffee and R. Scase (eds), *Entrepreneurship in Europe: The Social Process*, London: Croom Helm, pp. 105–30.

Brockhaus, R.H. (1982), 'The psychology of the entrepreneur', in C.A. Kent, D.L. Sexton and K.H. Vesper (eds), *Encyclopedia of Entrepreneurship*, Englewood Cliffs, NJ: Prentice-Hall, pp. 41–56.

Brockhaus, R.H. and Horwitz, P.S. (1986), 'The psychology of the entrepreneur', in D. Sexton and R.W. Smilor (eds), *The Art and Science of Entrepreneurship*, Cambridge, MA: Ballinger, pp. 25–48.

Cameron, A.F., Massey, C. and Tweed, D. (1997), 'New Zealand small business: a review', *Chartered Accountants Journal of New Zealand*, **76** (9), 4–12.

Cantillon, R. (1755), *Essai sur la nature du commerce en général*, London and Paris: R. Gyles; translated (1931), by Henry Higgs, London: Macmillan.

Carlsson, B. (1996), 'Differing patterns of industrial dynamics: New Zealand, Ohio, and Sweden, 1878–1994', *Small Business Economics*, **8**, 219–34.

Carsrud, A.L., Gaglio, C.M. and Olm, K.W. (1986), 'Entrepreneurs – mentors, networks and successful new venture development: an exploratory study', *Frontiers of Entrepreneurship Research*, Wellesley, MA: Babson College, pp. 229–43.

Castro, C., McMullan, W.E., Vesper, K.H. and Raymount, M. (1988), 'The venture generating potential of a university', in R.W.Y. Kao (ed.), *Readings in Entrepreneurship*, Toronto: Ryerson, pp. 178–87.

Chetty, S.K. and Hamilton, R.T. (1996), 'The process of exporting in owner-controlled firms', *International Small Business Journal*, **14** (2), 12–25.

Cochran, T.C. (1968), 'Entrepreneurship', in D.L. Sills (ed.), *International Encyclopedia of the Social Sciences*, London and New York: Macmillan.

Cole, A.H. (1959), *Business Enterprise in its Social Setting*, Cambridge, MA: Harvard University Press.

Cooper, A.C. and Dunkelberg, W.C. (1987), 'Entrepreneurial research: old questions, new answers and methodological issues', *American Journal of Small Business*, **11** (3), 11–23.

Coviello, N.E. and Munro, H.J. (1995), 'Growing the entrepreneurial firm: networking for international market development', *European Journal of Marketing*, **29** (7), 49–61.

Coviello, N.E. and Munro, H.J. (1997), 'Network relationships and the internationalisation process of small software firms', *International Business Review*, **6** (2), 1–26.

Cummings, S. (ed.) (1980), *Self-Help in Urban America: Patterns of Minority Business Enterprise*, Port Washington, NY: Kennikat, pp. 33–57.

Dana, L.P. (1995), 'Entrepreneurship in a remote sub-Arctic community: Nome, Alaska', *Entrepreneurship: Theory and Practice*, **20** (1), 57–72.

Dana, L.P., Korot, L. and Tovstiga, G. (2002), 'Toward a trans-national techno-culture: an empirical investigation of knowledge management', in H. Etemad and R. Wright (eds), *Globalization and Entrepreneurship: Policy and Strategy Perspectives*, Northampton, MA: Edward Elgar.

Dean, D., Gan, C. and Myers, C. (1998), 'An investigation of the relationship between a firm's perceived export barriers and stages of export development: an analysis of Canterbury manufacturing firms', *Journal of Enterprising Culture*, **6** (2), 199–216.

Dubini, P. and Aldrich, H.E. (1991), 'Personal and extended networks are central to the entrepreneurship process', *Journal of Business Venturing*, **6** (5), 305–13.

Dunning, J.H. (1995), 'Reappraising the eclectic paradigm in an age of alliance capitalism', *Journal of International Business Studies*, **26** (3), 461–91.

Ely, R.T. and Hess, R.H. (1893), *Outline of Economics*, New York: Macmillan.

Fleming, D. (1988), *Creating Entrepreneurs*, Sydney: Allen and Unwin.

Fletcher, H. (1999), 'How can New Zealand win the globalisation game?', *University of Auckland Business Review*, **1** (1), 74–81.

Gasse, Y. (1977), *Entrepreneurial Characteristics and Practices: A Study of the Dynamics of Small Business Organization and Their Effectiveness in Different Environments*, Sherbrooke, Quebec: René Prince.

Gasse, Y. (1985), 'A strategy for the promotion and identification of potential entrepreneurs at the secondary school level', *Frontiers of Entrepreneurial Research*, Wellesley, MA: Babson College, pp. 538–59.

Gibb, A.A. (1986), 'Understanding and influencing the business start-up process', *Proceedings of the First Canadian Conference on Entrepreneurial Studies*, Memorial University, St John's, Newfoundland, pp. 1–35.

Gomes-Casseres, B. (1996), *The Alliance Revolution*, Cambridge, MA: Harvard University Press.

Holm, D.B., Eriksson, K. and Johanson, J. (1997), 'Business networks and cooperation in international business relationships', in P.W. Beamish and J.P. Killing (eds), *Cooperative Strategies: European Perspectives*, San Francisco, CA: New Lexington Press, pp. 242–66.

Iyer, G. and Shapiro, J.M. (1999), 'Ethnic entrepreneurship and marketing systems: implications for the global economy', *Journal of International Marketing*, **7** (4), 83–110.

Jenkins, R. (1984), 'Ethnicity and the rise of capitalism in Ulster', in R. Ward and R. Jenkins (eds), *Ethnic Communities in Business: Strategies for Economic Survival*, Cambridge: Cambridge University Press, pp. 57–72.

Johannisson, B. (1987), 'Towards a theory of local entrepreneurship', in R.G. Wyckham, L.N. Meredith and G.R. Bushe (eds), *The Spirit of Entrepreneurship*, Vancouver: Faculty of Business Administration, Simon Fraser University, pp. 1–14.

Johanson, J. and Associates (1994), *Internationalization, Relationships and Networks*, Stockholm: Almquist and Wiksell International.

Kao, R. (1988), 'Can we teach entrepreneurship?', in R.W.Y. Kao (ed.), *Readings in Entrepreneurship*, Toronto: Ryerson, pp. 161–3.

Kets de Vries, M.F.R. (1977), 'The entrepreneurial personality: a person at the crossroads', *Journal of Management Studies*, **14** (1), 34–57.

Knight, F.H. (1921), *Risk Uncertainty and Profit*, Boston, MA and New York: Houghton Mifflin.

Knight, R.M. (1987), 'Can business schools produce entrepreneurs? An empirical study', *Journal of Small Business and Entrepreneurship*, **5**, 17–26.

Levine, H.B. (1985), 'Entrepreneurship and social change: implications from a New Zealand case study', *Human Organization*, **44** (4), 293–300.

Levine, H.B. and Levine, M.W. (1983), 'Socio-economic patterns and crayfishing zones: implications for managing the Stewart Island Crayfishery', *New Zealand Geographer*, October, 83–5.

Light, I. (1972), *Ethnic Enterprise in America: Business and Welfare among Chinese, Japanese and Blacks*, Berkeley, CA: University of California Press.

Light, I. (1980), 'Asian enterprise in America: Chinese, Japanese, and Koreans in small business', in S. Cummings (ed.), *Self-Help in Urban America*, Port Washington, NY: Kennikat Press, pp. 33–57.

Light, I. (1984), 'Immigrant and ethnic enterprise in North America', *Ethnic and Racial Studies*, **7** (2), 195–216.

Light, I. and Bonacich, E. (1988), *Immigrant Entrepreneurs: Koreans in Los Angeles 1965–1985*, Berkeley, CA: University of California Press.

Light, I. and Rosenstein, C. (1995), *Race, Ethnicity and Entrepreneurship in Urban America*, New York: Aldine De Gruyther.

Linowes, R.G. and Dixon, B.R. (1992), 'Small business management development for a newly deregulated economy: the case of New Zealand', *Journal of Small Business Management*, **30** (4), 131–6.

McGregor, J. and Gomes, C. (1999), 'Technology uptake in small and medium-sized enterprises: some evidence from New Zealand', *Journal of Small Business Management*, **37** (3), 94–102.

Mill, J.S. (1848), *The Principles of Political Economy with Some of Their Applications to Social Philosophy*, vols 1 and 2, London: John W. Parker; revised 1886, London: Longman, Green.

Min, P.G. (1984), 'From white-collar occupation to small business: Korean immigrants' occupational adjustment', *Sociological Quarterly*, **25** (3), 333–52.

Min, P.G. (1986–87), 'Filipino and Korean immigrants in small business: a comparative analysis', *Amerasia*, **13** (1), 53–71.

Min, P.G. (1987), 'Factors contributing to ethnic business: a comprehensive synthesis', *International Journal of Comparative Sociology*, **28** (3–4), 173–93.

Min, P.G. and Jaret, C. (1985), 'Ethnic business success: the case of Korean small business in Atlanta', *Sociology and Social Research*, **69** (3), 412–35.

Olm, K., Carsrud, A.L. and Alvey, L. (1988), 'The role of networks in new venture funding of female entrepreneurs: a continuing analysis', *Frontiers of Entrepreneurial Research*, Wellesley, MA: Babson College, pp. 658–9.

Oxenfeldt, A.R. (1943), *New Firms and Free Enterprise: Pre-War and Post-War Aspects*, Washington, DC: American Council of Public Affairs.

Portes, A. and Bach, R.C. (1985), *Latin Journey*, Berkeley, CA: University of California Press.

Portes, A. and Jensen, L. (1987), 'What's an ethnic enclave? The case for conceptual clarity', *American Sociological Review*, **52** (6), 768–71.

Portes, A. and Jensen, L. (1989), 'The enclave and the entrants: patterns of ethnic enterprise in Miami before and after Mariel', *American Sociological Review*, **54** (6), 929–49.

Portes, A. and Jensen, L. (1992), 'Disproving the enclave hypothesis', *American Sociological Review*, **57** (3), 418–20.

Reid, S.D. (1981), 'The decision-maker and export entry and expansion', *Journal of International Business Studies*, **11**, 101–12.

Robinson, P.B. and Sexton, E.A. (1994), 'The effect of education and experience on self-employment success', *Journal of Business Venturing*, **9**, 141–56.

Sadler, A. and Chetty, S. (2000), 'The impact of networks on New Zealand', in L.P. Dana (ed.), *Global Marketing Co-operation and Networks*, New York: International Business Press, pp. 37–58.

Sanders, J.M. and Nee, V. (1987), 'Limits of ethnic solidarity in the enclave economy', *American Sociological Review*, **52** (6), 745–67.

Say, J.B. (1803), *Traite d'économie politique ou simple exposition de la manière dont se forment, se distribuent, et se consomment les richesses*; revised (1819); translated (1830) by C.R. Prinsep, *A Treatise on Political Economy: On Familiar Conversations On the Manner in Which Wealth is Produced, Distributed and Consumed by Society*, Philadelphia, PA: John Grigg and Elliot.

Say, J.B. (1815), *Catechisme d'économie politique*; translated (1821) by J. Richter, *Catechism of Political Economy*, London: Sherwood.

Sexton, D. and Bowman, N. (1985), 'The entrepreneur: a capable executive and more', *Journal of Business Venturing*, **1**, 129–40.

Sexton, D. and Bowman Upton, N. (1990), 'Female and male entrepreneurs: psychological characteristics', *Journal of Business Venturing*, **5**, 29–36.

Shapero, A. (1975), 'The displaced, uncomfortable entrepreneur', *Psychology Today*, **7** (11), 83–9.

Shaver, K.G. and Scott, L.R. (1991), 'Person, process, choice: the psychology of new venture creation', *Entrepreneurship, Theory and Practice*, **16** (2), 23–64.

Taylor, D.B. (1993), 'Marketing: contrasting attributes of small and large manufacturers', *Journal of Small Business and Entrepreneurship*, April–June, 116–20.

Taylor, D.B. and Brooksbank, R. (1995), 'Marketing practices among small New Zealand organizations', *Journal of Enterprising Culture*, **3** (2), 149–60.

Timmons, J.A., Smoller, L. and Dingee, A.L.M. (1985), 'The entrepreneurial mind', in *New Venture Creation, A Guide to Entrepreneurship*, Homewood, IL: Richard D. Irwin, pp. 139–79.

Waldinger, R.D. (1984), 'Immigrant enterprise in the New York garment industry', *Social Problems*, **32** (1), 60–71.

Waldinger, R.D. (1986a), 'Immigrant enterprise: a critique and reformulation', *Theory and Society*, **15** (1–2), 249–85.

Waldinger, R.D. (1986b), *Through the Eye of the Needle: Immigrants and Enterprise in New York's Garment Trades*, New York: New York University Press.

Waldinger, R.D. and Aldrich, H.E. (1990), 'Trends in ethnic business in the United States', in R.D. Waldinger, H.E. Aldrich, R. Ward and associates, *Ethnic Entrepreneurs: Immigrant Business in Industrial Societies*, Newbury Park, CA: Sage, pp. 49–78.

Waldinger, R.D., Aldrich, H.E. and Ward, R. (1990a), 'Opportunities, group characteristics and strategies', in R.D. Waldinger, H.E. Aldrich, R. Ward and associates, *Ethnic Entrepreneurs: Immigrant Business in Industrial Societies*, Newbury Park, CA: Sage, pp. 13–48.

Waldinger, R.D., McEvoy, D. and Aldrich, H.E. (1990b), 'Spatial dimensions of opportunity structures', in R.D. Waldinger, H.E. Aldrich, R. Ward and associates, *Ethnic Entrepreneurs: Immigrant Business in Industrial Societies*, Newbury Park, CA: Sage, pp. 106–30.
Ward, R. (1987), 'Ethnic entrepreneurs in Britain and in Europe', in R. Scase and R. Goffee (eds), *Entrepreneurship in Europe*, London: Croom Helm, pp. 83–104.
Ward, R. and Jenkins, R. (eds) (1984), *Ethnic Communities in Business: Strategies For Economic Survival*, Cambridge: Cambridge University Press, pp. 105–24.
Werbner, P. (1984), 'Business trust: Pakistani entrepreneurship in the Manchester garment trade', in R. Ward and R. Jenkins (eds), *Ethnic Communities: Strategies for Economic Survival*, Cambridge: Cambridge University Press, pp. 166–88.
Wong, B. (1987), 'The role of ethnicity in enclave enterprises: a study of the Chinese garment factories in New York City', *Human Organization*, **66** (2), 120–30.
Wu, Y.L. (1983), 'The role of alien entrepreneurs in economic development: an entrepreneurial problem', *American Economic Review*, **73** (2), 112–17.

13 Entrepreneurship among graduates from business schools: a Norwegian case

Lars Kolvereid and Bjørn Willy Åmo

13.1 Introduction

During the past decade, entrepreneurship has become a widely taught topic in universities. Many business schools offer majors in entrepreneurship along with majors in more traditional areas such as finance, accounting and marketing. Bodø Graduate School of Business has offered a major in entrepreneurship as part of its Master of Science in Business (*siviløkonom*) program since the school was established in 1985, and the first students with a major in entrepreneurship graduated in 1987. The research questions addressed under the present circumstances are, to what extent has the entrepreneurship major been a success? More specifically, are business graduates with a major in entrepreneurship more entrepreneurial than students with other majors? To answer these questions and identify some practical implications, statistics from the student database and data collected from the alumni at five different points in time are used.

The first part of this chapter provides a brief introduction to the history of entrepreneurship education. This section points to the objectives and the intended effect of entrepreneurship education and discusses various measures suggested for measuring the effects from entrepreneurship education. The next section describes the investigated program in entrepreneurship at Bodø Graduate School of Business and the reasons for establishing this educational program. The subsequent section displays how the data was gathered for this study. The last section contains the conclusions. This closing section discusses the findings and the available measures of success regarding entrepreneurial training and education, investigating data for 16 years, five surveys and more than 2300 students.

13.2 Entrepreneurship training and education

There is rising interest among students worldwide for entrepreneurship (Fiet, 2000). Finkle and Deeds (2001) report a dramatic rise in number and status of entrepreneurship programs in business schools and universities. The popularity of entrepreneurship courses has also grown dramatically among graduate and undergraduate students.

Entrepreneurship teaching has a relatively short history, the first entrepreneurship classes were held in the US in 1947 (Katz, 2003). In 1953 the University of Illinois offered a course in 'small business or entrepreneurship development' and the first contemporary MBA entrepreneurship courses were introduced at Stanford and New York universities in 1967 (Katz, 2003). Entrepreneurship as a subject offered at universities came late to Europe compared to the US (Volkman, 2004). It was around 1980 that entrepreneurship started to be offered as a subject in European universities, and then mainly in those of Northern Europe (Volkman, 2004). As early as in the mid-1970s the first courses in entrepreneurship were taught in universities in Sweden (Landström, 2000). In Norway, courses in small business management have existed since the late 1970s, and entrepreneurship courses since 1985.

In 1985, when Bodø Graduate School of Business was founded, 253 colleges/universities in the US offered courses in entrepreneurship (Vesper, 1993). Growth in entrepreneurship courses and majors in Europe has been profound, but largely untracked (Katz, 2003). Even so, Katz (2003) claims that most of the educational programs outside the US were started after 1993. There was a considerable growth in the development of entrepreneurship education and training programs in Europe in the period 1988–93 (Garavan and O'Cinneide, 1994a). The interest since then has exploded and now courses in entrepreneurship are widely available (Katz, 2003; Landström, 2000). This makes it important to report on the progress and success of universities that have offered entrepreneurship for the longest time. The purpose of such reports should be to transfer knowledge about the effectiveness and efficiency of a long-established entrepreneurship education program, so that newcomers could benefit from the lessons learned from more experienced entrepreneurship educators.

In entrepreneurship pedagogy empirical tests of key propositions are in short supply and badly needed (Hindle and Cutting, 2002). There is a lack of research in the outcomes of education in entrepreneurship (Garavan and O'Cinneide, 1994a; Honig, 2004). Moreover, there has been little rigorous research on the effects from entrepreneurship training and education, utilizing large sample sizes, control groups, and long-term longitudinal studies (Peterman and Kennedy, 2003). Vesper and Gartner (1997) ask for research that points to which elements of the educational process influence selection decisions and actions in alumni start-ups. The present research meets two of the desired criteria for research on entrepreneurship training and education: it utilizes a large sample and is long term, covering a period of 18 years.

13.2.1   The objectives of entrepreneurship education

Economic growth heavily relies on entrepreneurship as a driving force and entrepreneurship training and education in particular can open major access routes to prosperity (Kourilsky and Esfandiari, 1997). Teaching and promoting entrepreneurship is potentially beneficial for society as entrepreneurship may be a possible solution to high unemployment rates and as a recipe for economic prosperity (Garavan and O'Cinneide, 1994b). McMullan and Gillin (1998) argue that entrepreneurship training and education may be one of the few unexploited, cost-effective, micro-economic tools governments have for developing local economies. Public policy within Europe aims to stimulate entrepreneurship through teaching (Rae and Carswell, 2001), and in Norway the government has introduced national strategies for innovation and for entrepreneurship in teaching.

The purpose of an entrepreneurship program in universities should be to contribute to the development of students' ability to discover/identify business opportunities and their ability to exploit these opportunities (Landström, 2000). Researchers differ between entrepreneurship training and entrepreneurship education. Entrepreneurship training comprises the planned and systematic processes which aim to modify or develop knowledge or skills that enables an individual to achieve an effective performance (Hynes, 1996). Entrepreneurship education is the processes which aim to enable an individual to assimilate and develop knowledge, skills, values and an understanding that allows a broader range of problems to be addressed (Hynes, 1996). Landström (2000) argues that the lowest level of learning is the 'know-what', then the 'know-when' and the 'know-how', the highest level of learning being the 'know-why'. Applied to entrepreneurship education, the 'know-what' is teaching the students the skills of registering a firm and how to write a business plan. The 'know-when' and the 'know-how' are teaching students the skills of identifying a business idea and how and when to exploit it. In our view this constitutes entrepreneurship training: the 'know-why' is therefore entrepreneurship education, that is, educating students about how to understand the entrepreneurship phenomenon and its place and purpose in society. The 'know-why' is teaching students the theory about why some prefer to start and run their own business and why some do not. The 'know-why' also includes how entrepreneurship influences society and people's living conditions. Johannisson (1991) argues that entrepreneurial education suffers from being focused on the 'know-what' element of entrepreneurial knowledge. The intention of the entrepreneurship program offered should correspond with the content of the program as it also should be reflected in the measurements utilized in investigations regarding the outcomes of the program.

13.2.2 The effects of entrepreneurship education

Béchard and Toulouse (1998) argue that the main research question in entrepreneurship is the extent to which entrepreneurship is a function of people with definite personality traits or whether entrepreneurship concerns knowledge and skills, which can be developed through education. This is the research question in focus here: is the behaviour of business graduates who have taken a major in entrepreneurship more entrepreneurial than those who have majors in other fields?

Current debates on entrepreneurship training and education tend to focus on issues such as achievements and output (Adcroft et al., 2004). It is necessary to determine which approaches to and models of entrepreneurship training and education are appropriate for universities (Volkman, 2004). Teaching contents and methods will be decisive factors of success for entrepreneurship teaching in the twenty-first century (Volkman, 2004). It is especially important to improve the exchange of experience with different models and approaches to entrepreneurship teaching in order to increase the effectiveness and efficiency of the programs offered (Volkman, 2004). Volkman (2004) argue for the importance of evaluation and comparative evaluation of the degrees of success of entrepreneurship programs. This study contributes towards this end by providing a thorough description of one of the longest established entrepreneurship programs in Europe, and the results from this educational program. While it is assumed that entrepreneurship can be taught, it is critical to ensure that quality teaching is implemented (Hynes, 1996). Reporting results for longitudinal studies from single institutions' entrepreneurships programs enables us to identify more effective didactic designs (McMullan and Vesper, 2000).

A well-established measure of success of entrepreneurial teaching is the rate of former students starting up their own business. However, several authors request better measures of success for teaching in entrepreneurship (Hynes, 1996; Menzies and Paradi, 2003). For an entrepreneurship educational program to be successful it has to address the following three core areas: (1) how to identify or recognize a market opportunity and generate a viable business plan to address the market opportunity, (2) how to gather resources, in the face of risk, to pursue the opportunity, and (3) how to create an operating business organization to implement the opportunity-motivated business idea (Kourilsky and Esfandiari, 1997).

Even so, it is important to measure output of entrepreneurial teaching in a broad sense in terms of skills-building, behavioural change, and the development of a more entrepreneurial graduate. Outputs should not be measured in the strict sense of business formation as there are more goals to strive for than just business formations (Hynes, 1996). Menzies and Paradi (2003) argue that venturing rates may not be as valuable to study as the number of successful businesses owned, when measuring the success of graduates with a major in entrepreneurship. There is also a call in the literature for opportunity identification to be included in entrepreneurship education, because creativity theorists have long recognized that individuals can be taught to identify opportunities (DeTienne and Chandler, 2004). The impact of entrepreneurship training and education on attitudes or perceptions of entrepreneurship still remains relatively untested (Peterman and Kennedy, 2003).

According to Klofsten (2000) there is one major difference between entrepreneurs and non-entrepreneurs. Entrepreneurs create organizations while non-entrepreneurs do not. Klofsten (2000) concludes that it is possible to stimulate entrepreneurial behaviour by education and training. Education is set up for medium- or longer-term outcomes, but in the case of entrepreneurship teaching one can get an early indication of success based on the likelihood of graduates starting up a business (McMullan and Gillin, 1998). One of seven success criteria suggested for ranking entrepreneurship programs were alumni start-ups (Vesper and Gartner, 1997).

Another possible measure of entrepreneurship teaching success is whether the program is popular or not (McMullan and Gillin, 1998). If the educational program is growing in terms of numbers of graduates, this is one way of measuring success in entrepreneurship teaching. Another measure of the success of an entrepreneurship educational program is if it is being copied by other universities/graduate schools of business (McMullan and Gillin, 1998).

Entrepreneurship is more about knowledge and procedures and less about motivation and personal competences (Garavan and O'Cinneide, 1994a). Knowledge about procedures and business opportunity identification or recognition, how to generate a viable business plan to address the market opportunity, how to gather resources, and how to create an operating business organization can all be taught. As the subject is complex and some part of it consists of formal procedures, experimental learning is particularly important to entrepreneurial education (DeTienne and Chandler, 2004). Even so, to reach higher-level learning, a solid base of theory is needed to fully understand the human behaviour that constitutes entrepreneurship, because entrepreneurs are required to solve problems that are poorly structured and open ended (Honig, 2004). Learning can be seen as a cognitive process of acquiring and structuring knowledge, of making meaning from experience, and of generating new solutions from existing knowledge (Rae and Carswell, 2001). The relationship between learning and achievement is significant (Rae and Carswell, 2001).

13.3   Bodø Graduate School of Business
There is an upward trend in the proportion of the population in Norway that obtains higher education. In 2001 56.6 per cent of the population had completed at least an upper secondary education, and 17.5 per cent had completed at least four years of college. Public colleges require no tuition fees. The cost is covered by the state via taxes. Bodø Graduate School of Business was the first business school in Norway to offer a Master of Science degree with a major in entrepreneurship. Bodø Regional University was established in

1971, offering bachelor degrees in business management, aquaculture and social sciences. In 1985 Bodø Graduate School of Business was established as a separate department at the university. From the outset, two majors were offered in the Master of Science in Business program: entrepreneurship and management control. In 1987, 25 students graduated, whereof 14 had a major in entrepreneurship. The business school has since then experienced steady growth.

In the fourth year of studies, Master of Science in Business students at Bodø Graduate School of Business are expected to select a major. The major accounts for 75 per cent of their work during the final year, and consists of 50 per cent course work and 50 per cent thesis work. The course content has varied from year to year, but new business formation, innovation and strategy have always been central components of the curriculum.

Regarding the 'know-what' element of entrepreneurship teaching, the Innovation Fair provides the students with hands-on knowledge about how to start a firm and how to make a business plan. The Innovation Fair also develops the 'know-who' knowledge, as the students are expected to team up and start an actual business and earn money from it. The profit from the businesses is used to pay for a study trip abroad. The 'know-who' is further addressed in the business development section of the course, which concerns conditions and methods used in development of new businesses and in improving established organizations. This is done with real entrepreneurs with real business ideas. An additional topic addressing the 'know-who' is a theoretical discussion of team building and resource-based theory. Other topics address the 'know-why' issues, such as regional development, gender and entrepreneurship, and the developments in definitions and theory of entrepreneurship.

The Bodø Graduate program was set up not only to train and educate future entrepreneurs, but also to provide candidates for the various businesses and social institutions that support entrepreneurs. However, graduates are expected not only to be job-seekers, but also job-creators. This entrepreneurship program model appears to be similar to the Stirling program in Scotland set up at about the same time, as reported by McMullan and Gillin (1998).

An entrepreneurship development program has been defined as a collection of formalized teachings that informs, trains and educates anyone interested in participating in socioeconomic development through a project to promote entrepreneurship awareness, business creation, small business development or to train the trainers (Béchard and Toulouse, 1998; Interman, 1992). In terms of Interman's (1992) classification of entrepreneurship development programs, the objective of the entrepreneurship major has been entrepreneurship awareness, small business development and training of trainers, more so than training in skills to create new businesses. Thus, it has not been the sole objective of the entrepreneurship major to encourage students to start businesses and become self-employed. The entrepreneurship program offered by Bodø Graduate School of Business could be classified as 'focused' by the classification of Volkman (2004). A program is focused if its faculty, students and staff are located in the area of business. The major offered by Bodø Graduate School of Business is not just an add-on to another curriculum, it is the curriculum itself.

Some of the core values that underpin the program are revealed in the course description. The program takes the perspective that participants should be motivated to think of the environment as something they can alter. The course objectives are described the following way in the students' handbook (2004/05):

> The course shall enable students to understand processes associated with innovation, strategy and entrepreneurship. This shall be achieved by scholarly lectures, which provide a theoretical foundation to understand the topics, guest lecturers who cover the themes by using their own practical experiences and examples, as well as project work. The learning strategies that are utilized in pursuing this educational goal are several. The course shall also offer practical experience in new business start-up through the annual innovation fair, in addition to participation in a new business development seminar.

In 2004, the school offered eight different majors and 152 students graduated with a Master of Science in Business degree. Of these, 28 had a major in entrepreneurship. It has been a policy of Bodø Graduate School of Business to limit the number of students in each major to 30, and to enrol students in the majors based on how they rank with regard to their bachelor grades. Entrepreneurship has always been among the most popular majors and some years the 30-student limit to the major had to be put aside. Table 13.1 shows the number of students who graduated from Bodø Graduate School of Business, by year, the number of graduates with a major in entrepreneurship, the percentage of the graduates with a major in entrepreneurship who are female, the accumulated number of students, and the accumulated number of students with a major in entrepreneurship.

In four years, 1992, 1993, 1994 and 1999, extra resources had to be allocated to the entrepreneurship major in order to meet the high demand for entrepreneurship education among students and to enable the school to enrol more than the set limit of 30 students in the major. The cumulative percentage of graduates selecting the entrepreneurship major fell gradually from 56 per cent in 1987 to 18 per cent in 2002, but has since remained constant. Hence, the entrepreneurship major has been and remains quite popular among students. While majors in areas such as marketing, international business, environmental management, information management and logistics in some years have struggled to attract a sufficient number of students, the entrepreneurship major has often had the opposite problem. There is little doubt that the entrepreneurship major has been successful using popularity among students as a criterion, as suggested by McMullan and Gillin (1998).

13.4   The surveys

Five surveys were administered, in March 1995, 1997, 1999, 2001 and 2003, addressing all the graduates with a major from Bodø Graduate School of Business. It was not possible to obtain the addresses from all the graduates at the times of the surveys, some graduates had moved abroad and some did not have a permanent address at the time of the survey. The purpose of the surveys was to reveal the graduates' need for additional education, possibly provided by the business school. Another aim of the surveys was to gather information about the career history of the graduates. The career history of the former graduates was gathered in order to inform potential new students about expected income and position after graduation. A third aim for the surveys was to monitor the success rate of the master program in entrepreneurship provided by the graduate school of business.

The response rates of the five surveys range from 49 per cent to 56 per cent of the graduates addressed. The response rates among the graduates with a master in entrepreneurship

Table 13.1 Graduates from Bodø Graduate School of Business, 1987–2004

Year	1987	1988	1989	1990	1991	1992	1993	1994	1995	1996	1997	1998	1999	2000	2001	2002	2003	2004
Total number of graduates	25	61	68	83	89	119	123	152	140	139	146	171	175	201	217	163	144	152
Accumulated number of graduates	25	86	154	237	326	445	568	720	860	999	1145	1316	1491	1692	1909	2072	2216	2368
Number of different majors offered	2	3	5	5	6	6	6	7	8	8	8	8	8	7	7	7	8	8
Graduates with major in entrepreneurship	14	21	14	17	20	31	36	34	22	21	19	19	37	22	25	19	24	28
Percentage of females among graduates with a major in entrepreneurship	21	33	29	0	40	58	33	38	36	19	11	32	24	32	32	42	54	57
Accumulated number of graduates with a major in entrepreneurship	14	35	49	66	86	117	153	187	209	230	249	268	305	327	352	371	395	423
Percentage of graduates with major in entrepreneurship	56	34	21	20	22	26	29	22	16	15	13	11	21	11	12	12	17	18
Cumulative percentage of graduates with major in entrepreneurship	56	41	32	28	26	26	27	26	24	23	22	20	20	19	18	18	18	18

Table 13.2   Response rates for surveys mailed in March every second year from 1995 to 2003

Year of survey	1995	1997	1999	2001	2003
Number of graduates	720	999	1316	1491	2072
Respondents addressed	668	1038	1262	1431	1798
Responses to questionnaires	374	520	626	772	883
Response rate	56%	50%	50%	54%	49%
Respondents with a major in entrepreneurship	105	115	138	152	224
Response rate major in entrepreneurship	56%	50%	51%	46%	60%

compared to the response rates of the other graduates is not significantly different (at $p<0.05$). Moreover, there is no statistically significant difference in response rates between male and female graduates. The response rates from graduates on surveys in years 1995, 1997, 1999, 2001 and 2003 are reported in Table 13.2. The surveys asked the respondents about their career history, for feedback on the usefulness of their study and about their need for further education.

There is a debate regarding what constitutes entrepreneurship. Shane and Venkataraman (2000) argue that entrepreneurship does not require, but can include, the creation of new organizations. The surveys reflect their view by including questions regarding business start-ups, continued entrepreneurship and opportunity recognition. The question measuring the number of business start-ups has been the same for all the five surveys: 'How many businesses have you established (either alone or together with an equal partner)?' In order to avoid problems with missing values, respondents were urged to answer '0' if they had not started a business. The number of business start-ups is calculated as the sum of all the businesses respondents report to have started. Business founders are the number of respondents reporting to have started a business. The question measuring businesses owned has also been the same through the five surveys: 'How many businesses do you own today (either alone or as an equal partner)?' Again, respondents were asked to answer '0' if they did not own a business at the time of the survey. Businesses owned are calculated as the sum of all the businesses reported to be owned. Business owners are the sum of all the respondents who report owning a business. Table 13.3 reports the number of businesses started and owned by graduates with and without a master in entrepreneurship as measured in five points of time.

As shown in Table 13.3, the surveys from 1995 and 1997 clearly indicate that graduates with a major in entrepreneurship are more likely to start and own a business than graduates with other majors. The data from 1995 was used by Kolvereid and Moen (1997), who found that having a major in entrepreneurship was statistically significantly related to the probability of starting a business in a logistic regression controlling for 23 different indicators of various personal and job characteristics. The first two surveys indicate that graduates with a major in entrepreneurship are about three times as likely as other graduates to start a business. The effect of having a major in entrepreneurship seems to be weaker in the most recent surveys, but entrepreneurship majors remain more than twice as likely to start and own a business than graduates with other majors.

Table 13.3 *Business start-ups and business ownership among business graduates*

Survey	Major	N	Business start-ups	Business founders		Businesses owned	Business owners	
				N	%		N	%
1995	Entrepreneurship	105	38	19	18.1	24	15	14.3
	Other	265	17	15	5.7	13	11	4.2
1997	Entrepreneurship	115	56	19	16.5	32	20	17.4
	Other	415	35	25	6.0	30	23	5.5
1999	Entrepreneurship	129	59	42	32.6	38	27	20.9
	Other	482	60	29	6.0	77	47	9.8
2001	Entrepreneurship	141	51	30	21.3	35	25	17.7
	Other	577	87	51	8.8	75	46	8.0
2003	Entrepreneurship	142	42	25	29.6	28	24	16.9
	Other	768	110	79	10.3	98	66	8.6
Average for all five surveys	Entrepreneurship	126	49	27	21.4	31	22	17.6
	Other	501	62	40	7.9	59	39	7.7

According to Landström (2000) one objective of education in entrepreneurship is to develop students' ability to discover/identify business opportunities. A question measuring business options discovered by the respondent were therefore added in the 2003 survey. The question was 'How many opportunities to establish or buy a business have you identified/discovered during the last five years?' Business opportunities discovered during the last five years are calculated as the sum of all the business opportunities discovered/identified during the last five years. Business idea holders are the number of respondents reporting to have discovered/identified one or more business opportunities. Among respondents to the 2003 survey, 142 entrepreneurship majors reported to have discovered/identified 264 business opportunities while 768 graduates with other majors reported to have discovered/identified 389 such opportunities. Moreover, 48.6 per cent of the graduates with a major in entrepreneurship reported to have discovered/identified at least one business opportunity, compared to 24.3 per cent business idea holders among students with other majors. Graduates with an entrepreneurship major also reported stronger intentions to start a business than graduates with other majors.

The 2003 survey also included questions regarding employee innovation behaviour. The measure and items of employee innovation behaviour was reported in a study of innovation behaviour among white collar workers (Åmo and Kolvereid, 2005). The measure consists of five items regarding employee involvement in innovation behaviour in their employing organization. Principal Component Analysis was used to build the components, the items loaded on one factor. The variance explained was 75.2 per cent and the Cronbach's alpha was 0.92. A T-test between the group of business graduates with a major in entrepreneurship (n = 164) and the other business graduates (n = 680) regarding their innovation behaviour at their workplace revealed no difference between the two groups at a 5 per cent significance level.

While the data show that entrepreneurship majors are more entrepreneurial than other majors, the data also reveal that there really are more similarities than differences between graduates with entrepreneurship major and other graduates. They have similar jobs, the same salary, and work in similar organizations. This finding indicates that entrepreneurship majors are as attractive to employees as graduates from more traditional majors such as management control, finance and marketing.

13.5   Conclusions

Entrepreneurship is a popular major with students from Bodø Graduate School of Business and has been so for 18 years. Even though there is a feedback loop between students enrolling on an educational program and business graduates, one should interpret popularity as a measure of success with caution. This popularity of an educational program among students could be regarded as one measure, among others, of the potential success, but not as confirmed success.

Even though the effect on the disposition to start and run a business of having a major in entrepreneurship seems to have declined in the most recent surveys, entrepreneurship majors remain about twice as likely as graduates with other majors to start a business and to become a business owner. These results coincide with previous research (Garavan and O'Cinneide, 1994a; Menzies, 2004).

The surveys indicate that business graduates with a major in entrepreneurship discover/identify more business opportunities and are more likely to have a business idea. Not only are graduates with a major in entrepreneurship more entrepreneurial than other graduates, they are as attractive as students with other majors employees in a large variety of organizations. This finding indicates success for the entrepreneurship major offered by the graduate school of business as students with a major in entrepreneurship are more versatile than the students with other majors. They are also more inclined to become entrepreneurs. Maybe the students with a major in entrepreneurship have a more informed choice whether to pursue a career as an employee or as an entrepreneur, as they know more about what it takes to become an entrepreneur than students with other majors.

This analysis focused upon the entrepreneurial behaviour of the business graduates, not on their attitude towards entrepreneurship. This was intentional, as the societal and individual purpose or goals of entrepreneurship educational programs is only achieved through action, that is, behaviour. This implies that the reported research has limitations; no measurements regarding the 'know-why' element of entrepreneurial education was included in the surveys. Furthermore, the surveys did not include items measuring whether the business graduates were involved in sculpturing the national or regional policies regarding entrepreneurship. Nor did it include items measuring to what degree the business graduates were involved in activities helping or guiding others to release their entrepreneurial potential. We encourage other researchers to include measures of such opinions and activity in future studies regarding the success of entrepreneurial educational programs.

Further research is needed in order to establish measures of what constitutes a good major in entrepreneurship. Moreover, future research should attempt to reveal the goals of the different stakeholders in education of entrepreneurship. To what extent are the goals of the students, the school, the professors, the entrepreneurship research community and the society providing funding for universities and business schools offering majors in entrepreneurship the same? Finally, future research should try to assess the quality of the businesses started by graduates. To date we have little empirical evidence that investigates performance, growth and survival of businesses started by graduates with a major in entrepreneurship compared to other graduates. This study also points to the need for better measures about the success rate of the firms established by graduates with a major in entrepreneurship compared with the success rate of the firms established by graduates with other majors. Such measures will enable the research community interested in entrepreneurship education to establish if the entrepreneurship students are given a better tool with which to judge opportunities to pursue.

References

Adcroft, A., Willis, R. and Dahliwal, S. (2004), 'Missing the point? Management education and entrepreneurship', *Management Decision*, **42** (3/4), 521–30.
Åmo, B.W. and Kolvereid, L. (2005), 'Organizational strategy, individual personality and innovation behavior', *Journal of Enterprising Culture*, **13** (1), 7–20.
Béchard, J. and Toulouse, J.M. (1998), 'Validation of a didactic model for the analysis of training objectives in entrepreneurship', *Journal of Business Venturing*, **13** (3), 317–32.
DeTienne, D.R. and Chandler, G.N. (2004), 'Opportunity identification and its role in the entrepreneurial classroom: a pedagogical approach and empirical test', *Academy of Management Learning and Education*, **2** (3), 242–57.
Fiet, J.O. (2000), 'The pedagogical side of entrepreneurship theory', *Journal of Business Venturing*, **16** (2), 101–17.
Finkle, T.A. and Deeds, D. (2001), 'Trends in the market for entrepreneurship faculty, 1989–1998', *Journal of Business Venturing*, **16** (6), 613–30.
Garavan, T.N. and O'Cinneide, B. (1994a), 'Entrepreneurship education and training programmes: a review and evaluation – Part 1', *Academy of Management Learning and Education*, **2** (3), 242–57.
Garavan, T.N. and O'Cinneide, B. (1994b), 'Entrepreneurship education and training programmes: a review and evaluation – Part 2', *Journal of European Industrial Training*, **18** (11), 13–21.
Hindle, K and Cutting, N. (2002), 'Can applied entrepreneurship education enhance job satisfaction and financial performance? An empirical investigation in the Australian pharmacy profession', *Journal of Small Business Management*, **40** (2), 162–7.
Honig, B. (2004), 'Entrepreneurship education: toward a model of contingency-based business planning', *Academy of Management Learning and Education*, **3** (3), 258–373.
Hynes, B. (1996), 'Entrepreneurship education and training – introducing entrepreneurship into non-business disciplines', *Journal of European Industrial Training*, **20** (8), 10–17.
International Management Development Network in cooperation with the United Nations Development Program and the International Labour Office (Interman) (1992), *Networking for Entrepreneurship Development*, Geneva: International Labour Office.
Johannisson, B. (1991), 'University training for entrepreneurship: Swedish approaches', *Entrepreneurship and Regional Development*, **3** (1), 67–82.
Katz, J.A. (2003), 'The chronology and intellectual trajectory of American entrepreneurship education 1876–1999', *Journal of Business Venturing*, **18** (2), 283–300.
Klofsten, M. (2000), 'Training entrepreneurship at universities: a Swedish case', *Journal of European Industrial Training*, **24** (6), 337–44.
Kolvereid, L. and Moen, Ø. (1997), 'Entrepreneurship among business graduates: does a major in entrepreneurship make a difference?', *Journal of European Industrial Training*, **21** (4/5), 154–60.
Kourilsky, M.L. and Esfandiari, M. (1997), 'Entrepreneurship education and lower socioeconomic black youth: an empirical investigation', *The Urban Review*, **29** (3), 205–15.
Landström, H. (2000), *Entreprenörskapets rötter*, 2nd edn, Lund: Studentlitteratur.
McMullan, W.E. and Gillin, L.M. (1998), 'Industrial viewpoint – entrepreneurship education', *Technovation*, **18** (4), 275–86.
McMullan, W.E. and Vesper, K.H. (2000), 'Becoming an entrepreneur: a participant's perspective', *Entrepreneurship and Innovation*, (February), 33–43.
Menzies, T.V. (2004), 'Are universities playing a role in nurturing and developing high-technology entrepreneurs?', *Entrepreneurship and Innovation* (August), 149–57.
Menzies, T.V. and Paradi, J.C. (2003) 'Entrepreneurship education and engineering students', *Entrepreneurship and Innovation* (May), 121–32.

Peterman, N.E. and Kennedy, J. (2003), 'Enterprise education: perceptions of entrepreneurship', *Entrepreneurship Theory and Practice*, **28** (2), 129–44.
Rae, D. and Carswell, M. (2001), 'Towards a conceptual understanding of entrepreneurial learning', *Journal of Small Business and Enterprise Development*, **8** (2), 150–58.
Shane, S. and Venkataraman, S. (2000) 'The promise of entrepreneurship as a field of research', *Academy of Management*, **25** (1), 217–26.
Students handbook (2004/05), *Studies Offered at Bodø Graduate School of Business*, Bodø Graduate School of Business, Bodø, Norway.
Vesper, K.H. (1993), *Entrepreneurship Education*, Entrepreneurial Studies Centre, UCLA, Los Angeles, CA.
Vesper, K.H. and Gartner, W.B. (1997), 'Measuring progress in entrepreneurship education', *Journal of Business Venturing*, **12** (5), 403–21.
Volkman, C. (2004), 'Entrepreneurship studies – an ascending academic discipline in the twenty-first century', *Higher Education in Europe*, **29** (2), 177–85.

PART IV

POLITICAL CONTEXT

14 Evaluation of entrepreneurship education: planning problems, concepts and proposals for evaluation design
Norbert Kailer

14.1 Introduction

Increasing the number of start-ups and business successions and improving the support for young entrepreneurs is internationally of high importance for the economy and the labour market (European Commission, 2004a; 2004b; Schauer et al., 2005). Numerous studies show a strong correlation between entrepreneurial competence and the success of start-ups (Fayolle, 2000, p. 171; 2004b; Garavan and O'Cinneide, 1994; Van der Sluis et al., 2004). The connection between implicit entrepreneurial knowledge (work experience, industry-specific know-how) (Onstenk, 2000, p. 33; Staudt et al., 1997) and economic success of new enterprises (Schulte, 2004) is especially well researched (Hendry et al., 1991; Henry et al., 2003, p. 54; Storey and Westhead, 1994).

Massive public investments led to an expansion of the support infrastructure and to a growth on the supply side of training, coaching, information and financing for nascent entrepreneurs and start-ups. Entrepreneurship education is a growth industry itself. However, it has to be noted that there exists no clear definition of entrepreneurship education. 'Generally, entrepreneurship education programmes focus on three main areas: education including degree and non degree-courses, research, and practical applications' (Hisrich, 1992, p. 27). Stampfl and Hytti (2002, p. 129) highlight the following functions: 'Learn to understand entrepreneurship, learn to become entrepreneurial, learn to become an entrepreneur.'

Innovative and growth-oriented start-ups are particularly expected from university graduates. Therefore, entrepreneurship education was also widely intensified at universities (Gibb, 1993; 1996; Jack and Anderson, 1999, p. 114; Klandt, 2004, p. 293; Koch, 2003). Surveys show a strong increase in entrepreneurship chairs in the USA as well as in the European Union (Katz, 2004; Klandt et al., 2005; Salomon et al., 2002; Twaalfhoven, 2000, p. 11; 2001; Wilson, 2004). According to Pleitner (2001, p. 1148), entrepreneurship is the fastest growing discipline at universities.

Braun and Diensberg (2003, p. 205), however, point out that the increase in importance of entrepreneurship education is also based on a hidden agenda. They argue that nobody can seriously criticize an improvement and expansion of educational offers, and the promoting administrations do not have problems with justifying their actions because there is no immediate need for proof of success. Hills and Morris (1998) identify a deficit in the assessment of the effectiveness of entrepreneurship education. Storey also criticizes the fact that most European small and medium-sized enterprises (SME) support programmes lack clear goals. Thus, evaluations are hardly possible. 'If public money is spent on SME support, then it is vital that evaluation of the impact of these initiatives takes place. Unfortunately, evaluation is not possible unless objectives that are clear and, in principle, measurable, are specified' (Storey, 2000, p. 190).

Owing to the high costs of awareness campaigns and support programmes for nascent founders and successors, proofs of the effectiveness and efficiency of these measures are rapidly gaining in importance. One example of this is the criticism concerning the impact of regional business plan competitions in terms of resulting start-ups (Boehme et al., 2005; Kaschube and Lang-von Wins, 1999). Sternberg and Klose (2001, p. 57) also point out that a large proportion of participants in subsidized programmes would have founded an enterprise anyway. Last but not least, crowding-out effects have to be taken into account. This results in an overestimation of effects of these programmes. Endowed entrepreneurship chairs also have to prove their impact when the subsidies expire or have to be renewed.

The boom in entrepreneurship education and the increasing criticism of missing data about the impact of these measures (Henry et al., 2003, p. 102) are the starting points of this chapter, which deals with the question how a practice-oriented model of evaluation can be developed and established. After discussing definitions of evaluation, section 14.2 gives an overview of recent empirical studies analysing the usage and deficits of evaluation. In section 14.3 evaluation studies of university entrepreneurship programmes are analysed. Section 14.4 discusses problems connected with the introduction of evaluation. In section 14.5, questions and decisions during the evaluation planning process are discussed and evaluation models are presented. The final section focuses on practical proposals for designing and implementing evaluation studies.

14.2   Usage and problems of evaluation

Very different definitions for evaluation can be found in the literature. Evaluation serves to trigger programme innovation, to control and optimize programmes, to forecast outcomes, to support strategic decision-making at policy level and at programme level (Neuberger, 1991, p. 273). Wottawa and Thierau (1990, p. 9) point out that evaluation is targeted and purpose oriented. It serves as support for planning and decision-making by assessing several alternative actions. The purpose is to assess the steps taken, in order to improve them. Owing to temporal and budgetary restrictions, this requires a concentration on specific aspects and criteria (Neuberger, 1991, p. 273). According to Weiss (1972), the purpose of evaluation research is to compare the effects of a programme with the intended goals. Evaluation contributes to subsequent decisions about the programme and to improve future programme planning. Easterby-Smith (1986, p. 13) differentiates evaluation into the functions of proving, improving and learning, and points out that evaluation is an integral part of the process of learning and development. Evaluation researchers also insist on evaluation measures which are adapted to the current level of scientific techniques and research methods (Beywl and Taut, 2000, p. 359; Wottawa and Thierau, 1990, p. 9). It is also intended to develop general standards for evaluations.

Evaluation of training and consulting has been dealt with in numerous publications. Evaluation concepts have been developed by Kirkpatrick (1976), Warr et al. (1971), Hamblin (1974) and Easterby-Smith (1986). Human resource development (HRD) manuals such as Craig and Bittel (1976) or Mumford (1986) already contained chapters about evaluation. Evaluation methods were especially developed for training and management development (Easterby-Smith et al., 1980; House, 1967; Smith and Piper, 1990; Stiefel, 1974; von Landsberg and Weiss, 1995). The importance of a target- and result-oriented approach in the area of HRD has been strongly supported by Ulrich (1990).

Entrepreneurship education evaluation concepts were developed by Hills and Morris (1998, p. 46), Henry et al. (2003, p. 189) and Fayolle (2004a).

Despite this vast amount of literature, recent studies (for example, Ashridge Management Center, 2005) still show a widespread deficit in evaluation practice. Training seems to be only loosely coupled to the overall strategic planning of organizations. There is a lack of planning routines in the management of training. Evaluation is carried out mainly in larger enterprises, mostly in the form of 'happiness sheets' at the end of the measures (Kailer, 2001).

These results also apply to the providers of entrepreneurship programmes. Hills and Morris (1998, p. 48) identified the following major deficits in entrepreneurship research:

* need for valid empirical measures of research variables and outcomes
* use of control groups without entrepreneurship education experience
* use of pre-tests prior to entrepreneurship education and post-tests immediately after, in addition to periodic follow-ups.

Storey (2000, p. 176) analysed European SME support programmes and discovered a far-reaching deficit of evaluation and goals. An analysis of non-European entrepreneurship programmes also showed a remarkable lack of evaluation. Planning is therefore mostly based on rules of thumb (Braun and Diensberg, 2003, p. 206). In the EU project 'entreva.net', methods for evaluating entrepreneurship education programmes were analysed (Hytti and Kuopusjärvi, 2004; Stampfl and Hytti, 2002). Most of the studies were classified as mere monitoring. Only one-quarter of all studies can be called evaluation.

> Monitoring was, however, more common than, 'real' evaluation. The preferred type of evaluation (in 66% of the evaluations analysed) was asking the recipients for their opinion concerning the programme. In many of the evaluations (50%) the recipients were also asked to give their view of the difference made by the programme. Also other types of evaluations emerged in our study. There were, for example, different types of comparisons, such as: A comparison of the participant's performance to that of persons who created a new venture in the framework of another programme; a comparison of the start up related attitudes and start up specific knowledge of the assisted before and after the programme; a comparison between the participants who have started-up a business and the participants who have not. (Hytti and Kuopusjärvi, 2004, p. 22)

14.3   Evaluation of entrepreneurship education programmes at university level

In 2005 the author conducted an exploratory Internet research concerning evaluation studies of university entrepreneurship programmes. As university courses usually include an obligatory evaluation (mainly written or oral exams and assessment of the lecturers by anonymous questionnaires), the analysis focused on the presence of impact indicators in evaluation studies.[1] The Internet research covered major universities, support institutions, networks and further training institutions in German-speaking countries, Scandinavian countries, France, Spain, the Netherlands, Denmark, Great Britain, Ireland, the USA, Canada, Australia and New Zealand. The results of other research projects, for example, the 'entreva.net'-database' (Hytti and Kuopusjärvi, 2004) covering evaluation studies in the field of entrepreneurship training in the European Union, were also included.

14.3.1   Overview of the results
Despite its exploratory nature, the study revealed a broad spectrum of entrepreneurship education programmes organized by universities, further training associations or regional networks. Although the course descriptions found on the Internet were detailed, hardly any information could be found which would allow the drawing of conclusions on the efficiency and effectiveness of the programmes (for example, rates of admission and quits, rates of foundations, further development of participants start-ups, total costs of the programme, and so on). Some programmes refer to evaluation data which are not published. As far as evaluation studies are available, they are mostly at the monitoring level. This is similar to the findings of Storey (2000), Braun and Diensberg (2003) and Hytti and Kuopusjärvi (2004).

- *Ex-post evaluation designs* clearly dominate. In most cases the studies are limited to a questionnaire sent out to students (BMBF, 2002; Ennoeckl, 2002; Franke and Luethje, 2004; Fueglistaller et al., 2004a; Golla et al., 2004; Richter, 2000; Schwarz and Grieshuber, 2001), to graduates or alumni of colleges or universities (Holzer and Adametz, 2003; Kolvereid and Moen, 1997; Leodolter, 2005; Nandram and Samson, 2004) or to graduates of a certain programme (CRS, 2003; Fletcher and Rosa, 1998; Lucas and Cooper, 2004; Mitterauer, 2003; Nakkula, 2004; Tohmo and Kaipainen, 2000). Questionnaires usually concentrate on their attitude towards entrepreneurship as well as their entrepreneurial potential, perceived hindrances and graduate's foundation rates. Since these surveys usually cover several subsequent study years, the development in the student's attitude towards entrepreneurship during their studies (Boissin, 2003; Klapper, 2004; Noel, 2001; Pihkala and Miettinen, 2002), as well as the development of start-ups of former participants (for example, number of employees, rate of survival, turnover) are analysed (Charney and Libecap, 2000; CRS, 2003; Holzer and Adametz, 2003; Mitterauer, 2003; Nandram and Samson, 2004).
- Evaluation *designs with pre- and post-test(s)* are rarely carried out: the National Foundation for Teaching Entrepreneurship to Youth (NFTE, 2005) examined participants, Carayannis et al. (2003) analysed changes in attitude of French business students with regard to entrepreneurship. Pihkala and Miettinen (2002) analysed Finnish students several times during the entrepreneurship course. In the CMI Enterprisers programme, which was developed by the Massachusetts Institute of Technology (MIT) and Cambridge University, changes in the attitude, in the personal assessment of one's entrepreneurial potential, and in the participants' intention towards foundation were evaluated with one pre- and two post-tests (Lucas and Cooper, 2004). The Irish Technology Enterprise Programme was evaluated by Henry et al. (2003) with four questionnaires during an evaluation period of three years. Fayolle et al. (2005) analysed changes in entrepreneurial attitudes with a pre- and post-test of course participants of a business school in France.
- In most cases merely *one instrument* is used (typically a questionnaire sent via snail mail). Combinations are rather rare: the NFTE (2005) combined seminar room observations, focus groups, pre- and post-tests as well as case studies with control groups. Charney and Libecap (2000) combined questionnaires for students and interviews for the teaching staff. Pihkala and Miettinen (2003) and Urbano et al.

(2003) interviewed young entrepreneurs. Frank and Luethje (2004) combined group discussions, expert interviews and questionnaires for students. Case studies were used by Leitch and Harrison (1999), and semi-structured interviews by Thakur (1995) and Fayolle et al. (2000).

- The evaluation studies rarely concentrate on the *programme impact.* On the output level in most cases the foundation rate of (former) participants and the jobs created through these start-ups are analysed (CRS, 2003; Fueglistaller et al., 2004a; Golla et al., 2004; Henry et al., 2003; Holzer and Adametz, 2003; Leitch and Harrison, 1999; Mitterauer, 2003; Puxi and Stetefeld, 2001; Sternberg and Mueller, 2004). Distortions caused by crowding-out effects or windfall gains for participants are hardly taken into consideration.

- Only in studies with a long observation period the survival rate and the *economic development* of the start-ups are analysed (Charney and Libecap, 2000; Henry et al., 2003; Nandram and Samson, 2004). More sensible data, such as turnover, sales or development of one's personal income are collected only in some studies (Charney and Libecap, 2000; CRS, 2003; Holzer and Adametz, 2003; Mitterauer, 2003).

- The studies rarely include a *cost–benefit analysis.* Mitterauer (2003) carried out a supplementary fiscal analysis: based on turnover sums estimations for the income tax and social insurance payments were made and the total tax revenue was compared to the total costs of the programme. The CRS (2003) estimated the effects of start-ups on the regional economy. Westhead et al. (2000; 2001) evaluated the participants' benefits of the Shell Technology Enterprise programme.

- *Control group designs* in the strict sense were not found. *Comparison groups,* however, were constituted in the following forms:
    – In surveys among graduates and students of an institution, the participants of a certain entrepreneurship programme were compared to (former) students of non-entrepreneurship courses (Charney and Libecap, 2000; Nakkula, 2004; Noel, 2001).
    – Start-up entrepreneurs were compared to graduates from the same programme which were not self-employed (Fueglistaller et al., 2004b; Leodolter, 2005).
    – Entrepreneurs with and without an 'entrepreneur's exam' were compared regarding the development of their enterprises (MKB and VNO-NCV, 1999).
    – Participants of an entrepreneurship programme were matched with a group of young entrepreneurs or students with similar features (Schamp and Deschoolmeester, 2002; Sternberg and Mueller, 2004; Westhead et al., 2001) respectively with participants of a similar programme (Tohmo and Kaipainen, 2000).

- A *regular repetition* of the survey is only intended by the University of St Gallen (Fueglistaller et al., 2004a; Golla et al., 2004) and in the ISCE Project (Fueglistaller et al., 2006).

- *International comparisons* are rare: Golla et al. (2004) compared Germany and Switzerland, Carayannis et al. (2003) France and the USA, Franke and Luethje (2004) students of the Vienna University of Economics, the MIT and the University of Munich. The ISCE Project was started in 2006.[2]

- Most studies concentrated on students, graduates or alumni as sources of information. In some cases the interview partners were representatives from universities or programme managers (Levie, 1999; Thakur, 1995).

14.3.2   Some examples of evaluation studies of entrepreurship education programmes at universities

14.3.2.1   Student surveys   A written survey was carried out among 5000 students from 10 German universities, which were supported in the context of the national EXIST programme. The attitude towards entrepreneurship and the interest in foundation were especially analysed (BMBF, 2002). The Swiss Survey on Collegiate Entrepreneurship is a web-based survey which is carried out among students of universities and universities of applied science in Switzerland every two years. The survey aims at analysing the future plans of the students, especially as far as entreneurship is concerned (Fueglistaller et al., 2004a). The Maison de l'Entrepreneuriat (Fayolle, 2003, p. 218) combines entrepreneurship education activities of five universities in Grenoble, France, with the goal of increasing the foundation rate. Boissin (2003) analysed changes of their students' attitude towards entrepreneurship using a questionnaire. In similar studies Klapper (2004) analysed students of the first and second year at the ESC Rouen and Carayannis et al. (2003) students from the ESCEM, France, and the George Washington University, USA, with a pre- and post-test. Pihkala and Miettinen (2003, pp. 139ff.) combined several standardized tests to analyse attitude changes of students from two Finnish polytechnics. At the University of Linz, Austria, two studies of business students were carried out to determine the impact of the activities of the entrepreneurship institute (Ennoeckl, 2002; Richter, 2000). A similar study analysed the entrepreneurial potential of students as well as the staff of the University of Technology of Graz, Austria (Bauer and Kailer, 2003).

14.3.2.2   Alumni surveys   Kolvereid and Moen (1997) conducted a survey of graduates with a major in entrepreneurship from the Bødo Graduate School of Business in Norway. A study at the University of Linz, Austria, covered the graduates of the last five years. Data about their studies and career and their inclination to found an enterprise, respectively, about their start-ups were collected (Leodolter, 2005). In a similar study, graduates of the Technical University of Graz, Austria during the last 14 years were analysed with a focus on their current contacts with the university and its staff (Holzer and Adametz, 2003). The Dutch University of Nyenrode also carried out a written survey amongst all alumni with a focus on the rate of foundations, their career as an entrepreneur, and the size and the progress of their company, and compared the results with the Dutch Global Enterprise Monitor (GEM) survey as a benchmark (Nandram and Samson, 2004). In a similiar study, Levie et al. (n.d.) compared a sample of alumni of the University of Strathclyde with data of the Scottish GEM survey.

14.3.2.3   Evaluation of subsidized entrepreneurship programmes for university students and alumni   In the Young Innovators programme in Baden-Württemberg, German university graduates are financially supported for one year. They also have access to university resources and coaching. Participants and graduates of this programme were interviewed by Sternberg and Mueller (2004), via telephone and the web, and matched with a control group of young entrepreneurs without financial subsidies in terms of level of innovation, age and company size. The comparison focused on the development of the enterprises (sales volume, R&D expenses, number of employees). The UNIUN project was carried out in Austria and Germany to promote start-ups in the environment of universities.

Workshops for potential and nascent founders were one component. After a process of administrative selection, these workshops were offered over a period of one year. The workshops were evaluated via standardized telephone interviews with the participants from the years 2001 and 2003. The foundation rate as well as the extent of the entrepreneurial activity were determined. The development of the start-ups was analysed by size, turnover and personal forecasts about the future development. In addition, a fiscal analysis included a comparison of the programme costs and the total tax revenue (income tax, social insurance taxes) generated through the start-ups. The extent of the crowding out effect and of windfall gains for participants was also estimated (Mitterauer, 2003). The American National Foundation for Teaching Entrepreneurship ran several evaluation studies on the effect of the entrepreneurship programme organized by the Koch Charitable Foundation at the Brandeis University. The methods used included seminar room observation, focus groups with alumni, pre- and post-tests with participants, as well as case studies with a non-participating control group (NFTE, 2005). The target group of a version of this programme were students of public high schools. This course was evaluated by the Harvard University Graduate School of Education with pre- and post-tests as well as psychological tests. Non-participating students acted as control group (Nakkula, 2004). Charney and Libecap (2000) conducted a written survey which included all 2500 graduates of the Eller College of the University of Arizona from 1985 to 1999. Among them, 450 had attended the Berger Entrepreneurship Programme. At the impact level, the intention to start an own business, the amount of start-ups as well as the development of these enterprises (sales, employees) were taken into account. The study focused on differences between participants and non-participants. University staff and the programme management were also interviewed. The CMI's Connections programme was developed by the Cambridge MIT Institute (CMI) to foster entrepreneurial spirit among students. This one-week programme was implemented and evaluated in 2003 at the University of Strathclyde, Scotland. There was no admission selection for the 55 participants. The design included a pre-test and two post-tests to analyse the knowledge transfer and focused on the assessment of personal competences (Lucas and Cooper, 2004). The assessment measures concentrated heavily on estimating the student sense of personal competency in both general skills and in their understanding of and capacity to undertake entrepreneurship; asked questions about their envisioned career; and sought the frequency of behaviours believed to be precursors of entrepreneurship (Lucas and Cooper, 2004, p. 6). Benchmark-data from other participating universities served as a substitute for a control group. The Shell Technology Enterprises Programme (STEP) offers traineeships for students and graduates in companies in the UK. The STEP participants of the year 1994 as well as their host organizations took part in a longitudinal study with a written questionnaire in 1997. Students which did not participate in STEP acted as the control group. The focus of the analysis was on the analysis of the benefit for the participating students and enterprises (Westhead et al., 2000; 2001).

In a longitudinal study amongst graduates of the SME programme of the Vlerick Leuven Gent Management School, Belgium, Schamp and Deschoolmeester (2002) gathered data on the effects of management training on managerial competence and the entrepreneurial behaviour of owners of Flemish SMEs. Young entrepreneurs were matched in terms of age, company size, industry and site and served as the control group.

14.3.2.4   Evaluation of other subsidized entrepreneurship programmes in cooperation with universities   An evaluation of labour market activities in Saxony, Germany, which were co-financed by the European Social Funds, was carried out via questionnaires. The items dealt with the professional career of the participants, the rate of foundations and the number of jobs created (Puxi and Stetefeld, 2001). The Irish Genesis enterprise programme of the Cork Institute of Technology is a one-year incubator programme for start-ups. The evaluation focused on the rate of foundations and rate of survival and the start-up's sales volume, investment volume, turnover and number of employees.[3] In Ireland, Henry et al. (2003) evaluated the effects of the Technology Enterprise Programme (TEP) in a three-year study. The evaluation design included a pre-test and two post-tests to allow estimations of the transfer effect and the development of the start-ups.[4] An internationally oriented university programme for executives and chief executive officers (CEOs) was organized and evaluated by Leitch and Harrison (1999) in Ireland. The benefit for participants as well as the participating enterprises was analysed using questionnaires several times during and after the programme. In addition, managers of the enterprises were interviewed and case studies were developed. Up to 2001, in order to become self-employed, a training course including an examination (*Midenstands* [Diploma]) was obligatory in the Netherlands. Five hundred entrepreneurs, who were already deleted from the trade register, were compared with entrepreneurs who had not fulfilled this obligatory requirement and with SME owners, who had no obligation to take this examination. The analysis focused on the development of the company and reasons for closing down the company (MKB and VNO-NCV, 1999).

14.4   Problems in the assessment of costs and benefits of programmes
Training managers identify the following main obstacles preventing a widespread use of evaluation (Kailer, 1991, p. 132; Kailer, 2001, p. 65):

- The 'dominance of the daily routine work' leads to lack of time (not only) for evaluation.
- As some training managers doubt whether there are suitable instruments to identify the benefits of the training programmes, they prefer not to control the costs either.
- They fear that the results of cost–benefit analyses could be misinterpreted or misused (this fear is widespread among organizations where the training budget has been cut down recently).
- To avoid cuts, the variable costs of training are 'distributed' to different accounts within the enterprise so that the total sum is not visible at first sight.
- A concentration on monetary and quantitative aspects could lead to a decreasing appreciation of the educational side of the evaluation process.
- It is assumed, that the contractors, that is, the top managers are not really interested in detailed evaluation results.

All these results show a clear connection between the importance of evaluation and the learning and development culture of the organization (Arnold, 1996; Neuberger, 1991, p. 273).

The analysis of costs and benefits of programmes leads to the following problems.

The *individual costs* of participants (for example training fees, literature costs, contributions in kind, opportunity costs for time spent in training) are often difficult to determine. In many enterprises the salaries for internal coaches and the costs of the training infrastructure are not adequately taken into account (Kailer, 1991; Kailer, 2001). Whilst it seems possible to measure direct benefits such as increased personal income or jobs created within an enterprise, it is extremely difficult to assess *indirect benefits*. For example, how can personal development or an attitude change towards entrepreneurship or intrapreneurship be adequately measured? Also, on the company level, the connection between training and an increase in sales or in profits is often very weak and difficult to determine. At a national economic level, the additional number of jobs, income, number and quality of innovations and business networks created are of primary interest. Nevertheless, crowding-out effects triggered by subsidized new businesses have to be considered. The question whether *indirect effects* on the customers and supplier level should be included is also highly important: according to an Austrian study, each new enterprise leads to a direct added value of 140 000 euros per year. If the indirect effects (for example, spending power effects) are also taken into account, the annual added value rises to about 320 000 euros per year (Getzner et al., 2003).

The question of *internal or external evaluation* is also of importance. It has to be taken into account that external evaluators are also dependent on the respective contract awarders. This too might influence the evaluation design as well as evaluation results.

The necessity of *programme goals* is also disputed. Storey emphasizes that goals are the base for any evaluation: 'A fundamental principle of evaluation is that it must first specify the objectives of policy' (Storey, 2000, p. 177). Here the problem of hidden and non-communicated goals of shareholders has to be taken into account. 'Not only is there a conspicuous absence of clear objectives for SME policy, but the implied objectives can often be conflicting' (Storey, 2000, p. 177). 'Goal free evaluation' (Easterby-Smith, 1986, p. 36), however, is based on the assumption that the officially declared goals are neither complete nor stable nor clear. Different groups of stakeholders have different goals and expectations. Therefore evaluators should not start out from the official goals, but instead try to make contact with stakeholders and participants in order to find the real benefit of the programme.

> In practice this might involve trying to avoid contact with the course director before and during the programme, and deliberately not looking at course brochures or proposals to validating bodies. Instead the evaluator should spend his time talking to participants and other stakeholders, and should attempt to observe carefully what takes place during and after the programme. (Easterby-Smith, 1986, p. 37)

14.5 Evaluation planning and evaluation concepts

By differentiating between the functions of 'proving', 'improving' and 'learning', Easterby-Smith (1986, p. 13) highlights that evaluation must be an integral part of the process of learning and development. Feedback based on evaluation data is a core element of the learning of companies (Nadler, 1997). The importance of feedback loops is also emphasized in concepts of entrepreneurial learning (Leitch and Harrison, 1999; Young and Sexton, 1997, p. 231) because the learning process of entrepreneurs basically can be considered as action learning (Fayolle, 2004b, p. 343; Johannisson, 1992, p. 99). Expecially, SME owners are used to this kind of informal learning (Donckels, 1993, p. 263). Concepts for entrepreneurship education at university level also underline the importance of reflecting and evaluating learning and work experiences (Gibb, 1996, p. 315; Johannisson, 1991; Johannisson et al., 1996, p. 3).

Feedback based on evaluation can, according to Argyris, trigger learning at different levels:

- Single-loop learning, where the feedback leads to a better input of resources, whereas the goals of the programme are not questioned.
- Double-loop learning, where the goals of the programme are critically assessed and therefore become an object of learning.
- Deutero learning, where the process of learning itself is discussed.

Only with the use of feedback at the level of double-loop or deutero learning, can the 'theory-in-use' be changed (Argyris and Schoen, 1978; Bateson, 1983, p. 219).

In this context it is important to keep in mind that the parameters of programme designs (for example, decisions about the definition of goals and target groups, selection principles, pedagogic decisions) contain an explicit or implicit learning theory. 'As purposive activities, programmes are intended to stimulate, cause or facilitate a process of learning that leads to certain learning outcomes' (Burgoyne and Stuart, 1978, p. 93). The efficiency of a programme therefore depends on the accordance of programme design with programme goals. This underlines the importance for the educational institution to develop an explicit programme philosophy (Stiefel, 1973). Twaalfhoven (2001) examined entrepreneurship programmes of leading US MBA schools, and extracted three distinct approaches used for programme development: the 'research-oriented model', the 'consulting model' and the 'teaching and practice-oriented student development model'.

14.5.1   *Questions and decisions in the evaluation planning process*
During the planning process the questions summarized in Table 14.1 have to be answered.

In practice, evaluations mostly concentrate on just a few of these questions, such as number of participants, participants' satisfaction with the programme or trainers, or the changes of participants' attitude towards entrepreneurship.

In the field of management development a number of concepts and models for evaluation have been developed during the last years. A transfer of those models into entrepreneurship education is advisable. Therefore, in the following sections some frequently used concepts of evaluation are discussed: Storey (2000) developed a model especially designed for evaluating SME programmes. The 'Four Levels of Evaluation' (Kirkpatrick, 1976; Kirkpatrick and Kirkpatrick, 2005) probably is the most popular tool for evaluation in the Anglo-American area. Easterby-Smith's model (1986) developed at the University of Lancaster, Great Britain, focuses on management development. Von Sassen developed the Learning Cycle, which is targeted on change processes in organization development activities, in the Dutch NPI (von Sassen, n.d.).

14.5.2   *Storey's six-steps model*
David Storey (University of Warwick, UK) has developed a model for the evaluation of SME programmes (Table 14.2). The six steps are ranked in terms of sophistication. Storey

Table 14.1   Questions in the evaluation planning process

Cause of evaluation	Triggered by a certain incident
	Systematically planned
Evaluation design	With and without control group(s) (matching)
	Before, during, at the end, after the programme
	Announced or secretly (for example, mystery shopping)
	Self-evaluation or third-party evaluation
Evaluation goals	Support of participant's learning
	Control of the current programme
	Changes in current or future programmes
	Assessment: participants, coach, training organization, accommodation, and so on
	Improvement of learning of (future) participants
	Proving programme effects on different levels: attitude changes, increased knowledge, changed behaviour at the workplace, effect on enterprise level, total economic consequences
Evaluation subject (who evaluates?)	Coach, programme planner, participant, evaluation expert
	External or internal evaluation
	Cooperative evaluation
Evaluation object (what and who is evaluated?)	Individual learning progress (intended, unintended)
	Individual change in behaviour (intended, unintended)
	Seminar climate
	Degree of transfer to the workplace
	Programme design (goals, contents, method, time)
	Trainer, training management, programme organization
	Environment (accommodation, seminar room)
	Training institute (provider)
Source of information	Participants, seniors, colleagues, documents, figures
	Trainer, training institute, principal (contract awarder)
Evaluation time	Workplace analysis and needs analysis
	Goal formulation and programme planning
	During or at the end of the programme
	After return to workplace or later on
Evaluation frequency	Pre-test, post test(s)
Instruments of evaluation	Questionnaire, interview, observation (standardized, open)
	Paper and pencil test, assessement of work assignment/job performance
	Critical incident technique, learning diary, document analysis
Data handling	Anonymous or not anonymous
	Data communication with(out) knowledge or consent

distinguishes between the preliminary stage of 'Monitoring' (steps 1 to 3) and real evaluation (steps 4 to 6). 'The difference between monitoring and evaluation is that the latter are attempts, demonstrating analytical rigor, to determine the impact of policy initiatives' (Storey, 2000, p. 180). From steps 4 to 6, the main focus is on the comparison with non-participants.

Table 14.2   Six-steps model of evaluation

Step	Questions	Problems
Monitoring		
Step 1: Take-up schemes	How many firms participated (sectors, size, location)? How much money was spent?	Almost no results concerning policy effectiveness or about satisfying objectives
Step 2: Recipient's opinions	Did course participants like it? Were there problems in the application procedure?	Satisfaction with course tells nothing about effectiveness Only results concerning policy delivery (which is not the key question)
Step 3: Recipient's views of the difference made by the assistance	Did firms think the course provided 'additionality' or would they have done it anyway? Does it cause 'displacement'?	Provide answers firms think you want to hear No way of checking the quality of answers Only snapshot of 'surviving' firms
Evaluation		
Step 6: Taking account of selection bias	Use of statistical techniques Use of random panels	Policy-makers feel uneasy about statistical adjustment, results are difficult to explain Use of random panels could mean public money is given to firms who will not benefit
Step 4: Comparison of performance of 'assisted' with typical firms	Employment growth, sales growth and survival rate of assisted firms compared with 'typical' firms	Assisted firms are not typical, self-selection bias has to be taken into account Administrative committee selection bias (depends on extent of competition for the funds and on the ability of selectors)
Step 5: Comparison with match firms	Compare assisted with 'match' firms on bias of age, sector, of ownership, geography over same period	Perfect matching on all four criteria very difficult, matching should take place immediately before policy implementation Sample selection bias (more motivated firms apply, attribution of differential performance to scheme and not to motivation)

Source: Storey (2000, pp. 180–90).

14.5.3   Kirkpatrick's four-step model

Kirkpatrick distinguishes four chronologically ranked evaluation levels. 'Evaluation changes from a complicated, elusive generality into clear and achievable goals if we break it down into logical steps' (Kirkpatrick, 1976, p. 18-2):

- *Reaction evaluation*: at this level the major aspect is the satisfaction of the participant with the programme, trainers and organizations. Evaluation is done most frequently with questionnaires for participants ('happiness sheets') at the end of the programme.

- *Learning evaluation*: the evaluation focuses on individual learning success. Which principles, facts and techniques were learned at the end of the programme? The most frequently used evaluation instruments at this level are written and oral exams.
- *Behaviour evaluation*: what changes in job behaviour in the workplace resulted from the programme? In other words, the success of transfer is evaluated at this level. The main instruments here are interviews with participants or persons from their environment and observation on the workplace.
- *Results evaluation*: what were the tangible results of the programme? Outcomes on the company level (for example, cost reduction, quality improvement, decrease in absences, increase in sales) are evaluated.

In his 'cycle of evaluation' Hamblin (1974) extends this scheme by including the planning and preparation phase. He regards evaluation as

> any attempt to obtain information feedback on the effects of a training programme, and to assess the value of the training in the light of that information. It should be noted that this definition includes investigation before and during training as well as after training. One can not assess training effects unless one knows something about the before-training situation for comparison with the after-training situation. (Hamblin, 1974, p. 8)

Warr et al. (1971, p. 16) elaborate these levels further in their CIRO model. They distinguish between

- **C**ontext evaluation (inquiry of the training needs and goals),
- **I**nput evaluation (resources used to reach the goals),
- **R**eaction evaluation and
- **O**utcome evaluation (immediate outcome: change of knowledge and attitude; intermediate outcome: change of behaviour at the workplace; ultimate outcome: effects on company level).

14.5.4   *Easterby-Smith's CAIPO model*
The CAIPO model of evaluation features five starting-points or levels for evaluation: **C**ontext, **A**dministration, **I**nputs, **P**rocess and **O**utcomes (Table 14.3). These levels do not substitute each other. The evaluators have to decide about the importance given to each level. 'The . . . framework is intended to distinguish a number of aspects of a programme or an event, each of which might form the primary focus for evaluation' (Easterby-Smith, 1986, p. 46).

14.5.5   *The NPI learning cycle*
This model has been developed at the Dutch NPI (Instituut voor Organisatie Ontwikkeling) (see Figure 14.1). The model's starting point is the difference between the 'world of working' (workplace) and the 'world of learning' (course, seminar) which causes a 'transfer gap'.

The NPI model emphasizes the importance of embedding evaluation in an overall planning and learning concept, based on the provider's explicit programme philosophy.[5]

Table 14.3   CIRO model

Evaluation level	Focus	Typical questions
Context	Circumstances outside and beyond the programme itself	Reasons for funding and running the programme Different aims and objectives of various stakeholders Reasons for evaluation of the programme
Administration	Specific training and developmental activities Programme management	Mechanisms of nomination, selection, briefing, follow-up activities Reasons for training and processes whereby participants come to the courses Administrative arrangements
Inputs	Methods, techniques and people involved	Potential impact of different methods Evaluation of the contribution of different methods, for example, lectures, role plays, business games, tutors and lecturers, counselling and appraisal sessions
Process	Processes during training and developmental activities	Description of processes Understanding of processes Investigation of specific aspects and dimensions of the process (for example, interaction process, hidden curriculum)
Outcomes	Participant's potential and implementation of the potential in the workplace	Description of changes in participant's potential: quantitative and qualitative learning and/or development (ability to learn from experience, confidence and self-efficacy) Implementation of the potential in form of behaviour, relationships, attitudes at work (including transfer problems).

Source: Easterby-Smith (1986).

In this model, evaluation is part of all phases of the learning cycle. The model emphasizes that the evaluation concept has to be formulated before the beginning of the programme.

Based upon an analysis of the work situation and a training needs analysis in step 1 the programme goals are formulated. Only a part of these goals can be operationalized. It also has to be considered that potential and actual participants as well as sponsors and trainers can pursue different goals, which might lead to serious conflicts. The problem of 'hidden goals' also has to be taken into account. In step 2 the programme is planned and organized according to the formulated goals.

By participating in the programme, intended as well as unintended learning results (changes in attitudes, knowledge or behaviour) will occur. This learning progress can be demonstrated through assessments and tests in step 3.

However, only a part of the learning results will be transferred successfully to the workplace. In order to reduce this considerable transfer gap, in step 4 measures to promote the learning transfer are of utmost importance. In this phase the professional and social environment plays a central role, for example, supervisors who act as mentors or promoters.

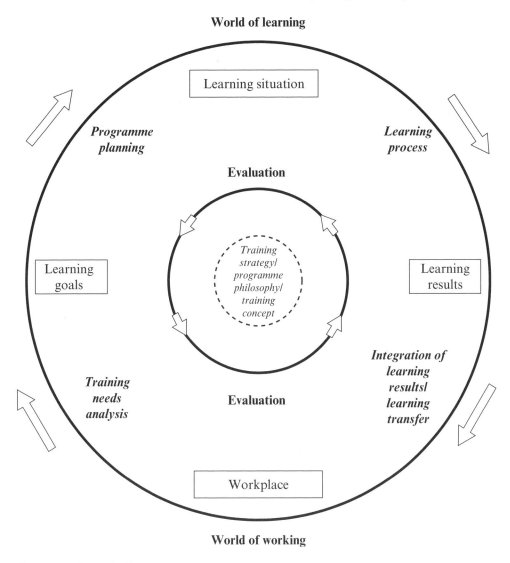

World of learning

Learning situation

Programme planning

Learning process

Evaluation

Learning goals

Training strategy/ programme philosophy/ training concept

Learning results

Training needs analysis

Evaluation

Integration of learning results/ learning transfer

Workplace

World of working

Source: von Sassen (n.d.).

Figure 14.1 NPI learning cycle

When the transfer from the programme to the workplace is successfully completed, the learning cycle can be regarded as complete (von Sassen, n.d.). Nevertheless, the changes of behaviour at the workplace or in the task or the working environment again will result in new training needs. Therefore this model can also be called a learning cycle.

Evaluation covers all phases of the model.

● Evaluation of needs analysis: were the goals derived correctly from the results of the training needs analysis?

- Evaluation of the programme planning: did the programme design, especially the pedagogic concept, adequately reflect framework conditions as well as the target group and the stated goals?
- Evaluation of the programme implementation: was the programme adequately executed, so that the set goals were accomplished?
- Evaluation of the learning transfer: to what extent were the learning results implemented at the workplace? Did the strategies used to facilitate the transfer have any effect?

The evaluation concept as part of the overall programme concept therefore has to deal with the following aspects:

- goals of the evaluation (of the respective stakeholders)
- coordination of the evaluation instruments used in the various phases of evaluation
- tasks and competences of the evaluators
- framework conditions of the evaluation (particularly time, budget).

14.6   Conclusion

Research on the Internet and in the respective literature revealed a broad range of entrepreneurship education programmes. Nevertheless, only a modest part of these programmes includes evaluation, clearly dominated by simple ex-post evaluation designs (in most cases only done with a single questionnaire). More sophisticated evaluation designs are rarely carried out. This also applies to the evaluation on the impact level (for example, creation of start-ups, development of these start-ups, fiscal analysis). Distorting effects caused by crowding-out effects or windfall gains are hardly taken into consideration.

Of course, limitations of the study have to be taken into consideration, such as the exploratory nature of the Internet research. More sophisticated studies about evaluation of (subsidized) programmes might be available, but – depending on various internal reasons – often remain unpublished.

During the past few years the focus of evaluation studies has shifted from input indicators to attitude changes as a prerequisite for transfer (Fayolle et al., 2005). However, senior managers, donators and governmental authorities in charge of the promotion of enterprises increasingly demand insights about the effect of entrepreneurship education programmes on the ultimate level/outcome level (Kirkpatrick, 1976). Therefore, programme designers should increase their efforts to develop and implement respective evaluation designs. To do so, the models presented in this chapter represent a cornerstone to build on. Future major points of interest in the field of evaluation research are different effects of programme designs and of various teaching methods in combination with different target groups (such as business and non-business students). Finally, the relationship between organizational culture and evaluation design would also require a closer look.

In conclusion, some practical proposals for designing evaluation studies are summarized:

1. *Include persons affected by the evaluation as soon as possible.* The persons concerned (programme managers, coaches, trainers, participants) should be involved in the formulation of evaluation goals and the design of the evaluation from the start (Easterby-Smith, 1986, p. 17). The variety of different viewpoints enables an

improved and widely accepted design and easier-to-use tools to be developed. The discussion of the focal points of the upcoming evaluation per se influences the attitudes and behaviour of the participants.

2. *Consider the target group's previous experience with evaluation.* Whilst planning the evaluation and choosing its instruments, it is advisable to take the target group's previous experience with evaluation into consideration to avoid resistance.

3. *Develop simple and manageable instruments.* To support evaluation by participants and coaches, the instruments should be designed to be as simple as possible with regard to usability and comprehensibility ('simple but not easy'). In addition, instruments for self-evaluation should also be provided. 'As programmes and their environments become increasingly complex, monitoring and control must become more systematic, but not too complex for field staff to respond to and understand . . . Systems can be simple, compact and sophisticated at the same time' (Paul, 1983, p. 102).

4. *Estimate costs and benefits of the evaluation.* Evaluation costs (including opportunity costs for evaluators and the target group for the whole process of planning, data collection and feedback) as well as potential benefits of a programme evaluation must be at least roughly estimated as a basis for decisions about the evaluation and its design. Facing increasing budget constraints, a decision to concentrate the evaluation on certain aspects or levels is more recommendable than a 'cover-it-all' approach which will lead to superficial data.[6]

5. *Use sophisticated evaluation designs.* The more instruments of qualitative and quantitative research are combined, the more often the evaluation is conducted (at least pre- and post-tests), and the more evaluation levels are addressed, the more valid will be the results. This, of course, allows more accurate conclusions to be drawn (Henry et al., 2003, p. 106) and to publish evaluation reports which meet the standards of the scientific community as well as those of the principals.

However, temporal and financial restrictions of the evaluation budget as well as different (and partly hidden) goals of the different stakeholder groups are important problems to solve. In this context the purpose(s) of evaluation should be clarified before starting any evaluative activity. One of the first strategic decisions in the planning process is the determination of the evaluation level(s) to be addressed (Easterby-Smith, 1986, p. 13):

(a) Evaluation can hardly be divorced from the process upon which it concentrates and should therefore be considered as an integral part of the learning and development process itself. With the primary aim of evaluation of 'learning', the evaluation should be designed to support learning processes of the participants (Argyris and Schoen, 1978; Nadler, 1997). Qualitative data are relatively easily to collect during the course (for example, semi-structured interviews and questionnaires, group discussions, self-tests). Examples are the use of pre-course questionnaires to design a 'tailor-made' course or instruments assessing the learning climate and individual learning progress which are administered during the course.

(b) A focus on 'improving' implies an emphasis on the improvement of the current or future programmes. Formative evaluation here serves as a decision aid for the programme designers and organizers, and provides trainers and coaches with information which will help them to increase their effectiveness.

(c)   A 'proving' focus aims at demonstrating that something has happened as a result of the programme. This is linked to the stakeholders' judgements of the programme value concerning effectiveness (was it the right activity for the intended goals?), efficiency (was the activity well done?) and the cost–benefit ratio (was it worth the costs?). Especially for the persons initiating and financing an entrepreneurship programme, it is essential to prove that the money has been well spent or that prolonging the subsidy is justified. The research should therefore focus on long-term effects including a cost–benefit analysis and pre- and post-tests. It is advisable to include additional post-tests to prove transfer effects on the workplace. Control groups and/or matching (Gensler et al., 2005) serve to single out selection effects. Garavan and O'Cinneide (1994, p. 5) suggest that longitudinal research designs with control groups of non-participating persons are needed to examine the lasting effects of the programme, whilst Storey (2000) advocates the inclusion of a control sample of matched firms. But it remains the danger that sophisticated designs and results are difficult to understand and to communicate. Finally, are stakeholders interested in obtaining rigorously researched evaluation data (including selection and crowding-out effects) or would they prefer to stick to mere monitoring data (for example, the number of participants) to minimize the danger of unpopular results?

6.   *Avoid 'evaluation bureaucracy'.* Combining a number of instruments and sophisticated evaluation designs will enhance the reliability of the results but might reinforce the impression of an evaluation bureaucracy (Hamblin, 1974, p. 67). This can lead to counter-productive consequences such as unwillingness to cooperate in the evaluation process or superficial feedback. Therefore, with the chosen evaluation goals and levels always kept in mind, only as many instruments as really needed should be implemented.

7.   *Use evaluation data actively.* The evaluation data should be used for a continuous external (potential participants, media, public) and internal (contract awarder, participant) marketing. This goes beyond the regular publication of a report of results, and underpins the necessity to identify the values and criteria of different stakeholder groups as a basis for selective information (Easterby-Smith, 1986, p. 15).

Notes

1.   For example, resulting number of start-ups, survival rates of founded enterprises, turnover, profit, sales of the enterprises, fiscal impact.
2.   The International Survey on Collegiate Entrepreneurship (ISCE) is a research project organized by the University of St Gallen, Switzerland, and the European Business School, Germany. It aims to identify the potential of students using an online questionnaire on a regular basis. Fourteen countries participated in the first round which started in 2006 (Fueglistaller et al., 2006).
3.   No evaluation report was published, source: www.gep.ie.
4.   See in detail Henry et al. (2003) and the contribution of Henry, Hill and Leitch in this book.
5.   Easterby-Smith (1986, p. 137) also highlights the importance of differentiation between the evaluation levels method, course/programme and policy.
6.   Easterby-Smith (1986, p. 18) published a checklist to assess the need for evaluation of particular courses, programmes or systems.

References

Argyris, C. and Schoen, D. (1978), *Organizational Learning: A Theory of Action Perspective*, Reading, MA: Addison-Wesley.

Arnold, R. (1996), Von der Erfolgskontrolle zur entwicklungsorientierten Evaluation, in J. Muench (ed.), *Okoenomie betrieblicher Bildungsarbeit*, Berlin: Schmidt Verlag, pp. 251–67.

Ashridge Management Center (2005), *Executive Education: Evaluating the Return on Investment*, www.ashridge.com/www./newsandevents.nsf, accessed 25 May 2005.

Bateson, G. (1983), *Oekologie des Geistes*, 6th edn, Frankfurt am Main: Suhrkamp Verlag.

Bauer, U. and Kailer, N. (2003), Gruendungsneigung von Technikern am Beispiel der Technischen Universitaet Graz und ausgewaehlten Wirtschaftsingenieurstudiengaengen, *Schriftenreihe BWL Education & Research*, No. 7, Graz, Austria.

Beywl, W. and Taut, S. (2000), Standards – Aktuelle Strategie zur Qualitaetsentwicklung in der Evaluation, *DIW-Vierteljahreshefte zur Wirtschaftsforschung*, **3**, 358–70.

Boehme, M., Tuertscher, G. and Pechlaner, H. (2005), Business Plan-Wettbewerbe als Instrument der Gruendungsforderung – Zufriedenheitsanalyse von Teilnehmern, in H. Pechlaner, H. Hinterhuber and E.-M. Hammann (eds), *Unternehmertum und Unternehmensgruendung*, Wiesbaden: DUV Gabler Edition Wissenschaft, pp. 136–57.

Boissin, J.-P. (2003), *Le concept de 'Maison de l'Entrepreneuriat' – Un outil d'action pour l'initiative économique sur les campus*, Direction de la Technologie du Ministère de la Jeunesse, Paris, www.entrepreneuriat-grenoble.org/servlet/com.univ.utils, accessed 9 March 2005.

Braun, G. and Diensberg, C. (2003), Evaluation und Erfolgsbewertung internationaler Entrepreneurship-Trainings, in K. Walterscheid (ed.), *Entrepreneurship in Forschung und Lehre*, Frankfurt am Main: Peter Lang Verlag, pp. 205–21.

Bundesministerium fuer Bildung und Forschung (BMBF) (ed.) (2002), *Studierende und Selbstaendigkeit – Ergebnisse der EXIST-Studierendenbefragung*, Bonn: BMBF.

Burgoyne, J. and Stuart, R. (1978), Management development programmes: underlying assumptions about learning, in J. Burgoyne and R. Stuart (eds), *Management Development: Context and Strategies*, Aldershot: Gower Press, pp. 93–114.

Carayannis, E., Evans, D. and Hanson, M. (2003), A cross-cultural learning strategy for entrepreneurship education: outline of key concepts and lessons learned from a comparative study of entrepreneurship students in France and the US, *Technovation*, **23**, 757–71.

Center for Rural Studies, University of Vermont (CRS) (2003), *NECFE – Northeast Center for Food Entrepreneurship, Client Outcome Report*, October, www.crs.uvm.edu/evaluation, accessed 10 March 2005.

Charney, A. Libecap, G. (2000), *The Impact of Entrepreneurship Education: An Evaluation of the Berger Entrepreneurship Program at the University of Arizona 1995–1999*, revised final report to the Kauffman Center for Entrepreneurial Leadership, Eller College of Business and Public Administration, University of Arizona.

Craig, R. and Bittel, L. (eds) (1976), *Training and Development Handbook*, American Society for Training and Development, New York: McGraw-Hill.

Donckels, R. (1993), *Pleins Feux Sur Les PME – De la théorie à la pratique*, Bruxelles: Roularta Books/Foundation Roi Baudoin.

Easterby-Smith, M. (1986), *Evaluation of Management Education, Training & Development*, Aldershot: Gower Press.

Easterby-Smith, M., Braiden, E. and Ashton, D. (1980), *Auditing Management Development*, Aldershot: Gower Press.

Ennoeckl, J. (2002), Hemmende und foerdernde Faktoren der Unternehmensgruendung durch Studierende, master thesis, University of Linz, Austria.

European Commission (2004a), *DG Enterprise 2004 Annual Management Plan*, Bruxelles: European Commission.

European Commission – Enterprise Directorate-General (2004b), *Final Report of the Expert Group 'Education for Entrepreneurship'*, October, Bruxelles: European Commission.

Fayolle, A. (2000), Exploratory study to assess the effects of entrepreneurship programs on French student entrepreneurial behaviours, *Journal of Enterprising Culture*, **8** (2), 169–83.

Fayolle, A. (2003), *Le métier de créateur d'entreprise – Motivations, Parcours, Facteurs clés de succès*, Paris: Editions d'Organisation.

Fayolle, A. (2004a), Value creation in changing student state of mind and behavior: new research approaches to measure the effects of entrepreneurship education, in U. Fueglistaller, T. Volery and W. Weber (eds), *Value Creation in Entrepreneurship and SMEs, Rencontres de St.-Gall 2004*, Swiss Research Institute of Small Business and Entrepreneurship at the University of St Gallen, St Gallen: Verlag KMU HSG,.

Fayolle, A. (2004b), *Entrepreneuriat – Apprendre à Entreprendre*, Paris: Dunod.

Fayolle, A., Gailly, B. and Lassas-Clerc, N. (2005), *Capturing Variations in Attitudes and Intentions: A Longitudinal Study to Assess the Pedagogical Effectiveness of Entrepreneurship Training Programmes*, EM Lyon Cahiers de Recherche No. 2005/11, Lyon.

Fayolle, A., Vernier, A. and Dijane, B. (2000), Les jeunes diplomés de l'enseignement supérieur sont-ils des créateurs d'entreprise comme les autres? *Revue Gestion 2000 – La Revue de Management pour Cadres et Universitaires – Dossier Entrepreneuriat*, No. Spécial, Mars–Avril, 39–55.

Fletcher, M. and Rosa, P. (1998), The Graduate Enterprise Programme: ten years on, in M. Scott, P. Rosa and H. Klandt (eds), *Educating Entrepreneurs for Wealth Creation*, Aldershot, UK and Brookfield, US: Ashgate, pp. 59–79.

Franke, N. and Luethje, C. (2004), *Entrepreneurial Intentions of Business Students: A Benchmarking Study, Working Paper*, Vienna University of Economics and Business Administration, Department of Entrepreneurship, Vienna.

Fueglistaller, U. et al. (2004a), *Swiss Survey on Collegiate Entrepreneurship*, KMU-HSG/START (eds), July, St Gallen.

Fueglistaller, U., Halter, F. and Hartl, R. (2004b), Unternehmertum im universitaeren Umfeld, in *IGA Zeitschrift fuer Klein- und Mittelunternehmen (Internationales Gewerbearchiv)*, vol 52, Berlin and St Gallen: Duncker & Humblot Verlag, pp. 15–31.

Fueglistaller, U., Klandt, H. and Halter, F. (2006), *International Survey on Collegiate Entrepreneurship 2006*, University of St Gallen (HSG) and European Business School (ebs) (eds), St Gallen and Oestrich-Winkel.

Garavan, T. and O'Cinneide, B. (1994), Entrepreneurship education and training programmes: a review and evaluation, Part 1, *Journal of European Industrial Training*, **18** (8), 3–12.

Gensler, S., Skiera, B. and Boehm, M. (2005), Einsatzmoeglichkeiten der Matching Methode zur Beruecksichtigung von Selbstselektion, *Journal fuer Betriebswirtschaft*, **55** (1), 37–62.

Getzner, M., Haber, G. and Schwarz, E. (2003), *Gesamtwirtschaftliche Effekte der Unternehmensgruendungen in Oesterreich 2003*, University of Klagenfurt, Austria.

Gibb, A. (1993), The enterprise culture and education – understanding enterprise education and its links with small business, entrepreneurship and wider educational goals, *International Small Business Journal*, **11** (3), 11–34.

Gibb, A. (1996), Entrepreneurship and small business management: can we afford to neglect them in the twenty-first century business school? *British Journal of Management*, **7**, 309–21.

Golla, S., Halter, F., Fueglistaller, U. and Klandt, H. (2004), *Gruendungsneigung Studierender – Eine empirische Analyse in Deutschland und der Schweiz*, Stuttgart: Proceedings of G-Forum 2004.

Hamblin, A. (1974), *Evaluation and Control of Training*, London: McGraw-Hill.

Hendry, C., Jones, A. and Arthur, M. (1991), *The Delivery of Effective Training: The Concept of Skill in Small-Medium Enterprises*, Centre for Corporate Strategy and Change, Warwick Business School, University of Warwick, Coventry.

Henry, C., Hill, F. and Leitch, C. (2003), *Entrepreneurship Education and Training*, Aldershot, UK and Burlington, US: Ashgate.

Hills, G. and Morris, M. (1998), Entrepreneurship education: a conceptual model and review, in M. Scott, P. Rosa and H. Klandt (eds), *Educating Entrepreneurs for Wealth Creation*, Aldershot: Ashgate, pp. 38–58.

Hisrich, R. (1992), Toward an organization model for entrepreneurship education, in H. Klandt and D. Mueller-Boling (eds), *Internationalizing Entrepreneurship Education and Training*, Cologne and Dortmund: Foerderkreis Gruendungs-Forschung, pp. 16–41.

Holzer, F. and Adametz, C. (2003), *TUG-AbsolventInnenbefragung 2003, Endbericht (Oktober 2003)*, Technical University of Graz, Graz.

House, R. (1967), *Management Development: Design, Evaluation, and Implementation, Bureau of Industrial Relations*, Graduate School of Business Administration, The University of Michigan, Ann Arbor, MI.

Hytti, U. and Kuopusjärvi, P. (2004), *entreva.NET – Evaluating and Measuring Entrepreneurship and Enterprise Education: Methods, Tools And Practices*, Small Business Institute, Business Research and Development Centre, Turku School of Economics and Business Administration, Turku, Finland.

Jack, S. and Anderson, A. (1999), Enterpreneurship education within the enterprise culture – producing reflective practitioners, *International Journal of Entrepreneurial Behaviour and Research*, **5** (3), 110–25.

Johannisson, B. (1991), University training for entrepreneurship: Swedish approaches, *Entrepreneurship and Regional Development*, **3**, 67–82.

Johannisson, B. (1992), Entrepreneurs as learners – beyond education and training, in H. Klandt and D. Mueller-Boling (eds), *Internationalizing Entrepreneurship Education and Training*, Cologne and Dortmund: Foerderkreis Gruendungs-Forschung, pp. 95–109.

Johannisson, B., Landstrom, H. and Rosenberg, J. (1996), University training for entrepreneurship – an action frame of reference, in H. Klandt (ed.), *Internationalizing Entrepreneurship Education and Training*, Lohmar and Cologne: Josef Eul Verlag.

Kailer, N. (1991), *Organisationsformen und Entwicklungstendenzen betrieblicher Weiterbildung in Osterreich*, Research Series Institute for Bildungsforschung der Wirtschaft No. 86, Vienna.

Kailer, N. (ed.) (2001), *Betriebliche Kompetenzentwicklung – Praxiskonzepte und empirische Analysen*, Vienna: Linde Verlag.

Kaschube, J. and Lang-von Wins, T. (1999), Erfahrungen aus einem Gruendungswettbewerb an Muenchner Hochschulen, in K. Moser, B. Batinic and J. Zempel (eds), *Unternehmerisch erfolgreiches Handeln*, Goettingen: Verlag fuer Angewandte Psychologie, pp. 245–62.

Katz, J. (2004), *2004 Survey of Endowed Positions in Entrepreneurship and Related Fields in the United States*, Kansas City, KS: Ewing Marion Kauffman Foundation.

Kirkpatrick, D. (1976), Evaluation of Training, in Craig, R. and Bittel, L. (eds), *Training and Development Handbook*, 2nd edn, New York: Mc Graw-Hill, pp. 18-1–18-27. (First edition: 1967.)

Kirkpatrick, D. and Kirkpatrick, J. (2005), *Evaluating Training Programs – The Four Levels*, 3rd edn, San Francisco, CA: Berret-Koehler.

Klandt, H. (2004), Entrepreneurship education and research in German-speaking Europe, *Academy of Management Learning and Education*, **3** (3), 293–301.

Klandt, H., Koch, L. and Knaup, U. (2005), *FGF-Report, Entrepreneurship-Professuren 2004, Eine Studie zur Entrepreneurshipforschung und –lehre an deutschsprachigen Hochschulen*, January, Cologne: FGF Forderkreis Gruendungs-Forschung e.V.

Klapper, R. (2004), Government goals and entrepreneurship education – an investigation at a Grande Ecole in France, *Education + Training*, **46** (3), 127–37.

Koch, L. (2003), Unternehmerausbildung an Hochschulen, *Zeitschrift fuer Betriebswirtschaft*, Supplementary Issue (2/2003), pp. 25–46.

Kolvereid, L. and Moen, O. (1997), Entrepreneurship among business graduates: does a major in entrepreneurship make a difference? *Journal of European Industrial Training Management*, **21** (4–5), 154–71.

Leitch, C. and Harrison, R. (1999), A process model for entrepreneurship education and development, *International Journal of Entrepreneurial Behaviour and Research*, **5** (3), 83–109.

Leodolter, M. (2005), UniversitaetsabsolventInnen als Unternehmensgruender und-uebernehmer – Eine empirische Studie an der Johannes Kepler Universitaet Linz, master thesis, University of Linz, Austria.

Levie, J. (1999), *Entrepreneurship Education in Higher Education in England – Survey 1999*, www.dfes.gov.uk/dfee/heqe/lbs.htm, 5 March 2005.

Levie, J., Brown, W. and Steele, L. (n.d.), *How Entrepreneurial are Strathclyde Alumni?* An international comparison, working paper, University of Strathclyde, Hunter Centre for Entrepreneurship, Strathclyde, Scotland.

Lucas, W. and Cooper, S. (2004), *Enhancing Self-efficacy to Enable Entrepreneurship: The Case of CMI's Connections*, MIT Sloan School of Management Working Paper 4489-04 (May 2004), Cambridge, MA.

Mitterauer, L. (2003), *Evaluation des Unternehmensgruendungsprogramms UNIUN – Gruendungsverlauf, Erfolgsbilanz, Fiskalanalyse der Programme UNIUN 1999 & UNIUN 2001*, final report for the Alumni-Society of the University of Vienna, Austria.

MKB-Nederland (SME Netherlands) and VNO-NCV (1999), Leren Ondernemen Loont (Studying entrepreneurship pays), MKB Nieuwsbericht 13 July, Delft, www.mkb.nl/Nieuws/287_102, accessed 20 May 2005.

Mumford, A. (ed.) (1986), *Handbook of Management Development*, Aldershot: Gower Press.

Nadler, D. (1977), *Feedback and Organization Development: Using Data-based Methods*, Reading, MA: Addison-Wesley.

Nakkula, M. (2004), *Initiating, Leading, and Feeling in Control of One's Fate – Executive Summary of Findings from the 2002–2003 Study of NFTE in Six Boston Public High Schools*, Project IF: Inventing the Future, Harvard University Graduate School of Education, Cambridge, MA, www.nfte.com/downloads/research_harvardexecsummary-01-02.pdf, accessed 22 May 2005.

Nandram, S. and Samson, K. (2004), Ahead of the pack, *Nyenrode NOW*, **2**, March, Breukelen: University of Nyenrode, pp. 10–11.

National Foundation for Teaching Entrepreneurship to Youth (NFTE) (2005), Brandeis University Research, www.nfte.com/impact/brandeisresearch.asp, 2 April 2005.

Neuberger, O. (1991), *Personalentwicklung*, Stuttgart: Enke Verlag.

Noel, T. (2001), *Effects of Entrepreneurial Education on Intent to open a Business*, Wichita State University, www.babson.edu/entrep/fer/Babson2001, accessed 3 March 2005.

Onstenk, J. (2000), Onderwijs En Ondernemerschap, CINOP Working Paper, Ministerievan Economische Zaken (ed.), Den Haag.

Paul, S. (1983), *Strategic Management of Development Programmes*, Management Development Series, No. 19, Geneva: ILO.

Pihkala, J. and Miettinen, A. (2003), Entrepreneurship education: does it promote entrepreneurial potential? A field study in Finnish polytechnics, in H. Klandt and A. Zaki Abu Bakar (eds), *Internationalizing Entrepreneurship Education and Training*, Lohmar and Cologne: Josef Eul Verlag, pp. 139–60.

Pleitner, H.-J. (2001), Entrepreneurship- Mode oder Motor? *Zeitschrift fuer Betriebswirtschaft*, **71** (2001/10), 1145–59.

Puxi, M. and Stetefeld, A. (2001), *Kontinuierliche wissenschaftliche Begleitung und Bewertung der im Freistaat Sachsen ueber den europaeischen Sozialfonds mitfinanzierten arbeitsmarktpolitischen Maßnahmen*, Annual Report 2000, Dresden: Saechsisches Staatsministerium fuer Wirtschaft und Arbeit.

Richter, J. (2000), StudentInnen und Unternehmensgruendung, master thesis, University of Linz, Austria.

Salomon, G., Duffy, S. and Tarabishy, A. (2002), The state of entrepreneurship education in the United States: a nationwide survey and analysis, *International Journal of Entrepreneurship Education* (1/2002), 65–86.

Sassen, H. von (n.d.), *Ausbilden und Lernen*, Working Paper 3639.774 HS/LG, NPI – Instituut voor Organisatie Ontwikkeling, Zeist, The Netherlands.

Schamp, T. and Deschoolmeester, D. (2002), *Building Blocks of Strategic Planning Effectiviness and the Growth of SME's – The Impact of Management Training on Strategic Targeting Proficiency and Accuracy Revisited*, Working Paper, Department of Management and Organization, Ghent University, Ghent.

Schauer, R., Kailer, N. and Feldbauer-Durstmueller, B. (eds) (2005), *Mittelstaendische Unternehmen – Probleme der Unternehmensnachfolge*, Linz: Trauner Verlag.

Schulte, R. (2004), Was ist 'Gruendungserfolg'? – Ueberlegungen zur Operationalisierung eines folkloristischen Begriffs, in J. Merz and J. Wagner (eds), *Perspektiven der Mittelstandsforschung*, Muenster: LIT Verlag, pp. 203–31.

Schwarz, E. and Grieshuber, E. (2001), Unternehmensgruendung als Berufsalternative osterreichischer Studierender, in S. Buchinger (ed.), *Gruenderland Osterreich*, Vienna: Bundesministerium für Wirtschaft und Arbeit, Center Wirtschaftspolitik, pp. 169–89.

Smith, A. and Piper, J. (1990), The tailor-made training maze: a practitioner's guide to evaluation, *Journal of European Industrial Training*, **14** (8), 2–31.

Stampfl, C. and Hytti, U. (2002), *Entrepreneurship als Herausforderung an das Bildungswesen – Ansaetze in Oesterreich und europaeischer Vergleich – Ergebnisse des Projektes ENTREDU*, Vienna: Schriftenreihe des Instituts fuer Bildungsforschung der Wirtschaft Nr. 123.

Staudt, E., Kailer, N., Kriegesmann, B., Meier, A., Stephan, H. and Ziegler, A. (1997), *Kompetenz und Innovation, Reihe Innovation: Forschung und Management*, vol. 10, E. Staudt (ed.), Bochum: Institut fuer Angewandte Innovationsforschung.

Sternberg, R. and Klose, B. (2001), *Evaluation des Programms zur finanziellen Absicherung von Unternehmensgruendern aus Hochschulen (PFAU)*, Cologne: Universitaet zu Köln, Wirtschafts- und Sozial geographisches Institut.

Sternberg, R. and Mueller, C. (2004), *Wissenschaftliche Begleitforschung zum Projekt 'Junge Innovatoren' des Ministeriums fuer Wissenschaft, Forschung und Kunst des Landes Baden-Wuerttemberg*, Cologne: University of Cologne.

Stiefel, R. (1973), *Fortbildungsphilosophie und Programmplanung*, Cologne and Bonn: Carl Heymanns Verlag.

Stiefel, R. (1974), *Grundfragen der Evaluation in der Managementschulung*, Frankfurt am Main: RKW.

Storey, D. (2000), Six steps to heaven: evaluating the impact of public policies to support small businesses in developed economies, in D. Sexton and H. Landstrom (eds), *The Blackwell Handbook of Entrepreneurship*, Oxford: Blackwell Business Series, pp. 176–94.

Storey, D. and Westhead, P. (1994), *Management Training and Small Firm Performance: A Critical Review*, Working Paper No. 18 (October), Warwick Business School – Centre for Small and Medium Sized Enterprises, University of Warwick, Coventry.

Thakur, S.P. (1995), Size of investment, growth opportunity and human resource management typologies in entrepreneurial firms: some observations, *Frontiers of Entrepreneurship Research 1995 Edition*, Babson College, www.babson.edu/entrep/fer/papers95/thakurc.htm, accessed 20 May 2005.

Tohmo, T. and Kaipainen, J. (2000), *Tyottomyydestae yrittaejyyteen. Evaluoinnin loppuraportti Polut yrittaejyy-teen – tiomenpisteestae ohjelmakaudella 1995–1999* (From unemployment to entrepreneurship. Final evaluation report on Priority 2, Measure 2 in the European Social Fund's Objective 3 Programme in Finland), Helsinki: Research centre of the Department of Economics and Chydenius Institute, University of Jyvaeskylae, www. entreva.net, accessed 28 May 2005.

Twaalfhoven, B. (2000), Entrepreneurship education and its funding – a comparison between Europe and the United States, report, European Foundation for Entrepreneurship Research (EFER) (ed.), June, available at www.efer.nl/pdf/EntreEduFunding.pdf, accessed on 12 February 2005.

Twaalfhoven, B. (2001), Developing entrepreneurship programmes in MBA Schools: a contrast in approaches, European Foundation for Entrepreneurship Research (ed.), Spring, available at www.efer.nl/res, accessed on 10 May 2005.

Ulrich, D. (ed.) (1990), *Delivering Results*, Boston, MA: Harvard Business School Press.

Urbano, D., Capelleras, J., Guallaarte, C. and Vergés, J. (2003), *Marco Institucional Formal de la Creación de Empresas en Catalunya* (Institutional formal frame for the creation of enterprises is Catalonia), Barcelona: Universidad Autonoma de Barcelona, http://webct.tukkk.fi/entreva/entredu/kirjallisuus/264.pdf, accessed 18 May 2005.

Van der Sluis, J., Van Praag, M. and Van Witteloostuijn, A. (2004), *Comparing the Returns to Education for Entrepreneurs and Employees*, Amsterdam: Tinbergen Institute Discussion Paper TI 2004-104/3.

Von Landsberg, G. and Weiss, R. (eds) (1995), *Bildungs-Controllung*, 2nd edn, Stuttgart: Schaeffer-Poeschel Verlag.

Warr, P., Bird, M. and Rackham, N. (1971), *Evaluation of Management Training*, 2nd edn Aldershot: Gower Press.

Weiss, C. (1972), *Evaluation Research. Methods for Assessing Program Effectiveness*, Englewood Cliffs, NJ: Prentice-Hall.

Westhead, P., Storey, D. and Martin, F. (2000), The Shell technology enterprise programme: student outcomes, *Education + Training*, 42 (4/5 2000), 272–81.

Westhead, P., Storey, D. and Martin, F. (2001), Outcomes reported by students who participated in the 1994 Shell Technology Enterprise Programme, *Entrepreneurship and Regional Development*, **13**, 163–85.

Wilson, K. (2004), *Entrepreneurship Education at European Universities and Business Schools – Results of a Joint Pilot Survey*, EFER/EFMD (eds), September, www.efer.nl/pdf/EuEntreEduPilotSurvey.pfd, accessed 10 March 2005.

Wottawa, H. and Thierau, H. (1990), *Lehrbuch Evaluation*, Bern, Stuttgart and Toronto: Verlag Hans Huber.

Young, J. and Sexton, D. (1997), Entrepreneurial learning: a conceptual framework, *Journal of Enterprising Culture*, **5**, 223–48.

15 Evaluating entrepreneurship education: play of power between evaluators, programme promoters and policy makers
Ulla Hytti and Paula Kuopusjärvi

Introduction

There is an increased need to carry out evaluation studies with respect to public policies and related instruments. Citizens are keen to know that their taxes are well spent on effective public policies. For this reason policy-makers need to conduct evaluations – systematic research – to find out what has happened in order to pass judgment on the policy (Venetoklis, 2002). This does not mean, however, that evaluations are necessary only in the public sector. If hundreds of millions of euros are spent on management training and development, then managers of those companies are entitled to ask why this should produce better employees and whether or not this will add to the long-term financial benefit of the company (Rowe, 1996). Accountability is not the only reason, however. Organizations that are involved in the planning and implementation of policies – whether as authorities or agents – also want some feedback that would assist them in improving the ongoing policy operations or planned operations in the future (Venetoklis, 2002).

The evaluation studies need to reflect the diversity in the objectives that enterprise education programmes can seek to achieve (Storey, 2000). These may be, for example, as follows: (1) increasing understanding of what entrepreneurship is about; (2) equipping individuals with an entrepreneurial approach to the 'world of work'; and (3) preparing individuals to act as entrepreneurs and as managers of new business (Hytti and O'Gorman, 2004). Therefore, the choice of indicators and measures needs to match these aims, which is a difficult and complex issue (Fayolle, 2005). If the programme aims at increasing understanding about entrepreneurship, it does not make sense to measure the start-up activity of the programme participants, at least in the short run. Besides the different aims in different programmes there is also another factor that influences evaluations, namely, the stakeholders involved in the evaluation process – evaluators, programme promoters and policy-makers – who may have different and conflicting views of the evaluated programme(s) (Abma, 2000).

In this chapter we aim to provide insight into the different perspectives of the different stakeholders involved in the evaluation process regarding enterprise and entrepreneurship education. Our analysis focuses on the different aims and needs as well as the arguments provided for the evaluations from the three different perspectives. The importance of stakeholder diversity has been acknowledged recently in the training and educational evaluation models (Michalski and Cousins, 2000). As a result, we will focus on the forces that shape evaluations and evaluation processes and the knowledge claims that follow it. Hence, we should become more critical of the power plays of which evaluation is a part (Segerholm, 2003).

   The chapter presents the results of a research project undertaken in six European countries. The study has been carried out as a part of a project, Entreva, financed under the European Commission's Leonardo Da Vinci programme.[1] The results of the study are more comprehensively presented in a research report (Hytti and Kuopusjärvi, 2004). The report in electronic format is available at www.entreva.net. The website also contains a web tool on how to plan and execute evaluations of enterprise education and training programmes that complements the report.

The different stakeholders and the notion of power

The research is based on the idea that evaluation is a politically contextualized act. Therefore, all aspects of evaluation – design, implementation, outcomes and uses – are shaped by the power relationships among the stakeholders (Cardoza Clayson et al., 2002). Stakeholders are the distinct groups interested in the results of the evaluation, either because they are directly affected by or involved in the activities, or because they need to make a decision about financing or running a similar training programme in the future (Michalski and Cousins, 2000). In this study we also include 'evaluators' as stakeholders in the process although they are not necessarily directly interested in or affected by the results of the evaluation per se. However, indirectly they are affected by at least the acceptability of the evaluation results to the other stakeholders – programme promoters and funders as well as the academic community in a more general sense. As a result, all the stakeholders in the process are vulnerable. Funders are accountable to, for example, the European Commission or national governments for the spending. Programme managers want to sustain and improve the programmes and evaluators want to conduct evaluations with high ethical and professional standards. All the stakeholders are vulnerable to political pressure and decreased funding as a result of their actions (Cardoza Clayson et al., 2002).

   The different stakeholders involved in the evaluation have different sources of power. While it is easy to accept that the programme funders have the greatest power when we consider their ability as a stakeholder to influence policy decisions of a programme being evaluated (Michalski and Cousins, 2000), it would be naive to assume that the other stakeholders are without any power. The programme promoters generally have direct contact with the programme participants and, therefore, they are in a key position when it comes to influencing their views and perspectives. Similarly, the evaluators have power in choosing particular research methods (surveys, group interviews, and so on) and of voicing the particular questions or results in their reports. The different stakeholders will define the programme in different ways and these definitions will change over time and place, and gain new meanings. As an example, policy-makers may understand enterprise education as a way to increase wealth and employment in society, programme promoters may understand it mainly as a tool to increase individual skills and well-being. In this sense, it is possible to acknowledge the asymmetrical and dynamic processes of power relations in and around evaluations.

Data gathering

Based on the results of the literature review conducted in the study, a template for interviews was developed which was applied when conducting the interviews. In all, 30 experts from six countries (Austria, Finland, Ireland, Germany, Norway and Spain) were interviewed to gain insight into evaluations of enterprise education and entrepreneurship training.[2] The experts were selected from three different groups involved in the evaluations of enterprise and entrepreneurship education programmes: programme promoters, evaluators and policy-makers. The different stakeholders are defined as follows. The programme promoters are the persons responsible for organizing enterprise and entrepreneurship training programmes. The evaluators are generally researchers who have some experience in internal or external evaluations of entrepreneurship programmes or a group of programmes. Sometimes the evaluators are also responsible for running the programme, so they occupy a dual position of a programme promoter and evaluator. Policy-makers are responsible for giving guidelines for carrying out and financing enterprise education and entrepreneurship training programmes, and sometimes also evaluations of these programmes.

In each country, a selection of experts for the interviews was carefully made. At least one interview with a representative from each category was carried out. In each country altogether four or five successful interviews were conducted. Then, the researchers in each country applied the template developed to document the contents of the interview. The researchers aimed at conveying the key messages with some illustrative quotes but did not try to fully translate the interviews. In this chapter, quotes from the documented interviews are used to illustrate our findings.

Analysis
We have conducted a qualitative analysis of the 30 interviews. In the analysis we focused on the arguments made by the three different groups: evaluators, policy-makers and programme promoters for conducting evaluations. Each sub-set of answers (programme promoters, evaluators, policy-makers) were then analysed comparatively. From each subset we identified different themes and arguments the respondents provided for conducting evaluations. The comparative analysis of the arguments from the different perspectives is presented in the research results. In the analysis we classified the answers by type, that is, we aimed at providing the answers that are typical for the different groups with regard to evaluations. These types are not authentic; they do not represent any single respondent's attitudes or perceptions but the type of arguments are possible for the group analysed, although not all the programme promoters, for example, consider that evaluation studies should solely assist in the programme planning and design questions (Eskola and Suoranta, 1998).

Use of evaluation studies
It is necessary to underline that evaluative inquiry is not just a method of collecting information but a way of debating the value of the programme or policy (Russ-Eft et al., 2002). We discuss both the process use and instrumental use of evaluation. It is necessary to underline that the instrumental use of evaluation, that is, that the evaluation results are applied to change the programme or policy, is not the only possible use of evaluations. The evaluation process in itself may have important consequences in a way that the actual conduct of the evaluation may lead to changes even before any results are produced or published. In short, process use refers to learning that occurs during the evaluation (Preskill et al., 2003; Russ-Eft et al., 2002). There may be different ways the evaluation leads to process uses (Russ-Eft et al., 2002):

- Enhancing shared understanding (for example, communication and discussion surrounding enterprise education). Patton refers to conceptual use of findings, which is defined as 'the use of evaluations to influence thinking and deepen understanding by increasing knowledge' (Patton, 2001, p. 332).
- Supporting and reinforcing the programme intervention (for example, the participants' satisfaction with the programme may increase if they have the opportunity to talk about the programme, or instant feedback from the evaluators on the problems identified may assist to correct the problems).
- Increasing engagement, self-determination and ownership, and programme and organizational development (for example, the evaluation itself – rather than the results – may trigger programme managers to develop their systems, practices and processes).

The instrumental use of evaluations is said to occur if 'a decision or action follows, at least in part, from the evaluation' (Patton, 2001, p. 332). There are differentiated needs for evaluations based on the phase in the policy-making process, and the objectives set for the evaluation. Diamond and Spence (1983) acknowledge four basic types of questions for evaluation research:

- programme planning questions
- programme monitoring questions
- impact assessment questions
- economic efficiency questions.

A really wide-ranging approach to evaluation would involve aspects of all four types of research activity, although, for obvious reasons, many evaluations only concentrate on a selection. Many researchers call for a step-by-step approach to evaluation, see, for example, Storey (2000). This approach stresses the point that it makes sense first to check that the programme has been executed as specified before measuring the impact, and then by the same logic to analyse first that there has been an impact before measuring effectiveness (Diamond and Spence, 1983).

A programme is then usually planned around these general goals, identifying the intervention methods, the interested stakeholders and the budget. This calls for evaluative procedures when aiming at identifying the appropriate methods, stakeholders and budget. Hence, the focus is on assisting in *programme planning*. The idea is that it is possible – and necessary – to evaluate the process, not only the outcome. *Monitoring evaluation* provides a systematic assessment of whether or not a programme is operating as intended in its design and whether or not it is reaching the target group. If the programmes deviate from their original intentions, much care must be taken in interpreting the results from the evaluation study. *Impact evaluation* is the form most commonly thought of with regard to evaluations. Impact evaluation gauges the extent to which a programme instigates change in the desired direction. This implies that we are not only interested in the effects, but also on their direction (Diamond and Spence, 1983, pp. 1–2). Diamond and Spence (1983) divide *economic efficiency* studies into two slightly different approaches:

- *cost–benefit analysis* – measurement of costs against the monetary value of the benefits

- *cost–effectiveness* – measurement of costs against the qualitative achievements: progress towards goal achievement.

Results
The different uses of evaluations are next reflected against the results from our compara-tive analysis of the different stakeholders in the evaluation studies: programme promot-ers, policy-makers and evaluators.

Programme promoters
From the point of view of the programme promoters, the quality of the programme and continuous improvement of it is by far the most important reason for conducting evalu-ation studies. 'Particularly, evaluation may be a very interesting instrument to anticipate changes and other needs and adapt the programmes to these changes' (Programme pro-moter, Spain).

Naturally, programme promoters are also interested in verifying the effectiveness of the programmes and learning of the results achieved. Through evaluations, decisions can be based on more objective information, not on subjective insights of the teachers. As the world changes, it is necessary to anticipate these changes and adapt the programmes accordingly. 'To look at the effectiveness of the programmes and to continuously improve them' (Programme promoter, Ireland).

Evaluations can be applied to discover why participants participate in a programme that may deviate from the official objectives set for the programme. This information can be applied to tailor the programmes and commit the participants in the programme. 'One reason is to find out the ultimate objectives of the participants, the truth why they par-ticipate in the project . . . Evaluation is one way of committing the participants in the project' (Programme promoter, Finland).

On many occasions, there are several lecturers, trainers and counsellors participating in the programme as instructors. Hence, the quality of the programme is largely dependent on the quality of these third parties. Evaluations can be applied to enforce a necessary pressure, even competition, between the trainers to achieve the quality requirements.

However, on many occasions this is not an end-result for the programme promoters but something that can be applied to justifying the need for the programme, to legitimizing the monetary contribution and support, and for marketing purposes. The evaluation results may be used to inform the different interest groups of the results of the training and the programme. It can be seen to be more objective than other marketing efforts such as programme brochures or advertisements. 'As a detail, we also apply the evaluations to pick out "testimonials" of the participants to be applied in the marketing' (Programme promoter, Finland).

Programme promoters claim that they will apply results from evaluation studies into practice if found useful. It is clear that from their point of view internal evaluation studies are considered more useful than external evaluations. Regarding external evaluations it seems that the programme promoters find that they do not meet their needs, that is, provide concrete and practical suggestions for improvement and further action. In general, over-load of information and lack of resources is hampering the in-depth use of results.

From the policy-making perspective the programme promoters are more interested in improving the innovativeness and distinctiveness of their training offer rather than in evaluating the programme. The drive is towards innovation and experimental approach rather than gradual improvement of existing programmes. The integration of evaluation into day-to-day work was also considered to be problematic in general; the programme promoters do not have enough time and/or other resources for evaluation since normal day-to-day work takes up all of their time. 'More attention is paid to the innovativeness and distinctiveness of programmes than evaluation. The problem is that no work team is dedicated to these issues so day-to-day work takes up all the time' (Policy-maker, Spain).

It is also argued that although programme promoters are interested in evaluations, they would need advice on how to evaluate and measure enterprise education and training. The evaluators criticized the planning of the programmes, which sometimes makes it impossible to evaluate the programmes afterwards. If there are no objectives set for the programmes in the first place, then the target becomes anything the programme happens to hit (Storey, 2000). 'It is sometimes very unclear what are the reasons and aims for entrepreneurship studies but this would have to be clear before any reasonable evaluation is conducted. This links to the general difficulty in measuring entrepreneurship education' (Evaluator, Finland).

The policy-makers feel that the programme promoters are not really implementing the results of evaluations, for example, negative results are sometimes hidden and not applied in the future development of the programmes.

The elements of vulnerability of programme promoters can be read from the analysis. In most cases, the promoters are dependent and accountable to two different groups. First, they need to reassure their funders that the programmes are run as planned and are able to meet the objectives. They fear that only the 'hard', quantitative elements are measured (for example, finance, money spent) and the 'soft' aspects remain unnoticed (for example, the subjective learning experiences of the participants). In this sense programme promoters feel that the financiers cannot identify the proper elements to be evaluated in the programmes.

Second, the programme promoters need to make sure that the participants will continue to enrol and to be satisfied with the programme. Evaluations are applied as a way of marketing and making sure that the aims of the participants are met, even if these are not originally in the programme. Hence, the programme promoters favour process use of evaluations. As a result, they look for evaluations that take into account these changes to the original aims. If the funders and evaluators seek to analyse only whether or not the original objectives for the programme are met without taking into account the specific requests of the participants, the results will not be very positive for the programme. Hence, the programme promoters need to balance between wishes of both the funders and participants of a programme, and aim to meet the needs of both groups. If these needs are not met, the punishment is either to be denied funding or the participants will no longer attend the programme.

Policy-makers and financiers
The policy-makers and financiers consider evaluations of enterprise education and training to be important as they give information on the future needs in the field and help to make funding decisions concerning the types of training to be resourced in the future. Economic efficiency is also important for financiers and therefore evaluations are also carried out to assess the return on investment.

Most importantly, however, the policy-makers are interested in measuring the impact of the training programme in question. This was, however, seen as a much more challenging task than merely controlling the use of finances or implementation of the planned actions in the programme. 'I can easily control that the programme is ran as planned but not that the desired effects of the programme have been achieved' (Norway 5).

The evaluations also help the financiers to control the use of funding and determine whether there is a lack of funding or whether the funding is excessive for certain types of programmes. The policy-makers also need evaluations to determine whether a programme is running as intended, whether it is running according to the budget guidelines and whether the promoter is capable of delivering the programme. This type of control use can also be regarded as process use. The mere awareness of the evaluation of the programme may have an effect on the programme promoter's actions in conducting the programme.

It should be noticed, however, that the individual policy-makers are not completely free in their decision-making with regard to evaluations. For example, the European Commission has rules and regulations that govern the policy-makers. There are also different practices if the evaluations are subject to bidding or if they are contracted from more or less the same research institutions. In practice, it might be easier and more reassuring for the policy-maker to contract the research from a known research institute with a long track record of working with policy research. As a result, there is concern if studies are contracted from a small group of researchers and institutes. In extreme cases, the programme promoters fear that institutes are chosen that are known to produce the desired results.

In most European countries the topic of enterprise education and training is currently high on the policy agenda and, therefore, there is an interest among policy-makers to present interesting innovations and provide empirical support for these innovations. As result, there is a risk that the methodology might be developed in order to 'falsify' positive results for projects. It is also argued that sometimes financiers aim to influence what is written in the reports or highlighted in the press releases, but skilled researchers do not fall into these traps. The worst-case scenario for evaluators is that the evaluations serve an alibi function for the policy-makers and are filed away without even being read. Evaluation studies are applied to defend their a priori beliefs (Grubb and Ryan, 1999). 'So, the problems with the evaluations from the evaluator perspective are (1) that the evaluations are not read and (2) the hidden aims that are not communicated to the evaluator' (Evaluator, Austria).

It was considered that the policy-makers apply the results of evaluation studies in the decision-making to some extent. Some problems may arise, however, if the financiers expect too many results within a short time frame. The policy-makers are generally accountable for their investment decisions and the related outcomes to, for example, elected officials in Parliament. As a result, they need to make sure that the financing decisions and regulations are followed, and that no misuse of finances occurs. Hence, the evaluation becomes more one of controlling the expenditure than learning from the real results achieved. The policy-makers focus on whether 'things are done in a right way', rather than on whether the 'right things are done'. Furthermore, different programmes are evaluated by using the same criteria, which is seen to be a problem.

Evaluators
The evaluators interviewed regarded evaluations important to assess the diffusion of programmes among the target group. Evaluations are also needed to assess the satisfaction of participants and the impact of the programme on, for example, business start-ups. It was also pointed out that it is important to find out reasons why certain people do not start up a company. It is also important to take the customer into account and find out whether their needs are met and the promises given kept. The instrumental use of evaluations was hence underlined. Besides the improvement of the programme and learning from previous experiences, evaluations can also be conducted to ensure continued access to funding. One of the evaluators suggested that the evaluations could also be used for spreading the entrepreneurial culture. The two examples could be understood as a form of process use.

Most evaluators adopted clearly an insider or an outsider perspective to the target of evaluation that bears consequences on their concept of the use and purpose of evaluations and the preferred ways for carrying out evaluations:

- action research to provide information for development of programmes (for programme promoters)/communicative purpose
- impact analysis to provide information of the impacts of an individual programme and/or institutional framework within a region/country for promoting entrepreneurship (for the policy-makers)/control purpose.

The promoters of ongoing action research were explicitly of the opinion that evaluations carried out after the completion of the programme are often superficial and not particularly utilized. Hence, they promoted the more frequent use of interim evaluations where information is continuously changing between the evaluator and the programme promoter. The evaluation was seen more as a learning process, which requires intensive cooperation between the programme promoter and the evaluator. As a result, they proposed the more pronounced process use of evaluations.

From the point-of-view of evaluators it is also necessary to acknowledge the altruistic interest in evaluations: conducting evaluations can be the core business for the research institute in question or at least there is a monetary element involved. Hence, it is suggested that the evaluators need to become more sophisticated with respect to issues of power and influence by understanding the political role of policy-makers, identifying parties at interest, and the ways they would be affected by particular proposed policies (Mustafa, 1994).

The availability of funding also influences the evaluators in another matter. Through funding the evaluators may specialize in different areas of evaluation, learn to know the substance area – enterprise education and training – develop suitable indicators and evaluation frameworks and conduct better evaluations. 'There are not enough competent researchers. There is a vicious circle: not enough money, no people who can qualify in the field' (Policy-maker, Austria).

The evaluators feel that they have a very limited influence on the ways evaluation studies are applied and used. The policy-makers in general seem to be interested in evaluations but sometimes the interest is not genuine but is geared towards secondary motives. The evaluators also recognized the problem in the compilation of evaluation reports and it was suggested that stronger emphasis should be put on recommendations.

Improving the use of evaluations
If evaluators and organizations want people to learn from evaluations, certain conditions and processes should be developed from the beginning to facilitate this process (Preskill et al., 2003). Several suggestions for the improvement of conducting evaluations and the use of the results were made. Besides allocating more time, money and other resources, a few interesting suggestions were made. Evaluation should be incorporated into tripartite discussion and other political forums. Discussing the evaluation and their (possible) results in a more open arena will help them to be misused or misunderstood and will give all the stakeholders involved the insights of all the agents (see also Grubb and Ryan, 1999). Workshops or other occasions where the programme promoters and other stakeholders could discuss the results and learn from each other could be organized. In order to develop the process use of evaluations these workshops could be organized at an earlier stage, at the beginning of an evaluation process. In these events the different stakeholders – programme promoters, policy-makers and evaluators – could together discuss the aims of the programme and how it should be evaluated, what could be the suitable indicators and results to be investigated. The usability of evaluations is hindered by the lack of commonly accepted criteria and measuring instruments, which would improve the transparency of evaluations. This would promote the dialogue and improve understanding of the different stakeholders involved. Furthermore, more systematic and longer-term approach is needed.

Evaluations studies should be more easily available, that is, the results and process considerations should be published externally, not only in internal research reports. It is suggested that evaluations should be more concerned with the processes that lead to the actual results (see also Grubb and Ryan, 1999). The usability of evaluation reports is also affected by the content and clarity of the reports. It is suggested that the use of comprehensible language ('non-jargon') and, for example, executive summaries would improve the usability of the evaluations conducted.

Discussion and implications
In this chapter we have discussed in depth the arguments and point of views of the different stakeholders in evaluation studies: programme promoters, policy-makers and evaluators. The evaluations are a politically contextualized act and all aspects of evaluation are shaped by the power relationships among the three stakeholders. We argue that it is not possible to escape the power aspect attached to evaluation. As we have shown, all the stakeholders in the process are vulnerable because all of them are accountable to someone else and face political pressure and fear of decreased funding as a result of their actions (Cardoza Clayson et al., 2002). The role of funding is central to this process.

Programme promoters generally regard running the programme as their first priority. They prefer internal and interim evaluations that continually provide information to assist them in programme planning and the implementation of the decision-making process. The programme promoters are cautious of evaluations that focus merely on financial issues and quantitative measures, but emphasize the appreciation of qualitative outputs. This reflects their position between two types of customers (funders and participants), which they are trying to satisfy. They are vulnerable to the loss of financing (if the funders are not pleased with the programme) and to the loss of participants (if the participants are not happy with the programme).

Policy-makers and financiers are primarily concerned with measuring the impact of programmes. They also need evaluation studies that inform them of existing programmes (control) and assist them in planning future programmes (policy-making). In general individual policy-makers are also accountable for their funding decisions. They need to demonstrate that the funding is spent as planned. This emphasizes their control focus. Secondly, policy-makers need to reflect if the right issues are financed in the long term.

Evaluators positioned themselves to support primarily either the decision-making of the programme promoters or of the policy-makers. In order to support programme promoters, an insider approach was the ideal (internal, interim evaluation), whereas to support policy-making an external approach was the best alternative (external, *ex-post* evaluation). The evaluators are also dependent on financing for two reasons: evaluation studies may be the core business for the research institute; funding for the evaluations enables specialization of researchers in the field that facilitates learning.

The theoretical implications of this chapter are twofold. First, it is necessary to acknowledge the different roles for the evaluation studies and differing perspectives of the stakeholders involved in the process. Therefore, it is not possible to strive for or ever achieve a 'one size fits all' type of evaluation processes of entrepreneurship education and training. Second, as a consequence of the different stakeholders and the play of power between them, the notion of objectivity of evaluations can be contested. Evaluation studies are always subjective as the decision as to what is evaluated is already dependent on subjective decision-making.

From the practical side we believe there is no escape from the politics and power play presented in this chapter. However, we do believe that it is possible to develop evaluation practices that openly acknowledge the different stakeholders in the process and aim to unite their perspectives in the processes. The different voices could be made visible and heard in evaluation studies (O'Sullivan and O'Sullivan, 1998). The different uses (instrumental and process use) should be made more visible. It is clear that a more open environment for evaluation studies is needed. The evaluation processes could start and involve workshops or other events where the programme promoters, policy-makers and evaluators could interact and debate the aims of the programme and the role of evaluation with regard to the programme. Furthermore, this debate should continue also for discussing the results of the evaluation with the evaluators. The evaluation reports should be understood as a source of learning and they should be published and distributed widely. In addition, the evaluators should pay more attention not only to identifying potential sources of problems and deficiencies in the programmes, but also to providing suggestions for further action and policy recommendations which would assist in implementing the results from the evaluation studies into practice. The work on developing indicators and measurement techniques for the different types of evaluation studies in the field of enterprise education and training should be continued. (See Hytti and Kuopusjärvi, 2004, for further examples.)

For this research we have asked the different stakeholders about the use of evaluation research and the potential barriers that hinder the process. We suggest that further research could benefit from a longitudinal research setting. Evaluation reports could be taken as a starting point for investigating which recommendations are taken into practice and how and why. It would be interesting to study if there are patterns or similarities across different evaluation studies in what recommendations are accepted or rejected.

Similarly, it would be interesting to analyse how the stakeholders themselves perceive the power element in the evaluation studies and research settings.

Notes

1. This project has been carried out with the support of the European Community (project number FIN/02/C/P/RF-82501). The content of this project does not necessarily reflect the position of the European Community, nor does it involve any responsibility on the part of the European Community.
2. Details and contact information for the research partners in the different countries is available from www.entreva.net.

References

Abma, T.A. (2000), Stakeholder conflict: a case study, *Evaluation and Programme Planning*, **23**, 199–210.
Cardoza Clayson, Z., Castañeda, X., Sanchez, E. and Brindis, C. (2002), Unequal power – changing landscapes: negotiations between evaluation stakeholders in Latino communities, *American Journal of Evaluation*, **23** (1), 33–44.
Diamond, D. and Spence, N. (1983), *Regional Policy Evaluation: A Methodological Review and the Scottish Example*, Aldershot: Gower.
Eskola, J. and Suoranta, J. (1998), *Johdatus laadulliseen tutkimukseen*, Tampere: Osuuskunta Vastapaino.
Fayolle, A. (2005), Evaluation of entrepreneurship education: behaviour performing or intention increasing? *International Journal of Entrepreneurship and Small Business*, **2** (1), 89–98.
Grubb, W.N. and Ryan, P. (1999), *The Roles of Evaluation for Education and Training: Plain Talk on the Field of Dreams*, London: Kogan Page/ILO.
Hytti, U. and Kuopusjärvi, P. (2004), *Evaluating and Measuring Entrepreneurship and Enterprise Education: Methods, Tools and Practices*, Small Business Institute, Turku School of Economics and Business Administration. A publication published in the Entrava –project, Leonardo da Vinci – programme of the European Commission, Turku, Finland.
Hytti, U. and O'Gorman, C. (2004), What is 'enterprise education'? An analysis of the objectives and methods of enterprise education programmes in four European countries, *Education + Training*, **46** (1), 11–23.
Michalski, G.V. and Cousins, J.B. (2000), Differences in stakeholder perceptions about training evaluation: a concept mapping/pattern matching investigation, *Evaluation and Program Planning*, **23** (2), 211–30.
Mustafa, H. (1994), Conflict of multiple interests in cost–benefit analysis, *International Journal of Public Sector Management*, **7** (3), 16–26.
O'Sullivan, R. and O'Sullivan, J. (1998), Evaluation voices: promoting evaluation from within programs through collaboration, *Evaluation and Program Planning*, **21** (1), 21–9.
Patton, M.Q. (2001), Evaluation, knowledge management, best practices, and high quality lessons learned, *American Journal of Evaluation*, **22** (3), 329–36.
Preskill, H., Zuckerman, B. and Matthews, B. (2003), An exploratory study of process use: findings and implications for future research, *American Journal of Evaluation*, **24** (4), 423–42.
Rowe, C. (1996), Evaluating management training and development: revisiting the basic issues, *Industrial and Commercial Training*, **28** (4), 17–23.
Russ-Eft, D., Atwood, R. and Egherman, T. (2002), Use and non-use of evaluation results: case study of environmental influences in the private sector, *American Journal of Evaluation*, **23** (1), 19–31.
Segerholm, C. (2003), Researching evaluation in national (state) politics and administration: a critical approach, *American Journal of Evaluation*, **24** (3), 353–72.
Storey, D. (2000), Six steps to heaven: evaluating the impact of public policies to support small business in developed economies, in D.L. Sexton and H. Landström (eds), *Blackwell Handbook of Entrepreneurship*, Oxford: Blackwell, pp. 176–91.
Venetoklis, T. (2002), *Public Policy Evaluation: Introduction to Quantitative Methodologies*, Government Institute for Economic Research, VATT-Research Reports 90, Helsinki.

16 Promoting enterprising: a strategic move to get schools' cooperation in the promotion of entrepreneurship

Bernard Surlemont

Introduction

Despite the encouragement of the European Commission, there is strong resistance from schools and educators to introduce entrepreneurship courses in education programmes of member states, particularly at the secondary level, where it is too often associated with an attempt to subordinate education to economic drives and commercial motivations. As a consequence, most countries experience many difficulties with implementing entrepreneurship programmes in the classroom.

This chapter explores how such resistance might be associated with the fussiness of what entrepreneurship really means. It supports the argument that it is crucial to make a clear distinction between the technical competencies, generally associated with entrepreneurship (that is, business planning, opportunity recognition, fund raising, money making, and so on), and the strategic competencies associated with enterprising (self-realization, perseverance, creativity, teamwork, and so on). That apparently subtle semantic nuance can make a substantial difference to how well entrepreneurship education is perceived and can be accepted by teachers and educators in secondary schools.

The analysis relies on the experience of the Foundation for Research and Education in Entrepreneurship (FREE), a Belgian foundation that promotes programmes to support entrepreneurship education in secondary and high schools. In particular, the foundation has recently conducted a large research project that investigates how teachers have been able to develop programmes, courses and pedagogical tools that favour the nurture of entrepreneurial attitudes in secondary schools.

This chapter develops the arguments to promote enterprising education in secondary schools as a way (1) to develop entrepreneurship skills and attitudes to pupils and (2) to ease the introduction of an 'entrepreneurship culture' in secondary schools. It opens with a summary of the key recommendations of the European Commission to develop entrepreneurship early on in education systems in Europe in line with the Lisbon 2010 objectives. Then, the reasons for schools resistance towards entrepreneurship education are introduced. The core of the chapter develops the key ingredients of an enterprising education, including its key success factors, consequences and benefits for schools, pupils and teachers. This analysis is fed by research conducted in Belgian schools about enterprising education. The chapter closes with some key implications and suggestions for further research.

Education as a lever to promote entrepreneurship in Europe

Since the pioneer research of David Birch (1981), which shows that in the US large firms are no longer the major providers of new jobs, many studies, including in Europe, have confirmed that the bulk of new jobs now emanates from small companies (Davis et al.,

1996; Gallagher and Stewart, 1986; Konings, 1995). This observation has progressively driven the attention of policy-makers to encourage entrepreneurship in order to create new jobs and support economic development.

In that respect, the Lisbon summit has pinpointed the necessity to revamp completely the European economy in order to improve its efficiency, generate wealth and create jobs. Among the key areas for actions, the promotion of entrepreneurship takes a central place. The Lisbon European Council and the European Charter for Small Enterprises have stressed this point. In particular, the latter commits the European Union (EU) to teach business and entrepreneurship at all school levels, and to develop training schemes for managers (EU, 2000).

In that context, the role of education to promote entrepreneurship has, increasingly, been placed under the spotlight (EU, 2004b). Indeed, several researchers, such as the Global Entrepreneurship Monitor (GEM) initiative (Acs et al., 2004), have pinpointed that the cultural framework is at the top of the list of obstacles against entrepreneurship in Europe. Since education is a strategic leverage to act upon culture, it has increasingly been under the scrutiny of policy-makers in the design of programmes to promote entrepreneurship. To mention but a few examples, France has recently launched an observatory of teaching practices for entrepreneurship (see www.entrepreneuriat.net). In Belgium, the Foundation for Research and Education in Entrepreneurship was created in May 2003 to promote entrepreneurship in secondary and high schools (see www. freefondation.be). In the UK, education is central to the policy programme developed by the Scottish Enterprise (see www.scottish-enterprise.com) and in Spain, entrepreneurship has been introduced in official programmes in secondary schools since 1994 (Ministerio de Education, 2003).

At the European level, the green paper on entrepreneurship exhorts European countries to develop entrepreneurship in curricula for primary school. 'Education and training should contribute to encouraging entrepreneurship, by fostering the right mindset, awareness of career opportunities as an entrepreneur and skills' (EU, 2003). The commission has been very proactive in that area. Since 2002, the Directorate General DG Enterprize has set up four task forces under the BEST procedure to analyse ways to promote entrepreneurship in education and to benchmark practices all over Europe. The first two reports on education for entrepreneurship (EU, 2002b; 2004a) propose a general review of entrepreneurship education and explore practices that promote entrepreneurial attitudes and skills through primary and secondary education. A recent report is focusing on the experiences of mini-enterprises among member states (EU, 2005). Lately, the commission launched an expert group on the development of entrepreneurship for non-business students in higher education. To some extent, the department for education has taken this part of the job to favour such initiatives. In the final report on its action plan for the follow-up of the objectives of educational systems in Europe, the council for education has a full section emphasizing the necessity of developing entrepreneurship at all education levels in order to promote initiatives and to train students in law to run a business (EU, 2002a).

In a nutshell, all these initiatives rely on the same rationale: Europe needs more job creation, hence more new companies. To promote the creation of new companies one needs entrepreneurs, and to increase the population of entrepreneurs we need to generate or facilitate more vocations by developing entrepreneurship courses in curricula.

The resistance of education systems to promote entrepreneurship in the classroom
If this rationale to promote entrepreneurship in education is making sense in theory, practice shows that it is not possible to implement actions without meeting with resistance
from education systems, particularly at secondary school level, which comprises the bulk
of the students population and where professional vocations often take precedence.
  Several factors explain the resistance of secondary schools:

1. Generally speaking, most secondary schools in Europe are in crisis. From a financial
    perspective, most schools are under strong financial pressures so that any new respon-
    sibility not accompanied by a corresponding financial and/or human resource is per-
    ceived as an additional pressure on budgets.
2. From a discipline standpoint, young students are becoming more difficult to handle.
    The role of teachers in society has been considerably downgraded over the last
    20 years. As a consequence, motivation has fallen among teachers, manifested in an
    increasing number of teacher resignations and psychological illnesses.
3. Too often, the promotion of entrepreneurship within school is organized from the top
    down and does not always take into consideration the key partners needed to achieve
    this objective, namely, teachers and school directors. Experience shows that there are
    indeed many more brakes to entrepreneurship in education systems than engines. In
    that respect, it has been largely demonstrated that a school culture that supports col-
    laboration and teacher participation in decision-making is most strongly related to
    higher morale, stronger commitment to teaching, and intentions to remain in the pro-
    fession (Weiss, 1999).
4. Exhortation to promote entrepreneurship in schools is often driven by authorities
    external to the education system, in particular from the business community or the
    ministry of economic affairs. These attempts are often interpreted as external pres-
    sures to have business considerations invading the classroom. Indeed, the attempt to
    promote entrepreneurship in school is also often interpreted as another attempt by
    the business community to penetrate school, to divert its aim and to corrupt the
    system. Teachers are consequently extremely cautious and susceptible about their
    academic independence.
5. This is not to mention that the theme of entrepreneurship tends to be extremely badly
    regarded in schools. It is associated with business, the drive for money and profit,
    commerce, exploitation of human beings, corruption, the dark face of globalization,
    and so on.
6. These perceptions are probably largely inspired by the fact that most teachers have
    only experienced schools and universities in their professional life, so that the educa-
    tional system is their unique frame of reference. Therefore, they have very little busi-
    ness experience and limited contacts with enterprises. This lack of communication
    generates some misunderstanding and resistance to entrepreneurship.
7. The pressure on school from the external environment has increased dramatically over
    recent years. Parents and society in general seem to consider that nowadays the role of
    schools is education as much as teaching. All over Europe, schools are solicited to play
    a role in areas like AIDS prevention, education in democracy, environment protection,
    sex information, racism prevention, and so on. In such a context, the demand to promote
    entrepreneurship in education is perceived as yet another responsibility.

8. Finally, secondary school administration is itself not particularly reputed to be organized as an entrepreneurial system. It is mostly a hierarchy that generates top-down directives that continue without innovations and where initiative is not particularly rewarded (Mintzberg, 1989).

As a consequence of such resistance, entrepreneurship education tends to be either confined to economic sections or to extra-curricula activities. It is therefore estimated that less than 10 per cent of the total potential population has been exposed to some dimension of entrepreneurship during their secondary school education (EU, 2005).

Enterprising versus entrepreneurship: more than a semantic nuance
In considering most initiatives that have been undertaken at the policy level, it seems that the definition of entrepreneurship has nowhere been a major concern. More precisely, most programmes seem to focus entrepreneurship on the ability to start or run a business. This is clearly the point of view of the green paper on entrepreneurship of the European Commission (EU, 2003). It is only recently that the Commission seems to have become aware of the importance of making a clear distinction between two concepts of entrepreneurship. In its recent report on 'Helping to create an entrepreneurial culture', the Directorate-General for Enterprise specifies that

> there seems to be a general recognition of the importance of including two different elements or concepts within the definition of entrepreneurship teaching:
> *   a broader concept of education for entrepreneurial attitudes and skills, which involves developing certain personal qualities and is not directly focused on the creation of new businesses; and,
> *   a more narrow concept of training in how to create a business. (EU, 2004b)

In other words, entrepreneurship in a broader sense refers to a set of attitudes, skills capabilities and competences such as creativity, teamwork, opportunity recognition, risk-taking, perseverance, passion and drive. This broad view of entrepreneurship, that we will refer to as 'enterprising' in the remainder of this chapter, can be applied in any area of life and work, and not just in business. Entrepreneurship in a narrow sense refers to a set of technical capacities and skills to start and run a business, such as business planning, market research, accounting and budgeting. That view of entrepreneurship is probably the one that has been the most widely referred to in research, education and policy-making. In practice, most national and European programmes promote specific projects that rely mostly on the narrow definition associated with the business-oriented concept.

In particular, only a few have made that distinction crucial for education purposes. As Paul Kearney mentions: 'It is recommended that the "broad approach" of helping all young people to develop their enterprising capacity for all facets of their lives be adopted, as opposed to the "narrow approach" which tend to encourage only some students to develop commercial enterprise skills, and mainly for commercial purpose' (Kearney, 1999, Book 1, p. 40). That recommendation is perfectly in line with the experience of FREE, which tries to promote entrepreneurship in education. Such wording nuance has its importance. It can make a substantial difference as to how well entrepreneurship education is perceived and can be accepted by teachers in secondary schools. The reasons for this are numerous:

- Developing broad enterprising attributes provides a solid basis for entrepreneurship. The reverse is not necessarily true.
- Favouring enterprising is likely to reduce the bias educators (and sometimes parents) have against the idea that entrepreneurship in school means encouraging commercial attitudes in young people. Evaluation in the UK has found that where institutions set out to implement a specifically entrepreneurial model of enterprise, as opposed to the broader view, they were more likely to encounter resistance from staff and students (UK Department of Employment, 1991).
- Enterprising does not imply overworking educators and schools. It does not imply doing new things but, instead, doing existing things differently. In that respect, it satisfies the requirements of education programmes and 'only' implies modifying the pedagogy in a way that develops enterprising skills.
- The way to teach enterprising may potentially concern every discipline in the curricula instead of being confined to economic education. In that respect, its potential audience is much broader.
- Kearney's research indicates that enterprising capabilities (that is, initiative, innovation, risk-taking and other critical skills) are best learned when a number of key learning principles are applied: 'Included in these key learning principles are notions of drawing on many disciplines (multiplicity), practising and reflecting in a diverse range of contexts (transference) and practising these capabilities often and regularly (common experience). Broad enterprise education approaches promote this type of learning, whereas narrow entrepreneurial education typically is confined to a subject area (e.g. business studies), focus on one context (the commercial) and happens as an occasional and isolated event for most students' (Kearney, 1999, Book 1, p. 41).
- Instead of showing resistance, schools may benefit greatly from enterprising pedagogy because of a regained motivation of students and teachers.
- Enterprising pedagogy capitalizes on the energy of passion that is too often hidden in classroom.
- Such pedagogy also helps students in their professional guidance and career choice; not to mention that it develops the necessary competences for students to succeed with their life as opposed to succeed in life.
- On a similar line, the broad approach develops the variables of employability since modern workplaces require workers to take the initiative, be innovative and take responsibility.
- Enterprising favours enterprise awareness, skills and behaviours in public and community organizations, as well as in the family and at the personal level. Narrow entrepreneurship places too much focus on the commercial context and makes little attempt to adopt the contexts and values of the non-commercial world, often resulting in a dissonance of systems and a cultural dissonance (Kearney, 1999, Book 1, p. 41).

Having, hopefully, made the case to support the idea that promoting enterprising is the way to go in schools, the question becomes: 'What does it mean to teach enterprising?'. In fact enterprising is not really something to teach, it is more a way to teach. Enterprising teaching relies on experiential and collaborative learning, student responsibility and reflective practices. It could take the form of a 'one session' module, be included in a full course or, ideally, be infused in the school culture and style of teaching. Our investigation of these initiatives concludes that educational systems that are at the forefront of enterprising teaching are found in Australia where Paul Kearney has made a substantial contribution in translating the key ingredients of ways to teach and learn enterprising (Kearney, 1999). To substantiate that pedagogical approach in a non-Anglo-Saxon environment, where entrepreneurship is probably lagging behind, the FREE conducted a large research project in the French-speaking part of Belgium to identify initiatives, tools and projects that contribute to developing the enterprising attitudes and skills of pupils (Aouni et al., 2005). This research has been done in close association with experts in entrepreneurship and in pedagogy. To conduct the research, the broad versus narrow definition of entrepreneurship was clarified. This contributed to the launch, in a close collaboration with the directors of education, of a large campaign of calls for project proposals from secondary schools. Then the research team visited and interviewed the teachers who had been referred as being involved in such projects. All projects that demonstrated some features of an enterprising pedagogy were selected.

These projects cover a wide variety of courses, pupils and tools. To mention just one example as a way of describing a typical project, we identified a course of 'sciences and technologies' offered to pupils in their fifth year of technical school. In this case, the topic relates to the solids and the problems of waste. The project was built into three phases:

1. Sensitizing: each pupil is invited to bring into class the contents of their domestic dustbin. The dustbin bags are opened and their contents are dispersed in the class. The analysis of the contents of these bags allowed us: (a) to show that there are several types of waste (plastic, organic, metal, and so on); (b) to measure the quantity of waste produced by the whole of the households of the pupils in the class over one week (sorted by types of waste); (c) to calculate, by extrapolation, the quantity of waste produced by the whole the Walloon population over one year (sorted by types of waste); (d) to realize the volume which this waste represents.
2. The pupils were then invited to go on the Internet to seek factual data relating to the problems of waste: who collects it? How is it collected? Where is it conveyed? For doing what? What are the risks? And so on. This is actioned by groups of two and results in the submission of a written report. Then, the pupils were invited to propose possible actions to cure the identified problems, and to justify the cogency and the relevance of their proposals in comparison with the problems of waste management. This exercise aims to identify what the pupils had retained from their research, while soliciting competences such as creativity, imagination and rhetoric (argument).
3. One of the key recommendations that came out of the class was the necessity to sensitize the young people to these problems and to encourage these adults of tomorrow to modify today their behaviours as regards waste management. The teacher took this opportunity to propose that the pupils give a course to third and fourth year classes in primary school (pupils aged 9–10 years). The enthusiasm of pupils for the idea was so high that the teacher contacted classes in the primary school to arrange the courses.

The benefits of this kind of project are potentially rich:

- For the pupils: (1) they all invested heavily in the project and acquired a much better knowledge of the matter than other pupils who saw the problems of waste in a more 'classic' way in a science course. This has been proven by the use of a control group; (2) they develop their creativity and imagination in the design of original teaching activities to illustrate the various facets of waste management (to present their project to younger pupils, all the groups chose a pedagogy organized around a game that was remarkable according to the primary school teachers' feedback).
- For the teacher, the satisfaction was enormous to have seen his pupils so motivated with the idea to teach in a primary school. By sharing confidence in the pupils and in giving them autonomy in the preparation of this project, he gained the respect of the whole class. Later on, the pupils attended the course with another motivation.
- For the school: in the primary school classes in which the courses were taught, all pupils asked not to go to recreation, so they could continue the course! This testifies not only to the interest that these children found in the problems of waste, but also (and especially) to the quality and impact of the work of the four groups of pupils who managed to transmit their knowledge to these children. In addition, this reinforces contacts between pupils of different ages, different schools and different teachers.

There is no doubt that such a project develops enterprising. It nurtures attitudes of creativity, autonomy, team spirit, curiosity, audacity and self-confidence. It requires students to learn to communicate (in writing and orally), to organize and to dare to teach and speak in public, to adapt the content of the message to the receiver and to practise the language clearly. The teacher was able to comply with the course requirements imposed by the official programme, for example: to seek and process data, to build a scientific, logical, reasoning in order to apprehend natural phenomena and technological processes, to use a rational argument on subjects such as waste, to evaluate the impact of daily acts on the environment, to explain the ecological impact of consumption, to identify the relationship between the polluting character of a material and its biodegradable character, and to describe the various modes of processing waste.

Generally speaking, the key characteristics of the projects that have been analysed are as follows:

- *Initiatives that provide a strong sense of ownership* from the point of view of students. This refers to the question of who is mostly responsible for the learning and who controls it. Generally the more 'say' and responsibility the students have in the learning, the more likely they are to practise their enterprise capabilities. These approaches tend to favour the taking of initiatives, creativity and responsibility. For instance, the tourism section of a technical school in Dinant (Belgium) answered a request for participation in the 'Days of the patrimony' of September 2004. In one week of preparation, the pupils were asked (and able) to welcome and accompany tourists, and inform them about the different sites visited by a bus travel tour. This project helped students to make sense of most of their courses and invited them to take many initiatives and self-responsibility.

- *Initiatives that support experiential learning.* Such an approach emphasizes learning at first hand through concrete experiences as opposed to second hand through abstractions. This tends to favour risk-taking. For instance, a project consists of a linguistic exchange between French-speaking pupils and Flemish-speaking pupils on the basis of emails and web cam conversations by which the pupils are asked to discover their counterpart. The pupils are then invited to introduce their correspondent in front of their class and are filmed. The film is sent to the corresponding class in Flanders (which carries out the same task). A twinning is then organized at the end of each year by the visit of French-speaking pupils in Flanders and Flemish-speaking pupils in Wallonia. The pupils profit from direct contacts with natives of the target language. The process of this course induces them to take risks, to get contacts with 'strangers' and to speak in front of a camera and a classroom.
- *Projects that support cooperative learning.* These refer to situations where students (1) learn with and from one another, (2) share learning tasks and (3) learn from adults other than teachers. These attributes favour teamwork. One of the projects consisted of solving (minor) violence and delinquency problems among students. In this case, mediation was managed directly by pupils. Voluntary pupils had a meeting place where they could offer to listen to and exchange opinions with other pupils to manage conflicts by mediation.
- *Projects that include reflective practice.* Indeed a trap of experimental learning is that too much time may be spent on carrying out the experience without consciously learning from it. The process of reflection helps students to learn to learn and to treat all experiences in the future as learning opportunities. For instance, in science and technology projects on waste management, at the end of their presentation in front of the children of the primary school, each pupil was invited to carry a self-evaluation in the form of a written report in which he expressed his opinion on the way he experienced the project and on suggestions for further improvements.

More than 40 projects have been analysed. The benefits and lessons from all these initiatives all point in the same direction and bring up interesting lessons and conclusions:

- Entrepreneurship is so much associated with business and commercial drives in school that the research team had to make strong efforts to explain the broader view. The bias was so strong that many teachers did not initially show up with their project, the reason being that, in their mind, what they were doing could not be associated with enterprising. This is why there were many latecomers to the project, and why many initiatives were revealed after the research had been closed.
- All students were significantly more motivated by their courses. They tended to invest much more time and effort in preparation and class participation. At least three factors explain such benefits: (1) students could make more sense of what they learned, (2) they go in with more self-confidence because teachers seemed to give more consideration to their opinion and the external exposure provided them some sense of pride, and (3) they were more proactive in the class process.
- Professors were also much more satisfied, mostly because of the enthusiasm shown by their students and the sense of escaping from routine.

- All projects and initiatives identified have been developed by teachers who themselves demonstrate entrepreneurial attitudes and behaviours. They are autonomous, curious, passionate, enthusiastic, modest, perseverant, take risks and responsibilities, give time, are open, like to share their experience and are open to the outside world.
- Projects and entrepreneurial behaviours have been manifested mostly in schools where the direction was supportive. Directors consider themselves more as human resource managers than an administrative body; they favour rooms for participation, are listeners, favour change and empowerment, and allow flexibility with respect to rules. This observation is in line with the research about corporate ventures that shows the strategic importance of the context to support bottom-up processes (Burgelman 1983; 1984).
- Another interesting observation is that teaching enterprising seems to work with any student regardless of their level of education, sex, discipline and capacity. In fact, the more spectacular results are obtained from students having troubles with academic education.
- One of the major obstacles for teachers to promote an enterprising pedagogy appears to be the education system itself. The pressure to respect the programme by the rules, the rigidity of evaluation systems, the lack of flexibility, not to mention the conservatism of parents' associations, are but a few illustrations of such inertia.

Implication and conclusion

In conclusion, it seems that being specific about what is meant by favouring entrepreneurship education is strategic. Developing entrepreneurship courses in secondary schools may not only face resistance in the school system, but also not obtain favourable priority. Indeed, it seems that nurturing the skills to start and run a business is a secondary objective compared with developing enterprising attitudes and competences. Of course, there is no evidence that enterprising education will make more entrepreneurs, in particular business-minded entrepreneurs. The argument however is that demonstrating enterprising skills and attitudes is a necessary, but not sufficient, condition to make an entrepreneur. Indeed, entrepreneurs manifest the basic skills and attitudes associated with enterprising education. If not inherited, these skills need to be nurtured and developed through education if one is willing to make a larger proportion of the population more enterprising.

The contention is that by favouring enterprising pedagogy in all disciplines will increase dramatically the proportion of the population being involved in a project, regardless of the nature of the project (business, social, art, sport, and so on) and, consequently, the proportion of the population having a business project. This may induce automatically an increased level of demand for entrepreneurship education from the students themselves.

In other words, policy-makers may achieve much deeper effects and reach their objective much more easily were they to support and promote enterprising pedagogy at all levels of the education system instead of forcing the case for entrepreneurship courses in only some curricula. This chapter calls for an increased focus on enterprising competences in all programmes that pretend to support entrepreneurship education in secondary schools. Such focus must go hand in hand with adequate information provided to teachers and school directors about the meaning and the benefits of enterprising education.

Consequently, by developing enterprising skills at school, society will increase the likelihood of generating more entrepreneurs. It follows from this argument that the introduction of 'traditional' entrepreneurship courses is probably necessary to teach students the basic competences that are important to becoming an entrepreneur but are not enough to really 'make' entrepreneurs. In other words, developing entrepreneurship courses is probably important *to enhance students' self-confidence in their ability to create and run a business*, which is so important to develop entrepreneurship activities. However, the exposure to enterprising education is likely to nurture *the desire to be entrepreneurial*.

In conclusion, the idea is not to make a total shift from traditional education to enterprising education. There should be variety in pedagogical approaches, depending on the specific material to be reviewed, the size of the class, the time available or teacher motivation. However, the development of new skills and attitudes requires time, maturation and commitment from the point of view of the school system. In that respect, it should be much more ingrained in the system than just having an introductory course or organizing an event to expose students to entrepreneurship.

In terms of research, this chapter calls for more interdisciplinary research associating scholars in entrepreneurship with researchers in pedagogy. The area addressed in this chapter is almost unexplored. We know too little about the links between education and drives for entrepreneurship. The validation of most pedagogical approaches is still questioned. Impact measurement is non-existent. Addressing these questions probably requires complex longitudinal research. Other areas of fruitful collaboration between pedagogy and entrepreneurship are: (1) the development of appropriate pedagogical tools and guidelines for teachers to develop and appropriate new tools, and (2) the development of 'training the teachers' programmes.

References

Acs, Z.J., Arenius, P., Hay, M. and Minniti, M. (2004), *GEM 2004 Global Report*, www.gemconsortium.org, published on 27 May 2005.
Aouni, Z., De Coster, E., De Poorter, X., Donnay, J., Lambert, A.-F. and Pirnay, F. (2005), *Réalisation d'une boîte à outils pédagogiques qui contribuent au développement de l'esprit d'entreprendre à l'attention des enseignants et étudiants de l'enseignement secondaire*, Centre de Recherche PME et d'Entrepreneuriat de l'Université de Liège, mai, 59.
Birch, D. (1981), Who creates jobs? *The Public Interest*, **65**, Fall, 3–14.
Burgelman, R.A. (1983), A process model of internal corporate venturing in the diversified major firm, *Administrative Science Quarterly*, **28** (2), 223–44.
Burgelman, R.A. (1984), Managing the internal corporate venturing process, *Management of Technology and Innovation*, **25** (2), 33–48.
Davis, S., Haltiwanger, J. and Schuh, S. (1996), *Job Creation and Destruction*, Cambridge, MA: MIT Press.
European Union (EU) (2000), Report adopted by the General Affairs Council and welcomed by the Feira European Council in June 2000, http://europa.eu.int/comm/enterprise/enterprise_policy/charter/index.htm.
European Union (EU) (2002a), *Résultat des travaux du: Conseil Education sur le programme de travail détaillé sur le suivi des objectifs des systèmes d'éducation et de formation en Europe*, doc. no. 6365/02 EDUC 27 20 février 2002.
European Union (EU) (2002b), *Training for Entrepreneurship*, November, European Commission Enterprise Directorate-General Unit B.1: Entrepreneurship (SC 27 3/4) B-1049 Brussels, http://europa.eu.int/comm/enterprise/entrepreneurship/support_measures/index.htm, accessed May 2006.
European Union (EU) (2003), *Green Paper: Entrepreneurship in Europe*, Commission of the European Communities, http://europa.eu.int/comm/enterprise/entrepreneurship/green_paper/green_paper_final_en.pdf, accessed May 2006.
European Union (EU) (2004a), *Education for Entrepreneurship: Making Progress in Promoting Entrepreneurial Attitudes and Skills through Primary and Secondary Education*, February, European Commission Enterprise

Directorate-General Unit B.1: Entrepreneurship (SC 27 3/4) B-1049 Brussels, http://europa.eu.int/comm/enterprise/entrepreneurship/support_measures/index.htm, accessed May 2006.

European Union (EU) (2004b), *Helping to Create an Entrepreneurial Culture: A Guide on Good Practices in Promoting Entrepreneurial Attitudes and Skills through Education*, European Commission Directorate-General for Enterprise Unit B.1: Entrepreneurship (SC27 3/4) B-1049 Brussels ISBN 92-894-6174-8 http://europa.eu.int/comm/enterprise/entrepreneurship/support_measures/training_education/index.htm, accessed May 2006.

European Union (EU) (2005), *Mini-companies in Secondary Education*, European Commission Enterprise Directorate-General Unit B.1: Entrepreneurship (SC 27 3/4) B-1049 Brussels.

Gallagher, C. and Stewart, H. (1986), Jobs and the business life cycle in the UK, *Applied Economics*, **18**, 875–900.

Kearney, P. (1999), *Enterprising Ways to Teach and Learn*, a series of books: Book 1, *Enterprise Principles*; Book 2, *Enterprise Activities*; Book 3, *Enterprise Briefs*; Book 4, *Enterprise Projects*; North Hobart, Tasmania, Australia: Enterprise Design Associates Pty Ltd, ISBN 0 958 5663 0 5.

Konings, J. (1995), Gross job flows and the evolution of size in U.K. establishments, *Small Business Economics*, **7**, 213–20.

Ministerio de Education (2003), *El espiritu emprendedor – motor de futuro*, Ministerio de Economia Centro de publicationes et Ministerio de Education Cultura y Deporte – Fundacion Coca-Cola, Madrid, Espana.

Mintzberg, H. (1989), *Mintzberg on Management: Inside our Strange World of Organizations*, New York: Free Press.

UK Department of Employment (1991), *Enterprise in Higher Education*, cited in P. Kearney, (Book 1, 1999).

Weiss, E.M. (1999), Perceived workplace conditions and first-year teachers' morale, career choice commitment, and planned retention: a secondary analysis, *Teaching and Teacher Education*, **15**, 861–79.

17 Explaining the intention to start a business among French students: a closer look at professional beliefs

Jean-Pierre Boissin, Barthélemy Chollet and Sandrine Emin

According to figures gathered in 2003 by the Global Entrepreneurship Monitor from 31 countries, France displays the lowest rates of entrepreneurial activity. In France, becoming an entrepreneur still remains an unusual career choice. Other figures show that young graduates accounted for only 12 per cent of all new ventures in 2002 (INSEE Première, 2003). Even if it is 4 per cent better than in 1998 (Tabourin and Parent, 2001), efforts still need to be made to better induce young French graduates to go into business.

Therefore, a number of questions must be asked on what the content of effective entrepreneurship courses should be. How should we teach entrepreneurship in the French context? We believe that the answer lies in the structure of students' professional beliefs. If students do not intend to go into business, part of the situation might be explained by the fact that they perceive entrepreneurship as problematic (either demanding or unattractive). We think that such a perception should be the starting point for education on entrepreneurship. Indeed, before designing course curricula on entrepreneurship, we ought first to understand those beliefs that students hold toward entrepreneurship; that is, we ought to know what students *think* entrepreneurship is. In other words, this chapter does not try to assess the effectiveness of existing education programs in the discipline. Rather, it aims at identifying which beliefs such programs should try to influence in order to promote entrepreneurial intention among students.

The chapter is based on a two-stage empirical study of 809 French students.[1] The first stage attempts to explain intention with three variables typical of the theory of planned behaviour: attitudes toward the behaviour, perceived social norms, and perceived behavioural control. In the second stage, we use regressions to identify professional beliefs that are key determinants for attitudes toward the behaviour and perceived behavioural control.

The first section builds hypotheses from intention models literature. The second section details our data and measures. The results are presented in the third section and are followed by a section set aside for discussion.

17.1 Applying intention models to entrepreneurial behaviour

Intentionality has previously been presented as key to entrepreneurial processes (Bird, 1988; Katz and Gartner, 1988). Therefore, intention models such as the theory of planned behaviour (TPB) (Ajzen, 1987; 1991) appear to provide the right framework, both simple and robust, to achieve a better understanding of entrepreneurship processes (Krueger, 1993). The TPB assumes that intention to perform behaviours of different kinds can be predicted with high accuracy from attitudes toward the behaviour, subjective norms, and perceived behavioural control. Intention, together with perception of behavioural

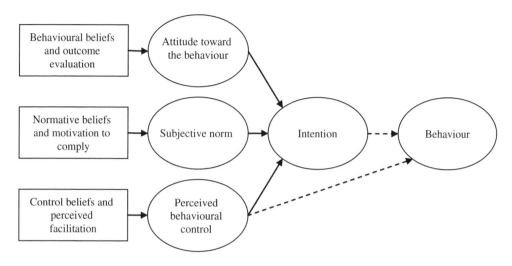

Source: Adapted from Ajzen (1987; 1991).

Figure 17.1   The theory of planned behaviour

control, accounts for considerable effect on actual behaviours. Attitudes, subjective norms, and perceived behavioural control are shown to be related to appropriate sets of salient behavioural, normative, and control beliefs about the behaviour (cf. Figure 17.1). They result from a set of personal and contextual variables (gender, social class, age, and so on).

We present the theory of planned behaviour and our hypothesis in two stages: first, we define variables predicting intention (section 17.1.1), and then we detail underlying beliefs structures (section 17.1.2).

17.1.1   Variables predicting intention

Intentions are assumed to capture the motivational factors that influence behaviour; they are indications of how hard people are willing to try and of how much effort they are planning to exert in order to perform the behaviour (Ajzen, 1991). The TPB assumes three conceptually independent determinants of intention: attitudes, subjective norms and perceived behavioural control. After a short presentation of these concepts, we describe the main results in the field.

Models and hypothesis   Attitude toward the behaviour refers to the degree to which a person has a favourable or unfavourable evaluation or appraisal of the behaviour in question (Ajzen and Fishbein, 1980). Subjective norm refers to the perceived social pressure to perform or not perform the behaviour. In our study, the social norm is defined by the degree of perceived approval or disapproval held by people whose judgement is important to the student. Personal attitudes toward outcomes of the behaviour and perceived social norms reflect the perceived desirability of performing the behaviour in Shapero's entrepreneurial event model (Shapero and Sokol, 1982) that measures the personal attractiveness of starting a business.

Perceived behavioural control refers to people's perception of the ease or difficulty of performing the behaviour at hand. More specifically, it is the perception of the presence or absence of requisite resources and opportunities needed to carry out the behaviour (Ajzen and Madden, 1986, p. 457). It is thus related to a perceived feasibility of performing the behaviour used in Shapero's model. Perceived feasibility is the degree to which one feels personally capable of starting a business. Such a concept is also compatible with Bandura's (1977; 1982) concept of perceived self-efficacy, which represents the confidence an individual has about his or her capacity to achieve actions required to obtain a given result (Bandura, 1977, p. 193) or is concerned with judgements of how well one can execute courses of action required to deal with prospective situations (Bandura, 1982, p. 122). Ajzen (2002) recently insisted on the differences between perceived behavioural control and perceived self-efficacy. Nevertheless, self-efficacy has been linked already, both theoretically and empirically, to many managerial issues, and to entrepreneurship. For instance, Hackett et al. (1993), cited by Krueger et al. (2000), reveal that the impact of gender and ethnicity on differences in career choices strongly depend on differences in self-efficacy. Bandura (1986) and Lent et al. (1994), both cited in Krueger et al. (2000), found correlations between self-efficacy and career intentions. In line with these authors, we retained in our study a measure of self-efficacy. Self-efficacy refers to the degree to which a student thinks he or she is able to carry out a new venture creation process.

With respect to the TPB, our first set of hypotheses is as follows:

H1a: The greater the attitude toward starting a business, the greater the level of intention to start a business upon graduation.
H1b: The more a perceived social norm is favourable to entrepreneurship, the greater is the level of intention to start a business upon graduation.
H1c: The higher the level of self-efficacy, the higher the level of intention to start a business at the end of student life.

These three hypotheses all assume a positive impact of the three variables, but we ought to keep in mind that we are more interested in their relative powers for explaining intention. Indeed, one of the aims is to locate key variables in order positively to influence intention through entrepreneurship courses.

Empirical findings in the literature   Several authors have applied intention models to the action of starting a business (Autio et al., 1997; Davidsson, 1995; Emin, 2003; Kolvereid, 1996; Krueger and Carsrud, 1993; Krueger et al., 2000; Reitan, 1996; Tounés, 2003). Some of these studies focus on students and, therefore, are of particular interest to this chapter (Autio et al., 1997; Kolvereid, 1996; Krueger et al., 2000; Tounés, 2003).

Kolvereid (1996) studied 128 business school students in Norway. Results show that intention to be self-employed was significantly correlated to attitude toward the behaviour, perceived social norms and perceived behavioural control. No demographic variable (gender, former experience as self-employed and familial background) significantly impacted intention, and they were all correlated to perceived social norms and perceived behavioural control. This is consistent with Ajzen and Fishbein's theory, assuming that such variables only have indirect influence on intention, through attitude, perceived social norms and perceived behavioural control.[2]

Krueger, Reilly and Carsrud (2000) tested Ajzen's model on 97 business school alumni facing a career choice. Perceived feasibility and attitude toward the act significantly predicted intention (with feasibility having a stronger impact than attitude). Social norms appear to be insignificant. Such results contradict Kolvereid (1996) who found a positive impact of social pressure.

Based on data from 1956 students (Scandinavians, Americans and Asians) of science, Autio et al. (1997) tested a model adapted from Davidsson (1995). Intention is the result of students' entrepreneurial conviction (a variable close to Shapero's feasibility and Ajzen's perceived behavioural control) and social context (with help provided by the university and several situational variables). Conviction is influenced by students' representations of entrepreneurship and by their general attitudes. Conviction is a concept close to attitudes toward the action (as defined by Ajzen) and perceptions of desirability (as pointed out by Shapero and Sokol). General attitudes refer to general psychological characteristics such as the need for achievement, autonomy and change, as well as economic motivations. Such elements are themselves influenced by personal variables such as gender, age, marital status, level of education, background experiences in professional life and familial background. Results show that general attitudes, especially the need for achievement and the need for autonomy, strongly impact entrepreneurial conviction. The most important personal variables appear to be the following: having worked previously in a small business, gender (with greater entrepreneurial conviction among men than women), and the existence of a role model (example: having a parent entrepreneur). Conviction is, by and large, the most significant explanatory factor of entrepreneurial intention.

17.1.2 *Determinants of attitudes, subjective norms and perceived self-efficacy*
According to intention models, attitudes and perceived behavioural control are explained by personal beliefs. After a presentation of these personal beliefs, we discuss hypotheses on belief structures.

Personal beliefs   Three kinds of salient beliefs can be distinguished: behavioural beliefs which are assumed to influence attitudes toward the behaviour, normative beliefs which constitute the underlying determinants of subjective norms, and control beliefs which provide the basis for perceptions of behavioural control. Such beliefs refer to information (true or false) someone has about his or her environment.

Attitude is assumed to depend on beliefs regarding the outcomes of an action. More precisely, someone forms a favourable attitude toward behaviours when:

- on the one hand, he or she thinks starting a business will bring about a certain outcome (example: he or she thinks it is a way to earn big money)
- on the other hand, he or she attaches value to such outcome (example: it is crucial to this person that a job can bring in big money).

Similarly, the more resources and opportunities individuals believe they possess, and the fewer obstacles or impediments they anticipate, the greater their perceived control over the behaviour should be. Specifically, perceived behavioural control is based on the product of two independent notions: control beliefs and the perceived power of the particular control factor to facilitate or inhibit performance of the behaviour. Using self-efficacy toward starting a business as the central concept, rather than perceived control, it appears to be a function of:

- the level of self-efficacy toward an array of tasks (example: the person at hand thinks of him or herself as capable of raising funds to start a business)
- the perception of whether such tasks are critical for success in the process of starting a business (example: he or she thinks that raising funds is a crucial task for succeeding).

Belief structures   There are two distinct ways of measuring such concepts. On the one hand, one can use global measures of attitude and self-efficacy, that is, the belief structures are combined into unidimensional constructs. On the other hand, one can opt for placing beliefs in the perspective of multidimensional constructs. Unidimensional operationalization has been used by key authors such as Ajzen or Krueger (Krueger et al., 2000), but it still remains highly criticized. Considering the underlying behaviour of motivations as conceptually separate (that is, the multidimensional approach) seems more relevant to this study for at least two reasons. First, a multidimensional approach to self-efficacy is more realistic. Some tasks might be perceived as considerably easy, while others might be perceived as serious barriers to feasibility. Studying intention among French public researchers, Emin (2003) showed that perceived self-efficacies for certain tasks had very distinct weights to explain perceived feasibility. Another argument is that understanding beliefs by seeing them in their various dimensions offers better chances for identifying recommendations for practice (Emin, 2003, p. 254). Assessing the weight of self-efficacy at each task is a precondition for knowing what we shall emphasize in entrepreneurship courses in order to develop entrepreneurial intention among students.

We can argue, in a similar way, that undertaking an anatomy of attitudinal beliefs is very insightful. Dividing professional beliefs into dimensions can give cues for the design of entrepreneurship courses, since it allows us to know what kinds of professional aspects of the entrepreneurial 'career' might decrease desirability of entrepreneurial behaviour. In a similar vein, Shimp and Kavas (1984) have provided empirical evidence that the multidimensional approach leads to a better model fit than the unidimensional approach.

For all these reasons, we opted for a multidimensional approach. Indeed, we state that attitudes toward starting a business are determined by a set of behavioural beliefs (H2a) and that self-efficacy toward starting a business is determined by a set of beliefs of self-efficacies (H2b). Of course, the added value of our tests lies rather on the identification of relative weights of various beliefs than the validation of hypotheses in and of itself.

To make clear the two-step logic of our tests, all relationships tested are mentioned in Figure 17.2. Note that all tests were carried out sequentially and separately: validation of H1 (step 1) and then validation of H2 (step 2).

17.2   Method

17.2.1   Sample and data

After a pre-test on 72 PhD students, the final version of the questionnaire was filled out by 809 French students from four universities in Grenoble (France). The questionnaire

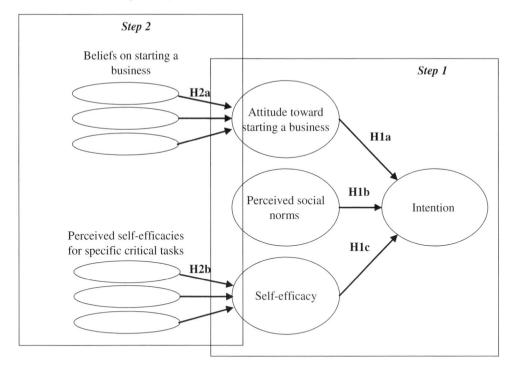

Figure 17.2   The global model

revealed that 32.7 per cent were studying Business Administration, 22.8 per cent Sport Sciences, 13.1 per cent Engineering, 10.9 per cent Humanities, 7.3 per cent Economics, 7 per cent Law, and 6.1 per cent Statistics; and 38.9 per cent of them had spent only one year at the university, 7.3 per cent two years, 31 per cent three years, and 22.7 per cent four or five years. We insist on the relative diversity in the composition of our sample. Until now, most of the studies have been carried out with samples limited to students in Business Administration (Kolvereid, 1996; Krueger, Reilly and Carsrud, 2000). All questionnaires were distributed by the authors to students at the beginning of classes.

17.2.2   Measures
Seven-point Likert scales were used for all measures. They are all described below.

Intention   Intention toward business creation has been measured, following Kolvereid (1996). According to Kolvereid, such measures must consider the dichotomy between two potential professional trajectories: employment in existing organizations versus self-employment. An intention index was created averaging scores on three distinct 7-point scales (Cronbach alpha = 0.685). The first scale measures how likely it is that the respondent would launch a new venture upon graduation. The second measures the likelihood of the respondent to pursuing a career as an employee in an organization or firm. The third scale measures the preferred choice between the two alternatives, provided that the respondent actually has such a choice (high scores indicating that the respondent would prefer going into business for him or herself rather than being employed by an existing organization).

Subjective norm   We used four 7-point scales (from 'very unfavourable' to 'very favourable'), each relating to one part of students' social environments (Cronbach alpha = 0.65): 'Suppose you start your own business: what would the opinion of the following people be: (a) your family, (b) your friends, (c) your teachers, (d) other people important to you.' The perceived social norm represents the average score on these items.

Attitude toward starting a business   Attitude was assessed with a single item measuring whether starting a business sounds attractive or not (see Krueger et al., 2000), from 'not attractive at all' to 'very attractive'. In order to measure underlying behavioural beliefs, we selected 23 items describing possible outcomes of career choice, adapted from Kolvereid (1996). For each item, respondents were asked to answer two distinct questions (7-point Likert scales, coded from -3 to $+3$):

- Does he or she value such an outcome as important for his or her future professional life? ('For each of the following items, tell if it is important for your future professional life.')
- Does he or she think that starting a business could lead to such an outcome? ('Do you think that starting a business would allow you to . . . ?')

Perceived self-efficacy   This was also measured with a single item: 'Do you think you are capable of starting a business?' (from 'not capable at all' to 'completely capable'). While it has become a key aspect of entrepreneurship theory (Boyd and Vozikis, 1994), the notion of self-efficacy has been measured in various ways. First, some authors do not choose to measure tasks that are specific to the act of going into business. De Noble et al. (1999) argued that authors in the field of entrepreneurship have frequently built measures on the basis of tasks which are non-specific to entrepreneurs and which could equally describe managers' work. Similarly, we feel that the available measures are not sufficiently oriented toward tasks which are critical to the new venture-creation process, and sometimes refer more to managing a business once it has already been initiated. We therefore created 14 items describing tasks deemed critical to starting a new business. For each task selected, respondents were asked to answer on a 7-point Likert scale, from 'not capable at all' to 'completely capable'.

17.3   Results
We first detail the structure of the surveyed students' professional beliefs and attitudes toward entrepreneurship. Second, we show how such a structure impacts the intention to start a business.

17.3.1   *Beliefs and attitudes toward starting a business*
As stated by hypothesis H2a, attitude is driven by a set of professional beliefs toward entrepreneurship. The next sub-section provides descriptive statistics on such beliefs. On the other hand, H2b states that perceived self-efficacy toward starting a business is the result of a set of beliefs about one's ability to carry out specific tasks critical to the entrepreneurial process. Figures on these beliefs are detailed in the second sub-section.

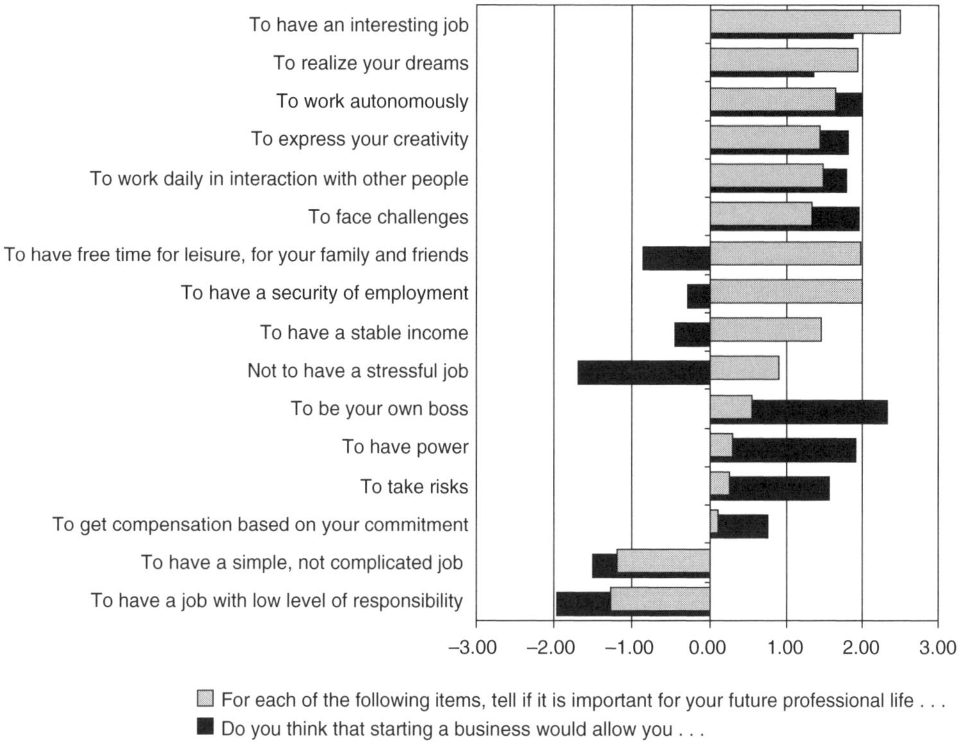
To have an interesting job
To realize your dreams
To work autonomously
To express your creativity
To work daily in interaction with other people
To face challenges
To have free time for leisure, for your family and friends
To have a security of employment
To have a stable income
Not to have a stressful job
To be your own boss
To have power
To take risks
To get compensation based on your commitment
To have a simple, not complicated job
To have a job with low level of responsibility
–3.00
–2.00
–1.00
0.00
1.00
2.00
3.00
For each of the following items, tell if it is important for your future professional life . . .
Do you think that starting a business would allow you . . .

Figure 17.3 Outcomes valued for career choice and outcomes expected from starting a business

Contradictions between outcomes expected and valuation This sub-section compares, on the one hand, the respondents' salient belief that performing the behaviour will lead to certain professional outcomes with, on the other hand, the respondent's evaluation of the outcomes (see Figure 17.3). Our results reveal a gap between what students expect from professional life and the perceived outcomes of an entrepreneurial career. Such tensions provide a partial explanation for the lack of French students' interest in entrepreneurship. Starting a business is perceived as a way to be exposed to challenging situations, to express one's creativity, and to perform interesting tasks. Meanwhile, students perceive an entrepreneurial career as incapable of securing a stable income and incapable of allowing for a satisfying extra-professional life. So these outcomes are precisely what they expect from professional life. On the opposite side, entrepreneurship is perceived as a risk-taking behaviour, a way of holding a position of power, but students do not value such outcomes as essential to making a career choice.

Self-efficacies for specific critical tasks Students appear to be rather self-confident in terms of their ability to innovate, to devote all of their time and energy to a project, and to locate helpful partners during the new venture-creation process (Figure 17.4). They feel much less able to gather all of the funding required for the new business.

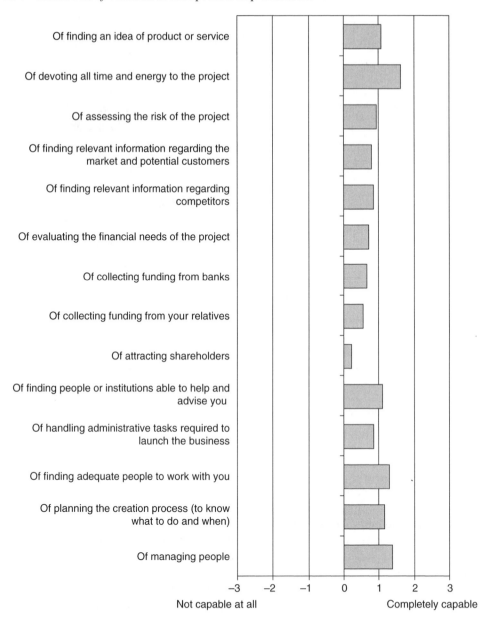

Figure 17.4   Self-efficacy toward tasks that are critical to the entrepreneurial process ('Do you think you are capable ... ')

17.3.2   Explanatory variables of intention
As stated in Figure 17.2, our analysis was performed in two stages. We tested the regression of attitude, perceived self-efficacy and subjective norms on intention (H1a, H1b and H1c). Testing H2a and H2b required the use of principal component analysis intended to summarize statistical information collected with the 23 items describing

Table 17.1   Regression upon intention

	Standardized coefficients (t)	Adjusted R^2	F
Attitude toward starting a business	0.446 (13.7) ****	0.433	199 ****
Perceived self-efficacy toward starting a business	0.289 (8.9) ****		
Subjective norms	0.035 (1.2) ns		

Note: **** $p < 0.001$; ns not significant.

possible outcomes of career choice and the 14 items measuring self-efficacies toward specific tasks. Such factor analysis resulted in a list of factors representing an array of beliefs used for a regression on attitude and self-efficacy.

Step 1 – Explaining intention (testing H1a, H1b and H1c)   Multiple regressions result in the validation of both H1a and H1c, but not H1b. Consistent with previous studies (Emin, 2003; Krueger et al., 2000), the subjective norm was not significant. In other words, motivation to start a business through stimulus from the social environment seems to have no impact on entrepreneurial intention. Generally speaking, results show the relevance of the TPB, since it appears to explain more than 40 per cent of total variance (cf. Table 17.1).

Attitude toward starting a business is by far the most important factor for entrepreneurial intention. This result is divergent with Krueger et al.'s (2000) study on a sample of American students, but consistent with Emin's (2003) results on a sample of French public-sector researchers in the sciences. This may reveal a cultural difference effect that would be stronger than the effect of professional occupations. Such possible cultural effects require further research.

If one of the aims of entrepreneurship courses is to increase entrepreneurial intention, our results suggest significant conclusions in terms of teaching practices. While it is of importance to convey essential skills for typical entrepreneurial tasks (hence increasing self-efficacy), we also consider new ways of promoting business creation as a desirable act for students. In other words, teachers should not limit their objectives to make entrepreneurship *possible*; they should also act in order to make it an attractive career choice.

Step 2 – Explaining attitude toward starting a business and perceived self-efficacy (testing H2a and H2b)   A factor analysis runs on the 23 items describing possible outcomes of career choice and the 14 items measuring self-efficacies toward specific tasks.

Regarding the topic of attitude, based on an eigenvalue of 1 as a cut-off point for factor extraction, we retained a five-factor solution, accounting for 60.3 per cent of the total variance. Factor 1 ('to avoid responsibility') refers to the level of responsibility and complexity of work. Factor 2 ('to achieve self-realization') depicts the need for interesting, creative and challenging jobs. Factor 3 ('to have decision-making power') includes items referring both to power and autonomy at work. Factor 4 ('to get economic benefits') refers to compensation expected from professional life. Factor 5 ('to have a high

Table 17.2   Regression on attitude toward starting a business

	Standardized coefficients	Adjusted R^2	F
To avoid responsibility	0.097 ***	0.211	43.83****
To achieve self-realization	0.217 ****		
To have decision-making power	0.239 ****		
To get economic benefits	0.069 **		
To have a high-quality work–life balance	0.098 ***		

Note: **** $p < 0.001$; *** $p < 0.01$; ** $p < 0.05$; * $p < 0.1$; ns not significant.

quality of life balance') depicts the willingness to devote energy to the job at the expense of other activities (leisure, family). Details about factor analysis are provided in Appendix 17.1.

The regression shows that the most important factors appear to be 'to achieve self-realization' and 'to have decision-making power' (Table 17.2). Meanwhile, economic incentives, avoiding responsibility, and securing a high-quality work–life balance have a much lesser impact on attitude toward starting a business.[3]

Insofar as perceived self-efficacy is concerned, the principal component analysis led to a four-factor structure. Factor 1 ('to build the project') refers to perceived self-efficacy for an array of tasks describing the initial stage of new venture creation, when the entrepreneur needs to gather and process information from various sources in order to conceive a viable business project (assessing risk, creating a business plan, knowing the market, and so on). Factor 2 ('to set up the organization') depicts tasks intended to give 'concrete birth' to the organization, handling administrative aspects, choosing a legal status, building a team, and so on. Factor 3 ('to raise funds') is a rather simple one: all items clearly refer to building relationships with financial partners. Factor 4 is more ambiguous, since it groups two items with seemingly poor conceptual relationships, namely, 'finding an idea of product or service' and 'devoting all time and energy to the project'. This factor appeared to us as a general notion expressing one's capacity to getting personally involved in the project, meaning devoting energy and time, but also managing to put one's personality into it in order to get a really distinctive product or service idea (therefore, we termed factor 4 'to get personally involved in the project'). Details about factor analysis are provided in Appendix 17.2.

As we previously stated, the regression was intended to evaluate the impact of these factors (measuring self-efficacies toward specific tasks) on a global notion of self-efficacy toward starting a business. We shall insist on the fact that self-efficacy refers to a respondent's *perceived* capacity to perform a task. Thus, the explanatory power of, say, the first factor in Table 17.3, is the impact of the perceived capacity of building the project on the perceived capacity of starting a business.

Our results demonstrate that self efficacy toward starting a business is chiefly influenced by the feeling of being able to set up the organization (administrative tasks, choosing legal status, building the founding team) and by the feeling of being able to get personally involved in the project.

Table 17.3   Regression on perceived self-efficacy for starting a business

	Standardized coefficients	Adjusted R^2	F
To build the project	0.185 ****	0.311	87****
To set up the organization	0.216 ****		
To raise funds	0.103 ***		
To get personally involved in the project	0.218 ****		

Note: **** $p < 0.001$; *** $p < 0.01$.

17.4   Discussion

It is our hope that several of our results will contribute to current debates on entrepreneurship studies, particularly for educators. One significant result is the prevailing weight of attitude in the explanation of intention. The impact of attitude is nearly two times the impact of perceived self-efficacy. This could lead to a very simple conclusion for teaching practices: while education regarding *how* to start a business appears to be a good way to stimulate entrepreneurial intentions, one should also not forget the attitudinal dimension. We need further study to understand how we could promote favourable attitudes, that is, how we could have entrepreneurship become not only a possible career choice, but also an attractive one.

Of course, this chapter does not describe course content for promoting entrepreneurship as a career choice. Innovative teaching practices still remain to be invented. Nevertheless, this study provides some clues. It gives information on students' professional beliefs regarding entrepreneurship and what students expect from their professional life. All kinds of beliefs can have an impact on attitude, but with very distinct significance. It would be of great interest to go further into belief analysis in order to know what kind of teaching content could positively influence them. It would also be very insightful to know which beliefs on entrepreneurship correspond to incorrect perceptions. We could imagine, for instance, further research contrasting with our results, gathered on a sample of students, focused on the way 'real' entrepreneurs perceive the underlying reality. Such entrepreneurs would be questioned about what brought about, in terms of professional outcomes, their choice of going into business.

The prevailing weight of attitude also asks whether entrepreneurship courses should be optional or compulsory. Should a course be optional, it is highly probable that a low level of desire to start a business would not be modified. Indeed, optional courses probably only attract people for whom starting a business is already a desirable act. In other words, optional courses might 'miss the target'.

Even though attitude is the predominant factor, we ought not to underestimate the role of perceived self-efficacy. Results show that it is strongly influenced by a set of self-efficacies toward critical tasks. Entrepreneurship teachers should focus on delivering skills on specific tasks that account for the strongest explanatory power. In the mean time, we ought to keep in mind that we are talking about perceptions, and that confronting such perceptions with the underlying reality as perceived by real entrepreneurs could be a logical follow-up to this research. This would be a way to make the distinction between, on the one hand, beliefs that correspond to reality, to which teachers should respond by providing corresponding skills and, on the other hand, beliefs to which we should react by 'setting the record straight' and dismantling prejudices and clichés on entrepreneurship.

Our chapter also has some limitations. Throughout our hypotheses, we opted for a rather determinist approach to intention, while other authors could argue that intention is sometimes tightly coupled to experimentation through action and that professional beliefs are permanently modified by experience. Further research is needed in order to shed light on such complexity, adopting a more process-based observation of intention formation.

Another limitation of intention models used in this chapter is that they do not tell anything about opportunity recognition and its relationship to intention formation. Is opportunity recognition (or elaboration) a precondition for intention to emerge? Alternatively, does the pre-existence of intention induce people to scan their environments more carefully in order to locate a business opportunity? According to Bhave (1994), both situations are possible in reality. In his model of the entrepreneurial process, he makes a distinction between externally stimulated opportunities and internally stimulated opportunities. Opportunity recognition is internally stimulated when it occurs as a result of entrepreneurial intention. The entrepreneur is willing to go into business, and starts a systematic processing of environmental information and opportunity elaboration. When opportunity is externally stimulated, the entrepreneur has identified new needs on the market, and then begins to consider going into business in order to take advantage of such an opportunity. Our approach is rooted in intention models and, therefore, does not offer the possibility of accounting for that kind of phenomenon. Further research should explore the interplay between intention and opportunity recognition in order to improve our understanding of how entrepreneurship courses could increase entrepreneurial intention among students.

Notes

1. Data were collected within the framework of an institutional program called Maison de l'Entrepreneuriat (House of Entrepreneurship), intended to promote entrepreneurship among French students (Boissin, 2006).
2. This is also why demographic variables are not included in regressions throughout this chapter, in order to fit the TPB which, as such, has already proven to be of direct relevance.
3. While the results on 'To achieve self-realization' and 'To have decision-making power' are no surprise, the positive sign of coefficients for 'To avoid responsibility' and 'To have a high-quality work–life balance' may seem counterintuitive. Once again, the variables are based on products. A descriptive analysis of the variables used to build these two factors reveals that hardly any of the respondents think that avoiding responsibility or having a high-quality work–life balance is a consequence of starting a business. In other words, they are almost all positioned on the negative part of the scale (from –1 to –3) for what regards outcome evaluation. Therefore, high global scores mainly concern those people who think that these aspects of professional life are not important (coded negatively, which leads to a $(-)*(-)$ product). Low scores represent people who think it is an important part of professional life (which leads to a $(-)*(+)$ product). Thus, the higher the score, the fewer people think that avoiding responsibility or preserving a high-quality work–life balance is an important criterion for career choice. The results are then no longer surprising.

References

Ajzen, I. (1987), Attitudes, traits, and actions: dispositional prediction of behaviour in personality and social psychology, *Advances in Experimental Social Psychology*, **20**, 2–63.
Ajzen, I. (1991), The theory of planned behaviour, *Organizational Behaviour and Human Decision Processes*, **50**, 179–211.
Ajzen, I. (2002), Perceived behavioural control, self-efficacy, locus of control, and the theory of planned behaviour, *Journal of Applied Social Psychology*, **32** (4), 665–84.

Ajzen, I. and Fishbein, M. (1980), *Understanding Attitudes and Predicting Social Behaviour*, Englewood Cliffs, NJ: Prentice Hall.

Ajzen, I. and Madden, T.J. (1986), Prediction of goal-directed behaviour: attitudes, intentions, and perceived behavioural control, *Journal of Experimental Social Psychology*, **22**, 453–74.

Autio, E., Keely, R.H. and Klofsten, M. (1997), Entrepreneurial intent among students: testing an intent model in Asia, Scandinavia and USA, *Frontiers of Entrepreneurship Research*, Wellesley, MA: Babson College, pp. 133–47.

Bandura, A. (1977), Self-efficacy: toward a unifying theory of behavioural change, *Psychological Review*, **84** (2), 191–215.

Bandura, A. (1982), Self-efficacy mechanism in human agency, *American Psychologist*, **37** (2), 122–47.

Bhave, M.P. (1994), A process model of entrepreneurial venture creation, *Journal of Business Venturing*, **9**, 223–42.

Bird, B.J. (1988), Implementing entrepreneurial ideas: the case for intention, *Academy of Management Review*, **13** (3), 442–53.

Boissin, J.-P. (ed.) (2006), Du concept à l'implantation des Maisons de l'Entrepreneuriat – diagnostic des réalisations en 2005, Contrat Ministère de la Jeunesse, de l'Education Nationale et de la Recherche, Université Pierre Mendès France (Grenoble II – Sciences sociales).

Boyd, N.G. and Vozikis, G.S. (1994), 'The influence of self-efficacy on the development of entrepreneurial intentions and actions', *Entrepreneurship Theory and Practice*, **18** (4) (Summer), 65–77.

Davidsson, P. (1995), Determinants of entrepreneurial intentions, RENT IX Workshop, Piacenza, Italy, November, pp. 23–4.

De Noble, A.F., Jung, D. and Ehrlich, B. (1999), Entrepreneurial self-efficacy: the development of a measure and its relationship to entrepreneurial intentions and actions, *Entrepreneurship Theory and Practice*, **18** (4), 63–77.

Emin, S. (2003), L'intention de crier une entreprise des chercheurs publics: le cas français, thèse pour l'obtention du doctorat en sciences et gestion, Université Pierre Mendés France de Grenoble.

INSEE Première (2003), Les créateurs d'entreprise en 2002, octobre.

Katz, J. and Gartner, W.B. (1988), Properties of emerging organizations, *Academy of Management Review*, **13** (3), 429–41.

Kolvereid, L. (1996), Prediction of employment status choice intentions, *Entrepreneurship Theory and Practice*, **20** (3) (Fall), 47–57.

Krueger, N.F. (1993), The impact of prior entrepreneurial exposure on perceptions of new venture feasibility and desirability, *Entrepreneurship Theory and Practice*, Fall, 5–20.

Krueger, N.F. and Carsrud, A.L. (1993), Entrepreneurial intentions: applying the theory of planned behaviours, *Entrepreneurship and Regional Development*, **5** (4), 315–30.

Krueger, N.F., Reilly, M.D. and Carsrud, A.L. (2000), Competing models of entrepreneurial intentions, *Journal of Business Venturing*, **15** (5/6), 411–32.

Reitan, B. (1996), Entrepreneurial intentions: a combined models approach, paper presented at 9th Nordic Small Business Research Conference, Lillehammer, Norway, 29–31 May.

Shapero, A. and Sokol, L. (1982), The social dimension of entrepreneurship, in *Encyclopaedia of Entrepreneurship*, C.A. Kent, D.L. Sexton and K.H. Vesper (eds), Englewood Cliffs, NJ: Prentice Hall, pp. 72–90.

Shimp, T.A. and Kavas, A. (1984), The theory of reasoned action applied to coupon usage, *Journal of Consumer Research*, **11** (3), 795–809.

Tabourin, R. and Parent, M.-F. (2001), *Enquête Jeunes, diplômés et créateurs d'entreprises*, Etude réalisée par INSEE-Direction régionale de Lorraine/consortium universitaire (Universités Nancy I, Grenoble I, Paris XI, Strasbourg I), Novembre, available at www.passeports-bretagne.com/Etd_1101_jd_creat%B0_insee.pdf.

Tounés, A. (2003), L'intention entrepreneuriale. Une étude comparative entre des étudiants d'écoles de management et gestion suivant des programmes ou des formations en entrepreneuriat et des étudiants en DESS CAAE, thèse pour l'obtention du doctorat en sciences et gestion, Université de Rouen.

Appendix 17.1:   Factor analysis for behavioural beliefs and outcome evaluation (principal components method with varimax rotation)

The factor analysis was carried out on the product of two scales:

V1   For each of the following items, tell if it is important for your future professional life.
V2   Do you think that going into business would allow you . . .

Items	Communalities	Loadings	Factors
To have a simple, uncomplicated job	0.694	0.823	To avoid
To have a job with low level of responsibility	0.648	0.791	responsibility
To have an interesting job	0.630	0.747	To achieve self-
To realize your dreams	0.643	0.744	realization
To express you creativity	0.598	0.738	
To be your own boss	0.627	0.768	To have decision-
To have responsibilities	0.675	0.643	making power
To have power	0.696	0.807	
To get compensation based on your commitment	0.591	0.757	To get economic benefits
To earn big money	0.634	0.770	
To have a perspective of career progression	0.575	0.700	
To not have to work a lot	0.614	0.620	To have a high-
To not have a stressful job	0.674	0.802	quality work–
To have free time for leisure, for your family and friends	0.604	0.722	life balance

Note: Explained variance = 63.6 per cent.

Appendix 17.2:   Factor analysis for self-efficacies toward critical tasks
(principal components method with varimax rotation)

Items	Communalities	Loadings	Factors
Assessing project risk	0.545	0.637	To build the
Finding relevant information regarding the market and potential customers	0.777	0.847	project
Finding relevant information regarding competitors	0.783	0.854	
Evaluating the financial needs of the project	0.551	0.589	
Finding people or institutions able to help and advise you (concerning administrative steps, law, business, etc.)	0.585	0.660	To set up the organization
Handling administrative tasks to launch the business	0.588	0.730	
Finding the adequate people to work with you	0.542	0.696	
Planning the creation process (to know what to do and when)	0.524	0.641	
Managing people	0.493	0.532	
Raising funds from banks/private funds/ business angels	0.650	0.675	To raise funds
Collecting funds from your relatives	0.687	0.801	
Attracting shareholders	0.592	0.683	
Finding an idea of product or service	0.609	0.726	To get
Devoting all time and energy to the project	0.596	0.752	personally involved in the project

Note: Explained variance = 60.9 per cent.

Index